Shapers
of
Southern
History

John Hope Franklin

Jack P. Greene

Anne Firor Scott

Bertram Wyatt-Brown

Bill C. Malone

Dan T. Carter

Charles Joyner

Pete Daniel

Peter H. Wood

Anthony J. Badger

Drew Gilpin Faust

Darlene Clark Hine

Vernon Burton

Suzanne Lebsock

Edward L. Ayers

Shapers of Southern History

Autobiographical Reflections

EDITED BY JOHN B. BOLES

The University of Georgia Press
Athens and London

Acknowledgments for the use of previously
published material appear on pages 1 and 135, which constitute
an extension of the copyright page.
© 2004 by the University of Georgia Press
Athens, Georgia 30602
All rights reserved
Set in Electra by Graphic Composition, Inc.

Printed digitally

Library of Congress Cataloging-in-Publication Data
Shapers of Southern history : autobiographical reflections / edited by John B. Boles.
  p. cm.
Includes bibliographical references.
ISBN 0-8203-2474-4 (alk. paper) — ISBN 0-8203-2475-2 (pbk. : alk. paper)
1. Historians — Southern States — Biography. 2. Southern States — Historiography.
I. Boles, John B.
E175.45.S45 2004
975'.0072'022 — dc22
2004010907

British Library Cataloging-in-Publication Data available

Paperback ISBN-13: 978-0-8203-2475-3

2017 hardcover reissue ISBN-13: 978-0-8203-5252-7

Contents

Preface   vii

A Life of Learning
JOHN HOPE FRANKLIN   1

The Making of a Historian
Some Autobiographical Notes
JACK P. GREENE   18

Chance or Choice?
ANNE FIROR SCOTT   40

Neither Priest nor Poet
A Search for Vocation
BERTRAM WYATT-BROWN   62

"Sing Me Back Home"
Growing Up in the South and Writing the History of Its Music
BILL C. MALONE   91

Scattered Pieces
Living and Writing Southern History
DAN T. CARTER   115

From Here to There and Back Again
Adventures of a Southern Historian
CHARLES JOYNER   137

Accidental Historian
PETE DANIEL   164

"Hey, Man, Where Did You Come From?"
Reflections on My First Three Decades
PETER H. WOOD   187

Southern History from the Outside
ANTHONY J. BADGER 203

Living History
DREW GILPIN FAUST 220

Up South in the Middle West
Toward a Cultural and Intellectual Autobiography
DARLENE CLARK HINE 237

Stranger in a Strange Land
Crossing Boundaries
VERNON BURTON 256

Snow Falling on Magnolias
SUZANNE LEBSOCK 284

Borders, Boundaries, and Edges
A Southern Autobiography
EDWARD L. AYERS 311

List of Contributors 333

Preface

Historians, philosophers, and social scientists of all sorts have shown us in recent years that memory is more complicated than many of us formerly thought. What W. J. Cash called "the great haze of memory" does not offer easy access to one attempting to explore it, but it beckons those who would understand themselves. It is not necessary to resort to voguish words like *problematize* to understand that memories do not exist, pristine, in some mental storehouse ready for us to retrieve and examine them with the same result any time we wish. The older, artifactual conception of memory was wonderfully captured by Wordsworth in his long poem *The Excursion:*

> Deposited upon the silent shore
> Of memory, images and precious thoughts,
> That shall not die, and cannot be destroyed.
>
> Book VII, 28–30

Instead, it now appears that remembering is primarily an activity of the present, performed in response to a present inquiry or self-conscious act of retrospection, in which the need of the moment selects, shapes, and gives meaning to whatever fragments of memory may be recalled. Relevant memories may in fact not be recalled at first, may not even at the time have been the obvious motivations of behavior, and may only become apparently relevant when we think long and hard to find an answer to, a reason for, or an insight into our actions, feelings, and predilections.

That said, I still believe that we can better understand the work of historians (and other scholars, artists, and so on) by consulting their carefully crafted autobiographical reflections on their own intellectual production. Not that such narrowly focused autobiographical inquiries capture the totality of a person: if one were asked to reflect autobiographically on one's role as spouse, or parent, or citizen, different aspects of the past would certainly be retrieved and displayed. Here, however, I am interested in the kinds of experiences, the choices recognized and made, the mentoring received, the situations rejected and desired, that fifteen prominent historians of the American South bring to their consciousness and share with us when asked—as my initial letter of inquiry to them put it—"to think autobiographically and ponder what in your background and life experiences helped determine you to become a historian of the South. How did your family background (especially gender, race, and class and where and how you grew up), teachers and mentors, colleagues, books you read, etc., shape both what you decided to write about and the general interpretations you developed?"

In part I see these essays as the raw material for scholars in the future who will write the intellectual history of modern southern historiography. But I also believe that contemporary interpreters of the South will find added nuance and deeper meaning in these scholars' existing work (and perhaps in their own) by seeing how the scholars themselves place their writing in personal, historical, and historiographical context. These essays suggest how historians define problems, address preexisting scholarship, mentor and are mentored to, and shape their careers at least part of the time by conscious choice. Despite our best attempts to be objective, if not neutral, about events of the past, all of us choose topics, analyze motivations, and see relationships between persons, ideas, and events based to some degree on our own life experiences. Unlike mathematicians, whose best work is typically done in their youth, historians practice a cumulative skill, and often their best, most seasoned work comes later in life, when there is a greater reservoir of lived experience upon which to draw. I believe that these essays are interesting simply as narratives of working historians' careers, but they are more than that. They shed light on the field of southern history as it has evolved and thrived in the last half of the twentieth century.

I do not wish to argue that these are necessarily the fifteen best or most influential southern historians or the only ones who have "shaped" the field. Obviously, these are highly talented, very significant scholars, but the list could have easily been doubled or tripled. I also knew that not everyone I asked to contribute would be able to or want to, so I began with a larger list of names than appears here. No doubt some readers will wonder why certain historians are not represented, but they should recognize that the editor is not the only one making decisions in this respect—not everyone accepts who is asked. I tried to choose historians from diverse backgrounds, doing different kinds of history, pursuing various careers. Perhaps this point deserves some elaboration.

I wanted to select eminent academicians who came from a variety of backgrounds — from Peter H. Wood, who grew up in a distinguished academic family first in St. Louis and then in Baltimore; to Bill C. Malone, the son of sharecroppers in East Texas; to Bertram Wyatt-Brown, who had a career-changing experience at Oxford University; to Darlene Clark Hine, whose black family was split between rural, southern attitudes and the urban lifestyle of Chicago; to Anthony J. Badger, coming of age in England. I wanted historians who reflected a variety of career paths, from consummate graduate-student director Jack P. Greene to museum curator Pete Daniel. I wanted scholars who had done pioneering work of various sorts, from John Hope Franklin's formative work in black history; to Anne Firor Scott, who practically invented southern women's history; to Vernon Burton's creative use of demography, family reconstitution, and computer-assisted statistics to produce a holistic account of a southern community; to Charles Joyner's application of anthropological methodologies to answer historical inquiries; to Edward L. Ayers's creation of a uniquely rich Web site of material exploring the origins of the Civil War in two counties, one northern, one southern, that straddled the Mason-Dixon Line. From Drew Gilpin Faust's exquisite excavation of a childhood letter to President Eisenhower, to Suzanne Lebsock's probing examination of the lives of free women in the antebellum industrial town of Petersburg, to Dan T. Carter's penetrating analyses of southern racism, the essays offer insights into some of the many ways historians make sense out of the past. Here are prominent, productive historian-teachers, male and female, black and white, northern- and southern-born, exploring diverse kinds of sources, asking various questions, utilizing disparate methodologies, studying different time periods, working from a range of institutional bases. All have published exemplary books that have widely influenced the profession. I believe these fifteen scholars fairly accurately represent the range of historical endeavors at the end of one century and the beginning of another.

I was frankly surprised, upon receiving the essays, to discover how similar politically this very diverse group was (actually, one historian who withdrew just before the final deadline was on the conservative end of the political spectrum). Liberalism, particularly on the issue of race, is quite typical of the academy (at least among faculty in the humanities) at present, however, so the essays accurately reflect the political climate on campuses.

I was also surprised by how many of the contributors came to be historians in decidedly roundabout and often serendipitous ways. Few were "born" to be

x Preface

historians. Instead, time and time again external political events, a charismatic professor, or a seminal book lit a spark in their intellectual development. Seldom do any of us think about the chance encounters and determinative moments that shaped who we became. Many of those who agreed to participate in this volume, even with some trepidation, were surprised, after they finished their essays, by how much they enjoyed the enterprise. I hope readers will have the same reaction.

A Life of Learning

JOHN HOPE FRANKLIN

As I began the task of putting the pieces together that would describe how I moved from one stage of intellectual development to another, I was reminded of a remark that Eubie Blake made as he approached his ninety-ninth birthday. He said, "If I had known that I would live this long I would have taken better care of myself." To paraphrase him, if I had known that I would become a historian I would have kept better records of my own pilgrimage through life. I may be forgiven, therefore, if I report that the beginnings are a bit hazy, not only to me but to my parents as well. For example, they had no clear idea of when I learned to read and write. It was when I was about three or four, I am told.

My mother, an elementary-school teacher, introduced me to the world of learning when I was three years old. Since there were no day-care centers in the village where we lived, she had no alternative to taking me to school and seating me in the rear of her classroom where she could keep an eye on me. I remained quiet but presumably I also remained attentive, for when I was about five my mother noticed that on the sheet of paper she gave me each morning, I was no longer making lines and sketching out some notable examples of abstract art. I was writing words, to be sure almost as abstract as my art, and making sentences. My mother later said that she was not surprised much less astonished at what some, not she, would have called my precocity. Her only reproach — to herself, not me — was that my penmanship was hopelessly flawed since she had not monitored my progress as she had done for her enrolled students. From that point on, I would endeavor to write and, through the written word, to communicate my thoughts to others.

This essay is a revised and enlarged version of the essay entitled "A Life of Learning," which as the Charles Homer Haskins Lecture was delivered before the American Council of Learned Societies in New York City on April 14, 1988, and printed in the council's *Occasional Papers, Number 4* (New York, 1988); it was subsequently reprinted in Franklin's *Race and History: Selected Essays, 1938–1988* (Baton Rouge, 1989), and is here reprinted with permission of Louisiana State University Press and Dr. Franklin.

My interest in having some thoughts of my own to express was stimulated by my father who, among other tasks, practiced law by day and read and wrote by night. In the absence of any possible distractions in the tiny village, he would read or write something each evening. This was my earliest memory of him and, indeed, it was my last memory of him. Even after we moved to Tulsa, a real city, and after we entered the world of motion pictures, radio, and television, his study and writing habits remained unaffected. I grew up believing that in the evenings one either read or wrote. It was always easy to read something worthwhile, and if one worked at it hard enough he might even write something worthwhile. I continue to believe that.

Two factors plagued my world of learning for all my developing years. One was race, the other was financial distress; and each had a profound influence on every stage of my development. I was born in the all-Negro town of Rentiesville, Oklahoma, to which my parents went after my father had been expelled from court by a white judge who told him that no black person could ever represent anyone in his court. My father resolved that he would resign from the world dominated by white people and try to make it among his own people. But Rentiesville's population of less than two hundred people could not provide a poverty-free living even for one who was a lawyer, justice of the peace, postmaster, farmer, and president of the Rentiesville Trading Company, which, incidentally, was not even a member of the New York Stock Exchange.

The quality of life in Rentiesville was as low as one can imagine. There was no electricity, running water, or inside plumbing. There was no entertainment or diversion of any kind — no parks, playgrounds, libraries, or newspapers. We subscribed to the *Muskogee Daily Phoenix*, which was delivered by the Missouri, Kansas, and Texas Railroad as it made its way southward through the state each morning. The days and nights were lonely and monotonous, and for a young lad with boundless energy there was nothing to do but read. My older sister and brother were away in private school in Tennessee, and one did not even have the pleasure of the company of older siblings. Now and then one went to Checotah, six miles away, to shop. That was not always pleasant, such as the time when my mother, sister, and I were ejected from the train because my mother refused to move from the coach designated for whites. It was the only coach we could reach before the train moved again, so my mother argued that she would not move because she was not to blame if the train's white coach was the only one available when the train came to a halt. Her argument was unsuccessful, and we had to trudge back to Rentiesville through the woods.

There were the rare occasions when we journeyed to Eufaula, the county seat, where I won the spelling bee for three consecutive years. There was Muskogee to the north, where I went at the age of five for my first pair of eyeglasses — the malady brought on, I was told, by reading by the dim light of a kerosene lamp. It was a combination of these personal and family experiences that forced my parents to the conclusion that Rentiesville was not a viable community. They resolved to move to Tulsa. First, my father would go, find a place, set himself up in the practice of law, and we would follow six months later, in June 1921, when my mother's school closed for the summer recess.

That June, however, we received word that in Tulsa there was a race riot, whatever that was, and that the Negro section of that highly segregated community was in flames. At the age of six I sensed from my mother's reaction that my father was in danger. We were all relieved several days later, therefore, when a message arrived that he had suffered no bodily harm, but that the property he had contracted to purchase was destroyed by fire. He practiced law in a tent for several months, and our move to Tulsa was delayed by four years.

In the month before I reached my eleventh birthday, we arrived in Tulsa. It was quite a new world, and although a city of less than moderate size at the time, it was to my inexperienced eyes perhaps the largest city in the country. I did not see much of it, however, for racial segregation was virtually complete. I thought that Booker T. Washington, the school where I enrolled in grade seven, was the biggest and best school until one day I saw Central High for whites. It was a massive, imposing structure covering a city block. I was later to learn that it had every conceivable facility such as a pipe organ and a theater-size stage, which we did not have. I also learned that it offered modern foreign languages and calculus, while our school offered automobile mechanics, home economics, typing, and shorthand. Our principal and our teachers constantly assured us that we need not apologize for our training, and they worked diligently to give us much of what was not even in the curriculum.

Now that the family was together again I had the example and the encouragement of both my parents. My mother no longer taught, but she saw to it that my sister and I completed all our home assignments promptly. Quite often, moreover, she introduced us to some of the great writers, especially Negro authors, such as Paul Laurence Dunbar and James Weldon Johnson, who were not a part of our studies at school. She also told us about some of the world's great music such as Handel's oratorio *Esther*, in which she had sung in college. While the music at school was interesting and lively, especially after I achieved the position of first trumpet in the band and orchestra, there was no Handel or Mozart, or Beethoven. We had a full fare of Victor Herbert and John Philip Sousa, and operettas, in more than one of which I sang the leading role.

Often after school I would go to my father's office. By the time I was in high school, the Depression had yielded few clients but ample time, which he spent with me. It was he who introduced me to ancient Greece and Rome, and he delighted in quoting Plato, Socrates, and Pericles. We would then walk home together, and after dinner he went to his books and I went to mine. Under the circumstances, there could hardly have been a better way of life, since I had every intention after completing law school of someday becoming his partner.

It was in secondary school that I had a new and wonderful experience, which my parents did not share. It was the series of concerts and recitals at Convention Hall, perhaps even larger than the theater at Central High School that I never saw. As in the other few instances where whites and blacks were under the same roof, segregation was strict, but I very much wanted to go with some of my teachers, who always held season tickets. My parents would *never* voluntarily accept segregation; consequently, the concerts were something they chose to forego. Even at court my father refused to accept segregation. Whenever I accompanied him, which was as often as I could, he would send me to the jury box when it was empty or, when there was a jury trial, have me sit at the bench with him. They took the position, however, that if I could bear the humiliation of segregation, I could go to the concerts.

Thus, I could purchase my own tickets with the money I earned as a paperboy. To be more accurate, I was not the paperboy but the assistant to a white man who had the paper route in the black neighborhood. It was at one of these concerts that I heard Paul Whiteman present Gershwin's Concerto in F while on a nationwide tour in 1928. I also attended the annual performances of the Chicago Civic Opera Company, which brought to Tulsa such stellar singers as Rosa Raisa, Tito Schipa, and Richard Bonelli. I am not altogether proud of going to Convention Hall; there are times, even now, while enjoying a symphony or an opera, when I reproach myself for having yielded to the indignity of racial segregation. I can only say that in the long run it was my parents who knew best, though later I made a conscious effort to regain my self-respect.

There were many sobering experiences at Fisk University, which I entered on a tuition scholarship in 1931. The first was my encounter with at least two dozen valedictorians and salutatorians from some of the best high schools in the United States. The fact that I had finished first in my high-school class did not seem nearly as important in Nashville as it had in Tulsa. Imagine my chagrin when a whiz kid from Dayton made all A's in the first quarter while I made two B's and a C+. My rather poor grades were somewhat mitigated by my having to hold three jobs in order to pay my living expenses. I was also absolutely certain that the C+ resulted from whimsical grading by the teaching assistants in a course called "Contemporary Civilization." As I think of it now I still become infuriated, and if there was anyone to listen to my case today I would insist that my examinations be reevaluated and my grade raised accordingly! I *was* consoled by my salutatorian girlfriend, later my wife of fifty-eight years, who over the years lent a sympathetic ear to my rantings about the injustices in that course. She could afford to be charitable; she received a grade of B+.

Another sobering experience was my first racial encounter in Nashville. At a downtown streetcar ticket window, I gave the man the only money I possessed, which was a twenty-dollar bill. I apologized and explained that it was all I had and he could give me my change using any kind of bills he wished. In an outburst of abusive language and using vile racial epithets, he told me that no nigger could tell him how to make change. After a few more similar statements he proceeded to give me $19.75 in dimes and quarters. From that day until I graduated, I very seldom went to Nashville, and when I did I never went alone. It was about as much as a sixteen-year-old could stand. I thought of that encounter some three years later, and felt almost as helpless, when a gang of white hoodlums took a young black man from a Fisk-owned house on the edge of the campus and lynched him. As president of student government I made loud noises and protests to the mayor, the governor, and even President Franklin D. Roosevelt, but nothing could relieve our pain and anguish or bring Cordie Cheek back. Incidentally, the heinous crime he had committed was that while carrying an armful of wood he brushed against a white girl, whose brother gave her a dollar to declare that Cheek had sexually assaulted her.

Still another sobering, even shattering, experience was my discovery at the end of my freshman year that my parents had lost our home and had moved into a four-family apartment building that they had built. I knew that the country was experiencing an economic depression of gigantic proportions, that unemployment had reached staggering figures, and that my father's law practice had declined significantly. I was not prepared for the personal embarrassment that the Depression created for me and my family, and frankly I never fully recovered from it. The liquidation of all debts became an obsession with me, and because of that experience my determination to live on a pay-as-you-go basis is as great today as it was when it was not at all possible to live that way.

Despite these experiences my years in college were pleasant if hectic, rewarding if tedious, happy if austere. Most classes were rigorous, and everyone was proud of the fact that the institution enjoyed an A rating by the Southern Association of Colleges and Secondary Schools. The faculty was, on the whole, first-rate, and they took pride in their scholarly output as well as in their teaching. Although the student body was all black, with the exception of an occasional white exchange student or special student, the faculty was fairly evenly divided between white and black. It was an indication of the lack of interest in the subject that we never thought in terms of what proportion of the faculty was white and what proportion was black.

Since I was merely passing through college en route to law school, I had little interest in an undergraduate concentration. I thought of English, but the chairman of that department, from whom I took freshman English, discouraged me on the ground that I would never be able to command the English language. (Incidentally, he was a distinguished authority in American literature and specialized in the traditions of the Gullah-speaking people of the Sea Islands. I was vindicated some years later when he chaired the committee that awarded me the Bancroft Prize for the best article in the *Journal of Negro History*.) My decision to major in history was almost accidental. The chairman of that department, Theodore S. Currier, who was white, had come into that ill-fated course in contemporary civilization and had delivered the most exciting lectures I had ever heard. I decided to see and hear more of him.

During my sophomore year I took two courses with Professor Currier, and my deep interest in historical problems and the historical process and what he had to say was apparently noted by him. Soon we developed a close personal relationship that developed into a deep friendship. Soon, moreover, I made the fateful decision to give up my plan to study and practice law and to replace it with a plan to study, write, and teach history. My desire to learn more about the field resulted in his offering new courses, including seminars, largely for my benefit. He already entertained the hope that I would go to Harvard, where he had done his own graduate work. I had similar hopes, but in the mid-1930s with the Depression wreaking its havoc, it was unrealistic to entertain such hopes. With a respectable grade point average (that C+ prevented my graduating summa cum laude) and strong supporting letters from my professors, I applied for admission to the Harvard Graduate School of Arts and Sciences.

Harvard required that I take an aptitude test that must have been the forerunner to the Graduate Record Examination. It was administered at Vanderbilt University, just across town but on whose grounds I had never been. When I arrived at the appointed place and took my seat, the person in charge, presumably a professor, threw the examination at me, a gesture hardly calculated to give me a feeling of welcome or confidence. I took the examination but cannot imagine that my score was high. As I left the room a Negro custodian walked up to me and told me that in his many years of working there I was the only black person he had ever seen sitting in a room with white people. The record that Fisk made that year was more important. The Association of American Universities placed Fisk University on its approved list. On the basis of this new recognition of my alma mater, Harvard admitted me unconditionally. Apparently this was the first time it had given a student from a historically black institution an opportunity to pursue graduate studies without doing some undergraduate work at Harvard. The university declined, however, to risk a scholarship on me.

Admission to Harvard was one thing; getting there was quite another. My parents were unable to give me more than a very small amount of money and their good wishes. I was able to make it back to Nashville, where Ted Currier told me that money alone would not keep me out of Harvard. He went to a Nashville bank, borrowed $500, and sent me on my way.

Shortly after my arrival in Cambridge in September 1935, I felt secure academically, financially, and socially. At Fisk I had even taken two modern foreign languages in order to meet Harvard's requirement, and in Currier's seminars I had learned how to write a research paper. Since I was secretary to the librarian at Fisk for four years, I had learned how to make the best use of reference materials, bibliographical aids, and manuscripts. Even when I met my adviser, Professor A. M. Schlesinger Sr., I did not feel intimidated, and I was very much at ease with him while discussing my schedule and my plans. After I got a job washing dishes for my evening meal and another typing dissertations and lectures, a feeling of long-range solvency settled over me. Although I had a room with a Negro family that had taken in black students since the time of Charles Houston and Robert Weaver, I had extensive contact with white students who never showed the slightest condescension toward me. I set my own priorities, however, realizing that I had the burden of academic deficiencies dating back to secondary school. I had to prove to myself and to my professors that the Association of American Universities was justified in placing Fisk University on its approved list. I received the M.A. degree in nine months and won fellowships with which I completed the Ph.D. requirements.

There were few blacks at Harvard in those days. One was completing his work in French history as I entered. As in Noah's Ark, there were two in the law school, two in zoology, and two in the college. There was one in English and one in comparative literature; there were none in the medical school and none in the business school.

The most traumatic social experience I had there was not racist but anti-Semitic. I was quite active in the Henry Adams Club, made up of graduate students in United States history. I was appointed to serve on the committee to nominate officers for the coming year, which, if one wanted to be hypersensitive, was a way of making certain that I would not be an officer. When I suggested the most active, brightest graduate student for president, the objection to him was that although he did not have some of the more reprehensible Jewish traits, he was still a Jew. I had never heard any person speak of another in such terms, and I lost respect not only for the person who made the statement but for the entire group that even tolerated such views. Most of the members of the club never received their degrees. The Jewish member became one of the most distinguished persons to get a degree in United States history from Harvard in the last half-century.

The course of study was satisfactory but far from extraordinary. Mark Hopkins was seldom on the other end of the log, and one had to fend for himself as best he could. I had no difficulty with such a regimen, although I felt that some of my fellow students needed more guidance than the university provided. In my presence, at the beginning of my second year, one of the department's outstanding professors verbally abused a student visiting from another institution and dismissed him from his office because the student's question was awkwardly phrased the first time around. Another professor confessed to me that a doctoral committee had failed a candidate because he did not *look* like a Harvard Ph.D. When the committee told him that he would have to study four more years before applying for reconsideration, the student was in the library the following morning to begin his four-year sentence. At that point, the chairman of the committee was compelled to inform the student that under no circumstances would he be permitted to continue his graduate studies there.

When I left Harvard in the spring of 1939 I knew that I did not wish to be in Cambridge another day. I had no desire to offend my adviser or the other members of my doctoral committee. I therefore respectfully declined suggestions that I seek further financial aid. It was time, I thought, to seek a teaching position and complete my dissertation in absentia. I had taught one year at Fisk following my first year at Harvard. With five preparations in widely disparate fields and with more than two hundred students, I learned more history than I had learned at Fisk *and* Harvard. I early discovered that teaching had its own very satisfying rewards. For some fifty-two years, there have been many reasons to confirm the conclusions I reached at Fisk, St. Augustine's, North Carolina College at Durham, Howard, Brooklyn, Chicago, Duke, and short stints in many institutions here and abroad.

After I committed myself to the study, teaching, and writing of history, I was so preoccupied with my craft that I gave no attention to possible career alternatives. Less than two years into my career, however, when I was working on my second book, the president of a small — but quite respectable — historically black liberal-arts college invited me to become dean of his institution. It was at that point that I made a response that was doubtless already in my mind but which I had not yet articulated. I thanked him and respectfully declined the invitation on the grounds that my work in the field of history precluded my moving into college administration. When the president received my letter, he sent me a telegram informing me that he was arriving the following day to explain his offer. During the three hours of conversation with him I had ample opportunity to state and restate my determination to remain a teacher and writer of history. Each time I did so I became more unequivocal in my resistance to any change in my career objectives. I believe that he finally became convinced that he was indeed wrong in offering me the deanship in the first place. From that day onward, I had no difficulty in saying to anyone who raised the matter that I was not interested in deanships, university presidencies, or ambassadorships. And I never regretted the decision to remain a student and teacher of history.

There is nothing more stimulating or satisfying than teaching bright, inquisitive undergraduates. It was puzzling, if dismaying, when a student complained, as one did at Howard, that my lengthy assignments did not take into account the fact that his people were only eighty-five years removed from slavery. It was sobering, but challenging, when an undergraduate asked, as one did at Brooklyn, if I would suggest additional readings since he had already read everything in the syllabus that I distributed on the first day of class. It was reassuring to find that some students, such as those at Chicago, came to class on a legal holiday because I neglected to take note of the holiday in my class assignments. It was refreshing, even amusing, when students requested, as some did at Duke, that the date for the working dinner at my home be changed because it conflicted with a Duke-Virginia basketball game. As Harry Golden would say, only in America could one find undergraduates with so much *chutzpah*.

There came a time in my own teaching career when I realized that with all my frantic efforts at research and writing I would never be able to write on all the subjects in which I was deeply interested. If I only had graduate students who would take up some of the problems regarding slavery, free blacks, the Reconstruction era and its overthrow, it would extend my own sense of accomplishment immeasurably. That was a major consideration in my move in 1964 from Brooklyn College to the University of Chicago, where for the next eighteen years I supervised some thirty dissertations of students who subsequently have published more than a dozen books. In view of Chicago's free-wheeling attitude toward the time for fulfilling degree requirements, there was a possibility that even years after retirement from that institution, I might have more doctoral students complete their work and write more books. Subsequently, I reveled in the excitement of teaching in still another type of institution, the law school at Duke University.

I could not have avoided being a social activist even if I had wanted to. I had been barred from entering the University of Oklahoma to pursue graduate studies, and when the National Association for the Advancement of Colored People asked me to be the expert witness for Lyman Johnson, who sought admission to the graduate program in history at the University of Kentucky, I was honored to do so. After all, it was easy to establish the fact that Johnson could not get the same training at the inferior Kentucky State College for Negroes that he could get at the University of Kentucky. Johnson was admitted forthwith. To me it was one more blow against segregation in Oklahoma as well as Kentucky. The defense argument collapsed when the University of Kentucky placed one of its history professors on the stand and asked him about teaching Negroes. He replied soberly that he did not teach Negroes, he taught history, which he was pleased to do!

Then, Thurgood Marshall asked me to serve on his nonlegal research staff when the NAACP Legal Defense Fund sought to eliminate segregation in the public schools. Each week in the late summer and fall of 1953 I journeyed from Washington to New York, where I worked from Thursday afternoon to Sunday afternoon. I wrote historical essays, coordinated the work of some other researchers, and participated in the seminars that the lawyers held regularly, and provided the historical setting for the questions with which they were wrestling. I had little time for relaxing at my home away from home, the Algonquin Hotel, but each time I entered this establishment, I made eye contact with an imaginary Tallulah Bankhead, Agnes DeMille, or Noel Coward, who were among the more famous habitués of its lobby.

The historian, of all people, must not make more of his own role in events, however significant, even if it is tempting to do so. It would be easy to claim that I was one of the 250,000 people at the March on Washington in 1963. I was not there, and perhaps the truth is even more appealing. Since I was serving as Pitt Professor at the University of Cambridge that year, I was something of a resource person for BBC television. On Richard Dimbleby's popular television program *Panorama*, I tried to explain to the British viewers what had transpired when James Meredith sought to enter the University of Mississippi. I suspect there was a bit of advocacy even in the tone of my voice. In the summer of 1963 I took British viewers through what the BBC called "A Guide to the March on Washington." Here again, with film clips on Malcolm X, James Baldwin, A. Philip Randolph, and others, I explained why the march was a very positive development in the history of American race relations. Finally, in 1965, I was actually on the Selma march. No, I did not march *with* Martin, as some imaginative writers have claimed. I doubt that Martin ever knew that I was there, far back in the ranks as I was. I was *not* at Pettus Bridge in Dallas County, but joined the march at the city of St. Jude on the outskirts of Montgomery. I took pride in marching with more than thirty historians who came from all parts of the country to register their objection to racial bigotry in the United States. And I want to make it clear that I was afraid, yes, frightened out of my wits by the hate-filled eyes that stared at us from the sidewalks, windows, businesses, and the like. It was much more than I had bargained for.

One must be prepared for any eventuality when making any effort to promote legislation or to shape the direction of public policy or to affect the choice of those in the public service. This came to me quite forcefully in 1987 when I joined with others from many areas of activity in opposing the Senate confirmation of Robert H. Bork as associate justice of the Supreme Court of the

United States. In what I thought was a sober and reasoned statement, I told the Judiciary Committee of the United States Senate that there was "no indication — in his writings, his teachings, or his rulings — that this nominee has any deeply held commitment to the eradication of the problem of race or even of its mitigation." It came as a shock, therefore, to hear the president of the United States declare that the opponents of the confirmation of Judge Bork constituted a "lynch mob." This was a wholly unanticipated tirade against those activists who had merely expressed views on a subject in which all citizens had an interest.

It was necessary, as a black historian, to have a personal agenda, as well as one dealing with more general matters, that involved a type of activism. I discovered this in the spring of 1939 when I arrived in Raleigh, North Carolina, to do research in the state archives, only to be informed by the director that in planning the building the architects did not anticipate that any Afro-Americans would be doing research there. Perhaps it was the astonishment that the director, a Yale Ph.D. in history, saw in my face that prompted him to make a proposition. If I would wait a week he would make some arrangements. When I remained silent, registering a profound disbelief, he cut the time in half. I waited from Monday to Thursday, and upon my return to the archives I was escorted to a small room outfitted with a table and chair that was to be my private office for the next four years. (I hasten to explain that it did not take four years to complete my dissertation. I completed it the following year, but continued to do research there as long as I was teaching at St. Augustine's College.) The director also presented me with keys to the manuscript collection in order to avoid requiring the white assistants to deliver manuscripts to me. That arrangement lasted only two weeks, when the white researchers, protesting discrimination, demanded keys to the manuscript collection for themselves. Rather than comply with their demands, the director relieved me of my keys and ordered the assistants to serve me.

Nothing illustrated the vagaries of policies and practices of racial segregation better than libraries and archives. In Raleigh alone, there were three different policies: the state library had two tables in the stacks set aside for the regular use of Negro readers. The state supreme court library had no segregation while, as we have seen, the archives faced the matter as it arose. In Alabama and Tennessee, the state archives did not segregate readers, while Louisiana had a strict policy of excluding Negro would-be readers altogether. In the summer of 1945

I was permitted by the Louisiana director of archives to use the manuscript collection since the library was closed in observance of the victory of the United States over governmental tyranny and racial bigotry in Germany and Japan. As I have said elsewhere, pursuing southern history has been for me a strange career.

While World War II interrupted the careers of many young scholars, I experienced no such delay. At the same time, it raised in my mind the most profound questions about the sincerity of my country in fighting bigotry and tyranny abroad. And the answers to my questions shook my faith in the integrity of our country and its leaders. Being loath to fight with guns and grenades, in any case, I sought opportunities to serve in places where my training and skills could be utilized. When the United States entered the war in 1941 I had already received my doctorate. Since I knew that several men who had not been able to obtain their advanced degrees had signed on as historians in the War Department, I made application there. I was literally rebuffed without the department giving me any serious consideration. In Raleigh, where I was living at the time, the navy sent out a desperate appeal for men to do office work, and the successful ones would be given the rank of petty officer. When I answered the appeal, the recruiter told me that I had all of the qualifications except color. I concluded that there was *no* emergency and told the recruiter how I felt. When my draft board ordered me to go to its staff physician for a blood test, I was not permitted to enter his office and was told to wait on a bench in the hall. When I refused and insisted to the draft board clerk that I receive decent treatment, she in turn insisted that the doctor see me forthwith, which he did. By this time, I had concluded that the United States did not need me and did not deserve me. I spent the remainder of the war successfully outwitting my draft board, including taking a position at North Carolina College for Negroes, whose president was on the draft appeal board. Each time I think of these incidents, even now, I feel nothing but shame for my country—not merely for what it did to me but for what it did to the one million black men and women who served in the armed forces under conditions of segregation and discrimination.

One had always to be mindful, moreover, that being a black scholar did not exempt one from the humiliations and indignities that a society with more than its share of bigots can heap upon a black person, regardless of education or even station in life. This became painfully clear when I went to Brooklyn College in

1956 as chairman of a department of fifty-two white historians. There was much fanfare accompanying my appointment, including a front-page story with picture in the *New York Times*. When I sought to purchase a home, however, not one of the thirty-odd realtors offering homes in the vicinity of Brooklyn College would show their properties. Consequently, I had to seek showings by owners who themselves offered their homes for sale. I got a few showings including one that we very much liked, but I did not have sufficient funds to make the purchase. My insurance company had proudly advertised that it had $50 million to lend to its policyholders who aspired to home ownership. My broker told me that the company would not make a loan to me because the house I wanted was several blocks beyond where blacks should live. I canceled my insurance and, with the help of my white lawyer, tried to obtain a bank loan. I was turned down by every New York bank except the one in Brooklyn where my attorney's father had connections. As we finally moved in after the hassles of more than a year, I estimated that I could have written a long article, perhaps even a small book, in the time expended on the search for housing. The high cost of racial discrimination is not merely a claim of the so-called radical left. It is as real as the rebuffs, the indignities, or the discriminations that many black people suffer.

When the drive for racial equality reached a new level of intensity in the years of the Black Revolution, I was among those who argued that if the American public were better informed of the role of African Americans in the history of this country, perhaps there would be a greater appreciation of and sympathy for the goal of racial equality. Colleges and universities began to offer courses in African American history. When there were no more qualified African Americans available to teach such courses, some historically white institutions turned to black laypersons and only reluctantly hired white historians as teachers of African American history. In due course the cadre of black and white professors teaching and writing about African American history was second only to the United States armed forces in the extent of its use of whites and blacks to fill the need for teaching personnel.

In accepting President Clinton's invitation to chair his advisory board on race, I had yet another opportunity to influence public policy. This task was so burdened by long-festering sores on the body politic on the one hand and a virtually impenetrable thicket of racial, ethnic, and moral conflicts on the other that it was unbelievably difficult to make any progress whatsoever. I learned much about the layers of prejudice and misunderstanding that characterize the debate on race in America. I learned a great deal about the power of the press, for example, to manipulate, misrepresent, and influence public opinion. I could only conclude that the only highly touted freedom that the press enjoys was by those who owned it. I also learned the extent to which the burden of race is connected in some way with every aspect of the history and the very existence of our country. By the time the life of the board had expired, the seven members, among whom were some of the ablest, finest, and most dedicated men and women in the country, had learned a great deal about life itself.

Many years ago, when I was a fledgling historian, I decided that one way to make certain that the learning process would continue was to write different kinds of history, even as one remained in the same field. It was my opinion that one should write a monograph, a general work, a biography, a period piece, and edit some primary source and some work or works, perhaps by other authors, to promote an understanding of the field. I made no systematic effort to touch all the bases, as it were, but with the recent publication of my biography of George Washington Williams, I believe that I have touched them all. More recently, I have started the process all over again by doing research for a monograph on runaway slaves.

Another decision I made quite early was to explore new areas or fields, whenever possible, in order to maintain a lively, fresh approach to the teaching and writing of history. That is how I happened to get into Afro-American history, in which I never had a formal course, but which attracted a growing number of students of my generation and many more in later generations. It is remarkable how moving or even drifting into a field can affect one's entire life. More recently, I have become interested in women's history, and during the winter of 1987–88 I prepared and delivered three lectures under the general title of "Women, Blacks, and Equality, 1820–1988." I need not dwell on the fact that for me it was a very significant learning experience. Nor should it be necessary for me to assure you that despite the fact that I have learned much, I do not seek immortality by writing landmark essays and books in the field of women's history.

Over the years I have had some great teachers in my pursuit of a formal education; and I have expressed my appreciation in a number of ways, ranging from public statements of gratitude to dedication of books to them. Four others, now all deceased, were deeply involved in what my father would call "my larger education" and were at the very core of the learning process as I experienced it. Two were my parents, who were patient and long-suffering in every respect, and I have earlier made several references to their role in my education. Another was Ted Currier, my Fisk mentor, who taught me the meaning of transcending race when, during the Black Revolution, the black students sought to run him away from Fisk University solely because he was white. Fearing for his well being, I said that I thought he should "disappear" for a few days. He calmly indicated to me that he had given his life to Fisk, which was more than the students could say; and he had no intention of succumbing to the temporary wrath of a group of students, many of whom did not know what real sacrifice meant. After I heard his declaration of intent, I was ashamed for having made the suggestion that he leave; and I apologized to him. In addition to all that he had previously taught me, I was grateful to him for demonstrating to me what real courage was.

I learned so much from my wife, whom I dated for nine years and to whom I was married for some fifty-eight years until her death in January 1999. I learned from her how to stand up to one's seniors when she advised me not to step down after I was elected president of the student body at Fisk. The dean had suggested that I "give way" to a so-called stronger (read "favorite") candidate. She merely said that I should do so only if I were able to explain to the students who had elected me why I should betray their trust that they had reposed in me. I had no explanation; therefore, I declined to step down. Years later, after we were married, I was attempting to write *From Slavery to Freedom* in a small apartment, with no office at the college and no workspace in the library. She suggested that I should go to the Library of Congress, rent a room in Washington, and complete the writing. She would send me money each week for my expenses. Without her advice, I could never have completed the book that, more than anything else, launched me on my career. It was so characteristic of her to make suggestions, offer advice, and stand willing to make sacrifices that would result in my success and our well-being. Small wonder that I called her President and CEO of the Aurelia Franklin Foundation.

I have learned much from my colleagues both at home and abroad. The historical associations and other learned societies have instructed me at great length at their annual meetings, and five of them have given me an opportunity to teach and to lead by electing me as their president. Their journals have provided me with the most recent findings of scholars, and they have graciously published some pieces of my own. Very early I learned that scholarship knows no national boundaries, and I have sought the friendship and collaboration of historians and scholars in many parts of the world. From the time that I taught at the Salzburg Seminar in American Studies in 1951, I have been a student and an advocate of the view that the exchange of ideas is more healthy and constructive than the exchange of bullets. This was especially true during my tenure on the Fulbright Board, as a member for seven years and as the chairman for three years. In such experiences one learns much about the common ground that the peoples of the world share. When we also learn that this country and the Western world have no monopoly of goodness and truth or of skills and scholarship, we begin to appreciate the ingredients that are indispensable to making a better world. In a life of learning that is, perhaps, the greatest lesson of all.

The Making of a Historian

Some Autobiographical Notes

JACK P. GREENE

In this postmodern world, scholars seem to feel compelled to spell out their personal relationship to their subjects of study, an impulse that I personally find wholly uncongenial. Stuart Schwartz, a historian of colonial Brazil, illustrates the process with a riddle: What did the postmodern anthropologist say to his informant? "But enough about you, let's talk about me." This drive to make oneself a part of the problem would be more engaging if scholars were more interesting people. We sit around in libraries and studies thinking and writing about intellectual problems and teaching students at various levels, but our lives are confined and routine. Hence, an assignment of this kind is especially difficult. Not much given to self-examination, more outer- than inner-directed, I am very convinced that any group other than my family or very close friends would find my autobiography—as opposed to the problems I have studied and what I have had to say about those problems—boring. Furthermore, for reasons elaborated below, I have never thought of myself as a historian of the South.

At the same time, however, even the life of the most closeted scholar can be analyzed in terms of questions of universal interest: how people choose the careers they do, how they pursue specific paths within their careers, how they bring their personal strengths to bear on career possibilities, and how a few people—I do not count myself among them—actually manage to redefine the nature of their chosen careers or professions.

My parents were the first generation in their families to move out of the traditional occupations of farming, storekeeping, or, in one case, being an unlettered Methodist minister. Driven by his aversion to the hard work of tobacco farming, my father was one of the first people in his community in Wilkes County, North Carolina, to go off to a university. As an agricultural engineer, he spent his professional life developing machinery to make the lives of farmers easier. My mother, from Lafayette, a small university town in northwest Indiana, regarded rural North Carolina as hopelessly backward. She worked in the restaurant business and shared my father's commitment to hard work and high standards. Both my parents' families regarded themselves as a bit better than their neighbors.

Being a good student was not difficult for me, although making straight A's like my mother was not something upon which I put priority. My father had been an athlete in high school, but I responded to his early efforts to turn me in that direction with a studied resolution, born of a deep contrarian strain in my personality, to be unathletic. I preferred playing with lead soldiers or cowboys and Indians over catching a ball. By the time I was nine or ten years old, however, I had developed a strong interest in sports. At first, this interest was vicarious and centered upon the football and basketball teams at Purdue University, where my father worked and where, during the labor-short years of World War II, I had my first paid job at age ten, driving a tractor pulling an experimental hay bailer on which my father was working. Eventually I also got deeply interested in major league baseball, hating the Chicago Cubs and, perhaps because I liked their names, rooting for the Cincinnati Reds and Pittsburgh Pirates. By the time I was twelve or thirteen I had athletic ambitions of my own, but in the large high school I attended in Lafayette, Indiana, I was too small ever to play on the school teams and had to content myself playing club football and baseball and YMCA and intramural basketball. Throughout my school years, however, I was always more interested in sports or drama or choir singing or even the Boy Scouts than I ever was in the academic side of school. Indeed, I found my job, beginning at age thirteen, as a bellhop and checkroom boy at the Purdue Memorial Union building, far more interesting than school. Most of my fellow employees were college students, many of them World War II veterans, and I reveled in the large and more adult world with which they brought me into contact. One learns a lot about life as a bellhop, even at a college hotel. By the time I was fourteen I was the head of the checkroom and bellhop corps with many far older college students working under me, and I assigned myself the job of watching the fire doors on Friday and Saturday nights when the big bands came to the Purdue Union. I recall teaching Doris Day the Purdue fight song when she was there with the Les Brown orchestra.

Unlike my father's generation, I never had any doubt that I would go to college. But for what purpose? My father wanted me to be an engineer, but I never shared his passion for understanding how machines worked. Whereas he thought that every man should know how to tear down and repair his automobile, I disliked getting greasy. My interests were not in machines. For a time, I thought they might be in structures. I loved contemporary architecture, which I subsequently learned was known as Art Deco. If I was expected to be an engineer, I thought I might be an architectural engineer and build sleek buildings of the kinds I saw in movies. But my lowest grades were usually in art or penmanship, and someone told me that you had to be able to draw well to be an architect. Thereafter, my ambitions veered off toward the performing arts—I thought I might be a crooner like Bing Crosby or Frank Sinatra or a dancer like Fred Astaire or Gene Kelly. Barring that, I aspired to be a baseball player or a sportswriter or a baseball executive. Had I known what it was, scholarship in any field would have held no interest for me. My aunt and uncle, who taught English at Davidson College, seemed to lead the most retired, arid, and boring lives. Yet, like my maternal grandmother, I was a public-library rat, and, although I principally read historical novels, I also read some historical biography and was fascinated by foreign and exotic places and peoples. When I was nine and ten, I often wrote little booklets (drawing my information from encyclopedias) on the lives of the great dictators of the 1930s—Hitler, Mussolini, Atatürk, Franco, and Salazar—or the explorers of the American West—Daniel Boone, Simon Kenton, Davy Crockett, and Kit Carson. But I was as likely to write little essays about my favorite animals—pandas and penguins—or places—Spain and Denmark.

By the time I was twelve a new interest in baseball statistics had supplanted these interests. When I was not working, playing sports, or hanging out with my friends at school or at the neighborhood drugstore, I was mostly keeping track of the daily averages of the top twenty-five National League hitters, something I did every day for four or five years. In those days, baseball averages appeared in the papers only on Sundays and then included only games through the previous Thursday, information that was not sufficiently up-to-date to feed the voracious appetite I had for professional baseball, an appetite that fed off the *Sporting News*, a weekly publication that I read from cover to cover. If these activities showed a bent toward scholarship, teaching people like myself, even— much less most of my school mates—was something I never once considered doing.

When I was fifteen, in 1947, I underwent an experience I thought would be traumatic, when my father moved from Purdue to North Carolina State University, yanking me away from Lafayette, Indiana, where I had a responsible job and enjoyed an independent lifestyle. I had strong family roots in western North Carolina. My grandparents lived in Clingman, a small hamlet in Wilkes County named for my great-grandfather, who owned the crossroad store around which much of the secular life of that community revolved. Throughout my youth I had spent at least two weeks of every summer at my grandparents' farm, and when I was turning twelve, my parents sent me off there to spend the whole summer. Although I adored my North Carolina family and developed an appreciation for the beauties of the Blue Ridge Mountains, I felt strongly alien in this rural world that was only slowly acquiring the amenities of electrical power and running water; had no institutions except the corner store, the Baptist church, the Masonic Lodge, and the Grange; and, to judge from the other young people I met, was educationally disadvantaged. These visits had powerfully impressed upon me that I was a midwesterner, not a southerner.

For that reason I was not enthusiastic about my family's move, although, recognizing that it represented a major promotion for my father, I kept my sentiments to myself. But my skepticism about living in the South was immediately reinforced when my father discovered that the only place he could find for us to live was on an old air force base at what is now the Raleigh-Durham Airport, where there was little to do except practice my jump shot and where I had to ride a bus to a small high school in what was then the rural backwater of Cary, pronounced *Cayree*. People from Raleigh, eight miles away, were a curiosity in Cary, and I was a genuine exotic. The good things about the year I spent in Cary were, first, that it forced me to adapt to—and showed me that I could adapt to—a culture that was vastly different from the one in which I had lived my first fifteen years and, second, the confidence I acquired as a result of playing on all the athletic teams. Whereas my athletic opportunities in Lafayette had been practically nil, in Cary I was the starting quarterback on the football team by the end of the season, the shooting guard or small forward on a basketball team that came within two points of winning the county championship in 1948, and the shortstop on the baseball team. I also had the major comic role in the junior school play. Educationally, however, the school was no challenge. Only a few people, mostly women, aspired to go on to college. Recognizing as much, my father proposed, actually insisted, that I skip the last year of high school and go to the university.

I entered the University of North Carolina at Chapel Hill a few weeks after my seventeenth birthday. I was too young and immature to get much out of college during my first five quarters. I recall during my first term listening to history lectures, thinking how simple the material was, and wondering why all my classmates were taking notes. Nothing was assigned for me to read in any course except textbooks, and only in science or literature classes did instructors seem to expect students to read the assignments. I darkened the door of the library rarely during my freshman year and not once during my sophomore year. I did learn to play bridge, went to movies at least once and sometimes twice a day, played a lot of intramural sports after I failed to make any of the athletic teams, got to be a far better dancer, and spent a lot of time thinking about women, who, because they could not attend the university until they were juniors, were few and mostly monopolized by the upperclassmen. Most useful, perhaps, by joining a fraternity I also learned that I was not a club or an organization man and not a social conformist.

Of course, I was concerned to know what I should be when I got out of college and became an adult, and I really had no clue. For this reason, I early wandered over to the university testing service, which gave me many tests, including a test known as the Kuder Preference Test, which was supposed to tell you what sort of life's work might be best for you. When I went by a week later to get the results, the counselor told me that I had three choices: college teaching, the ministry, or law. The first two seemed wholly out of the question. Having been around universities all my life, they held no attraction for me, and I regarded formal religious institutions in about the same way I would subsequently come to regard my fraternity. I was not interested in belonging to or working for any clubs, religious or otherwise. That left only the law, and my entire undergraduate career was spent in the expectation that I would go to law school and become a lawyer.

Several things combined to frustrate this plan. The first was that I did not know any lawyers and could not tell exactly what they did. This was before the era of television and Perry Mason. From what I could tell, they mostly seemed to look up property titles and record deeds, neither of which seemed very exciting. Defending criminals sounded more interesting, but, doubting that I would ever be sufficiently articulate to appear effectively before large audiences, I was frightened by the performance skills I imagined to be required in courtroom situations. Second, those of my classmates who were going to law school were mostly campus politicians and other stuffy and self-important types with whom I felt no rapport. Third, during the last quarter of my sophomore year I took a history course from Professor Hugh T. Lefler, a historian of colonial and Revolutionary America, whose enthusiasm for his subject was so infectious and whose skepticism was so appealing that I decided that I would major in history on my way to getting ready to go to law school.

Other than Lefler, none of the professors who taught the history courses I subsequently took in Chapel Hill were especially exciting. Some of them were decent lecturers, especially James L. Godfrey, who first taught me about the British Empire, and Samuel Emory, a historical geographer who used to weave fascinating tales about the American past designed to illustrate how that past had been influenced by the physical geography of North America. But none of them exhibited Lefler's deep cynicism, his delight in iconoclasm, his eager commerce with doubt. He did not lecture but instead had an expository teaching style in which he supplied his classes with a detailed outline of his course and then spent class periods with a running commentary on that outline. Astonishing as it may now seem, not one of these professors, including Lefler, ever required me to write a paper of any kind, research, critical, or whatever. When I later entered graduate school, I had never written anything in history since the little booklets I used to make up at the public library when I was nine and ten. Fortunately, I had done a few papers in a comparative religion class and in several political science classes taught by a lawyer named Edward Woodhouse, whose courses had little content but encouraged students to write short ten- to twenty-page research papers on aspects of American government, a project that I relished so much that I wrote several such papers.

Yet even two or three weeks before I graduated at age nineteen from undergraduate school (I took extra courses and graduated in three years because I wanted to finish college before I could be drafted for the Korean War), I was still headed to law school at the University of North Carolina. Over the previous year, however, I had gotten to know a few graduate students and had begun to think I would like to do an M.A. in history, but not with the intention of being a historian or a college teacher. Indeed, at that time I was thinking mainly about the foreign service as an alternative to law. After consultation with some of my professors, and unknown to my family, I applied to graduate school at both North Carolina and Indiana and was admitted to both. My choice of Indiana was dictated by two considerations. First, I thought that I wanted to do an M.A. thesis on the fur trade in the upper Ohio Valley during the French era, and Indiana seemed to me to be a more appropriate place for this subject. Second, and far more important, I wanted to escape from the South and return to the Midwest of my youth. During my four years in North Carolina I had acquired an appreciation for its physical beauties. Notwithstanding the fact that my time in Chapel Hill produced a genuine fondness for it, I never warmed up to the pine-infested and view-deprived landscapes of the vast Piedmont that takes up most of the state. But the seashore and the mountains seemed to me magnificent. Moreover, what I liked about Chapel Hill — its relative liberalism and rich intellectuality — were the very characteristics that seemed to distinguish it from the rest of the state. Deep down, I was deeply embarrassed to live in and go to school in the South. The injustice and social and economic effects of the entrenched system of racial segregation and the seemingly unquestioning religiosity of the population were elements in my distaste for the South, but it was chiefly driven by my conviction that the South was both culturally and economically backward and deeply provincial. Rarely did I miss an opportunity to tell people I met that, although my parents lived in North Carolina, I was from Indiana. Hence, my choice to go to Indiana was an easy one, and I managed to persuade my father to let me defer law school for a year and, more important, to pay my way to graduate school at Indiana.

Only when I got to Indiana did I begin to realize that it was every bit as provincial as North Carolina. Because of my North Carolina residence and education, people immediately stereotyped me as a southerner, and I had to learn to defend myself against charges that I was racist, anti-Semitic, poorly educated, and violent, even though the last two may have been true. Having experienced no such hostility when I moved to North Carolina from Indiana, I began to suspect that, except on the important issue of race, southerners might very well be considerably more tolerant than either the midwesterners or the easterners among my graduate-school classmates.

When I entered the graduate program at Indiana, I had just turned twenty and was hopelessly naïve about what thesis research might require. It had never occurred to me, for instance, that I might need to read French to work on the French in the Old Northwest. When my thesis adviser, a seemingly ancient man named Albert Kohlmeier, who may have been considerably younger than I am now, quickly established that I could not read French, he told me to study one of the classic themes of colonial history, the development of representative government, in my home state of North Carolina during the colonial era, which I did as my first serious work in colonial British American history, the field I would later pursue and make my own. More important, I lived in a housing complex with many graduate students in different fields and saw the commitment many of them had to their fields. As yet, I felt no such commitment, but I remained skeptical about law school and learned that many graduate students had fellowships and assistantships by which they could pay their expenses at graduate school. I still had no way to discriminate among graduate schools. As far as I knew, Harvard, Yale, Columbia, Johns Hopkins, and Chicago were places that had bad football teams. I had no idea that there might be good professional reasons to go to those places to take a doctorate. I did know that I did not want to stay at Indiana, where I had done very well during my two-semester M.A. program but knew that the graduate students in history seemed not to be as engaged and interesting as those I had known at North Carolina, although the basketball team was a lot better. I also knew that I wanted to work with a younger man, and one of my teachers told me I might consider trying to study with either Edmund S. Morgan, then at Brown, or John R. Alden, then at the University of Nebraska. I found the books of these two, Morgan's book on the Puritan family,[1] the significance of which I did not then appreciate, and Alden's three books on figures associated with the American Revolution.[2] Although I got admitted to Brown, I got a teaching assistantship from Nebraska, which, in any case, seemed like a much more exotic place to me than Rhode Island, which I associated with falling-down buildings, a decaying economy, and snobbish people who would have scant regard for an outlander like myself.

Hence I went eagerly to Nebraska, where I did my first teaching and grading and where I developed a close and happy relationship with my mentor, John Richard Alden, who did not mind my iconoclasm and who granted me the large measure of independence I subsequently came to realize is absolutely essential for the development of independent-minded scholars. Alden was principally interested in the American Revolution and in military history, neither of which much interested me. I wanted to do a dissertation on the subject of my M.A. thesis but focusing on all four of the British southern continental colonies from Virginia south to Georgia. Never insisting that I try to follow in his footsteps, he granted me my impulse and helped me get a Fulbright grant to do the research for my dissertation in England during the academic year 1953–54.

Nothing could have been more fortunate than this fellowship. My passion for historical research was entirely the product of my getting into the archives during that year, working through masses of unpublished documents, and acquiring a sense of how little historians knew about the early American past. As a result, I quickly reconceived of history, now largely thinking of it as a series of unresolved problems, and I began to develop a sense that I might be able to contribute to the illumination, if not the resolution, of a few of those problems, a business that to this day still engages my interest and enthusiasm. In England I also encountered among the other Fulbrighters a lot of other graduate students from all the major graduate schools and began to sense for the first time that, while I might be as smart and as accomplished as they, I was going to have a hard time competing with them for jobs because I would be getting my degree from Nebraska, which had a more visible, professional, and published history faculty than either North Carolina or Indiana but was hardly one of the top graduate schools. (I learned as much when several of my fellow Fulbrighters expressed considerable surprise that Nebraska had a graduate school.) Hence, I was delighted when, after another year in Nebraska, Alden took a professorship at Duke and took me along with him—back to North Carolina. At Duke, where I was for just a year, I added fields in early modern English history with William Baskerville Hamilton and colonial Latin America with John Tate Lanning, two men, who, along with Lefler and Alden, have had much influence upon my approaches to teaching and to the past. From Lefler and Hamilton, who was an even greater iconoclast than Lefler, I learned the value of doubt and came to appreciate the smothering effects of piety. From Lanning, I acquired reinforcement for my own enthusiasm for research in primary materials, a respect for the integrity of the past, an impatience with anachronism, and an interest in comparative colonial history. From Alden and Lanning, I learned that, with effort, one can learn to write better. Neither Lanning nor Alden was a noteworthy writer as a young man, but Lanning turned himself into a powerful writer and Alden made himself an elegant prose stylist. My young wife Sue, a Nebraskan and a literary scholar, taught me how to write good, grammatical sentences.

When I got out of graduate school in the spring of 1956, my education as a historian was only just beginning, but I had already developed a rather clear understanding of what sort of historian I wanted to be. My dissertation, a study of the development of representative government in colonial Virginia, South Carolina, North Carolina, and Georgia during the slightly more than thirty years from 1730, when both Carolinas became royal colonies, to 1763, had focused on the problem of governance in the eighteenth-century British overseas empire and the tensions between settler power and imperial authority. No historian exerted a more profound influence upon this work than Charles M. Andrews, widely and justly regarded at that time as the dean of colonial British American historians, whose broad imperial approach to the subject I found especially appealing.[3] Like Andrews, I thought of myself, first and foremost, as a historian of the American portions of the early modern British Empire. In working out the dimensions of my dissertation problem, moreover, I quickly became aware of the extent to which the American colonies were deeply enmeshed in the larger British Atlantic world and recognized the importance of the transfer of English institutions, ideas, and legal, constitutional, and political practices to America. Hence, I early recognized that to be an American colonial historian required more than a passing familiarity with English history. Virtually everything that happened in the construction of the societies and polities of colonial British America seemed to me fully comprehensible only in terms of their English heritage and their continuing interaction with that heritage.

Finally, by focusing upon the specific experiences of four colonies, I had both developed an acute appreciation for local variations in general trends and inadvertently stumbled into the realm of comparative history. Colonies, I had learned, not only needed to be compared to the metropolitan society from which they came, but also could be fruitfully compared with one another. For a time I toyed with the idea of doing a broad comparative study of the history of imperial governance. In undergraduate school I had studied Spanish. At Indiana, when I was thinking about a career in the foreign service, I studied Portuguese for a year as a strategy to give myself a marginal advantage on the foreign service exam (Portuguese, one of the five languages authorized by the foreign service, was the one taken by fewest applicants). In my doctoral studies I learned to read French and (marginally) German, which was said to be similar to Dutch, so I thought I had or could quickly acquire the linguistic skills needed for such a study. The skeptical reaction of the hiring committee at Vanderbilt when I told them that this might be my next project caused me to rethink my enthusiasm for going in this direction. But the comparative history of the Americas has remained a continuing interest of mine, while the comparative history of British colonization has been a central preoccupation.[4]

Several concerns influenced my thinking as I began to consider how I might turn my unwieldy dissertation into a monograph. My first consideration was to extend the temporal range, pushing the story backward to the Glorious Revolution and forward to the American Revolution, a decision that required as much new research as I had done for the dissertation and a far better knowledge than I had of the extensive literature on the coming of the American Revolution. Inspired by Andrews, my approach to my dissertation had been largely institutional; I quickly learned while writing it that such an approach was falling out of favor during the early 1950s. Hence, I was much concerned to find some different angles that would enable me to transcend that approach.

By requiring me to read the works of Sir Lewis Namier on the structure of politics in eighteenth-century England during the age of the American Revolution,[5] W. B. Hamilton had pushed me in one seemingly promising direction. I was much taken by Namier's prosopographical approach to the study of politics, which inspired me in a determination to "find out who the guys are." By discovering as much as I could about the men who composed the legislatures about which I had written, I aspired to transform my book from a study of government into a study of politics. I quickly discovered, however, that in the absence of adequate biographical dictionaries of the sort that have since been produced, I could never hope to complete this gargantuan task, which would have required the construction of prosopographies for about 2,500 men. It took me an entire summer just to find the necessary data for 110 members of the Virginia House of Burgesses I had identified as prominent members through an elaborate compilation and analysis of committee assignments.[6] In addition, I quickly found that prosopography and institutional history did not fit comfortably together.

More promising, as a result of my reading of the works of the constitutional historians C. H. McIlwain and Andrew C. McLaughlin,[7] I began to grasp that my study of the legislative development of the southern colonies had an important constitutional dimension. Conscious of the federal nature of the empire, both McIlwain and McLaughlin were sensitive to the constitutional tensions between provinces and metropolis, and their insights provided a starting point for me to work out the broader constitutional ramifications of the local developments on which I had focused. This approach provided the central framework for several articles and my books *The Quest for Power*, published in 1963, and *Peripheries and Center*, published in 1986.[8]

So far, this is scarcely the profile of a southern historian. My undergraduate degree and my doctorate were from southern universities. My dissertation had focused on four of the southernmost British continental colonies, and research for that study had taken me into the public archives, historical-society libraries, and major university collections in Virginia, North Carolina, South Carolina, and Georgia. Moreover, I had already committed myself to edit and publish the diary of Landon Carter, a colonial Virginia planter, whose papers I had encountered at the Alderman Library of the University of Virginia, and I had agreed to co-author a book on the political culture of Revolutionary Virginia with my friend Keith Berwick.[9] Notwithstanding all this interest in Britain's southern mainland colonies, however, I never once thought of myself as a southern historian. The fact that the colonies I studied were southern was entirely coincidental, a function of the fact that in terms of the specific developments I was investigating, those colonies had been significantly understudied. Moreover, I was entirely persuaded by the argument of Carl Bridenbaugh, one of the few colonialists ever to give the Fleming Lectures in Southern History at Louisiana State University, that, as he argued in the published version of his admirable lectures, *Myths and Realities: Societies of the Colonial South*,[10] not one but several Souths existed at the time of the American Revolution. Indeed, my principal reservation about that work was his inability to resist calling the disparate regions he described Souths, which seemed to me anachronistic. Nor was I persuaded by the ingenious argument of my mentor, John Richard Alden, in his published Fleming Lectures, *The First South*,[11] that the South emerged as a coherent and partially self-conscious region during the Revolutionary era. Whenever the South emerged, I thought, it had to have been after 1800, probably even after the 1820s. The prominence of Virginians on the national political stage before that time seemed to belie the existence of a self-consciously defensive "South" at odds with the rest of the country.

Of course, my ignorance of southern history was enormous. I had never taken a course in southern history nor had the remotest interest in doing so. During my year at Duke, I tended to make friends with those graduate students who seemed to be pursuing big subjects in colonial Latin American, early modern French, early modern English, and British Commonwealth history and, like most of them, regarded those who concentrated on the history of the South as parochial and local historians who had little interest in wider historical questions.

Nor did anything during my early academic career change this perspective. My consistent attendance at the Southern Historical Association's annual meetings had far less to do with my interest in southern history than with the fact that I found the casual atmosphere of those meetings especially congenial. Except for a year I spent at the College of William and Mary in 1961–62, editing the *William and Mary Quarterly*, all my teaching experience was in northern universities: Michigan State University (1956–59), Western Reserve University (1959–65), and the University of Michigan (1965–66). Indeed, not until I went to the University of Michigan in 1965 did I even have a colleague, W. W. Freehling, who taught or wrote about southern history.

This situation changed dramatically in 1966 when I moved to Johns Hopkins University. No person with even a casual acquaintance with the South could ever mistake Baltimore for a southern city or Johns Hopkins for a southern university. Yet the long-term presence of C. Vann Woodward, who wrote most of his important books on the history of the South while he was a member of the Johns Hopkins faculty, had provided Hopkins with a strong identification with southern history, and in the mid-1960s David H. Donald, who succeeded Woodward after he went to Yale earlier in the decade, was in the process of establishing the Institute of Southern History with a large grant from the Ford Foundation. The institute brought many promising young southern historians to the campus on year-long postdoctoral fellowships, and, together with Donald's legion of doctoral students working on southern history, they provided me with at least a rudimentary education in the history of this field. My engagement was always extremely limited, however. None of the institute's postdoctoral fellows worked in the era before 1820; none of my own growing corps of doctoral students, only a few of whom worked on the southern continental colonies, seemed to derive much edification from the activities of the institute; and the institute's focus on the antebellum era and after only served to confirm my earlier opinions that southern history began long after the Revolutionary era and that it was largely a self-contained and parochial enterprise with little relevance for the questions then engaging me.

For my own research and writing interests continued to be resolutely imperial, in the sense that they revolved around a group of related problems about the construction, character, and partial dissolution of the early modern English/British Empire. These included the transfer and adaptation of English culture to a variety of New World settings, the rapid economic and social development of colonial British America during the fifty years beginning about 1713, the American colonial contribution to the phenomenal success of the British Empire after the middle of the eighteenth century, the causes of the political rupture that eventuated in the separation from the empire of thirteen of Britain's eighteen continental North American colonies between 1776 and 1783, and the powerful continuities between the pre- and post-Revolutionary societies and polities that combined to form the United States during the last quarter of the eighteenth century. These problems had no special relevance to the colonies in those areas that later became the South. Indeed, as I repeatedly emphasized to my doctoral students, they were problems that could best be studied on a broad scale taking in the whole of Britain's American settlements from Barbados north to Nova Scotia. The specific topics that occupied me through most of my first decade at Hopkins were a general history of the American colonies from 1713 to 1763 and the British origins of the American Revolution, the first of which I eventually abandoned and the second of which remains unfinished.

Two other developments beginning in the late 1960s helped to turn my attention and that of my students away from the history of the South. The first was the rise of the new social history, which, among colonial British Americanists, was mostly inspired by the work of the Annales school in France and of the Cambridge Group for the Study of Population and History in Britain. This development diverted our attention ever more sharply away from the history of the United States and toward parallel studies on early modern Europe. Thereafter, we all thought of ourselves not as American historians but as early modern historians who happened to focus on the activities of Europeans and their descendants in the Americas. Doctoral students found fields in early modern Britain, France, Spain, or even Germany far more relevant to the preparation of their dissertation studies than fields in nineteenth- or twentieth-century United States history, including the South.

Largely internal to Johns Hopkins, the second development, the establishment of the Program in Atlantic History and Culture, was at once a response to the logic of the course of the intellectual development of contemporary historical studies and the success of the Civil Rights movement in the United States and elsewhere. At the same time that the aspiration of the Annalistes to achieve a *histoire totale* that would include all members of the societies of past times was stimulating a determination to break out of the paradigm of power that had dictated that the study of prominent men was more important than, for instance, that of poor women, the Civil Rights movement of the 1960s dramatically called attention to the massive contributions of African peoples to the formation and subsequent operation of American society and to the centrality of the institution of slavery in that process. Since the work of Charles M. Andrews and other "imperial" historians in the early twentieth century, scholars of colonial British America had been acutely attuned to the transatlantic dimensions of colonial history. By insistently pointing up those dimensions, the work of intellectual, economic, and political historians during the 1950s and 1960s had operated to enhance awareness of the powerful connections that had bound segments of Europe and America into transoceanic entities.[12] Considerably less well emphasized, however, were the equally powerful ties between Africa and the Americas, the study of which had been limited primarily to a few economic historians of the slave trade and a few cultural anthropologists. The Atlantic Program that we designed and implemented at Hopkins was open to studies involving societies and cultures all around the Atlantic world, but it had at its core the goal of promoting the study of the role of African peoples and their descendants throughout the Atlantic world.

In combination, the early modern orientation fostered by social history and the Atlantic program operated to call attention to the continuities and discontinuities in the movement of cultures from the old worlds of Europe and Africa to the new worlds of the Americas and to promote an interest in the comparative history of the various segments of the Atlantic world. Doctoral students in early American history now found themselves wanting and needing to know about parallel or contrasting developments in other Old and New World societies, which left little room for studies of later periods of United States national and regional (read, southern) history. The reorientation of colonial studies, which applied equally to non-British parts of the Americas, was facilitated by the fact that historians of the post-1800 United States were extremely slow to take up either social history or a broader Atlantic perspective.

Ironically, this broader orientation led me back to the study of some of the societies that eventually became part of the South. Initially, my participation in the Atlantic Program operated to refocus some of my scholarly attention on the British colonies in the West Indies, a vital part of the early modern Atlantic world. As I became increasingly knowledgeable about the West Indies and more and more attuned to the possibilities of social history, I began to develop an enhanced awareness of the extent to which the sugar colonies of the West Indies and the tobacco and rice colonies of southern North America formed one gigantic cultural entity in which white populations of varying sizes presided over a social, economic, and political system built heavily upon massive numbers of enslaved people of African descent. Within the British Atlantic world this slave-powered entity extended from Barbados north to the Chesapeake, with important extensions in New York and New Jersey and Rhode Island. Of course, no two of the societies that composed this entity were exactly alike. Indeed, there were radical differences between Jamaica, which was nine-tenths African, and Virginia, which was almost two-thirds white. Yet the centrality and extent of the enslaved populations and the extraordinary wealth they generated for the settler populations and for the metropolis gave them an underlying social and economic unity that suggested the desirability of comparative study, and in the mid-1970s I boldly commenced a project to study (comparatively and quantitatively and largely through the analysis of probate records and colonial budgets) wealth accumulation, private spending, and public investment in Virginia, Jamaica, and South Carolina, which were, in the mid-eighteenth century, Britain's three most profitable and most valued colonies. I conceived of these colonies as the core of what I came to call the greater West Indies or, if you will, the greater pre-South. But this project, turned down for funding by the National Endowment for the Humanities, largely, as I recall, because of its high costs and the reviewers' understandable doubts about whether I had sufficient quantitative expertise to carry it out, never got off the ground.

Nevertheless, I continued to think in terms of a large project that would study the development of those three colonies comparatively. My interest in the West Indies stretched all the way back to my days as a Fulbright student. While I was waiting for the Public Record Office to open, I used to spend time reading contemporary histories, chorographies, and travel accounts for the eighteenth-century southern continental colonies on which I was doing my dissertation, and, once I had exhausted those, I branched out to read similar materials about Jamaica, Barbados, and the Leeward Islands. What fascinated me most about this literature was the compulsion manifested by nearly every writer to assess the character of these new English societies and peoples who had settled them. This impulse, it seemed to me, was a device to measure the extent to which new climates and new physical settings had modified or reinforced traditional English conceptions of social, economic, and political organization and attributes of character or identity, to remark the ways in which, for instance, Virginia or Barbados had departed from English norms.

During the 1960s and early 1970s my investigation of the British origins of the American Revolution took me even deeper into British West Indian history. My extensive research on metropolitan-colonial relations between 1745 and 1765, which included the island colonies and Nova Scotia as well as all the continental colonies, revealed that many of the issues that would rend the empire in the mid-1770s had already in the 1750s and early 1760s been actively contested in Jamaica, where a vigorous local establishment opposed metropolitan political intrusions on the grounds that they violated the Jamaicans' inherited rights as Britons. They argued vociferously that they were entitled to consensual government, rule by the principles of English law, and all the other constitutional liberties enjoyed by people in the home islands. Only perhaps in their stridence and intensity did Jamaicans differ from the opposition the continental colonies were then offering to similar measures. Especially with regard to those plantation colonies that had large enslaved populations, the question that interested me was how people who came from a culture that defined itself in terms of the extensive participatory liberty it enjoyed and who were themselves so insistent upon preserving that liberty in the societies they were creating in the New World could reconcile that identity with chattel slavery.[13]

An invitation from Mercer University to deliver the Lamar Memorial Lectures in Southern History in 1976 provided me with an opportunity to bring these various interests together. Within the framework of my vision of a greater pre-South, I decided to explore changing settler identities in Virginia, Jamaica, and South Carolina during the eighteenth century. I chose an ironic title, "Paradise Defined," and a subtitle that signaled my intentions: "Studies in the Relationship between Historical Consciousness and the Emergence of Corporate Identities in Plantation America, 1650–1800." I approached these lectures by reading a lot of contemporary printed texts, principally histories, chorographies, and travel accounts, but I quickly realized that I was only scratching the surface of a vast pool of literature. Hence, instead of publishing the lectures I set out to read as extensively and fully as I could, and I spent the year 1979–80 trying to reduce these materials into a rather large book. At the end of the year I had written a lot of pages, but the book did not seem to be working, so I put it aside. Over the next few years I decided that the manuscript was not working because, although Jamaica and South Carolina made a nice comparison, I had no counterpoint for Virginia; so I decided to add Barbados, the mother colony of the British West Indies and of South Carolina. During the early 1980s I collected a vast amount of material on Barbados and wrote several chapters on the colony that I compressed into an article for a volume on colonial identities,[14] and in 1987 while I was a fellow at the National Humanities Center I made considerable progress in turning my growing manuscript into a multivolume book, two volumes of which I completed. But subsequent projects have diverted me from this project now for many years. If I ever finish it, it will probably be my principal contribution to the history of those colonies that would become part of the South.

Of course, my thinking about the southern colonies during the late 1970s and early 1980s was not limited to "Paradise Defined." Throughout this period, I had been trying to digest the new literature on social history, which, though it had initially centered on New England, was by the mid-1970s bringing forth a lot of new information about virtually every region of colonial British America. In several review essays I had begun by the mid-1970s to point out and comment upon some of the implications of one of the central discoveries of this literature.[15] Within the broad community of the early modern Anglo-Atlantic, the orthodox Puritan colonies, long celebrated by historians as the seedbeds of American culture, were wholly anomalous throughout most of the seventeenth century. Whereas the Puritan colonies were the products of a large family immigration, settled in reasonably close communities, had a profoundly religious orientation, and set out to create societies that would represent an improvement on the English world they had left behind, settlers in all the other English colonies—from Ireland to the Chesapeake, the West Indies, nonorthodox Puritan New England, and, later in the century, the Lower South and the Middle colonies—mostly came as single individuals, dispersed themselves over the landscape, were far more materially oriented than religious, and tried their best to recreate Old England in their new homes. To be sure, some of the early social-history works had judged places like Virginia and the West Indies in terms of a New England standard and thereby revealed how deeply entrenched and widely and unquestionably accepted was the idea that New England was normative. But the broad substance of this work revealed that New England was not a model for any other English colonial ventures in the seventeenth century, and this revelation raised profound questions about the foundations of American culture in the colonial era and, especially, about whether New England had been as influential as earlier historians had assumed.

This was the subject of my Walter Lynwood Fleming Lectures in Southern History at Louisiana State University in April 1981. Entitled "The Southern Colonies and the Formation of American Culture," these lectures provided a forum for me to develop the argument that, so far from being deviant or peculiar, the southern colonies were actually in the mainstream of colonial social development. I contended that a model first worked out in Ireland, Virginia, and Barbados early in the seventeenth century subsequently reappeared with pronounced variations in all the other English settler colonies in North America and the West Indies and Atlantic islands — with the single exception of the orthodox Puritan colonies of Massachusetts, Connecticut, and New Haven. Even Rhode Island, in its social development, was more similar to the Chesapeake than to its New England neighbors. This model privileged the pursuit of individual domestic happiness over all other cultural goals. Only in the eighteenth century did New England begin to conform to this ubiquitous model. I went on to suggest that the position of the southern colonies in the mainstream of Anglo-American social and cultural development helped to account for their prominence in the counsels of the United States during the Revolutionary and early national eras and to cast doubt on the widely entrenched historiographical trope that those colonies had always been socially distinctive. My contention was that the so-called peculiarity of the South must have been a function of some later development.

The development I had in mind, of course, was the widespread rejection of chattel slavery as an institution compatible with civilized societies, which occurred rapidly beginning in the 1760s and 1770s and reached full flower during the second and third decades of the nineteenth century. Only after the middle and New England colonies had abandoned slavery in the decades after independence or at least put it on the road to gradual extinction, I suggested, did the southern states, with their continuing commitment to the "peculiar" institution, become distinctive. Only then did they become part of a larger slave-favorable entity, the South. As comforting for present-day white Americans as is the idea that the essence of America derived from the largely nonslave cultures of New England and that the stain of slavery could be displaced entirely upon areas in the southern part of the continent that were distinctive in that regard, I contended, it now had to be deeply qualified by the acknowledgment that slavery had been at the heart of Anglo-American colonial development from early in the colonial era, an institution fostered by Britain, universally protected by law throughout the British colonial world, and sufficiently acceptable to the founding fathers that few leaders from non- or low-slave states hesitated to join in a political union with states having masses of slaves. No longer could we gloss over the fact that the American nation constructed between 1776 and 1789 was a slave republic.

In the mid-1980s I worked out and elaborated these ideas in my book *Pursuits of Happiness: The Social Development of Early Modern British Colonies and the Formation of American Culture*, published in 1988.[16] Some reviewers interpreted my argument about the cultural deviance of New England and the cultural centrality of the Chesapeake as a defense of the South, and I do not deny that one of the intentions of the volume was to bring the southern colonies into the mainstream of colonial development by showing the extent to which they conformed to the general developmental model that characterized social development throughout the early modern British world. For this reason, the volume may be regarded as a contribution to the history of the South or of those colonies that would become part of the South. My intention was considerably different, however. By mainstreaming the history of the southern colonies, I was endeavoring to rescue them from the parochial confines of southern history.

Since my first research in the history of the southern colonies, I have retained a strong interest in them, especially in the history of Virginia and South Carolina. Over the decades, I have always encouraged doctoral students to write dissertations in this still wide-open field of study, and 45 percent (thirty-four of seventy-six) of the people whose dissertations I have so far directed have done so. Throughout my seven-year association with the Program in the Lowcountry and the Atlantic World at the College of Charleston during the 1990s, I endeavored to promote the study of the history of the lowcountry — in its largest Atlantic context. Since publication of *Pursuits of Happiness*, however, I have not ventured much further into southern history per se than to express my hope eventually to finish *Paradise Defined*. If and when I do, however, my objective will be to treat the southern continental colonies not as the prefigurement of a South that would come into being after 1820, but as parts of the rich and slave-powered greater West Indian enterprise that contributed so mightily to the growth of British national power and wealth, brought free people — at least those who survived — remarkable opportunities for individual enrichment, and, in the process, enslaved thousands of African peoples.

Notes

1. Edmund S. Morgan, *The Puritan Family: Religion and Domestic Relations in Seventeenth-Century New England* (rev. ed., New York, 1966).
2. John R. Alden, *John Stuart and the Southern Colonial Frontier: A Study of Indian Relations, War, Trade, and Land Problems in the Southern Wilderness, 1754–1775* (Ann Arbor, 1944); *General Gage in America: Being Principally a History of His Role in the American Revolution* (Baton Rouge, 1948); and *General Charles Lee, Traitor or Patriot?* (Baton Rouge, 1951).
3. I was especially influenced by Andrews's *Colonial Background of the American Revolution: Four Essays in American Colonial History* (rev. ed., New Haven, 1931), and his last article, "On the Writing of Colonial History," *William and Mary Quarterly*, 3rd ser., 1 (October 1944): 27–48.
4. Manifestations of these interests are described more fully in my essay "Comparing Early Modern American Worlds: Some Reflections on the Promise of a Hemispheric Perspective," in the new online journal, *Compass* 1 (2003).
5. Sir Lewis Namier, *The Structure of Politics at the Accession of George III* (2nd ed., London, 1957), and *England in the Age of the American Revolution* (2nd ed., London, 1961).
6. Jack P. Greene, "Foundations of Political Power in the Virginia House of Burgesses, 1720–1776," *William and Mary Quarterly*, 3rd ser., 16 (October 1959): 485–506.
7. Charles Howard McIlwain, *The American Revolution: A Constitutional Interpretation* (New York, 1923); Andrew C. McLaughlin, *The Foundations of American Constitutionalism* (New York, 1932).
8. Jack P. Greene, *The Quest for Power: The Lower Houses of Assembly in the Southern Royal Colonies, 1689–1776* (Chapel Hill, 1963); Jack P. Greene, *Peripheries and Center: Constitutional Development in the Extended Polities of the British Empire and the United States, 1607–1788* (Athens, Ga., 1986).
9. Jack P. Greene, ed., *The Diary of Colonel Landon Carter of Sabine Hall, 1752–1778* (2 vols., Charlottesville, 1965). Only two chapters of my book with Keith Berwick were ever finished. They were published as Jack P. Greene, "Society, Ideology, and Politics: An Analysis of the Political Culture of Mid-Eighteenth-Century Virginia," in Richard M. Jellison, ed., *Society, Freedom, and Conscience: The American Revolution in Virginia, Massachusetts, and New York* (New York, 1976), 14–76, 190–201; and "'Virtus et Libertas': Political Culture, Social Change, and the Origins of the America Revolution in Virginia," in Jeffrey J. Crow and Larry E. Tise, eds., *The Southern Experience in the American Revolution* (Chapel Hill, 1978), 55–108.
10. Carl Bridenbaugh, *Myths and Realities: Societies of the Colonial South* (Baton Rouge, 1952).

11. John R. Alden, *The First South* (Baton Rouge, 1961).

12. For instance, Bernard Bailyn, *The New England Merchants in the Seventeenth Century* (Cambridge, Mass., 1955).

13. I have dealt with this theme in "'Slavery or Independence': Some Reflections on the Relationship among Liberty, Black Bondage, and Equality in Revolutionary South Carolina," *South Carolina Historical Magazine* 80 (July 1979): 193–214; and "Liberty, Slavery, and the Transformation of British Identity in the Eighteenth-Century West Indies," *Slavery and Abolition* 21 (April 2000): 1–31.

14. Jack P. Greene, "Changing Identity in the British Caribbean: Barbados as a Case Study," in Nicholas Canny and Anthony Pagden, eds., *Colonial Identity in the Atlantic World, 1500–1800* (Princeton, 1987), 213–66.

15. See Jack P. Greene, "Autonomy and Stability: New England and the British Colonial Experience in Early Modern America," *Journal of Social History* 7 (Winter 1974), 171–94 [review essay]; and "Economy and Society in the British Caribbean during the Seventeenth and Eighteenth Centuries: A Review Essay," *American Historical Review* 79 (October 1974), 1499–1517.

16. Jack P. Greene, *Pursuits of Happiness: The Social Development of the Early Modern British Colonies and the Formation of American Culture* (Chapel Hill, 1988).

Chance or Choice?

ANNE FIROR SCOTT

I was born fifty-six years after Appomattox and had two living great-grandmothers who had been young women during the Civil War, known to them as the War Between the States or the War of the Southern Rebellion. One, a dedicated believer in the Lost Cause, immediately enrolled me in the Children of the Confederacy. For all I know I am a member yet. I grew up in Athens, Georgia, in a massive run-down antebellum house built by slaves. The atmosphere of my early life illustrated Faulkner's well-known dictum: "The past is never dead. It's not even past."

How, then, did I become a historian whose work revised one of the most cherished images of the Old South? Or, indeed, become one of those sometimes despised characters known as "a southern liberal" and a strong supporter of civil rights? Do I understand the process myself? Can I understand it clearly enough to explain it to others, as the editor of this volume asks?

The recent proliferation of studies dealing with the complications of historical memory has done nothing to make this challenge less daunting. What does one "choose" to remember or to forget or to reconfigure? I turn to the journal covering most of my adult life and am puzzled that events now seen as of great historical importance hardly appear, while trivial occurrences received a degree of attention that is now mystifying. What unconscious motives have been at work over the years? The "facts," or the "reality" (the existence of both have been called into question of late), are elusive.

Once, in a different context, I coined a title—"History as Fiction, Fiction as History"—and tried to show that fiction written at the time came closer to telling the truth about late-nineteenth-century southern life than any historian had done. The words of that title and the issues they raise come back to me as I ponder: how much of what I might write here is "history"—sometimes described as "what really happened"—and how much have I (without meaning to) invented? And does the invented part tell a perceptive reader as much or more than the documented part? What will that reader learn that I do not know myself? When I review my several bits of memoir writing already in print, I am mortified to notice that they don't always tell the same tale. Therefore, I must take care as I write to avoid invention. One fiction I will surely not inflict on you is the idea that my development as a southern historian was well planned and linear, for it surely was not. Knowing all the hazards, I will do my best to tell the truth, but I do not minimize the difficulty of doing so. Nor should the reader. So — caveat lector.

In the beginning there was childhood. My mother's large extended family had southern roots going back to the eighteenth century. By the time I was born, my father, though raised in western Maryland, had lived in Georgia for nine years, and *his* father was known to have voted against Lincoln in 1860, a fact that had reconciled one of those great-grandmothers to my parents' marriage. Grandparents and great-grandparents were a living presence in our family storytelling.

In our family, reading to children began early. My father, who found children's books boring, began with such things as *Alice in Wonderland* and the *Just So Stories*. My mother inclined toward a semidramatic reading of *Uncle Remus*. Our sense that important things had happened before we were born was encouraged by his stories of wartime service in France and hers of going to school in Boston, where she had seen herself as an outsider. She spoke often of her mortification when, at the Armistice celebration, her lack of an ear for music allowed her to march happily to the tune of "Marching Through Georgia" until a classmate enlightened her.

By age five I had learned to read for myself and by seven or eight was immersed in such books as *Two Little Confederates, Red Rock, Miss Minerva and William Green Hill, Elsie Dinsmore, Lena Rivers,* even *St. Elomo* — and, no doubt, others that shared their general view of slavery as a beneficent institution, of Yankees as the root of all evil, of southern ladies as the epitome of gracious living. My best friend's mother, whose only interests in life were books and her garden, believed in encouraging children to read. Her library was at my disposal. She, like most of my female relatives, was a Daughter of the Confederacy, and some of her books reflected this fact. Happily, she was also well equipped with nineteenth-century English novels and a full set of G. A. Henty. Thanks to her I was never short of books. The only censorship I remember came when my mother said I should not read *Gone with the Wind*. Inspired by this prohibition, when she went to the grocery store I fished it out of its all too obvious hiding place and searched in vain for anything shocking. Could it have been Rhett Butler's "damn"?

I am puzzled now by the things that float to the surface of memory. As a young child, probably when saddled with some unpleasant chore, I reflected that having a slave to do one's work must have been very nice. In another quirk of memory I see myself at the dinner table begging to be taken to the movie *Birth of a Nation*; my mother firmly declined. I would like to think she objected to its message, but more likely she just thought it too violent for a young girl.

Even in the depths of the Great Depression there was always an African American woman in our kitchen and another who did our laundry in her own backyard. They were drastically underpaid but not, at least in the case of the cook/children's nurse, overworked. The washerwoman was another matter: she had to wash in an iron pot over an open fire, using water carried from a well. My impression was that her feet always hurt. I have a vivid memory of being rebuked for speaking of her as a "lady." She was, I was firmly informed, a "colored *woman*." Why do these moments come back when doubtless thousands of other fleeting thoughts are gone forever?

Georgia high schools in the 1930s did not demand extraordinary academic exertion. I have no recollection of what we learned in world history, though I do remember that the "other history teacher" (daughter of a university Greek professor) was said to be very inspiring while ours was not. My energies went less into academic exploration than into editing the school newspaper, a job with the fringe benefit of free movie passes, and into trying (quite in vain) to be popular. In the tight little world of high-school cliques with a class structure that would have been grist for a Trollope, I was always an outsider.

Impecunious in the extreme, I entered every essay contest that came along and, with a good bit of help from my father, won a few. The effort to write those essays and numerous editorials for the *Thumb Tack Tribune* revealed my budding aspiration to be a "writer," whatever that meant. Had I had a gift for fiction . . . who knows what might have come of those high-school years? I can imagine what a young Eudora Welty or a Reynolds Price might have made of my English teachers. They were sisters, known to generations of pupils as "Miss Ruby" and "Miss Martha." They were tall, spare women who spoke precisely and wore Phi Beta Kappa keys on long gold chains. They lived in austere circumstances with a brother, equally tall and spare, and did their best to instill grammar into the resistant young. Many years later when I had left the South and appeared to be developing a career, the taller and sparer of the two bent to tell my five-foot-two mother that she had always known I had talent. Needless to say, she had never communicated this to me when it might have made a difference.

Growing up in the midst of the Great Depression, I had no choice after high school but to live at home and enroll at the University of Georgia. Intrigued by what I read about Robert Maynard Hutchins and Mortimer J. Adler and their high-minded concentration on the great books, I yearned for the University of Chicago. I might as well have set my heart on going to the moon. As it was, most of my classmates were Georgians, and most were from small towns or farms. The College of Arts and Sciences was largely populated with middle-class students; the farm boys, some of whom paid their room and board with bushels of sweet potatoes or sides of ham, were at the Ag College. The term provincial might have been invented to describe most of us. I need hardly add that we were all white.

There were in those tumultuous years of the late 1930s a few homegrown radicals: one was nicknamed "Commissar Brown" in recognition of his politics, and, unlikely as it would have seemed at the time, several of my college friends were destined in later years to become sturdy advocates of civil rights. At this university that claimed to be the oldest state-supported institution of higher learning in the country, there were in the late 1930s very few cracks in the all-enveloping southern culture.

I had enrolled as a journalism major, but my father's repeated advice, "If you want to write it will be necessary to know something," pushed me to change to history. From time to time some history course truly engaged me, but not very profoundly. Since E. Merton Coulter gave me A's, either I adopted his view of the southern past or, more likely, his commitment to research was such that he never really read the papers he so often assigned. They were returned with suspicious speed. Now that I have been a teacher myself for five decades, how I wish one or two had survived so that I could see on just what those A's were based!

The course that truly inspired me came during a very hot summer and was taught by a saturnine professor who longed to have been born in the nineteenth century. He led the class through the Victorian Age, which turned out to be so intriguing that even his cynical view of the modern world did not keep me from reading and reading, memorizing reams of Browning, and finding that summer—devoted as it was to Carlyle, Ruskin, John Stuart Mill, and their contemporaries—to be the intellectual high point of my college years.

One thing is indisputable, both from my own journal and the memoirs and memories of some of my distinguished classmates: on our campus there was very little recognition of the question of race. We seem not to have been even dimly aware of the ferment going on around us, which in retrospect one can plainly see was laying the groundwork for the 1960s. Only one professor, a maverick teaching a class called "Contemporary Georgia," touched on that third rail of southern politics when he handed down the obiter dictum that in a hundred years everybody in Georgia would be café au lait, and he did not appear to find this insight at all disturbing. His offhand comment is the only thing I remember now about that course, and I do not think that any student rose to challenge him.

To be sure the Phelps-Stokes Foundation, based in the North, had already published some intriguing studies of what was called "Negro life in Georgia," but I only discovered their existence fifty years later. Nor did I pay much attention to the master's degree research of two friends who were making heavily statistical studies of black life in our town. I do not think I heard the name of W. E. B. Du Bois, or had any inkling of the existence of a black middle class. None of the early court cases dealing with the rights of black people were mentioned in our Constitutional history class, though *Plessy v. Ferguson* ruled our daily lives.

My undergraduate encounters with the outside world came from visiting speakers, some of whom were much engaged with moral questions; but none as far as my memory goes dealt with race as one of those questions. I read the *Atlanta Constitution* daily, never noticing that from its pages one would barely know that there were African Americans in Georgia. In fact, they constituted nearly half the population.

The only questions that reached me about the southern way of life, as it was called, came in the young people's program of the Southern Methodist Church, which was still separate from the northern branch, and also in the campus "Y." In summer camps and winter seminars I heard the first faint stirrings of concern for the rights of the fellow citizens we still called "colored people." At one Methodist summer gathering of college students I saw for the first time an educated black man speaking from the platform.

To complicate this picture, I must add that two of the black women who worked for our family have remained my friends for life. How could it be that they were, or seemed to be, as attached to me as I to them? With one at least, who had become a school teacher, I was finally in the 1950s able to have an open discussion of the problems of segregation, discrimination, and lynching. Much, much later—in 1999—she told my brothers and me the story of her eighty-five years of life, and how it was that she had come to be a college graduate. "I will wash as many clothes as it takes," her mother had said, and she did.

So it was for my first nineteen years. I learned the southern view of the past, lived with hot weather, segregation, poverty—in short, everything that made the South a region. I might well have grown up to be just another in a long line of southern ladies in my family who, with a couple of notable exceptions, were content with home, family, and church. Why did it not happen?

The first small break in the pattern came when I was twelve and went to eighth grade in upstate New York. My mother and her sister had traded children for a school year, believing that a winter in the South would greatly benefit the health of my somewhat fragile cousin. In the Syracuse junior high school I was an exotic creature, and with the help of my Georgia-born aunt I played that fact for all it was worth. The social-studies teacher, knowing her own ignorance and vastly underestimating mine, turned to me for information about that somewhat mythical region that she had never seen: the South. For some reason she wanted members of the class to learn about cotton and thought I could enlighten them. A distress call to my family yielded a box of cotton bolls, and my father's carefully typed description of how the stuff was produced. Knowing where the minds of eighth graders are apt to be, I presume I did not do too much damage as I tried to live up to my billing as an expert on things southern.

Assigned in English class to write a short story, I fell back on family legends about one great-great-grandmother's encounter with Ben Butler's army. My aunt collected such lore, and together we enthusiastically embroidered the facts. The woman in question, whose name was Judith Booten Hill, lived in Orange County, Virginia, on a plantation with the romantic name of "Glendalough," a place I had been taken at age five for a reverential visit. To this day I have not turned my historical skills to finding out if Ben Butler did in fact ever go near the place; but the family story was that when his men demanded flour, she, with feigned reluctance, provided a bag of lime, enjoying the vision of their first biscuits. Perhaps this story provided an early template for those strong southern women who would, so many years later, star in *The Southern Lady*.[1]

Another Civil War story my family liked to tell was of the Georgia great-grandmother, entrusted by her husband just as the war was ending with $10,000 Confederate dollars, who in the sad state of the southern economy was able to buy a whole city block with a fine house on it—both of which are still in the family. Another template perhaps.

I should note also that my Syracuse uncle-by-marriage, Ralph Volney Harlow, was an American historian who, during my New York year, was immersed in writing a biography of Gerrit Smith, a famous abolitionist. Looking now at the textbooks he was publishing at that time, it is clear that he shared what I have called the E. Merton Coulter view of the Civil War and Reconstruction. Or maybe one might call it the Dunning School. But in either case he was not likely to raise questions in my mind about the history I had been taught. Now decades later, I wonder what if anything I absorbed from dinner-table conversation as he examined, with my aunt as research assistant, the vast Smith papers.

No less an authority than C. Vann Woodward called the Smith biography a fine piece of work. Reading it today I observe that while Smith's abolitionist activities are covered in careful detail, his support for women's rights, or his support for his cousin Elizabeth Cady Stanton, is barely mentioned. Did anyone, in the 1930s, notice that omission? Perhaps my uncle's influence on me as a twelve-year-old was the vision he presented of a dedicated scholar at work.

All in all it was an exciting year, during which I encountered snow for the first time, met people quite unlike those I knew in Georgia, including my first Roman Catholics, and was exposed to the culture of a university history department (much different from the folksy gatherings back home), for my aunt was a sociable being who loved to entertain her husband's colleagues with gourmet dinner parties.

Whatever the consequences of that first foray into a new culture, they were at least temporarily buried when I returned to my southern family in the small university town that in the 1930s was not very different from its nineteenth-century self. Soon life was going on in its old patterns.

But I had come home, too, to my father the skeptic. He provided a more important part of my education than high school, or later, college. Trained in horticulture at the Maryland Agricultural College, he had educated himself in economics, became a college professor, organized and chaired a department at the university, and was interested in almost everything.

As a student it had been his custom to take the trolley from College Park to the Library of Congress there to read any book he had heard of or could find. As is common with autodidacts, there were things to which he had never been exposed, but he learned daily from new people, from new books, from questions his students asked. He had become famous as a teacher. Asked to account for his success in the classroom, he said that if the rumors of his effectiveness were true, it was because he and his students set out *together* to solve problems.

This was also his theory of child raising; in a sense he went through university with each of us in turn. When we were grown and scattered he continued the process with long letters, carefully tailored to the individual recipient. These letters survive for some patient descendant to decipher the execrable handwriting he blamed on the fact that in college he had found a job cataloging the college library by hand.

Though I did not realize it at the time, he introduced me to a whole range of experience that I would, years later, recognize as important for understanding the social history of the post-Reconstruction South. His work as an agricultural economist took him often into the countryside to visit farmers—and when I was a child the majority of Georgians *were* farmers. He liked company on these journeys down long dirt roads, and I have vivid snapshot memories of farm houses and farm families, black and white. In time he even jointly owned a farm with a black farmer. As we drove home, my father liked to reflect upon these visits—what the people were like, how they worked, why some did well and others did not, what they should be doing to improve themselves or the land, what the government or the agricultural college should be doing to help them, the revolution wrought by rural electrification, the sins of the U.S. Department of Agriculture. Though I doubt I understood half of what he was saying, these early encounters left me with a profound skepticism when later in life I began to read what people outside the South wrote about our rural people. Rereading now my introduction to the new edition of Margaret Hagood's *Mothers of the South*, written long after his death, I hear my father's voice.[2]

In a different vein, one of his surviving letters is a long meditation on the origin of southern manners. And in a journal that I only read after his death, there are long reflections on the lives of the black tenant farmers he knew. We all have some roads not taken; he had more than most. In different circumstances he would have been a great historian.

Finishing college in 1940, I went back to Syracuse for a visit, found a job, and stayed for six months. My southern accent, now restored (by the middle of my first year there I had acquired a perfect upstate New York speech), once again enabled me to play the role of visiting exotic, this time among university students. The area around Syracuse was lovely in spring, and I barely escaped marrying one of the young men who liked the way I talked. How would my life have evolved had I not, in the nick of time, realized that there was much more to see in the world than I had yet seen, and so left my Yankee beau behind? From a perch in New York State would I ever have become a student of southern women?

The Syracuse job ended. After a year working for the International Business Machines Atlanta office, and the U.S. entry into the war, came my next encounter with an alien culture. I had just turned twenty-one when I went off to study at Northwestern University. The midwesterners were extremely friendly but not much interested in the South. I was happy adapting to their world, which for me was one revelation after another: Socialist party meetings, the opera, the Chicago Symphony, ice skating—every day brought something Georgia had not offered. Study was the least of it, though I read my way through a good deal of what seemed to me, after my experience with a poverty-stricken southern university, an amazingly well stocked library. Any book I had heard of seemed to be in the card catalog.

In the winter of 1943 the war was going badly for the Allies, and as one by one the young men I knew went off to military service, increasingly I felt that Northwestern represented a retreat from reality. Searching for something that would satisfy my yearning to be closer to scenes of action, I found an internship program in Washington, which, because the war had siphoned off so many male candidates, was suddenly available to women.

Perhaps for the first time in my life being southern had an economic benefit: the four interns from south of the Mason-Dixon line were granted scholarships by one of the New York foundations influenced no doubt by FDR's ringing characterization of our region as "the nation's number one economic problem." Whatever the reason, we were not apologetic about the subsidy, and we were suitably impressed by our fellows who came from the Ivy League and seemed both richer and more sophisticated than ourselves.

The summer of 1943 was the most exciting time I had yet experienced— wartime Washington was filled with people I might never have heard of, much less met, in Athens, Georgia. The departure of more and more young men for the armed services continued to open unprecedented opportunities for young women.

The thirty-odd young people in the intern program came from all over the country. Some were avowed radicals, many thought themselves socialists. The political scientists in charge of the program assured us that we were being trained to be the leaders of the postwar world. A heady thought. Placed for my instruction in a congressman's office, I rapidly adopted the pseudo-sophistication of an insider and pontificated about public policy with the best of them. I undertook a night course in economics, but it tended to put me to sleep. I decided that working my way painstakingly through Lord Bryce's *American Commonwealth* was a better bet.

Washington itself, the so-called center of the free world, was an odd mix of world leadership and segregated life. It was often characterized as a southern city. As had been true in all my academic years, there was still very little attention on the part of our mentors to what a few perceptive observers had begun to identify as an overwhelmingly important issue for the United States: our treatment of our nonwhite citizens. Even under the shadow of Hitler's behavior, white Americans seemed, for the most part, to make no connection between his views and our own. Every day I took the Number 90 streetcar from the Capitol to Mt. Pleasant and was often the only white person on board. I don't remember being curious about what my fellow passengers were doing or thinking, but we were unfailingly polite to each other.

The fleeting twinges of conscience I had had growing up when something made me aware of the disparities between black children and myself developed more force as I encountered middle-class black bureaucrats who could not join me for lunch outside a government cafeteria. Now looking back I devoutly wish I had somehow met Pauli Murray, the Howard Law School activist who, that very summer, was organizing a sit-in in a Washington restaurant and would soon be refusing to move to the back of a bus in Virginia. But that wish is entirely retrospective. I had no idea that there were young black leaders whose work was foreshadowing the Civil Rights movement or how much I might have learned from them.

All summer, as the intern group was introduced to economics, to politics, to diplomats and journalists, to bureaucrats and congressmen, I do not remember that a word was said about race. Yet if we had spent much time reading *Time* magazine or other periodicals, we would have known that it was a summer of horrendous race riots. The various cabinet officers, heads of bureaus, congressmen, and leading political scientists brought in to educate us could have talked about the arguments over the Fair Employment Practices Committee or about the riots that were going on all summer. If anyone did, he failed to get my attention. Even Eleanor Roosevelt, who was already much involved in the debates over what would come to be called civil rights, in two long encounters with the intern group talked more about opportunities for women than about the needs of Negro citizens. There was irony even in this, since of all the people who were called upon to contribute to our education, she was the only female.

After the internship, and a brief return to Northwestern to write an M.A. thesis, in the summer of 1944 I went to work for the National League of Women Voters. (The thesis was an inadequate study of certain kinds of international organizations. I wonder, now, how my career would have developed if I had had the sense to take my father's suggestion that I write about the origin of the white primary in Georgia! I might have become a southern historian then and there ... but for reasons I can no longer remember, I shied away from that excellent idea and wrote an entirely unremarkable thesis.)

As for the league, again the war had opened doors in what had hitherto been high brick walls. The intensely intellectual old suffragists who led the organization in its first two decades had always staffed the national office with women who had advanced degrees and much experience. They in turn prepared erudite materials that were, with probably unrealistic expectations, distributed to local league members in keeping with the general proposition: learn first, then act. By 1943 not only had there been something of a revolution when the league's biennial convention had rejected the board's nominations and elected instead women who wanted a more democratic organization, but also the demands of the wartime State Department for trained people meant that the senior staff could show its contempt for the new wave by resigning as a body. The new president, with the usual limited budget of women's organizations, went about rebuilding her staff by recruiting bright young women whom she could train in the league way of doing things. Hence three of us, all in our twenties, took over the writing of material being provided for the edification of local league members. We also drafted congressional testimony, letters to various Cabinet secretaries, and the like. It was a heady experience, and one that in retrospect had a great deal to do with my later evolution as a historian of women.

At the time, however, my interests were intensely focused on the political process, on Congress and the White House as well as on the growing concern for international organization. My aspirations included running for office. No one among the perceptive adults who were my mentors at that point and who were concerned about my future would have forecast that I was bound to become a historian at all, much less a historian of the South. To be sure my closest friend on the league board was Martha Ragland, a remarkable woman from Tennessee. We compared notes often about the experience of growing up poor in the South (she too was a college professor's daughter), but neither of us connected these discussions with my future career. If she had had her way, I would have run for office sooner rather than later. Insofar as I thought about the future, I focused entirely on public affairs.

Looking at all this now, I see connections between my intense interest in politics and my later concern with the history of women. The league was itself the child of the suffrage movement, and in those days several powerful suffragists were still very active. They were, of course, political through and through. How else had they persuaded a virtually all-male Congress to approve a constitutional amendment to enfranchise women? In the process they had grown into extraordinarily interesting people. Two of my favorites — Katherine Ludington and Mary Foulke Morison — come to my mind's eye as I write. Off in New York, Carrie Chapman Catt was watching us and sending her thoughts. Maud Wood Park still lived, though in retirement in Maine. All these years later I see myself as part of a chain that began with Mary Wollstonecraft and Sarah Grimké, then moved to Elizabeth Cady Stanton and Susan B. Anthony, then to Catt and her colleagues, and finally in 1943 to Anna Lord Strauss (the league national president who hired me was a great-granddaughter of Lucretia Mott), and from her to me. So it was, perhaps, that my early interest in politics and the political process was never quite disconnected from my later life as a historian.

One other invaluable benefit of years with the league I can recognize now: the vice president, Kathryn Stone — who like the president, though a volunteer, worked every day in the office — was a stickler for clear, concise English prose. Sloppy writing offended her, and she combined affection for her young colleagues with a stern insistence that we "get it right."

Those years also gave me my initial understanding of the workings of women's voluntary associations, a subject that became important in all my historical writing. In addition to the league itself I worked with a host of other public affairs–minded women's groups: representatives of the American Association of University Women (AAUW), the Women's Trade Union League, and the Woman's International League for Peace and Freedom in particular became friends and colleagues. I also learned that jealousies and rivalries are not unknown in the most high-minded of organizations. All this was grist for a future not yet dreamed of.

When I began to have a dim inkling of how little I really knew about the subjects upon which I was so confidently writing, my reaction was to think that the cure would be more formal education. The University of Chicago offered me a graduate fellowship in political science. I planned to work with Leonard White, the broad-gauge historian of public administration, from whom I hoped to obtain more wisdom than I felt I possessed.

Fate had other plans. A former navy pilot named Andrew Scott, now a graduate student, turned up with an invitation I couldn't refuse: "Come marry me and go to Harvard." After an embarrassed and not altogether candid letter to Chicago, I was off to Cambridge and in short order had parlayed my Chicago application into a Radcliffe fellowship.

I have been known to say that I had to go to Harvard to truly discover the South. The condescension to southerners and the ignorance of faculty and classmates about my native region turned me overnight into an outspoken southern patriot. In my first history class Samuel Eliot Morison's lofty attitude toward my most famous ancestor, William Byrd of Westover, introduced me to Yankee provincialism. There was one literary scholar devoted to southern writing. With him I read *The Mind of the South*,[3] *The Road to Reunion*, and a whole string of southern writers of a type quite different from my early acquaintance with the works of people like Thomas Nelson Page. A. B. Longstreet, Johnson Hooper, Joseph G. Baldwin, Faulkner—here was another South than the mythical one of my great-grandmothers.

Seeking flexibility, I had enrolled in a somewhat loose-jointed program in the History of American Civilization within which students could choose a special field. I assumed mine was government. The most sympathetic faculty member I encountered was a constitutional scholar named Benjamin Wright, said to be a demon to women students unless they came from his native South. In the way these things develop, he came to be my mentor and would, we both assumed, direct my dissertation.

Through one of those life-shaping turns of fate, the day after my general exam Ben Wright was appointed president of Smith College. What to do now? Casting about for a new director, I had remembered two truly stimulating history courses (indeed I had taken only two; all the other courses had been in literature, philosophy, or government) taught by Oscar Handlin, a first-generation native of Brooklyn who then and thereafter had an outsider's sympathy for the South. He was also only six years my senior and still in the stage of welcoming graduate students.

My naïveté about dissertation topics would arouse a good deal of scorn if it turned up among today's graduate students. I don't think I came to that first interview with ideas of my own. Professor Handlin was curious about the neglected subject of southerners who had been part of the late-nineteenth- and early-twentieth-century Progressive movement. Possibly he had already embarked on what would be an innovative history text and felt he needed to know more about the South. Who knows? At any rate he suggested that I should look into the subject, and I dutifully agreed. He came up with a few names and a few half-remembered book titles and, with the kind of statement for which he would become famous, added "there is only one person doing decent history of the South — his name is Woodward." With that he was about to send me on my way when timidity was overcome by a sense of desperation. I admitted that I had never had a history seminar — up to that moment I had thought of myself as a student of politics — and needed instruction in historiography. He recommended Gibbon's *Autobiography*. I bought the book and was, as well as I can recall, somewhat puzzled as to what Gibbon had to say to me. Possibly the eighteenth-century prose and his tendency to drop into Latin was intimidating. Now, rereading, I see clearly what I was too inexperienced to understand then: Gibbon laid great stress on the virtues of self-education, of opposing one's own ideas to the accepted wisdom. "But every man who rises above the common level has received two educations," he wrote, "the first from his teachers; the second more personal and more important, from himself."[4] He also wrote with great feeling about the satisfactions of learning to work hard.

With such guidance, if it could be called that, I went to Widener Library and tried with limited success to figure out how one should proceed to write a dissertation. Though in my league days I had had no hesitation about bearding various congressmen in their dens, such was the aura of Harvard faculty that it did not occur to me to go back and demand help from Handlin. Perhaps unconsciously influenced by my father's example of self-education (or possibly even by what I had picked up from Gibbon), I struggled on, following every lead, and playing a great deal of tennis to escape my frustrations. I could only observe with envy as my husband typed in the attic for twelve hours a day finishing his dissertation in record time. Anxious for something that would feel like accomplishment, I dropped everything to type his final draft. In the days of five carbon copies that was no mean feat.

In the fall we moved to Washington where the Library of Congress became my venue and provided drawer after drawer of yellowed cards catalogued as "South: American." Day after day, perched on a high stool, I worked my way through those drawers only to discover that though the colonial South and the antebellum South were plentifully represented, almost none of these numerous publications dealt with the period that I was supposed to be studying. Except for some episodic attention to the Populists and Woodward's *Tom Watson*, southern history after 1877 seemed almost nonexistent. Something gave me the idea of moving on to the Manuscript Division, which turned out to be more rewarding than the card catalog. I discovered the papers of A. J. McKelway, one of those overlooked southern progressives, and went for permission to his son who edited the *Washington Star*. Trying to explain to him what I wanted to write about helped me begin to shape the topic for myself. I made friends with John Davidson, who was preparing for Arthur S. Link's grand project of editing the Woodrow Wilson papers. He sent me to see the ancient and formidable Mrs. Wilson for permission to read those papers while they were still at the library. She listened to my rationale and nodded her head. It would not be the last time that I was in the presence of a person who could have taught me a great deal if I had only known what questions to ask. In Wilson's papers I found the record of southern enthusiasm for his Progressive agenda.

The Manuscript Division itself was still in its early informal state when nobody worried much about protecting the documents and therefore allowed a great deal of browsing as well as chances to talk over my questions with other scholars. Someone must have pointed me to the newspaper room, and I spent hours being fascinated by back issues of the *Columbia State* and the *Atlanta Constitution*. (Reading the *Washington Star* for 1912, it was hard not to be totally distracted by the real-estate advertisements where one could trace the growth of the great brownstone city in the years just before the First World War.) Bit by bit I began to shape a topic.

Professor Handlin may have felt more responsibility for me than I realized, since he made sure that I went to the fall meeting of the Southern Historical Association and there introduced me to that one person whose work in southern history he admired: C. Vann Woodward. This was the beginning of what in time would become a long-lasting friendship, and — in retrospect — the beginning of my identification as a historian of the South. From Woodward and from David M. Potter, with whom I also began a friendship at that meeting, I began to learn to challenge the received wisdom about the South. Both helped me along the way in later years.

After these inspiring encounters, I might have made progress on the dissertation but for the fact that I was pregnant and by summer had become the mother of our first child, with all the attendant reorganization of life that comes with parenthood. Andrew was at his typewriter night after night, turning his dissertation into a book. Washington was in the midst of the Korean War and of Joseph McCarthy, distractions indeed. Then, in 1952, the Republicans won the midterm election, and in 1953 my husband gave up his career in international aid programs to join the faculty of Dartmouth College. I tried to console myself for leaving the interesting part-time job contrived for me by the League of Women Voters by vowing to at last finish the dissertation. New Hampshire had few resources for the study of southern Progressives, and we were barely there when I was again pregnant. With great effort I managed to write two chapters, but Professor Handlin was moved to inquire whether I planned to have a baby every chapter. It almost seemed that way, for when the next year we moved on to Haverford College, child number three arrived.

Three young children and no money — the dissertation almost vanished from consciousness except for constant low-level guilt feelings. Those years are a blur in my memory. Something to do with sleep deprivation, I suppose. Yet somehow in 1956, when the eldest went to first grade and a jewel of a nanny miraculously appeared, when the AAUW took a chance on a mother of three children under six years of age, I got back to work. (Then, as now, fellowships for part-time scholars were few, but in 1956 applicants were also few.) By this time I had a somewhat firmer grip on what research should be and managed to sharpen my topic and find a manageable focus. So it was that one way and another, eight years after those preliminary exams, I turned in a dissertation on the southern Progressives in the national Congress. The Harvard Committee on American Civilization declared itself satisfied, and so I had a Ph.D. degree.

Though I had learned a great deal in those eight years, the dissertation was more notable for ideas than for detailed research; it would not pass muster in today's graduate programs. But it did contain the germ of an important insight: in examining the varieties of reform in which southerners were involved over the years after 1890, I kept stumbling over women. The record had been there, in the sources, all along, but in the era when nearly all historians of the South were male, women's important part in creating southern Progressivism both before and after the adoption of the Nineteenth Amendment had gone unnoticed, even by me at first. Then I realized that the women I encountered in the sources were missing from the standard accounts. This seemed to me a serious oversight, one that distorted the history of southern politics.

This story might have ended when the dissertation was accepted but for another turn of fate that took my family to live in North Carolina: Andrew began teaching political science at the University of North Carolina. Rumor had it that the history department at UNC was totally opposed to the idea of women as faculty members (indeed, there was a good bit of historical evidence to support this view), but in 1959 the need for teachers was such that an unemployed Harvard Ph.D. arriving in the neighborhood — even though female — was seen as useful. I was soon teaching four sections of the American history survey.

A young member of the department had been assigned to organize the department's monthly faculty seminar. With somewhat mischievous intent he invited me, the only woman and the newest member, who had only the most tenuous appointment, to give a paper. I said yes and then began to wonder what I might talk about. The image of those overlooked southern women sent me to the Southern Historical Collection, where the category "women" was not even in the catalog. However, the staff of the collection, mostly female, was endlessly helpful. So, too, a young Duke professor who was there working on "my" period. My debt to Robert F. Durden is large. By treating me as an equal he almost made me believe I was a true scholar. And, like himself, a historian of the South.

Another piece of luck grew from a dinner party at which the other guests were Julia and Corydon Spruill. These two remarkable people became my friends and mentors. Julia had written what is still the classic work on colonial women in the South, and by the time I met her she was ready to do all she could to help me — I think she came to see me as her natural successor — to carry the story farther. There were others of that earlier feminist generation still alive and active in North Carolina in the 1960s: Jessie Daniel Ames, Gertrude Weil, and Kate Burr Johnson all played a part in my education. So, in time, did Guion G. Johnson who, next to Julia, knew more about the history of southern women than anyone alive. They pointed me to yet others of their co-workers who were dead, but for whom papers and records could be found.

With all this help and my growing conviction that the study of women's past would change the accepted view of southern history, I went to the faculty seminar with more confidence than might have been expected from a part-time instructor. I called the paper "The 'New Woman' in the New South," and to my surprise the all-male faculty took to the subject with enthusiasm and spent so much time telling me about their grandmothers that I never quite finished delivering the prepared essay.

It surely must have been on that evening that the glimmerings of an idea for a book about southern women began to float before my eyes. I think I was back in the library the next morning. But just at that point my husband accepted a Fulbright lectureship in Italy for the 1960–61 academic year. At the same time one UNC colleague asked me to expand my paper for a panel at the Southern Historical Association meeting scheduled for the fall of 1961. So I went off to Europe with a box full of notecards and wrote the paper at a desk looking out upon the busy street of an Italian city. Without quite aiming to, I had taken a giant step toward becoming a historian of the South.

While that paper was still aborning, a letter came from the chairman of the Duke University history department. He wrote that "a young man" in his department had received an offer the department had chosen not to match, and someone had suggested that since I lived nearby, perhaps I would come to teach "until we can find somebody." Hardly taking note of the assumption, I lost no time in saying yes.[5]

It is hard to convey to young women scholars today just how casually a career could come into being in the early 1960s. I had known one member of the Duke department in my graduate-school days when he taught at Harvard and my husband and I were his favorite babysitters. My other champion was the same Bob Durden with whom I had exchanged references and gossip for a year in the Southern Historical Collection. Search procedures were informal in those days, and somehow the department never got around to looking for the "somebody" mentioned in my original invitation.

I have often spoken of all this as luck. My husband reminds me that chance works for the prepared mind. As I trek through my past, it is clear that when opportunity presented itself, I was ready to seize it whether I quite knew what I was doing or not. Life, of course, was not always simple. By 1961 babies had become young children with the concomitant demands to be grade mother, den mother, chauffeur, and consoler as well as faculty wife and volunteer activist.

Though I was rapidly moving into academic history, my interest in politics had not diminished. Even as newcomers, my husband and I had done a little work for Terry Sanford when he ran for governor in 1960 and had met some of the young people around him. Nevertheless, I was taken entirely by surprise when in 1962 Governor Sanford proposed to appoint me chair of the Governor's Commission on the Status of Women that he was about to appoint. I was already fully occupied with teaching, child-raising, and the like — not to mention plans to write one book and edit another. I remember thinking, "Well, I can do the work on Sundays . . ." So I said yes. Of course I had no idea what I was getting into, or what I would in the end learn from the experience. It taught me a great deal about contemporary North Carolina women, and by extension about southern women generally, as well as about human nature. I can say, because it was the accepted view, that the report issued by the commission, *The Many Lives of North Carolina Women*, was seen in Washington as the best of all the state reports. The commission examined North Carolina women at work, at school, in politics, under the law, as volunteers, as members of a minority population. In every area there were problems of low pay, inadequate child care, discrimination on grounds of race and sex. Ten thousand copies of the report were distributed through the state and sparked many lively discussions of issues — for example, the deplorable differentiation in pay between men and women, the absence of white-collar jobs for black women, the growing number of working mothers and the shortage of day care — disparities that are now familiar but were then just emerging. For myself the term "southern women" became far more encompassing than it had been. The subjects raised by the commission have never since been off the state's agenda, and that early report is still today a useful historical document.[6]

As for me, the centipede might be a metaphor for my life in the 1960s, as I tried to keep all those many legs going in the same direction.[7] It was something of a miracle when, in spite of all the distractions, *The Southern Lady* finally emerged and in 1970 became, to my own astonishment, a book. Not only that, but a book that attracted attention from male historians as well as from representatives of the burgeoning feminist movement. Without quite understanding how it had happened, I found myself viewed as an expert. This sometimes follows when one comes early to a field in which there are as yet few others. More amazing still, there was a considerable lay audience for lectures on the history of southern women — nearly all, of course, initiated by women's organizations or by the lone woman in one or another history department.

About all this experience I again recur to Gibbon who, after reluctantly serving in the militia, wrote:

> A new field of knowledge and amusement opened itself to me . . . which both in my studies and travels will give me eyes for a new world of things which before would have passed unheeded. . . . What I value most is the knowledge it has given me of mankind in general and of my own country in particular.[8]

Both the governor's commission and the subsequent invitations to speak all over the state helped me learn what contemporary women were doing and thinking in a way that I could not have learned in a library.

At this point, young women will say with some vehemence, "But you make it sound easy . . . and *we* know from experience that combining scholarship and family life is hard enough without adding public service. Surely you are hiding something." I can only say that things were sometimes easier forty years ago. When I see young women now agonizing over the question of tenure, for example, I am a bit embarrassed to remember that I did not even know I had tenure for a year or so after it was granted. Then, too, I had so much help. When I began, academia was almost totally male-dominated, so it was hard to get one's foot in the door, but once in, southern men perhaps more than most were encouraging and endlessly supportive. Probably I benefited from being on the ground early; today a person in my situation would be lost in the mass of bright young women. I was thirty-seven when I first walked into a classroom, forty-two when my first scholarly article was published, and fifty when *The Southern Lady* came out. Academic careers now are expected to begin earlier, and a woman in her late thirties might have trouble gaining an initial appointment.

I should emphasize, too, the vital importance of a supportive husband and children. I have acknowledged in print several times the very important support that I had from Marie Alston Lee, a black woman who came to help with house and children in 1965 and is with us yet. Over the years we have each raised and educated children, we have become, I believe, mutually dependent, and in a number of ways we have both benefited from the feminist movement. I hesitate to think how much less I would have accomplished but for the good fortune of her presence.

After 1970, combining what I learned from books, documents, and people, I went on to write more about southern women with a side venture into the subject of southern urbanization. I have never been on a single track, for though my interest in the South has never flagged, I have written about women in many contexts, including some that had only a partial connection with southern history. Yet even a seemingly unrelated work such as *Natural Allies: Women's Associations in American History* (1991) contained a great deal more about the South than is usually the case in general monographs.[9] In recent years I circled back to the South when I published *Unheard Voices: The First Historians of Southern Women*.[10]

Now, in my eighties, I find myself again doing southern history in a slightly different way, focusing on the parallel lives of black and white women. I first became interested in black women's voluntary associations in the early 1980s. Before the Second World War a majority of these organizations (and indeed a majority of the African Americans) were in the South. I began to suspect that it was just these women's groups, so long ignored by white historians, that had a major part in shaping the growing (and also ignored) black middle class. This interest brought me in touch with some wonderful young black women historians who are still contributing a great deal to my education. Teaching a course on the subject of these parallel lives, first at Duke and then at the University of Mississippi, has been at least as enlightening for me as for the students. Indeed, I resort often to my father's advice: learn with your students. A new direction for research and reflection in one's ninth decade can be mightily invigorating.

How did all this come to be, this complicated life experience? How much was chance, how much was choice? Will I ever know? Perhaps it was all waiting there to happen on that day that Oscar Handlin pointed in a certain direction and I set out to learn about southern Progressives. But what if the streetcar from which I descended one summer evening in 1946 and there first met Andy Scott had been late? Suppose my husband had taken a job, as he several times came close to doing, in the Midwest or the Far West? Suppose I had never seen the Southern Historical Collection or met Julia Spruill and Guion Johnson (the first historians of southern women)? Suppose I had married, as might have happened, a medical doctor or (more likely) a politician? Or had given up writing the dissertation, as so often might have taken place without any overt decision. Suppose . . . suppose . . .

But none of those things happened. It even seemed chance that *The Southern Lady* was timely. I had taken nearly ten years to finish, and when I finally finished, the context was supportive. Thereafter, opportunities proliferated.

Support at critical moments is so important. Good health, a decent job, a supportive family—all these things matter. Only one thing is certain: had it not been for those intrepid women going back at least to Mary Wollstonecraft and coming through Elizabeth Cady Stanton, Jane Addams, or Carrie Chapman Catt, to name only a few, who defied public opinion and campaigned for women's rights, I would not at this moment be writing these words for publication. I have had three kinds of vital mentors: living women, women whose documents I have studied, and academic men and women. And of course my students, who have been central to the process of learning. I salute them all.

Notes

1. Anne Firor Scott, *The Southern Lady: From Pedestal to Politics, 1830–1930* (Chicago, 1970).
2. Introduction to *Mothers of the South: Portraiture of the White Tenant Farm Woman*, by Margaret Jarman Hagood (Charlottesville, 1996), iv–x.
3. I think it important to note that very few members of the Harvard faculty, or indeed of any of the eastern universities, had or have a profound understanding of southern history. I cringe now reading A. B. Hart on the subject, and even Paul Buck, whom I respected as a person, is often — by my lights — way off the track. There were of course notable exceptions: Potter and Woodward at Yale, and Frank Craven at Princeton come to mind — all born in the South.
4. John Lord Sheffield, ed., *The Autobiography of Edward Gibbon, Esq., Illustrated from His Letters, with Occasional Notes and Narratives* (New York, 1846), 81.
5. The UNC department had acquired a new chairman who did not seem inclined to reappoint me, so the Duke offer was indeed timely.
6. Governor's Commission on the Status of Women, *The Many Lives of North Carolina Women* (Raleigh, 1964).
7. I have detailed elsewhere all the side paths and distractions of my academic and personal life in the 1960s, so I will not repeat them here. See the epilogue to the twenty-fifth anniversary edition of *The Southern Lady* (Charlottesville, 1995).
8. Sheffield, *Autobiography of Gibbon*, 135.
9. Anne Firor Scott, *Natural Allies: Women's Associations in American History* (Urbana, Ill., 1991).
10. Anne Firor Scott, ed., *Unheard Voices: The First Historians of Southern Women* (Charlottesville, 1993).

Neither Priest nor Poet

A Search for Vocation

BERTRAM WYATT-BROWN

I never wanted to be a clergyman. Ordination into the Episcopal faith had no appeal. That calling, however, had been a prime family business, as it were, for over one hundred years. Professional communication with the divine had elevated the material and spiritual fortunes of the Browns from Barbour County, Alabama, where the Civil War had subdued the planter class of Eufaula, a small, once wealthy county seat close to the mouth of the Chattahoochee River. This ancestral background, about which I learned while growing up in the North, no doubt was the first sign of a lifetime interest in studying and teaching history, particularly southern history. In the course of my upbringing and early adult years, two alternative destinies—the clerical and the literary—arose and were eventually rejected. I repudiated the first more quickly than the second. The religious element has affected me deeply, however, both personally and intellectually.

During the waning years of the nineteenth century, my grandfather Eugene Brown, a member of the down-at-the-heels gentry, had reared a family of eight children on the meager salary of a country postmaster. He was demoted to assistant postmastership in Republican years, which seemed to be most of the time. He was a droll, intellectual South Carolinian with an apparently endearing vagueness. Somehow the funds were swept together to send two of his sons to the Episcopalian University of the South, in Sewanee, Tennessee, for both college and seminary. Entry into the ministry was one of the few ways for the genteel poor to recoup some standing from the ruins of war and the press of debts. It turned out that my father, Wyatt, the younger of the two seminary-bound sons, was most adept with a pool cue. Innocent-looking and obviously nearsighted, he could get a game going and sweep up the bets at the conclusion. That technique helped to meet tuition charges.

The family may have long had an intellectual bent to which I later aspired.

Family lore has it that grandfather Eugene Brown had once taught philosophy at the state college in Columbia, South Carolina. His wife, however, insisted on returning to her native Eufaula, where her father, General John L. Hunter of the state militia, had forcibly removed the Choctaws from the fertile lands. My great-uncle on my father's mother's side, Bertram Hoole, was the source of humanistic but not ecclesiastical possibilities. He had certainly begun on a very secular tack. In his youth he had been a horse-race enthusiast. He and a member of the aristocratic Ravenel clan had made a wager in Charleston sometime in the 1850s. Hoole's horse won, but the Ravenel bettor suspected some underhandedness. The stakes were high, one thousand dollars, an enormous sum in those days. After much fuming and stamping about, Ravenel at last gave great-uncle Bertram a choice: fight a duel or have his portrait painted at Ravenel's expense. With a bow to Sir John Falstaff, this pre–Civil War Bertram chose discretion over that other important virtue. Remarkable for its stiff rendition of a ruddy farmer face and an unfinished hand, his portrait was not worth a grand, then or now. Yet, in our dining room today, his penetrating blue eyes still stare glumly back at his observers.

Although trained in the antebellum years as both physician and attorney, after the Civil War Bertram Hoole practiced neither law nor medicine. The catastrophe had demolished whatever aspiration he ever had entertained. Imperceptibly he slid into what one might call an Ashley Wilkes syndrome of post-Appomattox despair. According to family legend, he studied and re-studied the works of Aristotle, Hume, Kant, Spencer, and other notable philosophers in lonely bachelorhood. As funds grew strained, he would sell off acres of his unplowed lands, until nearly all was gone. Upon his death the auctioning of his residence barely covered the expenses of the funeral. While I have perhaps avoided his melancholy proclivity, I feel a sense of intellectual kinship with this distant ancestor that ultimately led toward an academic career.

When I was born in March 1932, my father, Wyatt Hunter Brown, later the Episcopal bishop of Harrisburg, Pennsylvania, had christened me, not in honor of the reclusive Hoole, but for his older and most beloved brother. For a lifetime my uncle Bertram Brown was Episcopal rector of Calvary Church in Tarboro, North Carolina. The Rev. Wyatt Hunter Brown looked up to his elder brother as superior in a godliness hard for anyone on this earth to match. Uncle Bertram's congregation felt pretty much the same way. A sundial stands in a corner of Tarboro's courthouse square in his memory. He died in 1937 from heart failure, a dismaying, repetitive family malady. Both brothers had rare senses of humor and loved telling jokes and laughing uproariously. The subjects of their hilarity usually involved the proverbial Pat and Mike, an ethnic favorite no longer allowable, or hapless churchmen rejected for one ridiculous reason or another at the pearly gates.

Uncle Bertram had a successful missionary's common touch. One famous story, at least as family members used to tell it, has him visiting an old and dying farmer deep in the county backlands. The clergyman stepped out of his dusty Model T, loaded with uplifting tracts and Bibles, soon to be liberally dispensed. He entered the plain-board farmhouse to pray with and minister to the dying man. Before he could begin the Communion of the Sick, a service in his well-worn Book of Common Prayer, the old farmer touched his arm. He croaked that he had one final request. How much the ancient would dearly love to taste the flesh of a quail before he entered his heavenly home. When just about to confess his inability to deliver the miracle, Uncle Bertram was astonished to witness a bird fly through the open window. The creature plopped down, conveniently expiring, at the foot of the deathbed. Whether it was actually a quail or not was long a matter of local dispute. I disclaim any affirmation for the truth of the Franciscan incident.

Inheriting his father Eugene's absentmindedness, Uncle Bertram was notorious in town for leaving things here and there and forgetting appointments. On one occasion when he left the church, he was unable to locate where he had parked his Model T and aimlessly wandered about in a fog of wonderment. Eventually he had to walk home. Actually, the parishioners had hauled the vehicle off as a community and most un-Episcopalian disgrace. With a torn canvas roof, seats with burnt holes from his cigar ashes, a broken headlight, and a general air of decrepitude, the vehicle's parking space was now occupied by a spanking new Ford model. It was the surprise gift of the Calvary vestry. Somehow, I became the next and sole family heir of the mischievous trait of mental haziness.

Another from the family storehouse of legends illustrated Uncle Bertram's locally famous generosity. The anecdote explains how his wife, Julia, had presented him with a handsome, warm, silk-lined, black overcoat. After her numerous but easily evaded inquiries regarding where he could have left it, Julia spotted the missing garment weaving bibulously down the street. Uncle Bertram had to confess the intended loss. He had given it to the town drunk, who had complained of the cold—despite his generous intake of spirits.

A more revealing incident concerned the Rev. Bertram Brown's spiritual drive. It suggested some tension between the two brothers, no matter how genetically and spiritually connected they were. Preoccupied with the climb from ecclesiastical obscurity, my father in 1915 had become rector of the Church of the Ascension in Pittsburgh. Earlier he had shepherded a flock at St. Phillips in Asheville, North Carolina. Father's blazing sermons caught the attention of Andrew Mellon, then visiting the nearby Vanderbilt estate. He was the Pittsburgh Ascension's senior warden. Sometime after my father's installation at the new downtown church, he invited brother Bertram to preach to his well-heeled congregation. On the Saturday before the Sunday service, however, Uncle Bertram mysteriously vanished. After some frantic searching, someone in the family located him singing and preaching to the homeless with members of the Salvation Army on a downtown street corner. Cornet, trombone, and drum punctuated the impromptu missionizing. Who could be the more otherworldly seemed to be the unspoken issue between the two brothers. Such were the stories of pious dedication that circulated in the family, no doubt repeated many times for my own religious edification. If so, the lesson did not take.

In our household, sabbatarian duty commanded that there be an early Holy Communion service, with Father presiding at what always seemed to be the crack of dawn. Then Sunday school and eleven o'clock morning prayer followed at St. Stephen's Cathedral in Harrisburg or, in the summer, at the Church of the Transfiguration, Blue Ridge Summit, Pennsylvania. As the church calendar dictated, during the week various saints' days and other holy occasions added more liturgical requirements. Bishop's Court, as the wealthy bishop James Henry Darlington had dubbed our residence on Front Street, contained a consecrated chapel with marble altar and a stained-glass window with a dove descending. Even our summer place at Blue Ridge Summit, another diocesan legacy, had a room on the third floor fitted out for early morning Holy Communion, where I was assigned the job of acolyte. I scarcely minded these repetitions of spiritual routine as much as one might expect. Indeed, I have never lost faith or interest in religious matters but continue to regard true spiritual insight as something to be sought after, even if never, as in my case, fully mastered. Yet the very abundance of ceremonies did not encourage me toward an existence of perpetual performance of them.

As if the familial models of churchly tendencies were not discomfiting enough, my two brothers also snapped on the backward-facing collar. Charles

Mathews Brown (later Charles Wyatt-Brown) followed the example of Father and Uncle Bertram. He took holy orders upon graduation from seminary at Sewanee. (Father had our name legally changed in 1940 from Brown to Wyatt-Brown.)[1]

Charles loved people with a heartfelt sincerity that remains a marvel seldom to be observed. In any case, to the admiration of the rest of us, his parishioners returned that endearing quality by showing great affection for him. The hardworking rector officiated over highly southern and largely Republican parishes in Beaumont and Houston, Texas. Charles introduced his congregations to a spirit of tolerance, fairness, and empathy that surely they would not have easily reached on their own. Armed with a portable communion set, he was known to pursue the Beaumont church's truants preparing to embark at Sunday dawn for a full day of concentrated fishing. He would then lead them in Holy Communion on the marina wharf. Charles labored endlessly for Alcoholics Anonymous and the founding of a successful drug-addiction program for teenagers on the premises of strait-laced Palmer Memorial Church across the street from Rice University.

Formerly "Wyatt" but then "Hunter, Junior," the eldest brother, twenty years my senior, followed his brother and father's vocation after service in the U.S. Navy during World War II. He also went to St. Luke's Seminary, Sewanee. Hunter is still remembered fondly in Maryland, where he held three successful rectorships before moving to Florida. There he founded a boys' school, St. Andrews, in Boca Raton.

These four exemplary models of dedication to the cloth beckoned me toward the godly way. Yet their examples were far beyond my much more secular inclinations. Nevertheless, I found myself constantly asked by well-meaning churchwomen, "Bertram, aren't you going to be a clergyman like your father, uncle, and brothers?" *Not if I could help it*, was the immediate internal reaction. I kept that testy refrain to myself. Instead I usually mumbled something noncommittal in reply.

Thus, early on, any feasible alternative to a life devoted to clerical routine and spiritual inspiration seemed preferable. Yet the academic career is not all that different from the religious. In both cases, an interest in people is required, along with a degree of articulateness. The Episcopal faith, however, seems to prefer the mind-numbing homily that often has neither a clear beginning nor a climactic end. The novelist Ellen Glasgow once declared somewhere that

Episcopalian authorities would allow anyone to do as they liked except *think*. Also, both professions are equally ill-paid and poorly pensioned, but, unlike the business life, some compensation is derived from security in office.

Four years at the University of the South, the family's ongoing collegiate obligation, prepared me not for history but for English literature. I took history courses whenever mandatory literature classes did not stand in the way. But the heavy textbooks on English history or European civilization were extraordinarily deadening and pedantic in style, even though the subject matter was potentially quite interesting. Most of the instructors of that period in the Sewanee history department were equally dull. One or two staggered into class either unprepared, hung over, or both. John Rison Jones, a recent graduate of Sewanee, knew his subject well but was just learning the teaching craft. "Smiling Tom" Govan, a Jacksonian expert on Nicholas Biddle, had us all suffer through the European survey. He knew too little about it and only half-heartedly tried to fill the gaps. Yet he entertained us with sheer bull without revealing his ignorance, which I came to realize only later. Nevertheless, even as he handed back papers marked "D" to unfortunate freshmen, that petrified smirk never left his face.

The choice to major in English was determined not only by career plan but by association with my classmates. By and large these friends were the more earnest intellectuals at the college. All of us found English the subject with the best and most stimulating instruction. Most galvanizing was Dr. Charles Trawick Harrison. Heavy-lidded and gray-haired, his manners betokened an awesome dignity. Wearing a tattered black gown, Harrison punctuated his discourses on the religious poems of John Donne or the verses of Andrew Marvell with flicks of his chain-smoked cigarettes. He would meaningfully raise and lower his eyebrows to accentuate delivery of a weighty sagacity. With reference to some epiphanic verse, he would pronounce such words as "ingratiating—ah, most ingratiating" with signal and unquestionable finality. We were mesmerized. He was a brilliant teacher. I learned more from him than from any other instructor at Sewanee and hoped one day to emulate his example of intelligence and erudition.

Harrison presided over the required written and oral examinations before graduation. To prepare for the exam, a group of us English majors would gather for lunch or dinner at Gailor Hall. We quizzed each other on such slippery matters as naming who wrote some verse or created which fictional character or who had authored this or that highly "sentient" comment, another of Harrison's favorite adjectives. Some of these very competitive seniors went on to graduate studies in the humanities and prominent teaching careers themselves. But I was the only one to stay up half the night before the comprehensives to read Sir Walter Scott's *The Heart of Midlothian*. On the following day in the spring of 1953 I sat in Clark Hall before the examiners, all of us in the black regalia that was required for every imaginable formality at Sewanee. The faculty members included Charles Harrison from Alabama; cigar-chomping Abbott Martin from Georgia; Tudor Seymour Long and Maurice "Boothead" Moore, both from South Carolina; and Monroe K. Spears from Tennessee, the most published and distinguished of them all. As anticipated, among the many questions to be answered was, "Have you read any Walter Scott?" I replied confidently that I had and proceeded with remarks drawn from a hasty midnight gallop through that lengthy romance. At commencement not long afterward, I carried off the Alexander Guerry Medal in English Literature. Others, who had unwisely abstained from Scott's fiction, deserved the prize much more than I. Yet that answer no doubt won over the English faculty members still submerged in the mists of the Old South. It was a state of mind perpetuated at Sewanee, where Scott had retained his prominence unchallenged, along with the faded Confederate banners hanging in the university chapel.

After graduation, two mind-draining years in the U.S. Navy followed. It was the era of the Korean War, but the fighting had ceased. As a result, I never left the continental shores. Upon release in the summer of 1955, I had to decide what to make of my life. Journalism almost beckoned. I had relished working for the *Sewanee Purple*, the college weekly. My chief assignment was writing a gossip column, chronicling forgettable fraternity debauches and other ephemera of Sewanee doings. Sometimes doggerel poems in dismal imitation of Alexander Pope's heroic couplets appeared under my name. Poetry, however, was definitely not my calling.

Then Lucas Myers, a close friend whom I had known since 1940, provided another possibility. He and I had been enrolled in his mother's Sewanee elementary school, called Bairnwick. Years later we graduated in English in the same class from the University of the South. Sometime that summer of 1955, Lucas wrote me how intellectually fulfilling were his current experiences at Downing College, Cambridge University. Perhaps sensing my half-conscious unease about entering graduate school immediately upon mustering out of the navy, he advised that I should join him at Cambridge. For some reason, I jumped at the chance. Taking advantage of his detailed suggestions, I applied to several Cambridge colleges as a prospective candidate in English. Thanks to Lucas's interviews with those in charge of admissions, I received four positive responses but accepted the invitation to King's College. The letter from the Roman classicist L. P. Wilkinson, Senior Tutor, was the first to reach me. At the time I was stationed at the Harbor Defense Unit on the Little Creek Amphibious Naval Base, Virginia. Soon afterward, I crossed the Atlantic in the aged *Queen Mary* and arrived at Cambridge in September 1955.

Being enrolled for the two-year undergraduate program for those already equipped with a B.A., I thought a second sojourn along the same lines would be carefree and easy. But complications seemed to multiply for many reasons. First was the problem of cultural and social adjustment. When King's College accepted my papers, I had no idea what an enormous change from the Sewanee experience lay in store. Two years in the military provided little preparation for English university life. I had taken a correspondence course in Shakespeare out of the University of Chicago and also had tried to brush up my French while stationed in Virginia. But my tutor, a young and very beautiful bride, sadly explained that her husband objected to her working. She terminated our weekly sessions. Remember, these were the 1950s. In any event, a heady mixture of exhilaration and perplexity in the foreign surroundings greeted me in the new atmosphere.

When I put my bags down at the rambling St. Botolph's Rectory on Summerfield Road, Lucas, my sponsor and friend, had been living there for the past year. As a veteran himself, Myers had finagled his way out of Downing College lodgings and settled at Botolph's. (He had convinced John Raven, in charge of new students at King's, to let me join him there. Like Lucas, I was a veteran and older than most undergraduates.) Our landlady was the happily unshockable Mrs. Helen R. Hitchcock. With eyes fluttering constantly while she talked, the stately and kindhearted widow of the late curate of St. Botolph's Church on King's Parade lived by renting every available space on the property. Rates were low. I paid only 3 pounds, 10 shillings a week for my broom closet of a room on the second floor. One had to enter sideways because the bed was so close to the door. A tiny desk and chair were wedged under a small window. Earlier that year, Lucas had occupied the rectory's chicken coop. It was charmingly set adjacent to a small orchard of apple and peach trees and vegetable rows that were rented out to neighbors. A workman's handcart resided comfortably under some nearby bushes—for an inconsequential parking fee. Lucas, though, was exempted from even such small sums of rent in exchange for stoking the coal fires and replenishing the huge Aga stove. Before my arrival he had lived in a tiny garden shed back of the rectory.

I soon discovered that Lucas was closely affiliated with a brilliant group of young poets. In the fall of 1954, a year before my appearance, Lucas Myers of Downing, Daniel Huws of Peterhouse, and Ted Hughes of Pembroke all had poems published in *Chequer*. That circumstance brought the trio together. They were soon exchanging poems and treasuring long conversations in the orchard at St. Botolph's Rectory. Hughes often returned from London to see his friends. He was then working at various ill-paying, menial jobs, the most interesting of which was at the Pinewood Studios for J. Arthur Rank, reading submitted screenplays and potentially film-convertible books. With barely enough income to live on, Hughes was accustomed to sleep under Lucas's bed in the Botolph garden quarters on his frequent visits. Hughes later claimed that a residue of chicken droppings had fouled, as it were, a favorite corduroy jacket. Lucas, though, denies all responsibility. By the time I had arrived, however, Lucas had graduated from the orchard hutch to the dining room in the house itself.[2]

Around Myers and Hughes gathered several more aspiring young poets. I remember very clearly that on my first afternoon at Botolph's, this scruffily clad band was in the back yard. They were smoking smelly Gauloises and Woodbine cigarettes. The group chatted of this or that, while brushing away the pesky midges or mosquitoes that haunt the East Anglian outdoors until first frost. Following the example of prior cigarette exchanges all round, I passed around my last American Marlboros for everyone's appreciation. It was an automatic British custom that I found to be a new, slightly coercive but ultimately companionable ritual.

Much more convivial and insect-free were the dusks spent at the always crowded Anchor on Silver Street. The pub overlooked the River Cam, and the proprietor rented out shallow draft boats called punts. In good weather, punters poled themselves and dates under the succession of bridges. Everyone was put in a very sunny frame of mind whenever Ted Hughes appeared to expand on his abundant treasury of stories. Lucas has lately written that Ted "had a good voice, with a unique, often ironic modulation that gave [storytelling] an additional dimension." The poet often held his audience transfixed, as if each listener were mesmerized.³ This was a new world to me. These young people were so engaging and animated, and it was a delight to be around them.

At this point I was pretty happy specializing in English literature. Strange as it may seem nowadays, that subject was then at the top of the academic heap. The pronouncements of Lionel Trilling, Ivor Winters, William Empson, Cleanth Brooks, Allen Tate, and the priestly Canadian Northrop Frye reigned supreme. At places like Harvard, Oxford, and Cambridge, a preeminence of English studies lasted until about 1970. It then retreated everywhere from the study of literature proper and resorted to what some outsiders have considered swampy theoretical backwaters. Under the still enduring influence of Sewanee's Charles Harrison, I thought English was a subject in which I could flourish.

For Ted and then my friend Lucas to repudiate the authority of the giants in the discipline was a revelation to me, setting an example of how it was possible to move from one academic major to another. After enduring two years in the hands of tutors of English prose and poetry, Ted had found the academic style not just irrelevant but repellent in its soul-shriveling pretentiousness. He switched fields and won his degree in social anthropology in the spring 1954. Lucas had pursued the same migration and earned his degree the year afterward. I was quite surprised. He had been one of Charles Harrison's most treasured students at Sewanee. Indeed, Lucas had disappointed our undergraduate professor's fondest hopes. Yet in all fairness, anthropology was highly vigorous at Cambridge then. The prolific structuralists, Edmund Ronald Leach, Edward Evan Evans-Pritchard, and Meyer Fortes, were all holding forth.⁴ To my astonishment, Lucas, working under Leach, and Hughes knowledgeably discussed the warrior songs of the Nuer clans in Ethiopia, the social arrangements of the Tallensi in the Trans-Volta, and the strange customs of various groups in South India and Burma. It was all novel to me and far different from what I had expected of these recent apostates from English. The University of the South did not even have an anthropologist on the faculty. In all four years on the Sewanee mountain, never had I heard a single reference to Bronislaw Malinowski, Émile Durkheim, Franz Boas, or Margaret Mead.

Meantime, I had my first meeting with George Rylands, my tutor in English. The result was scarcely promising of a term-long compatibility. A tall, ruddy-faced, rather loose-wristed bachelor, "Dadie" Rylands was then famous as a producer of Shakespearean plays for BBC television. His rooms were made graceful with decorations by Dora Carrington, a friend of Virginia Woolf. I thought Rylands quite old then, but he only died recently at age ninety-six. "Mr. Wyatt-Brown," he asked, "do you know Mr. Sweeney here at King's?" "No, I'm afraid not," said I, having arrived just two days before. "He's *another* American," Rylands complained in the most Oxfordian of Oxford English. "I regret to say he does not do veddy well in his studies." And he eyed me thoughtfully. The implication was unmistakable. Actually, Sweeney turned out to be a delightful, athletic-minded fellow—no genius but certainly no academic misfit. This encounter with another side of the English literature fortress, as it might be called, presented something of a challenge. Dutifully, perhaps belligerently, I began writing essays on Thomas Carlyle, Matthew Arnold, Thomas Hardy, and other Victorian notables for the once-a-week meetings with Rylands.

Despite this somewhat off-putting relationship, I found that literary studies at Cambridge could supply very exciting moments. I grew thoroughly engrossed in the subject. The Cambridge high priests of literary criticism were most impressive. C. S. Lewis had settled there, having recently left Oxford. He lectured on medieval English poetry to sixty of us. Lewis predicted, however, that the number would gradually diminish over the Michaelmas term—and it did. I disappeared from the ranks halfway through. Though truly awe-inspiring, the author of the *Narnia* series, *The Screw-Tape Letters*, and other classics was one of the driest lecturers in any of the classrooms on Mill Lane. On the other hand, David Daiches, a Scots literary critic, was both accessible and enthralling on the podium, particularly with regard to Virginia Woolf. Her suicide in 1941 had temporarily set her reputation back until Daiches almost singlehandedly revived it. With only a small light on the lectern to see by, he dramatically read passages from *Mrs. Dalloway* in a way never to be forgotten. We will not see his kind of understated inspiration ever again.

By far the most fearsome and yet intriguing member of the university's English faculty was F. R. Leavis of Downing College. His lectures always drew something like two hundred undergraduates, if memory serves. A diminutive, wild-haired, and disheveled creature, he would stride down the aisle with a precariously balanced pile of texts in his arms. Meanwhile, an assistant was distributing a printed page or two of poems and excerpts from novels, each unit consisting of five or six lines. By style and syntax, we were supposed to identify both author and poem or passage. I was usually at a complete loss but determined to master the arcane mysteries of literary identification. Meantime, the graduates from the English public schools had no trouble completing the exercise. They had done this sort of thing, I imagined, at Eton, Harrow, or Shelburne.

Leavis was a devotee of the New Criticism and of its leading proponent, I. A. Richards, who had left Cambridge for Harvard not long before. Like Richards, Leavis stressed the hierarchical ranking of English literature, the sanctity of texts, and the irrelevance of the author's personality and circumstances in judging the artistic success or the unworthiness of the document under close scrutiny. Though opinionated and scorchingly harsh in his judgments of what he regarded as inferior, Leavis was often dazzling. He could reveal hidden connotations, mark the originality and appropriateness of a metaphor, or point out the deliberate and shadowy literary derivations from works of earlier writers, classical and otherwise. His expositions on the poems of Lord Byron, Alfred Lord Tennyson, and T. S. Eliot were especially stunning. Moreover, he drew out meanings and literary echoes in James Joyce's *Ulysses* that few specialists in the Atlantic world could hope to equal. His influential study of D. H. Lawrence, just published that year, informed some of his most outstanding lectures. The poets who met at St. Botolph's Rectory and with whom I associated denounced him, however, as a sanctimonious knave. As Lucas reported, Leavis split the world "into those who didn't exist, a large category, and those who did—there was no room for temporizing." For a while in 1954, Leavis had been his tutor at Downing. Leavis had a snappish streak. According to Lucas he had once declared to his pupils in tutorial that their momentarily absent fellow student, the poet Christopher Levenson, was nothing but "a complete ass."[5] It was scarcely the wisest method of instruction, but that degree of censoriousness was perhaps better applied to Leavis himself.

Meanwhile, I began to feel an odd disassociation from the Cambridge surroundings. The existing English order of society was so strange to an American—in terms of unfathomable social and linguistic rankings, somewhat confusing national politics, and a general cultural aloofness. It seemed as if the purpose of English college life was to squeeze out those who did not somehow "belong" because of alleged deficiencies of mind or some class-based, accent-derived defect. The English mentality can be a curious mixture of brutality and unpleasant one-upmanship, as Stephen Potter was famously satirizing in the mid-1950s. Like Leavis, Dadie Rylands, my English tutor, represented that national trait which perhaps had its roots in class and public-school distinctions. For instance, Antony Victor Brown, a pioneer in ITN television newscasting, once had felt the sting of his wit. The undergraduate had gone to Rylands's elegant chambers for a working out of the next assignment, a reading of the weekly essay—and a glass of sherry. "I never received any advice or criticism from him," Brown recalled. "When I got a bad degree—a third—I asked him why I had not done better. 'Because you're not very intelligent, dear Antony,' he replied."[6] It seemed to me then that refined etiquette, high breeding, and unbelievably breathtaking rudeness all jumbled together in the English character.

Also at that time, one must recognize, England still harbored a sense of world leadership. Americans were judged as wayward colonists with regrettable and undecipherable dialects and pushy manners. Rylands's comment about Sweeney fell into that category. The Suez crisis of 1956 was a rude awakening that had yet to sink into the British psyche. I remember that when the United States firmly and successfully opposed the French, English, and Israeli adventure to seize the Suez Canal, a King's College graduate student from Egypt and I crowed with satisfaction at Britain's humiliation.

In addition, there was something particularly troubling in the preciousness of King's, as I then interpreted it. As some readers may already be well aware, the college was the sole surviving redoubt of the Bloomsbury set, that collection of remarkable, intellectual Edwardians. They had once included Lytton Strachey, Rebecca West, Virginia Woolf, Julian Bell, Duncan Grant, and others, but there was an aging remnant at King's. The then recently deceased economist Lord Maynard Keynes, the college bursar, was still a presence to be felt. He had tripled the endowment of King's College, much to my later benefit in the form of a second-year scholarship. The most famous of the Bloomsbury crowd at King's, however, was the novelist E. M. Forster, then closeted in the fashion of that time, though everybody knew. Unforgettably, Forster wore pants that always revealed his skinny ankles. A man of gentle habit who loved the musical life in Cambridge, he later became a friend of mine but definitely not at this time. King's College seemed at times too inbred, too enclosed. While none of the students that I know of were practicing gays, such was not the case with regard to the reputation of the college fellows. For instance, the chaplain, brother of the Archbishop of York, was a nervous, bald-headed, middle-aged clergyman. During that Michaelmas term, he had leaped from one of the King's College Chapel's famous towers. He fell to the stone pavement some ninety feet below. It was rumored that he had been arrested in London the night before in a raid on a rent-boy hangout. It was said, too, that Boris Ord, the aged but gifted choir director, had earlier been caught in a similar sting but somehow escaped public exposure.

The elegant George Rylands and the short, plump classicist Sir John Shepherd, with long white locks and a mischievous eye for male beauty, were also surviving relics of the sexually diverse Bloomsbury group. After the sudden death of his predecessor, an Egyptologist, the college dons elected the impressive and articulate Noel Annan as provost, joined by his brilliant wife, Gabriele. Annan, whom one might call a latter-day Bloomsburian, contributed greatly to the sophistication and the remarkably self-satirizing peculiarity that made King's a very special, even beloved place, although it was an English social and intellectual tradition that, in my first term at Cambridge, I did not at all value. A genuine appreciation of the many things King's had to offer would not emerge until months later.

Despite, or because of, the array of literary geniuses to impart their wisdom, I found myself sinking slowly into unknown literary seas. I began to question how I could manage graduate studies at Harvard after experiencing the scorn of literary studies of my Botolph friends on the one side and the lofty anti-Americanism of Dadie Rylands and company on the other. I was still very much aware that Dr. Harrison of Sewanee expected me to do as he had done, that is, complete graduate studies at Harvard as I had originally intended. Yet if I did pass the exams in Anglo-Saxon and compose a dissertation on William Cowper, Henry Fielding, or George Meredith, could I really devote my life to trying to emulate giants like Leavis, whatever these friends thought of him? Still more discomforting was the feeling that, in my essays for Rylands, I was simply repeating what I had already learned at Sewanee under Harrison, "Abbo" Martin, or "Boothead" Moore. I spent the Christmas break on the ski slopes of Lech, Austria, but that reprise brought no permanent relief from a growing sense of disengagement.

By far, though, the major factor that led to a disillusionment with the subject of English literature was association with the Botolph group. Besides Lucas Myers occupying the dining room, the poet Daniel Huws and his future wife Helga had separate rooms at Botolph's on the second floor. Helga Kobuszewski, a Polish refugee from the Russian army's advance in the Second World War, knew how to cook superbly on spare, penny-pinching resources. Poor as we all were, we greedily dined — and noticeably and advantageously thinned —

on her feasts of liver sausage, fried with onions and potatoes. Thus, a kind of literary headquarters was established. Lucas Myers once referred to it as a "spiritual home" for himself, Ted Hughes, Daniel Huws, Danny Weissbort, David Ross, Than Minton, and others drawn to the poetic circle. On further reflection, Myers now dubs St. Botolph's "a center of intrigue" but also "a place of good humor and freedom of invention."[7] Its members kindly included me.

These friends were very gifted and high-spirited. Huws presented the most striking figure. I always thought of Dan as the reincarnation of a defrocked medieval monk with a certain devilishly intelligent look in his face. As a brilliant Celtic-language scholar, Dan quite appropriately later became Keeper of Manuscripts at the National Library of Wales, Aberystwyth, in Cardiganshire, and has published several books of poetry as well as learned studies of early Welsh literature. Lucas describes him dressed in "old clothes with wire in his brogans." He notes that "Dan had limited respect for privilege or accepted institutions and their established representatives either in elder generations or in our own." That theme actually came close to defining us all.[8]

What chiefly set the group apart was a conspicuous hodgepodge of backgrounds. That was indeed an anomaly in tight little monarchical England. Daniel Weissbort and Than Minton were Jewish; Colin White, Scots; Terence McCaughey, Irish; and David Ross, a wellborn Londoner but a rebel nonetheless. Ted Hughes came from Yorkshire, a provincial backwater by establishment standards.[9] Most of them, like Hughes and Myers, had either deserted English or had never planned on taking it. Literary criticism was constantly derided as beneath contempt because it harbored only the favored few and exuded a false sanctity.

And then there were the Americans, Lucas Myers, me, and later on that winter, the poets Sylvia Plath and Jane Baltzell, a Marshall Fellow from Pembroke College at Brown. Jane, who was Sylvia's friend and housemate, proved to be more level-headed than any of us other Americans. Like all of us, Jane reveled in college life but also felt some sense of alienation. She refused an opportunity to stay on as a tutor at Newnham College where she and Sylvia Plath studied English literature. Some Americans abroad tend to become more Anglo than the English. Yet another style compels one to be "a latent patriot," as C. Vann Woodward later put it with regard to his contemporary experience at Oxford University.[10] I found my half-southern, half-Pennsylvania-Dutch dialect becoming ever more pronounced.

I suppose there was ample reason for English anti-Americanism. We had come out of the doldrums of the Great Depression and horrors of World War II prosperous, dominant—and naïve about world affairs. In contrast, England of the mid-1950s was depleted from the unbelievable bloodshed of two world wars. The nation was just emerging from near penury and severe rationing, with a weakened industrial base and a collapsing empire. It was a dreary, rain-drenched, melancholy country. But like other Americans abroad, I considered American hegemony simply part of the natural scheme. Yet I and perhaps many others from across the seas resented the implications of class and cultural inferiority that our English hosts attached to us.

Among the Botolph members, a dislike of regular English studies was matched by an equal disdain for politics. Like them, I, too, grew apolitical, even antipolitical. That was not unusual for young people belonging to the so-called "Beat" Eisenhower generation. But poets were then particularly mistrustful of politicians of any stripe. Most of the clique were on the socialist left during this time of Tory reaction in England and rampant McCarthyism at home. Colin White alone favored communism but without carrying a card. He, though, was the only one of us actually to have experienced the brutalities of war and was scarred by it in a way that probably affected my outlook. During the Korean conflict, Britain contributed troops to the United Nations forces. First Lieutenant White had been assigned to lead a company of English convicts. They had been released to kill Chinese and North Koreans in lieu of their civilian compatriots back home. But in fact they were known to turn their weapons on their own officers or set lieutenants' tents afire. Colin related the occasion when his troops had held a farewell blowout the night before he went home. One reeling corporal recalled Colin's arrival as commander and asked whether he remembered the bullet that whizzed within inches of his head. "That was me," the ex-con confessed. "I am glad I missed and didn't frag you then; you turned out to be a bloody good bloke after all."

Colin made light of that experience. Clearly, though, the battle-scarred veteran was subject to what we nowadays call post-traumatic stress disorder or, in the language of that time, battle fatigue. On one occasion in midwinter 1956, for instance, he whacked Lucas Myers in the left eye. It bruised so badly that Lucas's vigilant tutor assumed he had initiated a street brawl. Charitably disposed, however, Myers now says that Colin "had struck" him quite "unintentionally."[11] The Scotsman's fury against the world, however, would surface after downing a pint or two of bitter. His truculence accentuated my own reasons for feeling disconnected from the other undergraduates.

Egged on by Colin's Scottish heckles, all of us were most derisive with reference to the so-called "crums." These were the Cambridge student aristocrats and nobility like the Duke of Buckingham's son, a member of my college. I once went to a tea party in his digs and was amazed to be passed a plate of crystallized violet petals. On a quite different occasion, we Botolphians, if the term is permitted, found ourselves in a melee with some high-toned undergraduates at a Queens' College party. Colin and several of us had crashed the event. True to form, Colin had started the quarrel. The legitimate guests chased after us. Hearing the racket all the way to the porter's lodge, the Queens' College "bull dogs," as they were called, clamped on their bowler hats and lumbered after us. We hurled ourselves successfully over the college's stone wall, which was surmounted with wrought-iron barbs of particular sharpness.

In spite of the high times at Cambridge, we all were angrier, more hostile, more censorious—and more uncertain of ourselves—than we realized. So it looks, at least, in retrospect. There was abroad a spirit of near violence or at least intense disillusion, the full origins of which elude me. Certainly alcohol played a part. On one occasion, Philip Hobsbaum, editor of *Delta*, another poetry outlet at Cambridge, had invited some Botolph people to a party sponsored by the magazine. Lucas Myers recalls that Colin again grew agitated and tried to bash a wine bottle over the host's head. Ted Hughes, however, caught the upraised arm before a possibly fatal blow was struck. Apart from Colin's own private war, maybe the rest of us were worried about the resilience of our manhood. A post–World War II fear that we were not up to the mark of our older, veteran brothers could have played a hidden role. It would seem that Sylvia Plath, who entertained a greater storehouse of fury, had other reasons for distress.[12] Of course, during this time, we had no clue about that.

To be sure, these ravening fears were not in constant motion. As Sylvia Plath's housemate Jane Baltzell (now Jane Baltzell Kopp) put it years later, we were caught up in the "hugger-mugger of youth, enthusiasm, excess and adventure of every kind."[13] Yet a mood of uncharted discontent also had much to do with the founding of the *St. Botolph's Review* and the party that followed its appearance. The publication was to set the group apart from the rest of the artistic community and lead to serious matters for Ted Hughes and Sylvia Plath. For me, that wild night had much to do with what I was later to regard as a momentous decision.

Ted Hughes, Daniel Huws, and Lucas Myers were desperately vexed about the state of the poetic scene that seemingly slighted them. As a result, they set retained. In any event, after the Christmas break I realized that a decision dealing with the future loomed ominously. The school year was more than half over. Resort to action, though, had less to do with intellectual than purely social and psychological factors.

The critical event was an undergraduate party at Cambridge in celebration of the launching of the *St. Botolph's Review*. That bacchanalia later became rather famous, at least in literary circles. The circumstances must be quickly summarized. There was some difficulty finding the money for putting out the magazine that had been planned at King's Lynn. Nobody had a shilling to spare. I was in no position to help as I had recently been denied GI Bill funding on the grounds that I was merely getting another B.A. Luckily, David Ross's father picked up the tab for the publication. Even so, Ted Hughes was particularly concerned. In his poem "St. Botolph's," in *Birthday Letters*, he writes, "I had predicted / Disastrous expense: a planetary / Certainty, according to Prospero's book."[15] Much to our relief, however, *St. Botolph's Review* made its debut on February 25, 1956. David Ross, Danny Weissbort, Dan Huws, Than Minton, Ted Hughes, and Lucas Myers all had entries. Hughes's "Fallgrief's Girl-friends" and "Soliloquy of a Misanthrope" and Lucas Myers's "Sestina of the Norse Seaman" and "Fools Encountered," with salty, gripping imagery, still seem to me the best realized of the poems in the one-issue journal.

I was very elated to sell some seventy-five copies up and down Silver Street and King's Parade. But pride mingled with disappointment. I had had nothing to contribute. The weather began sunnily enough, but it later turned bitter cold. Meantime, the poetic despisers of all such crass hustling—Myers, Hughes, Ross, and Minton—nervously solaced themselves with quantities of beer at the Anchor, much to my envy and dismay. Since Daniel Weissbort had the flu, I excused him but took some satisfaction from the commercial incompetence of most everybody else.

As is well known, Ted Hughes and Sylvia Plath met each other for the first time at the publication party that evening in Falcon Yard. Sylvia was to be the author of the autobiographical novel *The Bell Jar* (1962) and such books of poetry as *The Colossus* (1962) and *Ariel* (1965). Her collected works won a posthumous Pulitzer Prize in 1982. Ted would become England's poet laureate from 1983 until his death from cancer in 1998. A victim of chronic bipolar depression, Sylvia was to commit suicide in 1963, after seven years of marriage to Ted. A Hollywood film, with Gwyneth Paltrow and Daniel Craig in the leading roles, Christine Jeff directing, is currently being screened in art theaters. It

plans afoot to produce this new magazine. I joined the others on a trip
Lynn on the storm-swept coast of the North Sea sometime in early Ja
a freezing cottage belonging to David Ross's parents, we ate fish a
wrapped in newspaper, drank the local brew, and plotted the over
Christopher Levenson, F. R. Leavis, Stephen Spender, and others. T
regarded as unworthy guardians of the Poetic Establishment. The tr
ists were labeled the "Movement," but in the poet-rebels' opinion a
rigor mortis was all that actually moved. Whether there was more
enlightenment in such views I cannot now say. These very establish
were closely associated with the poetry magazine *Granta*. The e
turned down Lucas Myers's poems but did publish Sylvia Plath's. Be
typical of that day, we deplored her efforts as trivial and immature
what woman could ever write lasting poetry? How hopelessly misg
wrong we were. Apart from me, none of the Botolphians knew her
at that point. That oversight scarcely counted as they grumbled ceas
she was demeaning the poetic profession by publishing in the *N
Ladies' Home Journal, Mademoiselle*, and other middle-brow a
outlets.[14]

The problem for me in dealing with such intrigues was double.
realized I could not function effectively in this poetic milieu, for al
attitudes and great times. The poets spoke a language that I could
half the time. Dan Huws, Lucas, and Ted, for instance, carried Ro
The White Goddess in their hands as if it were their version of Hol
I still have my Penguin paperback. I had no idea what they foun
ing. Graves's anthropological conjectures about ruling matriarch
cient world might be as brilliant as Dan Huws and company saw
the theory did not seem credible.

Quite clearly, though, these poets were learning their craft wi
dedication that naturally and unthinkingly excluded others less a
elements of mythology, literature, and personal experience with p
ture than they were. These sources were invaluable—indeed in
in the development of their poetry. At the same time, I knew that
fields of either English or history had little of the permanence c
tual, emotional, and lyrical depth that poetry could draw forth.
rizing of disciplines, the best histories, with depressingly few exc
temporal and quickly forgotten as the leading works of literary cri
enough, poetry surmounts the erosions of time. That is a positio

romanticizes their impassioned first encounter at the Botolph gala and their later, tragic lives.[16]

Yet the event at the time had a much different meaning for me. I had known that Sylvia was coming to Cambridge even before I had arrived. Charles Gardner, an old friend from Blue Ridge Summit days, and his wife, Amy, had alerted me that I should meet her. They had both known Sylvia at Smith College. As I was dating Sylvia's friend Jane Baltzell, I guess I was introduced sometime that Michaelmas term on a visit to Newnham College's Whitstead Cottage, where they both were in residence. Earlier in the afternoon Sylvia had seen me hawking something on a Silver Street corner. She stopped her bike to inquire why I would be outdoors huckstering in the growing chill. Assuring her that it was not a theological tract but a collection of poetry, I sold her a copy that cost one shilling and six pence, as I recall. It is now thousands of times more valuable than its initial price. As the afternoon wore on, back in her attic room at Whitstead, Sylvia grew ever more excited about the prospect of meeting Hughes. She pedaled her bicycle back furiously in her customary style to my location outside the Anchor. I recall her blonde hair and coat billowing in the wind. Sylvia asked me if I knew any of these poets, especially Hughes and Myers, whose poems she most admired. I invited her to join us at 8:30 that evening for a party at the Cambridge Women's Union, just off Market Square. Meantime, Ted, Lucas, I, and perhaps a couple of others gathered in Lucas's dining-room quarters. There we downed a fifth of Bellows Bourbon, which, through the auspices of a naval friend of mine, had been obtained from the U.S. Embassy exchange in London. So fortified, we headed off, picked up dates, and gathered at Falcon Yard on Petty Cury.

The birth of the *Review* should have inspired a bright festival of song and dance. Instead, it became a sinister affair, far out of control. Among us there moved a mood of desperation and cruel bitterness. It surfaced like a serpent from the depths. Such are the perils of youth and immaturity. From nearly fifty years' distance, I suspect that we all had our different and private reasons for being unsettled. Rejected in the undergraduate literary press, the poets were very anxious. How might the public respond to the poems? They feared the worst. Somehow we all knew that a new era in poetry might be dawning—or possibly aborted. I had the still worse fate of finding myself a stranger to the community of poetry writing while in the midst of luminous talent. The lonely consolation was selling the *Review*.

According to Sylvia and my friend Jane Baltzell Kopp, whom I had escorted to Falcon Yard, the festivities began in a mood of dejection. At some point, though, the tempo picked up. The manic rhythms of a first-rate jazz band filled the rooms. Dan Weissbort was on piano and Michael Boddy, another friend of Ted's, took the trombone. By the time Sylvia arrived, the crowd had become quite boisterous and lavishly alcoholic. With Hamish Stewart, her Canadian date, Sylvia arrived already very drunk. "*Falcon's Yard*, and the syncopated strut of a piano upstairs, and oh it was very Bohemian, with boys in turtle-neck sweaters and girls being blue eyelidded or elegant in black," Plath reported in her diary the next day. "Bert was looking shining and proud as if he had just delivered five babies, said something obvious about having drunk a lot, and began talking about how Luke [Lucas Myers] was satanic after we had run through the poetry in St. Botolph's and yelled about it." Indeed, Lucas was gyrating about in a mad sort of way—"the hog-wild jitterbug," I remember he called it. In this fashion, he danced with Sylvia for a while. She had flattered him by reciting his Botolph poems verbatim over the racket. Sylvia recorded, "I started dancing with Luke and knew I was very bad, having crossed the river and banged into the trees, yelling about the poems, he only smiling with that far-off look of a cretin satan."[17] Sylvia's fervor immeasurably intensified the Dionysian air.

As if things were not already getting out of hand, Sylvia lunged toward that "big, dark, hunky boy, the only one there huge enough for me," as she later put it. It was Ted, of course. She shouted to him over the cacophony, shrieking lines from his poems which, like Lucas's, she had committed to memory. As Plath wrote in her journal, Ted answered "in a voice that should have come from a Pole, 'You like?'" A few minutes later he kissed her savagely on the mouth— "bang smash," Sylvia exclaims—and then on her neck. At that point, to use Sylvia's words, "I bit him long and hard on the cheek, and when we came out of the room, blood was running down his face. . . . Such violence, and I can see how women lie down for artists."[18]

For her part, Sylvia observed that most of the crowd of poets were almost uniformly dressed in shabby drabness. Myers was arrayed, she reported, in "checked baggy pants and a loose swinging jacket" and sporting "dark sideburns and rumpled hair. His smile resembled Beelzebub." In fact, many of them—Ross, Weissbort, Huws, Minton, Myers, and even Hughes himself—appeared hellishly dark and alien. Shortly before the sensational assault on Ted's cheek, she had tottered into the room where I was busily filling the dual role of bartender and consumer. She ran up, as she describes it, to the "smug shining bulb face of dear Bert." Did she mean that I was a light shining into the blackness of my allegedly dark and devilish friends? Somehow that is too flattering a view.[19] Obligingly I sloshed brandy into her glass.

The next day everybody gossiped about Ted's bloody cheek. In *Birthday Letters*, he recalls "the swelling ring-moat of tooth-marks / That was to brand my face for the next month."[20] And that was literally the case, as I, for one, can testify. One and all we dismissed Sylvia as overly dramatic, un-English, and, who could deny it, stereotypically and vulgarly American. But a measure of ferocity had been lurking in the mood of all of us, not just Sylvia. She merely added something extra.

All of us staggered about the Women's Union a while afterward. We were raucously singing some of Terrence McCaughey's and Colin White's randy Scottish and Irish ballads, smashing glasses and even some Victorian stained-glass windows. We left in the early hours, but the university proctors were blessedly too late to catch those responsible. Otherwise, I and several other miscreants would have been in very deep peril of being rusticated, as expulsion was then labeled. The next day, bulky Michael Boddy, Ted's trombone-playing friend, convinced the Cambridge Police that some rugger yobs had caused the outrageous damage after the party, not us placid, ethereal poetic types.

Jane Baltzell recalls that much of the discontent that evening arose from the "long hard winter," which had left "everyone's nerves . . . cranked up pretty tight." Jane had gone to an earlier party of celebrating intramural crewmen. At that affair, she had witnessed "rampaging students" who smashed into "where the boats from the race had been stored and burned them all on the fens in a big clearing. It was a wild night." I knew nothing of that incident, being too busy causing mischief elsewhere. Clearly, though, the Botolph gala was not the only site of "latent violence," as Jane put it in a letter to her parents.[21]

Although more or less innocent of the shambles created at the Women's Union, Lucas Myers took the brunt of it. His "Moral Tutor" at Downing forced him out of St. Botolph's. Obviously, it was headquarters for trouble. Lucas resettled in a miserable flat on Barton Road.[22] Unworthy recipient of my friend's misfortune, I left my second-floor cupboard of a room to inherit the splendor of the dining room. With a long table for spreading out work, the new quarters were brightened by Mrs. Hitchcock's glass animal figurines on the marble-top mantle. The room also boasted a wide, leaded casement overlooking the garden, soon resplendent in spring with apple blossoms. These appointments were enviably spacious by comparison with my former monk's cell. The transfer signaled a physical change that accompanied an intellectual one.

Once a blazing hangover subsided, I finally took the long-contemplated step. In part I was no doubt influenced by the antipathy toward English studies that my friends exhibited. At the same time, I was aware, especially after the Botolph celebration, that their vision of art and the world was something I could not share. Their interests in the occult and esoteric were not mine. As in the calling of my clerical kinsmen, they were reaching for the ineffable. Such ambitions were far out of my grasp. In any case, history seemed a much more congenial recourse. It was down to earth, based on tangible data, grounded in reality, no matter how grim or tragic that might be. A conference with George Rylands proved less threatening than expected. Though vexed at first, he realized that the discipline of history might suit my capacities better than literature. Graciously he arranged with the King's Fellows that, since it was so late in the university year, I could stand for one less exam than other students.

At once, I hastened to the Mill Lane Lecture Hall to hear the spirited presentations of J. H. Plumb on eighteenth-century English politics and to absorb the profundities of Herbert Butterfield, then expounding on French Enlightenment ideas. I also thoroughly enjoyed my first history tutor, J. R. Stevens, a retired editor of the *New Delhi Times*. I took his suggestion to begin with Luigi Albertini, *The Origins of the War of 1914* (1952) to bone up voraciously on the causes of World War I. Then I plunged into the achievements of Johann Georg IV, Elector of Saxony (1668–1694). To many readers that might all seem very boring. I found it both refreshing and liberating. Cambridge exams were always set with fifteen to twenty questions of which the student was required to respond to just a couple. They were all narrowly focused. One knew the answers or was left completely in the dark. With so little time to prepare, I had to rely on depth of study into just a few topics out of the scores available. To my delight, the examiners set a quotation from Count Alexander Isvolsky, the Russian ambassador in Paris, reporting to the foreign office in St. Petersburg, in August 1914. The idea was to elicit the various complications of Russian, German, French, and Austro-Hungarian diplomacy on the eve of the Great War. I knew the circumstances of his report well and sketched a detailed response. Magically, "The Great Elector of Saxony" also appeared on the printed exam page. In the early summer when the results were listed in the London *Times*, I discovered that I had ranked in the First Class category. Luck of the draw more than comprehensive knowledge explained my success, never to be repeated on any other exam. Meantime, the Botolph crowd had dispersed. Only Lucas Myers and I kept in touch afterward.

The following year in history need not detain us long. Suffice it to say, I moved out of Botolph's and into new King's digs at the first-floor corner of Bodley Court close by the Backs—that is, the River Cam. When Michaelmas term began in the fall of 1956, I was invited to join the Chetwin Society. It was a drinking club with a racially and nationally mixed group of interesting students from around the globe. That was not exactly the Cambridge norm. Finding a richer environment within the college walls than I had ever thought possible, I partially lost the sense of alienation that had growled so fretfully the previous year. Nevertheless, such Americans at King's as the late Warren Zimmerman (a future U.S. ambassador to Yugoslavia), Richard Yoder, and I found ourselves conversing at dinner and lunch or in the Combination Room with Egyptians, Indians, New Zealanders, and South Africans. Like us, they were part of the old colonial empire—and therefore outsiders. The English students I liked best also happily failed to qualify for old-boy status.

The Ten Club, a dramatic reading group that included E. M. Forster among its members, was also much more egalitarian than I had expected upon admission. Occasionally Forster and I discussed a concert we had both attended or we companionably had tea together, along with other undergraduates in his rooms at King's. Motoring toward Huntington for a memorable picnic of the Ten Club, I was obliged to sit in Forster's lap. In his prewar Bentley, the rotund figure of Donald Beavis, another Fellow of King's, had taken up so much of the front seat that Forster and I had to share the remaining space as best we could. I was determined not to break the octogenarian's fragile bones. It was fairly straining, however, to lift up long enough to relieve him of my weight.

Disappointments there were as well. Along with a few others, I had been selected for a special seminar under Denis Brogan, then a well-known American specialist. It met only a few times, but after hearing some undergraduate drone on with an oral presentation, Brogan would immediately fill the remaining time with a dreary monologue. None of us could wedge in a word. On one occasion, I think it was the last, he was ranting away while he picked up his coat and umbrella, headed for the door, and slammed it. We could still hear his voice trailing away as he marched down the stairs.

On the other hand, there were great compensations. First of these was my second-year tutor, Vice Provost John Saltmarsh. He was a chubby, round-faced fiftyish bachelor. Saltmarsh's muttonchop whiskers resembled a throwback to Zachary Taylor and General Ambrose Burnside. Unlike the more casual Rylands, Saltmarsh had a genuine editorial eye. Meticulously he taught me how to construct an argument, a lesson not always, alas, remembered well. No less stimulating was the Special Subject seminar for the History Tripos, as a major is called. Denis Mack Smith of Peterhouse, England's most distinguished scholar of modern Italian history, skillfully taught primary research. He worked us through piles of government documents, publications, and memoirs related to Count Cavour, Mazzini, Garibaldi, Ricasoli, Minghetti, Plombières, the battle of Solferino, and other personalities and events of the Risorgimento. I was sorely tempted to become an Italian expert and daydreamed about writing a biography of Prime Minister Francesco Crispi (1818–1901).

About midyear, a new focus developed. I was invited to join the Political Society, a history honors club. It was then under the supervision of Christopher Hibbert. He was the author of some twenty or more popular history books on a wide range of military and political subjects. As an initiate, I was obliged to present a paper. For reasons not remembered, I chose the Nat Turner Rebellion of 1831, although the materials available at the Kings's and University libraries were inadequate, poorly written, and highly racist. The result was scarcely memorable. Jane Baltzell told me so in the gentlest way possible. When she delivered the bad news, it was a sunny afternoon. We were seated on a green bank of the Cam behind King's, a sight that alleviated the letdown.

No matter how inept that effort was, researching it had placed me in the stacks where resided works in southern history. I pulled out C. Vann Woodward's Harmsworth Lecture at Oxford University, just delivered and printed only a year earlier. It was entitled *American Attitudes Toward History* (1955). Here was a historian who wrote with authoritative insights. Unlike most others, he could illuminate them in a distinctively artful style. What a contrast his lecture was to the plodding prose and outworn prejudices of William Sidney Drewry, *The Southampton Insurrection* (1900). Retrieving other Woodward publications, I determined to work with him if possible. He seemed to understand the South and its many troubling aspects in a way that was quite breathtaking and utterly new to me. I had long been drenched in the ancient lore of Lee, Davis, and Father Abram Ryan's lugubrious poems of Confederate loss.

Yet I never felt at ease in the milieu of plantation myths and Rebel glory. After all, I was not a native southerner, despite the family's roots in the regional soil. In my thinking, elements of Pennsylvania sometimes warred powerfully with those of Tennessee and Alabama.

Not long thereafter I wrote to the graduate history authorities at Johns Hopkins University. I specified a hope to work under Dr. Woodward. An interest in the reunification of the sections during the early post–Civil War years filled the application essay. I do not think I knew what I meant exactly. I had had no American history course since the senior year at St. James School in western Maryland. So that initial idea had little to do with my understanding of Reconstruction politics. Instead, I was influenced by Mack Smith's seminar on the Italian effort to unify that country's North and South during the same mid-century years. Anyhow, since I was successful in the application to Hopkins, it was certifiably the soundest choice I had ever made. Joyously, I left any notions of being priest or poet far, far behind and looked forward to graduate study in the state of Maryland that straddled North and South.

Yet those earlier possibilities did not altogether disappear. In subsequent years, I often treated issues of religion and social conventions, both North and South—from the evangelicalism of the 1830s abolitionists to the southern Anti-Mission Baptists, from the rituals of slaveholding to the romantic but warped ideals of the Populist Tom Watson. I have been privileged to work with some thirty doctoral students at Case Western Reserve University and the University of Florida. Over a dozen of them have dealt with many of these same areas of American culture, North and South. I should add that the ethic of honor, another theme with which I have been much concerned, grew mostly from prior and also later events and influences rather than directly from the sojourn abroad. Yet the experience of being in alien surroundings for two years afforded me a chance to contemplate another culture with some critical detachment. Living in England during the mid-1950s mixed elements of both distance and familiarity in very much the same way that residing in Pennsylvania and Tennessee had struck me at an earlier time.

Literature, the other concentration, has drawn me backward, too. In most of my published work, matters of imaginative art have figured conspicuously. The suicide of Sylvia Plath in 1963 occurred seven years after our brief acquaintance in Cambridge. In later years, Lucas Myers and I came to interpret that tragic event quite differently. In a memoir, he notes, "I didn't see things just as he

[Bert] did and told him so bluntly."[23] Despite this always friendly disagreement, I still contend that creating works of imagination could possibly be linked both genetically and environmentally to deeply rooted emotional torment. It has long seemed to me a subject worth pursuing. Seven years of research that ranged from the Rosenberg Library in Galveston, Texas, to the Public Record Office in Kew Gardens, London, resulted in a lengthy study of the Percy family of Mississippi. Its members included poets, memoirists, and novelists, from Catherine Ann Warfield to William Alexander Percy and Walker Percy. The study, covering six generations of both suicides and substantial artists, concerned the interrelationship of honor, melancholy, and imagination, as the subtitle announces. Another, more recent, study traces the depressive character of nineteenth-century and early-twentieth-century southern writers from Edgar Allan Poe to Willa Cather. *Hearts of Darkness*, however, is perhaps too oriented toward history, biography, and psychology to meet the strictures of departmental English discourses, which have become increasingly theoretical.[24]

In any event, if only Charles Harrison were still alive to forgive my exodus. In his lifetime he had gradually come to tolerate the apostasy but with many a sigh. Were he to appear again on earth, I hope he might twitch those eyebrows meaningfully once more and emphatically pronounce this homeward turn of mine to be "sentient." Or better still, he might add, "ingratiating—ah, most ingratiating."

Notes

I wish to thank Anne Wyatt-Brown for her patience and her acutely constructive critiquing of more drafts than either of us would care to remember. Lucas Myers, Jane Baltzell Kopp, Margaret Macdonald, Jay Langdale—my capable research assistants—and also Leonard and Kerstin Trawick, Gil Hinshaw, Michael O'Brien, and George Bedell—all lent substantial assistance. Denis Donoghue's bluntly dismissive but sadly applicable appraisal of an earlier version was both appropriate and, in the end, helpfully challenging.

1. In 1930–40 difficulties with the Nazi Bundists in Pennsylvania led my father, a vocal opponent of Adolf Hitler, to change his name from Brown to Wyatt-Brown. The circumstances are revealed in "Sewanee: How to Make a Yankee Southern, Memories of the 1940s," in William Leuchtenburg, ed., *American Places: Encounters with History, A Celebration of Sheldon Meyer* (New York, 2000), 365–88.

2. Lucas Myers, *Crow Steered Bergs Appeared* (Sewanee, Tenn., 2001), 4; Lucas

Myers, appendix 1, "Ah, Youth . . . Ted Hughes and Sylvia Plath at Cambridge and After," in Anne Stevenson, *Bitter Fame: A Life of Sylvia Plath* (Boston, 1989), 309; Elaine Feinstein, *Ted Hughes: The Life of a Poet* (New York, 2001), 23, 24.

3. Lucas Myers, "Where the Bones Lie," unpublished manuscript, 1–2. I acknowledge, with gratitude, his permission to quote from this memoir in preparation. The revision is an expansion of Myers, *Crow Steered*.

4. For their works published during this post–World War II period, see Meyer Fortes, *The Web of Kinship among the Tallensi: The Second Part of an Analysis of the Social Structure of a Trans-Volta Tribe* (London, 1949); Edmund Ronald Leach, *Political Systems of Highland Burma: A Study of Kachin Social Structure* (London, 1954); Edward Evan Evans-Pritchard, *Kinship and Marriage among the Nuer* (Oxford, Eng., 1951).

5. Myers, "Where the Bones Lie," 13.

6. Obituary for Antony Victor Brown (1941), *King's College Cambridge Annual Report 2002* (Cambridge, Eng., 2002), 34; Miranda Carter, *Anthony Blunt: His Lives* (New York, 2001), 57.

7. Myers, "Where the Bones Lie," 31. See Frank Raymond Leavis, *D. H. Lawrence: Novelist* (New York, 1956), and his most famous exposition, *The Great Tradition: George Eliot, Henry James, Joseph Conrad* (New York, 1950). Ivor Armstrong Richards led the forces of New Criticism with *How to Read a Page: A Course in Effective Reading* (New York, 1942), *Practical Criticism: A Study of Literary Judgment* (London, 1929), and *Principles of Literary Criticism* (New York, 1938).

8. Myers, *Crow Steered*, 6.

9. Hughes's forty works need not be cited here, but the literary efforts of other Botolph writers include Daniel Huws, *The Quarry* (London, 1999), *North: Poems* (London, 1972), *Five Ancient Books of Wales. H. M. Chadwick Memorial Lectures No. 6* (Cambridge, Eng., 1995); Daniel Weissbort, *Lake: New and Selected Poems* (Riverdale-on-Hudson, N.Y., 1992) and ten other books; David Ross, *Letters from Foxy* (New York, 1968).

10. C. Vann Woodward, *Thinking Back: The Perils of Writing History* (Baton Rouge, 1986), 104.

11. Myers, "Where the Bones Lie," 31.

12. See Bertram Wyatt-Brown, "Reuben Davis, Sylvia Plath, and Emotional Struggle," in Peter Stearns and Jan Lewis, eds., *An Emotional History of the United States* (New York, 1998): 431–59; and "Sylvia Plath, Depression and Suicide: A New Interpretation," in Frederico Pereira, ed., *Fourteenth International Conference on Literature and Psychoanalysis* (Lisbon, 1997), 177–97.

13. Jane Baltzell Kopp to author, August 21, 2002.

14. Some of Ted Hughes's verses had appeared in *Granta*, but he had used a pseudonym, "Daniel Hearing." Lucas Myers speculates that Hughes did so because he was not

convinced that they were as flawless as he thought he could achieve (Feinstein, *Ted Hughes*, 34; phone conversation with Lucas Myers, September 20, 2002).

15. Hughes, "St. Botolph's," in *Birthday Letters* (New York, 1998), 14.

16. Ted and Sylvia's daughter Frieda and Ted's second wife, Carol Hughes, very much opposed the filming and the alleged sensationalizing of Sylvia's suicide. See the *Albuquerque (N.M.) Journal*, February 4, 2002; and Greg Dean Schmitz, "Previews" in "Ted and Sylvia" Web site, *Yahoo! Movies: Ted and Sylvia—Greg's Preview*. For two of the many biographies of Sylvia Plath, see Anne Stevenson, *Bitter Fame* (Boston, 1989), and Linda Wagner-Martin, *Sylvia Plath: A Literary Life* (New York, 1999).

17. Entry for Sunday, February 26, 1956, Sylvia Plath, *The Unabridged Journals of Sylvia Plath, 1950–1962*, ed. Karen V. Kukil (New York, 2000), 210, 211; phone conversation with Lucas Myers, September 22, 2002. On the dancing, see "Lucas Myers, Earth/Moon: Lucas Myers? Additional Note . . ." in *Earth Moon: A Ted Hughes Website*, http://www.uni-leipzig.de/_angl/hughes/memo_myersadd.htm (a citation no longer on site).

18. Entry for February 26, 1956, in Plath, *Journals*, 211, 212.

19. Plath, *Journals*, 211. The Kulik edition says "smug shining blub face" which could have meant something less flattering. Sylvia could be mean-spirited.

20. "St. Botolph's," in Hughes, *Birthday Letters*, 15.

21. Jane Baltzell Kopp, e-mail to author, March 21, 2003, quoting from a letter to her parents dated "2 March 1958 [1956]." Jane's recollections of Leavis, Lewis, and the mood of the times parallel mine, but she found English women more difficult to deal with than the men: "The English women at Newnham (both faculty and students) struck me as almost repellant. (Sylvia made the same judgment.) Seems a strong word, I know, but they all seemed humorless and deliberately—aggressively even—unattractive, physically as well as otherwise. I found them incomprehensible, and I didn't make a single friend among them." She and Sylvia, however, made friends with Canadians, South Africans, and two brilliant Scots, Isabel Murray and George Henderson, whom we all admired.

22. Myers, "Where the Bones Lie," 32. After six weeks he moved to digs on Tenison Road, where he frequently entertained Ted and Sylvia, separately and together.

23. Myers, "Where the Bones Lie," 102.

24. Aside from some relevant essays and essay reviews, the studies I have in mind are *Lewis Tappan and the Evangelical War against Slavery* (Cleveland, 1969); *Southern Honor: Ethics and Behavior in the Old South* (New York, 1982); *Yankee Saints and Southern Sinners* (Baton Rouge, 1986); *The House of Percy: Honor, Melancholy, and Imagination in a Southern Family* (New York, 1994); *The Literary Percys: Family History, Gender, and the Southern Imagination* (Athens, 1994); *The Shaping of Southern Culture: Honor, Grace, and War, 1760s–1890s* (Chapel Hill, 2001); *Hearts of Darkness: Wellsprings of a Southern Literary Tradition* (Baton Rouge, 2003).

"Sing Me Back Home"

Growing Up in the South and Writing the History of Its Music

BILL C. MALONE

I am not one of those Texans who denies his southern roots. You know the kind. They argue that Texas is an exceptional place that somehow escaped the sin, guilt, and hidebound traditionalism that marks the southern experience. This argument, of course, is central to the Texas Mystique. In country music scholarship, the denial comes from those who rail against the corporate Nashville establishment and instead stress the alleged freedom and experimentation of such Texas musicians as Bob Wills and Willie Nelson and the Austin Outlaws, and argue that this spiritual and psychological expansiveness derives from the vastness of the Texas landscape and the diversity of its culture. This conception is essentially a *West* Texas vision and is of course linked to the romance of cowboys and the limitless western range.

My little corner of sandy and red-clay East Texas soil, though, with its wide variety of deciduous and pine trees, was thoroughly southern until the oilmen, bankers, and developers came in and appropriated the land and its resources. It was settled by folks who began coming into the area before the Civil War from thoroughly southern places like north Alabama and Mississippi, Tennessee, and North Carolina. If they knew for sure where their ancestors came from across the waters, they seldom passed the information on to children and their offspring. Local surnames such as Browning, Maxfield, Starr, Boyd, Bogue, Nipp, Goode, Owens, and Malone suggest that they came from various parts of Ireland, Scotland, England, Wales, and even the European continent. The Foshees on my paternal side, for example, apparently arrived on the South Atlantic coast as part of a Huguenot French immigration. Some of the people claimed an Indian admixture, and my relatives were no exception. My mother spoke proudly of her grandmother's alleged Indian extraction. I suspect that most white people represented that glorious and untraceable mixture of ethnicity that virtually defined the South. Some of the white settlers brought slaves, and the culture that they created bore the marks of an interrelation between the two peoples — in folklore, foodways, religion, speech patterns — that had begun long before the trek to East Texas was made.

Most black people in our area lived nearby, only a couple of miles down the Willow Flat Road in the Clear Springs community. Blacks and whites frequently worked side by side, in the fields or at clearing off the land. White people often attended revivals at Clear Springs, in the Baptist and Church of God in Christ congregations, sitting in segregated sections. As a child, it was exciting to hear the music and watch the black church people dance, but for me, the most joyful aspects of the revivals were the stands that sold fried catfish and homemade ice cream. I would never presume, though, to romanticize this relationship. Even though some miscegenation occurred, and my parents could point out individuals who were the progeny of such relationships, we remained keenly aware of a social line that could not be crossed. White supremacy and racial segregation prevailed. Children easily absorbed the etiquette of racial relations and the hurtful attitudes that accompanied them. I remember one day when a fire broke out down in the pasture. A small cousin and I reflexively agreed, "I bet them niggers did it." The older folks had an even more malevolent heritage to deal with, because they still talked about a grim and grisly incident from the not-too-distant past, the burning alive of a black man on Tyler's courthouse square. In some ways that shameful incident paled before another local event, because it involved people that we knew. A man and his son, presumably drunk, went into a black home, began tossing an infant to and from each other, purely for sport, until the child died from a head injury. They were taken into custody but ultimately went unpunished.

We called our little community "Galena," and for a brief period around the turn of the twentieth century we even had a post office bearing the name. I don't know why the name was chosen. As far as I know, no lead deposits were ever found there. The name just sounded pretty, I suppose, although most people I knew pronounced it G'leener. One does find occasional references to a nearby two-room school, Elm Grove (pronounced Ellem Grove) or to the Wells' Gin Community (inspired by one of the names given to the cotton gin that long thrived there), and, recognizing a habit that was well-nigh universal among young and old, male and female, and blacks and whites, some observers called it "Snuff City." If a poll had been taken among local farmers selecting America's most renowned men, the name of the great snuff maker, Levi Garrett, would have ranked very high.

Located about twenty miles west of Tyler, and eighty miles east of Dallas, Galena consisted of widely scattered farmsteads that extended across the Smith and Van Zandt county lines. Paul Terry and Verner Sims, in their study of a similar community in Alabama, *They Live on the Land* (1940), had described such entities as "Open-Country Communities." Galena had no central or easily definable core, although at least three local institutions provided some social cohesion: the cotton gin that was located at the intersection of Willow Flat and Carroll Roads; the Elm Grove two-room schoolhouse; and the Tin Top Pentecostal Church. Cotton ruled the economy, and although a few semi-prosperous men owned their farms, most people lived as sharecroppers and tenant farmers, paying the owners a share of what they produced. When the Great Depression arrived in 1929, people in my part of East Texas already knew hard times and deprivation, a legacy of Civil War defeat and one-crop agriculture.

A rough equality prevailed at social gatherings — in church, at the cotton gin, at the little country store that functioned at the crossroads, or at country dances — but tenants and other poor farmers paid deference to their "betters" with respectful words and a tip of the hat. People always knew who ranked above and below them. If humble farmers recognized the existence of those above them on the social scale, they also knew that some white people deserved only contempt. Poverty itself was not a disgrace, because most people were poor. I don't remember ever hearing the word "trash" used to describe poor farmers. The preferred word was "sorry," and it was reserved for those who would not work, or who let their livestock run freely into their neighbors' fields, or who led morally contemptible lives.

I entered this world on August 25, 1934, the third son of Cleburne and Maude Owens Malone. I was born at home on the Bracken place (owned by a family in Tyler), in a little four-room, tin-roofed "boxed" house (with walls made secure by one-by-three strips of wood nailed over the cracks between vertically aligned one-by-twelve boards). A porch, or gallery as we described it, ran along the front of the house, about two feet off the ground, and just high enough that our dogs could find refuge there during rainstorms or the blazing heat of summer. Since the interior walls were unlined, Daddy placed cardboard on the walls of the "living room" to lend some insulation and protection against winter winds. A few pictures, some religious mottoes with inscriptions like "Only one life it will soon be past. Only what's done for Christ will last," and some hoary and long out-of-date calendars that had pleasant or comic illustrations, decorated the walls.

The floors had no rugs or linoleum, and the cracks were so wide in some areas that we could see the chickens scratching underneath the house. Only one room — the front room — had a ceiling. In the other three we could see the rafters, and the rain often seeped through. Our interior furnishings can best be described as modest and minimal: two beds, a few straight chairs (with seats generally made of closely woven binder twine), a kitchen table that Daddy had made, a small desk, a dresser, a sturdy high chair that was passed down from son to son, a kitchen pie safe (complete with built-in flour sifter), and a couple of wires strung up in the bedrooms where our meager supply of clothes hung. Privacy was hard to come by in this little house. My brothers slept with each other in one bed, and I slept with my father and mother in the other one. I do not recall where visitors slept, but I'm sure that pallets were often called into use.

My mother certainly would not have viewed it so, because she spent too many precious moments bending over it, but to the rest of us the most cherished centerpiece in the house was the big iron kitchen cook stove. Since the rigors of farm work required it, meals were always substantial and, because we generally managed to maintain a garden, relatively balanced. We produced our own pork and poultry and sometimes had fried catfish or perch caught from Caney Creek down in the pasture or from Boyd Water (a locally named portion of the Neches River). Beef was highly prized but seldom consumed, largely because of the difficulty of preservation. During much of my childhood on the Bracken Place we had no icebox but instead wrapped a quilt around a block of ice and kept it in a firebox (where kindling for the fireplace was kept). We kept milk fresh by placing it in a tightly sealed syrup bucket, wrapping it securely with burlap, and lowering it into the well. At the time I did not comprehend just how much backbreaking labor and ingenuity had gone into the production of things that I took for granted. I only knew that the cornbread, fluffy biscuits, white gravy, sausage patties, pinto beans, homemade tomato soup, and Christmas pastries that graced our table when times were good were among the most sublime elements of country life.

My southernness and sense of history seem to have been Malone traits. My father, Patrick Cleburne Malone, named for a martyred Confederate general, was the son of Laura Foshee and Thomas Jefferson Malone, who in turn was the son of William Carroll Malone (named for a one-time Democratic governor of Tennessee). My parents were born in Van Zandt County, Texas — Daddy near the now-vanished community of Owlet Green, and my mother in the similarly defunct village of Primrose, not far from Edom. If opposites attract, then their union seems foreordained. He was quiet, and she was talkative. He generally held back his feelings but could explode into a furious rage. She was impulsive, and we always knew what was on her mind. He resisted going to church; she was passionately religious. He couldn't carry a tune; she was a wonderful singer. Both were intelligent and gifted individuals whose talents went unfulfilled or unrecognized, partly because of poverty and inadequate education, but also because they lacked the will to seek new challenges. My mother longed to go places and see new things, but she never learned how to drive and permitted herself to remain confined most of her life to a relatively narrow strip of East Texas soil. My father spent most of his life as a farmer but could master any mechanical puzzle put before him. Yet he would take few risks and consequently remained a wage laborer all his life. The marriage was probably a mistake, but they stayed together for forty-eight years, until she died in 1971.

The house where I was born, and where I lived for the first ten years of my life, was about a mile and a half from the crossroads where the cotton gin and little country store sat. Daddy was a cotton tenant farmer, working the land with a mule and plow, and relying on the help of his wife and my two older brothers, Wylie and Kelly, for picking, hoeing, and other tasks related to farm life. The crop year began with a visit to Tyler and the general supply store, Caldwell, Hughes, Delay and Allen, where Daddy bought on credit needed merchandise for the coming year — cotton sacks, overalls, plow lines, bridles, and related material. After the cotton was ginned, he paid his bills and invariably found himself in debt, a situation that was carried over from year to year. Ours was a semi-isolated existence until 1939, when Daddy bought our first battery-powered radio. I remember going to Dallas only once during the ten years that I lived on the farm, but if we could hitch a ride with some neighbor — usually Jess Starr, who owned an old beat-up truck — we might make it in to Tyler, twenty miles away, a couple of times a year (usually around Christmastime and during the East Texas Fair). Through the blessings of rural free delivery we did receive newspapers, religious and political tracts, and the Sears and Montgomery Ward catalogs, and periodically a peddler made his rounds in the countryside, bringing us useful household items, candy, and gossip from the outside world. Otherwise, we were a true folk community that depended on its own resources and the time-tested traditions of our ancestors. Our lighting came from coal-oil lamps, our heat from woodstoves, and our water from a backyard well. The alum-infested water, however, was distasteful to drink and hard to wash clothes with. Mama caught some rainwater in a barrel, but she often went down to a spring in the pasture to wash our clothes. Wylie or Kelly would hitch one of the mules to a sled and transport the big black washpot and our load of clothes down to the spring.

We permitted no blade of grass to grow in the yard but instead kept it swept clean with a rake and a home-made broom. I'm not sure that anyone ever stopped to think of why we did it — it was just one of the traditions we inherited — but swept yards were easier to maintain than grass-carpeted ones and would not harbor snakes. When we felt the call of nature, we made the trek to the outdoor privy, using pages from magazines or Sears catalogs as our toilet paper. On very cold nights, though, we had to resort to the appropriately named slop jar. As a consequence, bodily needs were too often repressed for much of the night. Medically, our treatment can only be described as substandard. We never went to the dentist and consulted a doctor only for the most severe ailments. Some of our neighbors occasionally visited old Mrs. Blackstock, who had the reputation of being a healer, someone who could cure complaints with her homemade concoctions or with appropriate scriptural incantations. One biblical verse, it was said, could even stop bleeding. My mother preferred to trust her own prayers, or those of her friends, but sometimes we had to resort to professional medical assistance. Dr. Montgomery occasionally drove his Model A Ford coupe down from Van to make house calls when we were seriously ill, but most problems were treated with coal oil, liniment, Alka-Seltzer, Grove's Chill Tonic, castor oil, or other patent medicines or home remedies.

One finds little romance, then, in those farm days in East Texas in the late 1930s and early 1940s. Life was often hard and lonely, but it was enlivened by periodic occasions of social intercourse — Christmas (the only time that oranges and apples entered the house), baseball games, fish fries down at Boyd Water, house parties (the commonly used designation for country dances), all-day singings, brush arbor revival meetings, quilting parties, ice-cream suppers, funerals, Sunday gatherings at Grandma Malone's, school closings, domino games (the new game of "42" was all the rage in the mid-1930s), and occasional trips to Canton for First Monday, a mule-trading day that has since become a giant flea market. Visiting, though, was the most common form of conviviality, and even unscheduled trips were welcomed. I was always bemused when Miss Winnie Smith visited, because in her mind all useful philosophy came from the Holy Scriptures. During one of my childish frustrations, for example, she declared, "Just remember, Billy, as the Bible says 'if at first you don't succeed, try, try again.'" If a family's visit came at a time when the crops were "laid by," or when no urgent farm task was impending, the host family would often pack up the wagon and immediately follow the visiting family back home.

Hog-killing day was in many ways the most special occasion of all. On the days leading up to the event, Daddy and the older folks seemed to be watching the sky and judging the position and color of the sun. I suppose they were merely looking for the coldest day of the year, when the meat could be easily preserved, but somehow it all seemed magical to me. Neighbors and relatives typically gathered to share both the tasks and the fun. Sheltered from the most grim aspects of the day — the actual butchering of the hog — I instead reveled in the more festive aspects of the occasion, the grinding of the sausage, the preparation of the pork for the smokehouse, the rendering of the lard in the big black washpot, and the making of the lye soap that was used in the cleansing of our heavy work clothes.

My father began each day by going out on the front porch, at about six o'clock in the morning, and hollering at the top of his voice, as if to announce to neighbors far and wide that Cleburne Malone was ready to confront the world. Like most southern men of his generation, he found his diversions outside the house, often in communion with other males — fishing, hunting, drinking, gambling, playing practical jokes, and spinning tall tales. The stories about Halloween were particularly fascinating, and they make accounts of today's trick-or-treating seem especially tame. Setting fire to an outdoor toilet when it had an occupant or dismantling a neighbor's buggy or wagon and reassembling it on the top of his house were harmful enough, but using a "dumb bull" to frighten people was almost diabolical. Someone would remove the bottom from a wooden keg, stretch a rawhide tautly across the top like a drumhead, cut a small hole in it, and then pull a cord made of horsehair through the narrow opening. When rosin or a fingernail was rubbed against the cord, a horrifying sound akin to that made by a wild beast was produced. Fiendish young men delighted in taking a dumb bull to the woods, or making the terrible sound near some black family's home. Those who heard it were convinced that a panther or some other predatory varmint was lurking nearby. Of course, plenty of material existed to supply the wants of local storytellers. Ghost stories, family feuds, murders, and violent retribution were the stuff of enthralling tales. One such story involved our nearest neighbor, Aaron Smith, who was shot to death by his brother-in-law outside his home, just across the pasture from our house.

Mama found her consolation in religion. Her life had always been hard. She was about a month old when her mother died, a victim of childbirth complications. Mama was virtually abandoned by her dad, an engineer for the Cotton Belt Railroad, and was reared by her paternal grandparents on a bleak farm in Primrose. She worshiped her grandfather, but too often he spent his meager Confederate pension on whiskey and kept his little family in dire straits. She had a love-hate relationship with her dad, recognizing his imperfections but nevertheless fascinated by his life as a railroad man. She never ceased to be thrilled by the sound and sight of a locomotive engine, and she may have thought of her absent father when she heard and sometimes requested songs like "Black Jack David" and "Rattlesnaking Daddy" that described rakish or devilish men.

Mama was raised a Methodist, but she and her grandmother were converted to Pentecostalism in about 1915 by an itinerant band of missionaries that came through East Texas. Regular church services were not always an option, but my mother prayed constantly, went to prayer meetings in her friends' homes, and often went down to the woods to pray alongside her friends or with her sister-in-law, my Aunt Erna. The Tin Top Pentecostal Church convened irregularly, with services conducted usually by local volunteers or by visiting evangelists. Pentecostalism was rough and scary in those days, and its adherents were convinced that both demons and angels peopled the world they inhabited. As I was growing up, my mother still talked about the time a wanderer remembered only as "Frenchy" (probably a Cajun) came to a revival meeting, made fun of the scene he saw around him, and pretended to speak in tongues. What seemed to be a blatant act of blasphemy cast both sinners and believers into an awestruck silence. When the man was found dead in his room the next morning, they were convinced that God had struck him down.

Shouting, testifying, glossolalia (speaking in tongues), and the various physically emotional manifestations that had inspired the term "holy rollers" marked the emotion-laden services. The music was wondrously spirited. Sometimes, only a guitar accompanied the singing, but often the music was performed a cappella, with the driving rhythm provided by tambourines and handclapping. The spirit could not always be contained within the walls of the church or confined by the limits of a church service. Heading home late at night after the congregation had been dismissed, Mama and Aunt Erna would shepherd their children through the dark woods (the shortest distance between church and home), and would continue to sing the cherished gospel songs at the top of their voices: "I'm in the way, the bright and shining way, I'm in the Glory Land Way. Telling the world that Jesus saves today."

Music, then, was also her salvation, as it was for me. She sang to dispel her loneliness, to voice her frustrations, and to praise her God. I don't know where she learned all of her songs, in those days before we obtained a radio. She knew a few pop songs, like "Red Wing," "San Antonio," and "Pony Boy," and some scattered verses of folk songs such as "Roll On Buddy" ("Old Diamond Joe, he was an old fool. He spent all his money trying to break Jay Gould"). She remembered most of her songs in fragmentary form, and probably learned them from friends and relatives. Like many rural people of her generation, she also copied down the lyrics of favorite songs in a school tablet or composition book. A sizeable number, such as the sentimental parlor songs "The Little Rosewood Casket," "Two Little Orphans," and "The Letter Edged in Black," came from "the Young People's Page" of the *Dallas Semi-Weekly Farm News*, in which people exchanged the lyrics of old songs. An even larger percentage of songs came from revival meetings or church-singing schools and were preserved in the paperback hymnals distributed at monthly singing conventions or sold in bulk quantity to rural churches. No songs were more soul-satisfying or emotionally uplifting to her than such items as "Farther Along," "No Never Alone," and "Leave It There." I realize now that the assemblage of songs in her repertory typified the music remembered throughout the rural South in the decades before 1920. These were the "old-familiar" tunes that made their way on to the early phonograph recordings and radio broadcasts when country music was in its commercial infancy.

Then came the Philco battery radio. It arrived in our household in 1939, bringing with it the awareness of another and more exciting world. The radio delivered auditory confirmation of the society we saw displayed in Sears-Roebuck and Montgomery Ward catalogs or in the Dick and Jane readers. It helped to dispel the loneliness and alienation that too often marked the lives of rural farm women. The radio's effects on my mother's life were incalculable, and she immersed herself in the soap operas, dramas, and comedies that were radio's standard fare. And it fed the imaginative universe that I inhabited, adding to my already fertile storehouse of make-believe with its stories and professional sports. Above all, it brought me into the universe of hillbilly music.

We began each day with the live hillbilly shows broadcast from Tyler, Dallas, Fort Worth, Shreveport, and Tulsa, and we brightened our noon-time dinners with the gospel music of the Chuck Wagon Gang or the Stamps Quartet. Each Saturday night, of course, we listened to the Grand Ole Opry from Nashville, and occasionally picked up a syndicated segment of the National Barn Dance from Chicago. Each weekday night we generally heard some Mexican border programming, from XERA and XEG—Cowboy Slim Rinehart, the Herrington Trio, Mainer's Mountaineers, and the Carter Family. Such radio hillbillies as the Shelton Brothers, the Callahan Brothers, Peg Moreland, the Chuck Wagon Gang, and Ernest Tubb were virtually members of the family. These entertainers fostered that illusion with their homey patter, down-home humor, and moralistic messages, and we were loyal to them. We bought their songbooks and picture postcards, gossiped about them, and faithfully patronized the flour manufacturers, cough-syrup makers, laxative distributors, and other businesses that sponsored them.

My brothers have similar affectionate recollections of the battery radio and of the music it dispensed, and their guitar strumming and earnest renditions of songs like "The Last Letter" and "The Great Speckled Bird" enlivened our household at the end of the 1930s. Otherwise, their memories of farm life are not nearly so sanguine. They had gone to the fields almost as soon as they started school. They were eight and nine years older than me and bore most of the work as well as the hard discipline that Daddy meted out. His frustrations with poor crops, bad weather, boll weevils, and stubborn mules were sometimes taken out in bursts of rage at his wife and sons. Consequently, my brothers were restless, uninterested in reading, but anxious to see the outside world. They never graduated from high school and left home as teenagers on a few occasions to work briefly in Dallas and Wichita Falls. When he was seventeen, in July 1943, Wylie begged and cajoled my parents into letting him sign up for service in the Navy Seabees. As the baby of the family, and almost an only child because of our age differences, I was sheltered from the hardest farm work and grew up much closer to my mother than they did. My mother dreamed that I might become a preacher, and as I child I must have encouraged that hope with some of my play. I often put a bible and hymnbook on top of the high chair that Daddy had built, and regaled her with my earnest prayers, songs, and sermons.

With much time on my hands and no playmates, I often retreated to an imaginary world peopled with ideas and scenes inspired by my reading and the radio. One of my flights of imagination wrought considerable damage to our already-strained economic condition. One day after I watched our landlord's hired hands brand some of their cows, I decided to play cowboy. I found a long stick, ignited it from a fire under my mother's washpot, and set out to do my own "branding." Our dogs Jake and Wimpey refused to cooperate, so I branded a cotton bale that was sitting in the backyard. Daddy had to take the bale back to the gin for re-ginning. I was an adult before I got up enough nerve to confess to him that the fire had not been caused by a spark from the washpot.

My imaginations usually assumed more benign manifestations. My Neverland was a vast world that contained nations that fought wars against each other but also competed in all the big-time sports. I even made a map of this land, created countries both real and imagined, and bisected them with a vast river, the Satin River, which was large enough to host huge naval battles. I also conjured up a mythical family, the McLemore Brothers, who combined my chief interests. They were detectives who captured criminals, incarcerated them in their own prison, and in their spare time sang and harmonized over their own radio station, in a fashion similar to that of the Sons of the Pioneers. When World War II came, I began writing a history of the conflict, made up of both facts and a great mixture of fiction, and became a Chinese detective named Mr. Wing who solved crimes great and small. When Wylie went off to war, I peppered my letters to him with references to spy-catching, and signed them as "Mr. Wing." To the end of his days, when I was in my forties, my dad still liked to call me Mr. Wing.

Even before the war came, the forces of modernization were already intruding upon our lives. Rural electric lines did not extend past the crossroads at the cotton gin (probably because only a few white families like ours lived on that section of the Willow Flat Road), but the battery-powered radio had introduced us to sounds and experiences that came from far-off and often romantic places. Oil had been discovered in 1929 at nearby Van. Although no one among my relatives had ever prospered from the discovery, the event nevertheless affected our lives. Van built the most modern school complex in our part of East Texas and began consolidating most of the little rural schools in the region. As the one and two-room schools were swallowed up, the communities around them surrendered their identities. Nearby Elm Grove had ceased to function by 1940, and so I trudged off the first day of school to catch the bus that would take me to Van. Although we had been forced to consolidate, the Van school nevertheless would not send a bus a mile and a half down the Willow Flat Road to pick us up. Bus service and rural electrification both ended at the Galena crossroads. I must confess that I missed school that first day, crying and holding back to the point that my brother Kelly, who had been entrusted with my care, also missed the bus — probably to his delight.

I also missed most of the other days that year, and as a result failed the first grade. I simply was not prepared psychologically to take leave of my mother, which she wisely understood. One day when my teacher drove down into the country to inquire about my absences, Mama said to her, "Billy doesn't want to go to school, and we don't make him." By the time the next school year rolled around, I was more than ready to attend, and spurred on by my mother's tutelage had already learned how to read. My love affair with reading and books has never ceased.

When I finally settled into the regimen of learning at Van, I could look out through the windows of the first-grade classroom and see the future of Texas being dynamically dramatized by the pumps of the Pure Oil Company as they busily extracted their precious supplies of black liquid from beneath the schoolgrounds themselves. Certainly I was not prescient enough to recognize the significance of what I saw, but I was literally witnessing the end of our way of life and the beginnings of modern Texas. By 1943 my family had become part of the host of rural folk who abandoned their lifelong moorings in the country to begin new lives as urban blue-collar dwellers. By this time Galena's population had already been severely depleted, a victim of migrations to the industrial and war plants of Dallas, Fort Worth, Houston, and the Gulf Coast, and by the entry of its young men and women into military service. Daddy had even done two short stints as a wage laborer, in Wichita Falls as a construction worker, and in Velasco at the Dow Magnesium plant, but had come back home to make one last attempt at farming. His efforts failed, and that last Christmas on the farm was indeed bleak. The apples and oranges that usually came into our house only at Christmas were absent this time, and I remember getting only one present, a paperback book, which he bought for thirty-five cents at a drugstore in Van.

Wylie's absence in the Seabees meant one less field hand and an aching loneliness in my mother's life. Once the inevitable decision was made to leave, we borrowed Jess Starr's truck and set out for Tyler. Adding insult to injury, the truck caught fire near Carroll, and some of our meager store of goods were damaged or destroyed. We settled into a little rental house, also without electric lights, on the old Van Highway right on the edge of Tyler's western city limits. The entire time my family lived in Tyler, from 1943 to the mid-1950s, we lived at addresses defined by the linkages to rural communities surrounding the city. We moved from the Van Highway to the Old Garden Valley Road to the Old Longview Road, and we remained on the margins of Tyler society, socially and economically as well as geographically.

World War II revolutionized life for southern rural people. The economic and social consequences of the war generated new opportunities and new forms of wealth. The move to town, though, evoked varying responses and adaptations, often according to gender, age, and race. Many rural men, including my father and brothers, never fully adjusted to the pace, regimentation, and discipline of town life; they remained rural people in the city. Daddy and Kelly both worked briefly for Norman-Ford on Erwin Street, a small plant that made prisms for bomb sights, but Daddy soon moved from there to the Gordon-Sewell wholesale grocery house, where he did back-breaking warehouse work. By the time we left Tyler for Dallas, about ten years later, he was working as a mechanic and shipping clerk for East Texas Auto Supply, making only a dollar an hour and still wondering if the move into town had been wise. Fortunately, C. E. Owen, the owner of East Texas Auto Supply who had invested heavily in the Lone Star Steel Company near Daingerfield, talked Daddy into buying one hundred shares of stock, at a dollar per share. Daddy's only speculative venture proved providential. Dividends and occasional sales of stock helped to finance my first years at the University of Texas in Austin.

My mother never doubted the decision to move to town. She ardently embraced the changes. Town life meant ready-made clothes, a telephone, washing machine, and a refrigerator; it generated more opportunities to go to church and promised the end of her social isolation. Sometimes when Daddy reminisced about the past, and said, perhaps not too jokingly, that if he could get a mule and plow he would move back to the farm, Mama would quickly respond, "If you do, you'll move without me."

On Saturdays my mother and I generally took the bus into town. I might go to one or more of the five movie houses that sat on or near the courthouse square. Waiting for Daddy to get off work, we often sat on the benches outside the courthouse visiting with friends or listening to the religious arguments waged by old men, usually Baptists or Campbellites (the name usually given to members of the Church of Christ). Almost always, we ate a hamburger and drank a Barq's orange at a little café right off the square, bought broken and discounted peanut patties at a local candy factory, or went into the bowling alley on Spring Street to watch the bowlers and listen to the jukebox. Certain songs endure as vivid memories of that period: Gene Autry's "I'll Wait for You," Tex Ritter's "Have I Stayed Away Too Long?" and Wiley and Gene's "When My Blue Moon Turns to Gold Again," all speaking directly to the loneliness felt by my mother as she thought about her boy far away in the South Pacific in military service. When Wylie left home at the end of his first furlough, and right before he went overseas, we sat in the bowling alley listening somberly as he fed nickel after nickel into the jukebox, playing only one song, "When My Blue Moon Turns to Gold Again." We then walked over to the old Dixie Highway, where he hitched a ride to Dallas that would take him off to an unknown fate. To this day he still talks about watching my mother as she walked down the highway waving to him until the car got our of sight. We did not know until some time later that he had overextended his leave and was AWOL.

Religion remained all-important to my mother. She listened faithfully to the radio preachers and went to the tent revivals when they came to town. The years immediately following the war marked the age of such charismatic evangelists as Oral Roberts, A. A. Allen, and Jack Coe, who attracted immense throngs with their messages of divine healing and biblical prophecy. An unending stream of events seemed to bear out the proof of the ominous sermons that they conveyed. The euphoria that accompanied victory over the Axis powers was soon dimmed by the rise of militant communism and the knowledge that the Soviet Union had developed an atomic bomb. A third world war no longer seemed unthinkable. The birth of Israel in 1948 only added to the conviction that the prophecies in the Book of Revelation were being fulfilled, that the end of time was near and that Christ's return was imminent. Pentecostalism, in short, had come to town but was as scary as ever. Its messages could even be heard in some of the hillbilly songs that received airplay in the late 1940s. Roy Acuff, for example, sang "This World Can't Stand Long," and the Bailes Brothers declared that "We're Living in the Last Days Now."

Except for having to make new friends, I was immensely happy with our move to town. My attendance at a country school called Dixie, just outside Tyler, somewhat cushioned my transition to town life. There I encountered a number of students whose family histories were much like mine. As a fat kid, of course, I always had to contend with a painful self-consciousness, but I found ready retreats in the radio, sports, popular culture, reading, and country music. A sports fanatic at the time, I bought every sport magazine that was available, memorized reams of statistics, and followed the exploits of the local Class C baseball team, the Tyler Trojans. Although I was usually very shy (and was in fact voted "Most Bashful" in my tenth-grade class at Dixie), I nevertheless loved to show off, particularly in spelling matches and singing. My debut as a solo singer came during a school assembly at Dixie, where in my boy soprano voice, I sang Tex Ritter's "Gold Star in the Window," a lament about a son killed in military action.

Since Dixie curiously had only ten grades, I transferred to Tyler High School in my junior year. In Tyler I encountered a considerably more class-differentiated environment, with kids from Dixie, Noonday, Chapel Hill and other nearby country schools sharing classrooms with the sons and daughters of bankers, oilmen, and businessmen. It was not uncommon to sit side by side in class with the future rose queens and duchesses of the city's annual and elite Rose Festival. I didn't always spend my hours at Tyler High School (now John Tyler) productively (I spent too much time daydreaming about the Grand Ole Opry and the New York Yankees), but I was fortunate in having Miss Sara Marsh as my twelfth-grade English teacher and having the Carnegie Public Library available for browsing while waiting for Daddy to get off work at East Texas Auto Supply. Miss Marsh was the most demanding teacher I ever had — a comma blunder guaranteed an F even if the rest of your essay was perfect — but she sharpened my writing skills and encouraged critical thought. At the Carnegie Public Library I discovered Irving Stone's *Clarence Darrow for the Defense*, a biography that has won few words of praise from professional historians but which nevertheless shaped my sympathies for organized labor and radicalism. Very briefly, I toyed with the idea of becoming a lawyer, but only if I could spend all of my time promoting social justice and defending unpopular causes.

With my high school years ending, my thoughts were riveted on going on to college. At a junior year career day convocation, I had told one of the interviewers that I wanted to go to the University of Texas in Austin to become a history teacher. My parents, however, remained socially conservative, poor but proud, afraid of large ambitions, and reluctant to support any venture that might ultimately cause me disappointment or frustration. Perhaps they were also wary that I might breach the unthinkable but unspoken social code, "Don't get above your raisin'." Above all, they were leery of any venture that might be too costly for their working-class pocketbooks. My mother tried to talk me into taking a six-month course at one of the local business colleges in preparation for a career as a bookkeeper. That kind of career would enable me to wear a white shirt each day and live a much more secure and comfortable life than had ever been available to them. Besides, I could save some money and *then* go on to the university. Remaining stubbornly persistent, I was permitted to attend the local Tyler Junior College. On the first day of registration, my father dropped me off at 7:00 A.M. at the college on his way to work, but only after leaving me with these words of advice: "Son, don't sign up for anything big, like lawyer."

During my two years at Tyler Junior College, I buckled down to work with a passion that I had seldom displayed in high school. Somehow, this experience caught my attention as being much more serious than anything that had come before. Two teachers were immensely influential: Dr. Wiley Jenkins, who taught American history, and Dr. J. C. Henderson, who taught biology and chemistry. Actually, Professor Jenkins rarely taught history, but instead spent almost every class hour talking in a pompous but endearing way about football and current events. Nevertheless, his comments whetted my interest in public affairs and sharpened my intellectual curiosity. Professor Henderson was a gentle human being and a marvelous lecturer. I had little aptitude for either biology or chemistry, but he impressed me with his ability to give an absorbing and highly detailed lecture from only one three-by-five card. Most important, both men were strong Democrats at a time when Tyler, and the nation, was shifting toward the Republican Party (today, the Democrats don't even bother to run candidates in Tyler). My encounter with an article included in a political science anthology, Henry Steele Commager's "Who Is Loyal to America?," furthered my commitment to dissent and critical thought. The populist, New Deal philosophy inherited from my parents was gradually evolving into liberalism.

Although academic studies now consumed much of my time, my deep love for country music never wavered. The years that ran roughly from 1945 to 1956 marked the heyday of what we now call "hard country music." Even such "soft," quasi-pop singers as Eddy Arnold used instruments that seemed to evoke the ambience and sound of the barn dance or honky tonk, and the music seemed redolent of working-class experience. Today as I listen to the recordings of that era, I hear how effectively the songs mirrored the aspirations and frustrations of people who were trying to adapt to new jobs and new ways of living. Electric amplification was becoming the norm in almost every style of country music, but fiddles and steel guitars abounded in virtually all performances. My brothers and I still described the music as "hillbilly," but the terms "country" or "country and western" (reflecting the concerns of those who longed for respectability) were becoming the preferred labels of both musicians and "music industry" representatives. Not only did the music still express the often-ambivalent concerns of a culture in transition, it was also intruding into markets and regions where it had never before been heard. Recalling that era in one of his songs, when his own musical tastes were being shaped, Merle Haggard declared that "Hank and Lefty crowded every jukebox." He concluded with, "That's the way it was in '51."

Hank Williams also figured strongly in my life. As songwriter Dallas Frazier phrased it, "I never met old Hank but we were awful close." Hank had come to Tyler in about 1949 as part of the cast of the Louisiana Hayride, a Saturday night show that normally broadcast from Shreveport but which occasionally took its programs to other cities in KWKH's listening orbit. This particular night Hank, Kitty Wells, the Bailes Brothers, and other Hayride regulars sang from the stage of the Tyler High School auditorium. Even though Hank's songs soon became popular all over the nation, and even moved into the repertoires of sophisticated lounge singers like Tony Bennett, it always seemed to me that he was a profoundly "rural" singer and that he understood the little anxieties and frustrations that troubled my teenage soul.

I heard all the performers, old and new, who sang on such radio barn dances as the Grand Ole Opry, Shreveport's Louisiana Hayride, and Dallas's Big D Jamboree, or whose records were played on such shows as Hal Horton's "Hillbilly Hit Parade" in Dallas. Disc jockeys like Horton, Tom Perryman in Gladewater, or Paul Kallinger down on the Mexican border still affected informal down-home styles, peppered their speech with rustic aphorisms, and conveyed the impression that they and the musicians they played on their shows were part of your family. Longing to know more about the stars and to learn their songs, I bought *Country Song Roundup* magazine and any other music journal that became available. Of course, I did not realize that I was unconsciously involved in research that could be of great use in my later formal study, so I tended to clip out certain interesting or appealing songs and then discard the rest of the magazine.

While new performers were always interesting to me, my preferences turned increasingly to older entertainers and their styles and to the roots of the music I loved. Fortunately, one of those legendary performers, the Grand Ole Opry's Uncle Dave Macon, came to Tyler in about 1949 as part of a tent show that also included Curly Fox, Texas Ruby, and comedian Lazy Jim Day. At about the same time we obtained our first record player, part of a radio console purchased from a railroad salvage store. Among the cache of 78 rpm records that I brought into the house was an album of songs by Jimmie Rodgers, the Mississippi Blue Yodeler, first recorded in the late 1920s and early 1930s, but whose recordings since his death in 1933 had largely lain dormant. Rodgers had been country music's first star and was now widely heralded as "the Father of Country Music." From this point on my search for the music of the pioneer performers, or for what I considered to be "real" country music, became virtually a crusade.

If I had any illusions about the permanence of the country music that prevailed during the early 1950s, I should have known better because of two events that occurred early in that decade. Rhythm-and-blues tunes by the likes of Fats Domino, Chuck Berry, Clyde McPhatter, Big Mama Thornton, and Lloyd Price dominated the jukebox at the Wigwam, the little student center at Tyler Junior College. While I devoted my nickels to such songs as "Jambalaya" and "It Don't Hurt Anymore," my classmates more often listened to such items as "Honey Love," "One Mint Julep," and "Work with Me, Annie." In July of 1954 Elvis Presley made his first Sun record in Memphis, the first dramatic evidence that young southern whites were beginning to appropriate the rhythms of black performers and to incorporate them into other musical styles. By the end of the year Elvis was making personal appearances throughout East Texas and was drawing enthusiastic hordes of young fans. The full implications of these stirrings of social revolution, in both the habits of young white people and in the nature of American popular music, were not immediately apparent to me. As I set out toward Austin and the University of Texas in September, having completed the two years at Tyler Junior College, I probably felt that the kind of country music I knew and loved would last forever. Hank Williams was now dead, but hard country singers like Kitty Wells and Webb Pierce were still turning out their heart-wrenching laments of hard times and lost loves.

By September 1954, thanks to a $35 a semester tuition fee and money derived from the sale of Lone Star Steel stock, I was in Austin and enrolled as a history major at the University of Texas. My parents never anticipated that my college stay would extend to eight years, through the bachelor, master's, and Ph.D. degrees, nor were they ever able to respond conclusively when relatives would periodically ask, "Is Billy about through down there at the university?" The inevitable second question was even harder to answer: "Do you think he'll ever do anything with all that education?" I'm not sure that I could answer the question either, but I was nevertheless having the time of my life. The move to Austin was liberating in many ways, even though I had no automobile and generally made the trip from home to the Capital City via Continental Trailways bus or by catching a ride with a student from Tyler. I encountered Mexican food for the first time, met my first genuine atheist (a graduate student who lived across the tiny hall in the garage apartment where I lived), spent countless hours at Home Drug drinking coffee and talking politics and literature, gloried in the triumphs of the Longhorns, reveled in the rich resources of the giant University of Texas Library, and, of course, went to as many country music shows as my limited means and transportation would permit. Lest I be misunderstood, I also went to class faithfully and was fortunate enough to take two courses with the legendary historian of the West, Walter Prescott Webb.

Any lingering doubts about Elvis Presley's effects on American youth and country music were completely dispelled on the night of January 19, 1956, when I saw him at the Austin Coliseum. I had gone to the coliseum to see and hear my current hero, Hank Snow, but was appalled when his show was cut short in order to accommodate the huge crowd standing outside who had come to hear Presley. I was troubled even more when I saw the reactions made by many of the young women in the auditorium when Presley made his most blatant sexual movements. Old-fashioned prudishness, of course, explains my discomfort at the sight of women screaming and rushing the stage. In my double-standard way of viewing human emotions, I felt that women should not behave in such a manner or aggressively express their sexuality.

Otherwise, my negative feelings arose from the fear that Presley's style was endangering "traditional" forms of country music. His performances evoked positive reactions from his youthful audience, and the country music industry was already rushing to find other musicians who could successfully emulate his success. For a brief period my suspicions seemed confirmed, and fiddles, steel guitars, and hard-country singing styles began to disappear from jukeboxes, records, and radio shows. As traditional country music faded from public view, my own quest for older-sounding or roots-based musicians intensified. I delighted in any evidence that the older forms still thrived, or that younger musicians, such as George Jones and Ray Price, were able to create new and commercially viable sounds out of older materials. Like many concerned fans, I also retreated to bluegrass and found both musical and spiritual satisfaction in its acoustic-based high lonesome sound. I will never forget the thrill I felt when I first heard the Stanley Brothers singing "White Dove" and "Gathering Flowers for the Master's Bouquet."

Above all, I continued to express my affection for country music through my own singing, which did not begin in earnest until 1956 when graduate school contributed to the illusion that I had a lot of free time on my hands. I bought a used Stella guitar from a budding novelist and English graduate student, Bill Casey, but until I learned to pick passably enough, I generally relied on other people for instrumental accompaniment. Singing at beer parties for countless hours, I wore out the fingers of good friends Tom Crouch and Willie Benson, who strummed as I sang. I took immense pride in knowing hundreds of songs, mostly sad ones such as "Unloved and Unclaimed," "Wreck on the Highway," and "The Knoxville Girl," and described myself as the Tragic Balladeer. Listeners often asked me, "Why is country music so sad?" mistaking my personal preferences for the total country songbag.

Sometime during this period my browsings in the Austin Public Library brought me in contact with the Folkways *Anthology of American Folk Music*, the most important body of reissued commercial recordings made in the twentieth century. Based on a collection amassed by Harry Smith, and graced by his quirky and idiosyncratic liner notes, this assemblage of hillbilly, blues, gospel, and Cajun recordings from the late 1920s and early 1930s introduced a large number of young people to the world of American roots music. I was particularly impressed with the collection because it lent validity to hillbilly music by linking it to the word "folk," a term with immense snob appeal. I found some familiar names from my childhood, such as Uncle Dave Macon, the Carter Family, and the Skillet Lickers, and encountered for the first time such vital entertainers as Buell Kazee, Clarence Ashley, and Kelly Harrell. Like many other young fans and singers, I soon began singing songs—such as "Wagoner Lad" and "Engine 143"—that I had learned from the anthology. To our additional delight, we soon discovered that many of these performers, who had either been unknown or presumed dead, were still alive and still capable of making good music.

Although I could always be coaxed into singing at a party or beer bust, my chief venue for music-making by the end of the 1950s was a little bar in North Austin called Threadgill's. Threadgill's was a converted filling station that reputedly had received the first beer license in Travis County when Prohibition was repealed in 1933. The owner and genial host was a man named Kenneth Threadgill, who knew a storehouse of Jimmie Rodgers songs and other old-time pieces, and who could sing and yodel them with a sweet but bell-like clarity. Threadgill's was basically a working-class bar, but by the end of the 1950s it began to be caught up in what has since been described as "the folk music revival," first when a few of my graduate school friends (Stan Alexander, Ed Mellon, and Willie Benson) and I began singing there on a weekly basis and, next, when offshoots from the university folk-music club, including the now-legendary Janis Joplin, arrived a few years later. We sat around the big circular tables in front of the bar and, without the aid of microphones or electrical amplification, sang our hearts out until Kenneth Threadgill felt sufficiently caught up with his work to join us with a few of his favorite songs.

The folk revival began in earnest in 1958 when the Kingston Trio recorded their immensely popular version of an old North Carolina murder ballad, "Tom Dooley." Everywhere, young people began trying to learn the guitar, banjo, or some other string instrument, and began experimenting with traditional or traditional-sounding songs. The quest for "authenticity" inspired some people to look beyond the Kingston Trio and other singers like them who seemed pale and superficial, and to search for *real* folk songs performed by *real* folk musicians. That search inevitably led fans to the old 78 rpm records of the 1920s and 1930s—that is, to the same kind of material heard on Harry Smith's collection—and to the contemporary musicians who were trying to recreate that tradition. In 1958 a trio of young New York musicians (Mike Seeger, John Cohen, Tom Paley) began their career as the New Lost City Ramblers, playing string-band tunes and ballads and love songs learned from old hillbilly records. Through Folkways recordings, numerous concerts in folk-music clubs and on college campuses (including the University of Texas), and a songbook that contained the bulk of their recorded songs, the Ramblers inaugurated a revival of old-time string-band music that has endured in America.

I became absorbed in all of the elements of the folk revival and borrowed from everything I heard — anything that seemed old. All the while, I thought that what I sang was more "authentic" than most of what I was hearing. I was skeptical of any so-called folk singer who did not grow up in a southern working-class environment and was suspicious of anyone who did not realize that people like Ernest Tubb, Hank Williams, and Kitty Wells were the natural inheritors of the hillbilly tradition that was now in fashion. Consequently, when I sang I generally made a point of singing songs like "Driftwood on the River," "Mansion on the Hill," and other products of the modern commercial country music era. Everyone I knew abhorred the music of the Kingston Trio, the Brothers Four, and other acts that seemed to be little more than pale reproductions of music borrowed from the "real" folk. On the other hand, we listened avidly to the New Lost City Ramblers, and I even got to jam with them one night at Threadgill's during their Austin visit. We sometimes couldn't resist poking fun at these New York City boys, who had only recently discovered *our* music, but we borrowed freely from their storehouse of recorded songs, bought their songbook, and carefully pored over the liner notes of their albums. The folk revival encouraged historical documentation, and record liner notes became valuable sources of information concerning early hillbilly recording sessions. The Ramblers usually listed the sources from which they obtained their songs, providing the names of recording artists and record release numbers. While we enjoyed New Lost City Rambler performances, we longed to hear the music of the people who had inspired them — Charlie Poole, Gid Tanner and the Skillet Lickers, Dock Boggs, the Monroe Brothers, and other early hillbilly musicians — and at least a few of us yearned to know more about the culture that had produced this music. My research into this music was punctuated by a strong sense of personal pride, because I was convinced that I was delving into the culture of my own people and, in the process, lending dignity and worth both to their lives and to their contributions to the American musical legacy.

Despite my immersion in the music and culture of hillbilly music, it scarcely entered my mind that this passion could become the basis of an academic career. Another graduate student, Ronald Davis, it is true, was preparing a doctoral dissertation on opera, but that topic was eminently respectable. Most of my history graduate-student friends had embarked on political or economic studies, and few of them really enjoyed what they were doing. Topics like "abandoned short line railroads" or "Texas crude oil pipe lines" (the names of actual theses written at the time in the University of Texas history department) might make useful contributions to knowledge, but they could hardly engage the full emotional and intellectual capacities of the researcher. After I passed my preliminary examinations for the Ph.D. in November 1960, I began a tentative search for a suitable dissertation topic, probably in the realm of southern labor history. No topic had firmly coalesced in my mind when I rode to Houston in December with Joe B. Frantz, my supervising professor, and a few graduate-student friends to see the Longhorns play Alabama in the Bluebonnet Bowl football game. I was already notorious in the history department for being a country music fanatic, and had even written a few political parodies and topical songs such as "The Ballad of John Glenn." That notoriety, and the fact that I was able to sing just about any country song requested on the way to the game, seems to have prompted Professor Frantz to ask me the fateful question, "Why don't you write a history of Nashville Publishing?"

Frantz had only a casual interest in country music and probably thought that its cultural importance was marginal at best. But as a business historian (a specialty that he shared with his expertise in western history), he could only be impressed with the economic vigor that the music was then demonstrating. Energized by a new and aggressive trade organization called the Country Music Association (CMA), and by a group of emerging publishing houses and recording studios that prompted the description of Nashville as Music City, USA, country music had rebounded from the blows dealt by rock and roll and was becoming an economic phenomenon that was respected around the world. I had mixed feelings about this economic success story. I was pleased that the men and women of country music were enjoying a prosperity that had long been denied them, but troubled by some of the diluted styles that had been passing as country music. I wanted to go far beyond the music-business history that Professor Frantz envisioned, to write a study that would encompass the full dimensions of the country music story, would delve into questions of identity and authenticity, and would demonstrate the vital link between the music and southern working-class people. I doubt that I ever mentioned my ambitious goals to Professor Frantz, but fortunately, in the years that followed, he never resisted my decision to write a general history.

My venture into formal country music scholarship, then, was clearly a consequence of events that occurred in the late 1950s and early 1960s. Almost nothing in my academic training prepared me to write on country music. I had no courses in anthropology, folklore, or music, and my history courses, although strongly concentrated on southern subjects, scarcely delved into the lives of plain people. Fortunately, I discovered the writings of Frank Owsley, Howard Odum, Bell Wiley, and W. J. Cash on my own. Cash's *Mind of the South* was revelatory because, although his purview was that of Piedmont Carolina, it sounded like he had an intimate insight into the lives and thinking of my own people. Without the folk-music revival, though, few people in academia would have recognized the legitimacy of the study and documentation of roots music, and without the resurgence of country music as a vital economic phenomenon, Professor Frantz probably would not have suggested the utility of a study of the genre. More than likely, I would have become a southern political or economic historian and would have remained a frustrated fan of country music.

Although the immediate social context in which I lived made it possible for a country music history to be written, the chief perceptions and overall thesis of my work were shaped years earlier by my East Texas experiences. I could not separate the music from the memories of growing up poor on an East Texas cotton farm and finding escape and diversion in the sounds of hillbilly music. I could not forget the thrill of being awakened and energized early each morning by the radio sounds of a fiddle, steel guitar, and lonesome voice, or of hearing my mother express her loneliness through the words of a gospel song. Nor could I ever forget the importance that the music held for the working people whose sacrifices made it possible for me attend college and to live a life of relative ease. Their story and that of country music were closely intertwined. That story did not cease when communities like Galena vanished. The music followed the people into the cities and into blue-collar life, and it now accompanies their children and grandchildren as they try to cope with suburban existence and ways of life that seem alien to me. Whether the music can survive this evolutionary process with any recognizable identity left intact is anybody's guess. Clearly, the questions of identity and authenticity that intrigued me forty years ago, when I diverged from the task assigned by Professor Frantz, continue to inspire and stimulate my scholarship. And it is immensely satisfying to have converted a lifelong passion into a field of academic study, and to be as ardently committed to it as I was in the beginning.

Scattered Pieces
Living and Writing Southern History

DAN T. CARTER

Looking back, I see myself as a child, standing halfway between two large mirrors. As I glanced from side to side, I realized that my image — reflected from one mirror and then back to the other — repeated again and again, growing smaller and more indistinct with each repetition. Well over a half century later, I remember this moment with an astonishing clarity. But I cannot recall how old I was, where I was standing, or anything that preceded or followed this moment. Like the shards of a broken pot, we retrieve our past in scattered pieces. All of us could think of moments in our lives that remain with us and, in some cases, that haunt us. In others we are only mystified by their intensity. Why do we remember this moment and not others? And why do we forget?[1]

In my study of George Wallace and American politics, for more than 150 hours I talked to dozens of individuals, asking them to relive their experiences in the 1950s, 1960s, and 1970s. I found their stories sometimes humorous, sometimes moving, and almost always revealing. But I also immersed myself in the more contemporary sources of the past. As I listened to my interviewees describe the events of those years, I recognized the great chasm between their recollections and what I knew to be true. And with each interview, I learned an important lesson about memory. It is not simply that we forget; the more fundamental problem is that we constantly recreate memory so that our past can live comfortably with the present without the jarring dissonances that inevitably accompany change through time. Like Shakespeare's monster Caliban, we drift into reveries of a past that is so comforting that when we wake we "cry to dream again."[2] No wonder Oliver Goldsmith called memory that "fond deceiver."[3]

Skeptical about the reliability of such recollections, I am also uneasy at the prospect of drawing a direct connection between my historical writing and the story of my own life. Like novelists who rebel when individuals try to link the characters of their lives to their fictional creations, I resist the notion that there is an unmediated line that stretches from my personal experiences to my work as a historian. Nevertheless, if that connection is not always clear, I have come to accept the fact that my childhood, my political awakening in the 1960s, and the graduate training I received all helped to shape what I have written and taught about during my career.

I was born in rural eastern South Carolina in the early summer of 1940 and spent my childhood and adolescence on a midsized tobacco farm. The Pee Dee River gave this corner of South Carolina its name and shaped its character. From the time when only Native Americans roamed this land, creeks and swamps have punctuated the sandy soil of mixed pine and hardwood stands and isolated it from the flat open lands to the south and east. Although the rural community where I grew up was less than a hundred miles from the seventeenth-century cosmopolitan city of Charleston, it remained a backwoods frontier until the 1820s, when the land was cleared as the cotton culture spread through the state. Toward the end of the century, the introduction of light flue-cured cigarette tobacco brought a second agricultural transformation and a modest economic upturn. Still, it remained a relatively poor agricultural region.

My family on both my mother's and father's sides drifted down from eastern North Carolina and settled in the region in the 1760s. The Lawhon, Purvis, and Langston ancestors of my mother were small-scale but respectable yeoman farmers for generations, and my mother's father was a college graduate, an accomplishment generally restricted to women schoolteachers in this rural setting. I traced my Carter ancestry four generations back to Giles Carter, a landowner of considerable wealth who accumulated several thousand acres and more than one hundred slaves by the 1840s. But that wealth slipped away during the Civil War and in the years that followed. By the time I was born at the tail end of the Great Depression, my father had spent the first thirty years of his life struggling to save a farm — the old homeplace we called it — that had been a part of our family for generations.

As a small child, we still drank from a hand pump on the back porch; in my earliest and haziest memories I can even recall the privy that sat out behind the house. Three times a week, Sunday morning, evening, and again on Wednesday night, I attended the same Baptist church where my mother's family had worshipped since the early nineteenth century. Like my mother, grandparents, and great-grandparents, the church minister had baptized me in the cypress-darkened waters of Lynches Creek. The building where I went to grade school — two grades to the class — would be condemned in many Third World countries; my high school was a ramshackle wooden frame building heated by pot-bellied coal stoves stoked each morning in a rotation shared by the nine male members of my graduating class. However primitive the physical setting, the education I received ranged from adequate to exceptional. In the South of the 1950s, teaching was the most prestigious position for a woman who wished to work, and many of the women (and several men) who taught me were exceptionally well read and committed to their students in a way that I still find remarkable.

My childhood was also a place of safety and freedom. I roamed the woods and fields with few restrictions. With only a quick good-bye to my mother, I would get on my Schwinn bike and travel for miles across country roads to visit friends and cousins. My parents may have worried about the possibility of a hunting accident — I got my first shotgun at fourteen — or the dangerous lure of the cool waters of Lynches Creek where I swam and rowed a flat-bottom boat along the borders of our farm. But there was no concern about strangers; the roads surrounding my home were dense with cousins, aunts, and uncles, honorary relatives and neighbors who had known my parents and my grandparents for generations. My parents were born in the age of the horse and buggy and the kerosene lantern, while I grew up in the atomic age of the late 1940s and 1950s; but in terms of the rhythms of my childhood life, I think our worlds were only modestly different.

In that setting — so linked to the past — I had my first history lessons on our front porch as I sat, spellbound, listening to stories from my grandfather, Claudius Quintillius Carter. Ruggedly handsome even when I knew him in his seventies and eighties, he had a broken nose that came (he proudly boasted) from dozens of fracases in which he proved he was the best bare-knuckles fighter in Florence County. He told me of his struggles to wrest a living from the land for his wife and eleven children. Each winter he had cut trees on the farm, dragged them to the edge of Lynch's Creek, lashed them together into a raft, and then drifted downstream into the great Pee Dee and to the sea at Georgetown before making the trip back — fifty miles on foot. Sitting beside him on the front porch of our house, I heard — again and again — tales of the great war always climaxing with the story of Pickett's charge at Gettysburg, where my great-grandfather had been wounded but stayed at the bedside of his dying cousin, writing down his last words, helping wash and lay him out, and then kissing him goodbye before standing aside as an army carpenter hammered shut the top of the crude wooden coffin. In fact, I was ten before I realized that his harrowing tales of the Civil War were retellings of his father's adventures.

Only in later years did I get a glimpse of the silences that always lay behind these stories. He proudly told me that he had become postmaster of my local community in 1897 at the astonishingly young age of twenty-seven, a responsible and relatively well-paying position that was widely sought in that impoverished community. Until my own son did research on his history honors thesis, however, I did not consider the fact that my grandfather had been appointed postmaster by a Republican president at a time when virtually all whites had closed ranks in the Democratic Party and most Republicans were black; that — in this small, close-knit community — he had almost certainly known his predecessor, a local black political activist named Frazier Baker. After my grandfather's appointment, Baker moved from Effingham to a larger post office in Lake City thirteen miles away, only to be brutally murdered by a white mob the next year for daring to keep what had become a "white man's job" in the late 1890s. This I learned from my son's research. But I had heard nothing of this from my grandfather.[4]

If the tales my grandfather told me were half-myth and half-truth, I think they shaped me in ways I did not understand until many years later. He was a natural storyteller who understood the lure of detail, atmosphere, narrative momentum, and dénouement. And though I have tried to penetrate those myths that he had come to believe, I have never forgotten the power that narrative can create.

Although my childhood seems carefree in retrospect, it was not the life of a feckless Huck Finn. From the time I was six or seven, I had a long list of chores around the farm. By my ninth year I was working in the tobacco fields, from dawn to dusk during harvest season. Lest I raise echoes of a barefoot past straight out of Erskine Caldwell's *Tobacco Road*, I should note that my mother was an honor graduate of Winthrop College for Women who had taught Latin and whose mastery of the rules of English grammar still shames me by example. My father farmed, but by the time I was six or seven he had begun to earn a comfortable living as a small-scale building contractor. Both encouraged me to read, to think independently, and to dream of a world beyond the intimate community that had been the home of the Carters and the Lawhons for more than 150 years. In the impoverished rural world of my childhood we were comfortably middle class, and I worked long hours in the fields not because of economic necessity but because my father believed that manual labor — particularly grueling work in the fields or on one of his construction sites — created inner reserves of fortitude and self-discipline even as it taught essential lessons about the dignity of labor.

The universe in which I lived as a child and a teenager was the world of the segregated South, though I use the term segregated with a full awareness of the irony of the word. It was certainly an oppressive culture in which blacks were relegated to the bottom rung of every economic ladder and barred by law from the schools of my childhood and by custom from the ballot box of my community. But it was hardly segregated. I saw, talked with, played with (and occasionally fought) black children from the time I can remember. Beginning the summer I was nine, I worked ten-hour days, five days a week in the fields, side by side with black men and women and girls and boys of my own age.

Each year, at the end of the summer's long tobacco harvest season, at least two of the landlords for whom we had worked would stage a "last cropping" dinner. With the tobacco securely hung in the barns, we would go over to the pump and freshen up while the landowner and his wife spread out the meal. There would be fish stew, a spicy mixture of freshwater bream and redbreast cooked in a rich tomato sauce and poured over rice — all washed down with sweet iced tea and loaf after loaf of soft, sliced bread. I can still smell the wood fires under the black pots of stew and the pungent sweetness of the barns, saturated from generations of curing tobacco with oak-wood fires. As I sat with the other children, teenagers, and womenfolk and finished off the evening with a plate of fresh hand-churned ice cream, I would watch the men as they drifted away out under the trees and began passing mason jars of corn whiskey, laughing nervously like little boys away from the censoring eyes of womenfolk and respectability.

I saw nothing incongruous about the promiscuous mixing of black and white or the absurdity of those nuanced cultural conventions that decreed that — since the sky was overhead — it was permissible to eat side by side in a way that would have triggered a riot in one of the handful of restaurants in nearby Florence. And when I saw the two mason jars of corn whiskey passed around — one for blacks and one for whites — I saw, but I did not understand.

Still, there were disquieting moments. In the summer of 1952 I traveled to Charleston on a Greyhound bus for a week's visit with one of my favorite aunts. As we rolled through the flat land just east of Lake City, an older black woman hailed the bus and from a tightly bound handkerchief, she carefully counted out the fare for (I presume) her granddaughter to ride to a small town less than thirty miles away. As we drove away, I watched in surprise as the eight- or nine-year-old girl tentatively sat down on the empty front seat of the near empty bus. At first the driver did not see her; when he did, he gruffly mumbled "move on back." Either she did not hear, or she simply didn't understand the taboo she had violated. When she remained seated, he suddenly pulled the bus to the side of the road, stood up, and towered over her: "I told you to move to the back of the bus," he shouted. Paralyzed with fear, she remained in her seat, crying softly. From the back of the bus an older and poorly dressed black man moved up the aisle and gently took her hand: "Come on back here with me, honey," he said. Until she got off the bus thirty minutes later, I sat with eyes carefully averted as I heard her sobbing slowly subside. I remember this as vividly as anything from my childhood. I also recall that my indignation was not against a system that allowed such brutalities but against the driver's bad manners. Even as a twelve-year-old, I knew that we were supposed to be "polite to colored people."

And that same fall, I glimpsed the explosive links between race and sex. For a rural child of the 1940s and the 1950s, few events were more eagerly awaited than the annual county fair. Since I raised cattle and showed them in the livestock exhibition, it meant essentially a week away from school, often sleeping in the barns and slipping away during the afternoons for walks through the carnival booths and rides. At ten or eleven, for a prepubescent adolescent, the highlight of these excursions on the sawdust-covered midway was to move to the edge of the crowd facing one of the two burlesque tents in which a dozen skimpily clad girls paraded across the platform to the constant patter of the barker, who promised those who paid their fifty cents ("Men only over the age of 18") a far more revealing look inside the tent. I say two burlesque shows, because one was white and the other was black, or "colored" as it was called.

The week afterward, I spent a Saturday afternoon fishing on Lynch's Creek with my cousin and two young black teenagers. They were a little older than me; one would say they were "boys" like me except for the painful twist of meaning that word has come to have for black men. All of us, it turns out, had been to the fair. It did not occur to me that it was peculiar that there was a single "colored day" set aside for my black friends. That too was simply part of the world in which we lived. I began talking about how beautiful I had thought the "colored girls" were at the fair. I did not mean my comments in a predatory way; I thought of it as a compliment. I, as a white boy, was generously recognizing the beauty of an inferior race. I do not remember what my black friends said, but I distinctly remember that both recoiled as though they were physically struck. One stood and simply walked away without saying a word.

Afterward, still bewildered, I told the story to my mother. She groped for some way to try and help me understand the taboos I had unknowingly violated. Finally, she said: "What if they had started talking about how beautiful the white girls were at the fair?"

Then my world—the world of the white South—turned upside down one morning in the spring of 1954. Mr. M. L. Anderson, the principal of the little school I attended, called together the seventh through twelfth graders in the rickety auditorium to announce that the Supreme Court of the United States had passed a decision outlawing the separation of the races in the schools. We were likely to encounter "colored friends" or acquaintances who might be boastful or taunting, he warned, and we must respond with restraint as young ladies and gentlemen, implicitly young white ladies and gentlemen.

There were no taunts, however, only silence as a wall of fear and anger divided black from white. And as the first halting challenges to the racial status quo emerged, I became a part of the white South as it mobilized for massive resistance. It is difficult to recreate the memories of those special pleasures of oppression. What did the northerners know of us? Why did they taunt and abuse us? Our colored people were happy and contented; it was those hated Yankees, those outside agitators who were creating turmoil and conflict where only peace had prevailed. Why did they seek to turn our tranquil lives upside down? By us, of course, I meant "us" in a tribal sense: the white South.

While the battles to maintain the southern way of life, my way of life, were fought in distant places—Montgomery, Alabama, and Clinton, Tennessee, and Little Rock, Arkansas—there were closer skirmishes as well. In the nearby town of Florence, a local white policeman known sardonically by the black community as "Mr. Thug" badly beat a black man after he had—in the words of the officer—"sassed me." When a group of angry young black men smashed several windows in the downtown block-long black shopping district, baton-wielding city police and the sheriff's department mobilized a show of force that would have done justice to one of the great urban riots of the next decade. Like most whites, I thrilled to the mobilization of white resistance. After nearly three years of passivity in the face of growing black "impudence," it was a chance to strike back.

Several weeks after this very tame civil disturbance, my cousin James was back in South Carolina for the Christmas holidays, visiting from his home north of Miami. James was fourteen years older than me. My parents had taken him in during his teenage years after his father had kicked him out of the house at age fifteen. In 1943 he had enlisted in the Seabees, the navy's construction and engineering arm. At Tarawa and later on Iwo Jima he worked round the clock constructing runways, several times under Japanese sniper fire. In the 1940s he was a war hero; in the 1950s he became — to me at least — a romantic adventurer as he moved to Florida, bought a 120-foot schooner, and sailed the Caribbean carrying supplies to remote out-islands. I worshipped him with the kind of intensity most youngsters today seem to reserve for sports heroes or rap stars.

As I described with some enthusiasm, I am sad to say, the way in which local police had showed those "niggers"—and that is the word I used—who was in charge, James stopped my account in midsentence. During the war, he told me, navy units were segregated in the Pacific. But under the desperate pressure to throw up airstrips and emergency housing, the black and white labor battalions of the Seabees worked side by side. In late 1944, said James, he became desperately ill with fever and dysentery and was sent off to an understaffed field hospital where he thought he was going to die; where he wished, he said, he could die.

But for the next week, every spare moment they had, two of his black friends took turns sitting with him, helping him to the latrine, feeding him, cleaning him when he fouled himself, and nursing him back to health. In many ways, I suppose, it was a clichéd story straight out of a Hollywood script: white sailor, saved by black friends, abandons racism. However banal, for him it was real. "When I got better," he said as he looked intently at me, "I swore I would never again use that word that way. I grew up hearing it day and night: the 'niggers' did this, the 'niggers' did that. Someday you'll understand. It's a kind of sickness. And people think the only cure is to find somebody to hate."

I wish I could say that this gentle rebuke became an epiphany; that, like Paul on the road to Damascus, the scales from my eyes dropped away. They did not. I was simply embarrassed and hurt at the shaming administered by someone I loved. But I like to think in retrospect that my cousin had planted a time bomb that ticked away silently over the next three years.

If so, the change for me came completely in four intense years between 1958 and 1962. During those first two years I attended night classes at a local extension branch of the University of South Carolina while I worked as a reporter at the *Florence Morning News*. Much of the work was the usual regimen of a rookie reporter: writing obituaries, covering the local tobacco warehousemen's convention, and the latest multiple-car accident. But on the eve of my employment at the newspaper, local klansmen had driven editor Jack O'Dowd out of town for daring to argue that *Brown v. Board of Education* was the law of the land. If O'Dowd's successor, James Rogers, was more cautious in his editorial policies, he and most of the reporters with whom I worked were openly disdainful of the threadbare rationale for white supremacy.

I learned much during those two years. My two editors, Dew James and Joe Dabney, struggled to teach me the pitfalls of adjectives and the superiority of active-voice verbs, but their greatest gift was to introduce me to the astonishing possibility that I could be critical of my culture without becoming a traitor to its best values. On the surface, whites in the small town of Florence seemed united in their defense of segregation, but appearances were deceiving. Over endless cups of coffee at a downtown coffee shop, I came to know and to be instructed by men (and a couple of women) who had a vision of a South without racism. In some cases, their convictions sprang from deep religious conviction; others had served in the military or lived outside the region at some time in their lives and, as in the case of my cousin James, had a direct experience with black men and women that challenged their early assumptions about white supremacy. Publicly they may have spoken cautiously; privately they peeled away my half-hearted defenses of the "southern way of life." In the end, there would be no Damascan experience, but in the spring of 1960 as a nineteen-year-old reporter, I stood in a Kress five-and-ten-cent store photographing raucous whites who screamed obscenities at the dozen well-dressed black young men and women sitting quietly at the lunch counter. "Which side are you on?" asks the old union rallying song. As I took those photographs, there was no longer any doubt in my mind about which side I had chosen. In two short years, the racial moorings of a lifetime had been severed.

My next two years at the University of South Carolina in Columbia completed that transformation. Despite the fact that political pressure had led to the firing of two outspoken professors in the late 1950s for condemning segregation, faculty members like Raymond Moore in International Studies and historians Robert Ochs and Bill Foran made little effort to hide their contempt for the state's commitment to maintaining white supremacy. (Jack Thompson, my American history teacher at the university's branch campus at Florence, was even more withering in his comments about what he called the "Neolithic mossbacks" who ran the state.) Within months after my arrival at the university, I gravitated toward a small group of students who openly challenged segregation, a system that most white South Carolinians saw as the bedrock of their society. Only later did I realize how fortunate I was to meet and work with an extraordinary group of men and women over the next two years: James McBride Dabbs, the Maysville, South Carolina, planter turned author and civil rights leader; Ella Baker, the inspirational NAACP and later SNCC activist who inspired hundreds of black and white young people to act upon their best convictions; John Lewis, the SNCC organizer and founder whom I first met at a civil rights retreat in Highlander, Tennessee; and civil rights activists (and later authors) Will Campbell and Connie Curry were some of the other individuals I encountered in those hectic two years. And there were my three roommates. Hayes Mizell went on to become a field organizer for the American Friends Service Committee's Southern Project and a lifelong activist for human rights; Charles Joyner, who ultimately captured the memory of a low-country slave community in his eloquent book, *Down by the Riverside*; and fellow historian Selden Smith, whose good humor reminded me that commitment need not become self-righteousness. Most of all, I have kept with me the memory of those women who had struggled so hard to keep alive the dream of racial justice during the height of racial reaction in the 1950s and early 1960s: Alice Spearman, the head of the South Carolina Council on Human Relations; Libby Ledeen of the university's YWCA; and Mae Gautier, a young University Methodist chaplain.

Encouraged by Spearman and Ledeen, I joined a loose-knit group of thirty or forty black and white students from the state's colleges and universities. Rather grandly, we called ourselves the "South Carolina Student Council on Human Relations" and elected Charles Joyner as our first president. (He claimed it was because he could play the guitar and knew most of the words to the freedom songs.) From the fall of 1960 until I went away to graduate school at the University of Wisconsin in 1964, there was a continuous round of Saturday "conferences" and evening meetings in Columbia and civil rights workshops at Monteagle, Tennessee; Dorchester, Georgia; and Penn Community Center, near Beaufort, South Carolina. (Penn Center was the only place in the state where integrated groups could safely meet overnight.) It is difficult to recall how daring we felt as we assembled — black and white — to plan for a day when segregation would be only a bitter memory. In truth, there were many meetings, a great deal of talk, constant singing, and little concrete action, but it transformed the lives of those of us who saw another possibility for the South and its place in the nation.

All of us were caught up in a feverish questioning that led us to act (and think) in new ways about southern and American politics. In retrospect, it is possible to construct an "intellectual genealogy" in which the books that shaped my thinking are arranged in a neat ascending order. The truth is that it was all haphazard, and it is difficult at this point to recall which people and which written works were most important to my thinking as a future historian. Clearly, a few writers and their works were critical: C. Vann Woodward's *The Strange Career of Jim Crow* and *The Burden of Southern History*; W.E.B. Du Bois's *The Souls of Black Folk*; James McBride Dabbs's *The Southern Heritage*; and — however dated it now may seem — W. J. Cash's *Mind of the South*. At the same time, Michael Harrington's *The Other America: Poverty in the United States* awakened me to the larger dimensions of economic as well as racial inequality in America.[5]

But my real immersion in the story of the American South did not come primarily from historical works but through the reading of novels and short stories. I had encountered little serious fiction until my junior year in high school, when I devoured Thomas Wolfe's *You Can't Go Home Again* in one long weekend and began haphazardly reading works by authors as disparate as John Steinbeck and Ayn Rand. In my college freshman English class, my teacher (and later friend and colleague) Jack Russell — a native of New Jersey — was shocked, however, to discover that I had read nothing by William Faulkner except a couple of short stories in high school and college English anthologies. "Here," he said, as he loaned me his dog-eared copy of *Absalom, Absalom*. "Read this."

It was tortuous. Out of a sense of shame at my inadequacy I plodded through page after page, struggling to grasp the identity of the shifting voices, the confusing chronology, the maddeningly indirect dialogue. Halfway through I confessed that I couldn't finish; it was too difficult. Go back again and stop obsessing about whether I understood every line, Jack said. "Just keep listening to the voices. It will come." I think it was that same night when I reached that extraordinary moment in *Absalom, Absalom* when William Sutpen — in order to realize his grand design — refuses to acknowledge Charles Bon, his Haitian-born son. (Too late, Sutpen learned that the daughter of the Haitian planter he had married was tainted with a drop of African blood.) Two decades after that abandonment, Bon has ingratiated himself with Sutpen's legitimate heir, Henry, and through him met and made plans to marry Sutpen's daughter, Judith. What Henry and Judith do not know is that Bon is their half-brother/half-sister. When Henry Sutpen learns from his father the truth — that the man he has come to love like a brother *is* his brother, that he is tainted with that ineradicable drop of black blood, and that he is intent on marrying Judith — he faces a horrific choice. Bon, who has created the crisis in a desperate attempt to force his father to acknowledge him as a son, offers the butt end of his pistol to his half-brother; "*do it now.*" Henry replies in anguish, "*You are my brother.*" To which Bon has the devastating response, "*No I'm not. I'm the nigger that's going to sleep with your sister.*"[6] Reading those last pages of *Absalom, Absalom*, I came to understand — viscerally — that crazed fear of blackness (Bon: "*So it's the miscegenation, not the incest, which you cant bear*"). That fear had led William Sutpen to renounce his son; it caused Henry Sutpen to kill his own brother, and it had sent the white South, and the nation, tumbling through a 200-year nightmare.

Certainly there was an element of naïveté in my hope (and that of my friends) that sweeping away the vestiges of segregation and overt discrimination and encouraging community development with a few Great Society programs would undo centuries of oppression and racism. But I have little patience with the criticism of the "sixties" that often comes from contemporary conservatives and from some disenchanted liberals and radicals. I don't think I ever lived in a dream world of impractical idealism, because my political commitments, my view of the past, and my hopes for the future were always tempered by what I came to understand about the complex history of the South through my reading of Faulkner, Robert Penn Warren, Richard Wright, Eudora Welty, Carson McCullers, James Agee, Ralph Ellison, and Flannery O'Connor.

For me and most of my fellow white students from the Deep South, a commitment to civil rights inevitably caused conflict with family members. It certainly led to tension in my case. My father's politics had been shaped in the hardscrabble New Deal era and, despite the fact that he was a farmer and small businessman, he proved surprisingly liberal on some economic issues. Perhaps because of his own difficulty in obtaining work in the midst of the Great Depression, he consistently defended the notion that the federal government had an obligation to guarantee jobs for unemployed workers during economic downturns. Still, his racial views were typical of his generation. If he treated his black workers fairly and with considerable cordiality, he also defended segregation as "best for both races" and shared the view of many fellow white southerners that communists had infiltrated and manipulated the Civil Rights movement in an effort to foment discord between the races. Fortunately, my mother had far more moderate views on race and the good sense to know that this was a conflict of views that could not be resolved in the short run. At one point, after a polite but intense argument with my father, she took me aside and called for a temporary cessation of discussion on the issue. "You love your father and he loves you," she told me. "And I don't want either of you to say things that you will later regret." As in so many things, she was right. As a local school board member, my father began working closely with black board members, and eventually his views changed. I think others were not so lucky.

The changes that my father made in his thinking were one of the things that gave me great hope in the 1960s and 1970s. No one who grew up in the midst of the cruelties of the Jim Crow South of the 1950s could fail to be hopeful. I was also optimistic about the future of the South because I knew that nestled together with the racial cruelties of my childhood were memories of a loving world of kinfolk, neighbors, and friends; a world governed by obligations and responsibilities to family, church, and neighbors. In that world, even the harshest edges of racial hatred could be softened by the daily human exchanges of the rural South. In the summer of 1962 I was a pollworker in my local community for that year's Democratic primary. Over the previous two years the number of black registered voters in that rural precinct had gone from less than a half dozen to more than one hundred. As we set up the tables and ballot box and stacked the blank ballots, my uncle — who was in charge of the voting — groused about all the "Kennedy-loving" blacks who would be casting their ballots. But when those black voters came to pick up their blank ballots, he greeted them with a smile, a joke, and a solicitous question about their children or the state of their tobacco crop. As we counted the ballots afterward I teased him a bit, and it was his turn to be embarrassed. "Well, most of 'em are neighbors," he said apologetically.

To be sure, there was disappointment and frustration. If we did not understand the full implications of what was called "white backlash," we certainly knew that there was continuing resistance — North and South — to equal rights. And how could anyone who cared about civil rights not be depressed at the election of Richard Nixon as president in 1968 and his overwhelming reelection in 1972? Still, there was also a sense that the South of my childhood had turned a corner in the 1960s, and I was heartened by the sight of integrated public facilities, desegregated public schools, and growing biracial political activism. As African Americans moved (if all too slowly) into the mainstream of the southern economy, the future seemed possible.

In some ways that mixture of impatience and hope was the background to my career as a historian. From the beginning, my work was shaped by my belief that an understanding of the past could help in the search for a morally just society. I don't agree with intellectual historian David Harlan that we should be unconcerned about the truthfulness of our re-creation of the past, but I do share his view (and that of Tolstoy's) that history is ultimately a form of moral reflection.[7] Instinctively, without thinking through the intellectual implications, I believed that we could better understand who we were as a people, as a nation, by engaging in a conversation with that past. And that conversation might do more than inform us about what people had said and done; it might help us make decisions about how we *should* live.

This did not mean that I embraced the notion that "history" was simply a rhetorical weapon to be used as a tool in a struggle for ideological dominance. In that respect, my own training was conventional — even conservative — and I think it served as a healthy counterpoint to my passionate commitments. At the University of Wisconsin where I received my M.A. degree, I took a seminar under the avowed Marxist William Appleman Williams (there weren't too many of those in South Carolina!). But I also studied under the quixotically conservative William B. Hesseltine, and most of the other teachers who strongly influenced me — Merrill Jensen, Leon F. Litwack, David A. Shannon, and Avery O. Craven at Wisconsin and later Joel R. Williamson, Ralph Lee Woodward, and George B. Tindall at the University of North Carolina — were above all committed to the importance of careful historical research and documentation as well as balance and fairness in their findings. Tindall, as my major professor, was particularly important in helping me to see that some degree of empathy was essential in understanding people with whom you identified as well as those individuals you found morally repugnant. To explain, he would argue, you have to understand.

My dissertation and my first book, *Scottsboro: A Tragedy of the American South*, was an initial attempt to find my own voice as a historian.[8] In it, I tried to tell the story of one of the great civil rights cases of the twentieth century. The case began in the early spring of 1931 when Alabama authorities arrested nine black teenagers in the little town of Scottsboro. The youths, who ranged in age from thirteen to nineteen, had been hoboing across north Alabama on a train looking for work in the midst of the Great Depression; and they had the misfortune to share the freight cars with two white women who concocted a phony story that they had been raped. Within less than a week after their arrest, eight of the nine had been sentenced to die in Alabama's electric chair. The all-white jury deadlocked in the case of the youngest black teenager after several jurors refused to accept the prosecutor's recommendation for a life sentence. (Seven of the jurors demanded the electric chair for the thirteen-year-old.)

Although I had hoped, as I said in the preface, to explain something of what that nightmare meant to those nine black teenagers caught in the web of white injustice, it now seems hesitant in its attempts to probe the inner meaning of the experience for them and for other African Americans. The narrative momentum of the story lay in my efforts to understand and describe the destructive impulses that led white southerners — many of them decent, God-fearing, and kindly people — to countenance the most brutal and inhumane acts.

My second book moved back three-quarters of a century, to the aftermath of what my grandfather called the "War of Northern Aggression." In *When the War Was Over*, I examined the ways in which white southern leaders responded to defeat and emancipation, but the subtext was still the same: why did white southerners act as they did?[9] In some respects, my research led me to move against the grain of my own political sympathies and convictions. Writing in the 1960s and 1970s, scholars intent on revising the traditional and racist Dunning school of historiography had concluded that white southerners had learned nothing from their defeat; presidential Reconstruction was little more than another chapter in which they had sought to maintain their authority in a world without slavery. As I studied the white elites who struggled to rebuild their lives in the immediate aftermath of the war, however, I found their story more complex than the one I had learned and taught and in some ways even more instructive. Most white southerners were blinded by their racist assumptions, but they reacted to a world turned upside down in quite different ways. And if there was not the possibility for a complete "solution" to the enormous challenges posed by emancipation, enfranchisement, and postwar reconstruction, I came to believe that there were other, less tragic outcomes possible.

Through the years I continued to write and to work with documentary filmmakers, but inevitably I kept returning to the same theme: the fears and hatreds that ignited the legal persecution of the nine Scottsboro defendants and that had served as the foundation for the policies adopted by the white southern leadership in the aftermath of the Civil War. I had grown up immersed in that evangelical religious culture that, however captive to the culture around it, seemed incompatible with the worst cruelties of white supremacy. What compulsion, I kept asking myself, drove my great-grandfather and his brothers and kin and most of the men of his generation to acts that did such harm to the black men and women in their midst?

Most reviewers described *Scottsboro* and *When the War Was Over* as bleak and depressing stories — and they were — but I still believed when I wrote those books that telling these stories could help us understand something of the weight and complexity of our nation's heritage of racial oppression and discrimination. I believed that truth-telling about the southern, *and American*, past could make a difference in shaping people's commitments and their actions.

For years, I kept above my desk a quotation from a speech Robert Kennedy had given at the University of Cape Town, South Africa, in 1966, when the only future for that country seemed a bloodbath as whites fought to the death to maintain their privilege and power, and black South Africans seemed to confront an equally grim choice: submission to oppression or a death struggle that would leave the country a wasteland. Kennedy confronted that despair head-on. The great danger that all of us face, he said:

> [is the despairing] belief there is nothing one man or one woman can do against the enormous array of the world's ills — against misery and ignorance, injustice and violence.... [It is true] that few will have the greatness to bend history itself; but each of us can work to change a small portion of events....

It is from those numberless diverse acts of courage and belief that human history is shaped. Each time a man stands up for an ideal, or acts to improve the lot of others, or strikes out against injustice, he sends a tiny ripple of hope, and crossing each other from a million different centers of energy and daring these ripples build a current which can sweep down the mightiest walls of oppression and resistance.[10]

In the mid-1960s — even as late as the election of Jimmy Carter — I still looked to a day when a racially healed South might offer to the nation an opportunity for redemption instead of an object lesson in hate. But as the events of the 1970s and 1980s unfolded, it was clear that Alabama governor George Wallace, not Georgia's ex-president Jimmy Carter, was the southerner whose mark had been left upon American society.

I suppose I will always be described as a "southern" historian, but my study of George Wallace made me rethink many of my earlier assumptions about the South as a distinct region.[11] Of course it has a different past, but I came to believe that historians' focus on the uniqueness (and perniciousness) of antebellum slavery and legal segregation through the mid-twentieth century had sometimes obscured the ways in which differences between "North" and "South" had been eroding for nearly a century. John Egerton had it right when he came up with the title of his 1974 book, *The Americanization of Dixie: The Southernization of America*, and few things better illustrated that theme than the career of George Wallace.[12]

There was never any likelihood that the Alabama politician would be elected president of the United States; he was too raw, too crude, too southern. But he had been one of the great transitional figures in American politics: poltergeist and weathervane in the America of the 1960s and 1970s. His speeches and campaigns combined the traditional conservative agenda — a bellicose foreign policy, low taxes, and a limited federal government — with the new social agenda. It was George Wallace who first articulated the full range of this new political agenda: from anger over the Supreme Court's rejection of prayer in the schools, through angry denunciations of busing, outrage over pornography, and resentment over the expenditure of public resources for the poor. The neoconservative political movement of the 1970s and 1980s had many sources, but it was George Wallace who furnished the passion and paved the way for later politicians. He had foreseen the tide on which Ronald Reagan sailed into the White House. When Wallace retired from public life in 1986, the nation's newspaper of record, the *New York Times*, argued that it was Wallace who had "sniffed out early the changes America came to know by many names: white backlash . . . the silent majority . . . the alienated voters . . . the emerging Republican majority."[13]

Most of all, with a skillful use of euphemisms and code words, he had made it possible to use race in a way that seemed to be disappearing in the late 1960s. In tracing the line that ran directly from George Wallace's 1963 "Stand in the Schoolhouse Door" to Richard Nixon's "Southern Strategy," through Ronald Reagan's amiable harangues against "welfare queens" to George H. W. Bush's use of the Willie Horton case in 1992 to George W. Bush's attack on affirmative action, I came to see that the racial fears of white northerners and white southerners had come together in a way that I could not have anticipated in the 1960s. As we move further into the twenty-first century, the connection between the southern past and present remains, but it is no longer fixed in a distinctive history of "northern" or "southern" history set resolutely in apposition to each other. (And in truth it never did.)[14]

This is not to say that Wallace-style racism has triumphed in American politics. In my southern childhood the "single drop" theory of race was almost unchallenged. Black was black. Period. The elevation of African Americans and Hispanics to positions of authority in the presidential administration of George W. Bush shows that money, education, and shared ideology "whitens" some black and brown people in the eyes of a growing number of whites. And the unseating of Senator Trent Lott from his position as Senate Republican leader in December 2002 for his comments endorsing Strom Thurmond's 1948 Dixiecrat campaign points to the political eclipse of classical racism in its cruder guises. Assumptions about race continue to play a continuing role in our culture, but these covert assumptions are increasingly smothered by a rhetoric of racial equality.

Even though the vocabulary of equal rights is shared by most Americans — even though "racial integration" may be practiced on an individual level — race remains the great dividing line in American society. The social-science data is conclusive: in our schools, in our churches, in our social organizations, and in our neighborhoods, black and white are becoming *more* segregated. But that return toward racial separation is no longer a matter of great concern to most Americans. Certainly most of my white students believe that racial issues are a historical problem of their grandparents (at most their parents') generation.

Neither are issues of economic inequality. I have often found it ironic that the outcry over economic as well as racial inequality came in the 1960s when the gap between rich and poor (if not between black and white) was less than at any time since the 1920s. Yet today, when each year brings new statistics confirming the triumph of the super-rich and the continuing struggles of the poor to survive, questions about economic inequality are as intellectually remote to most of my students as the controversy over Anne Hutchinson's expulsion from the Massachusetts Bay Colony for her antinomian beliefs. And not surprisingly, for they have grown up in a world in which the worshipful euphemisms of "free enterprise" have replaced the complex realities of capitalism and the rhetorical promises of the "opportunity society" obscure (what I believe to be) the dispiriting reality of a society increasingly divided between the super-rich, a comfortable upper-middle class, a large but precarious middle class, and millions of Americans struggling to survive from one week to the next.

At the same time, the "freedom revolution" of the 1960s and 1970s has been severed from its original belief that grassroots civic involvement could transform society. As we begin the twenty-first century, most Americans — certainly most white Americans — reject the notion that government can play a role in ameliorating racial and economic inequality. "Freedom" has come to mean a liberation from social responsibility as well as from repressive social conventions, and liberalism increasingly survives as the libertarianism of the self-obsessed. As novelist George Packer put it, "Freedom is the bottom line in America: freedom to earn, freedom to spend, freedom to start a new life." Throughout our history, one of the vital forces was a yearning for a future America variously described as "community" or "the beloved Republic" (or even socialism). Today such ideas can only be described with irony and enclosed in quotation marks. With the collapse of a broad faith in the earlier promises of social democracy, we are left only with the uneasy hope that capitalism's market mechanisms can save us from our future.[15]

"Books," wrote the English essayist and dramatist Joseph Addison, "are the legacies that a great genius leaves to mankind, which are delivered down from generation to generation, as presents to the posterity of those who are yet unborn."[16] Most of us are not geniuses, however, and few historians write today in ways that speak beyond their own generation. In my own case, I have never been particularly comfortable with many of the conventions of my profession. Creating a distinctive historical interpretation (often utilizing new literary or social-science theory) has become increasingly important in staking out a position within the community of historians. Whenever such issues emerge in spirited historical debate, however, I often find myself assuming that pleasant but rather vacant expression I'm sure all of you have seen when a childless guest is trapped by a particularly enthusiastic older colleague just back from a visit with his or her new grandchildren. The truth is that I'm basically interested in telling a story, in much the same way my grandfather told his stories on the porch of my home in Effingham a long time ago.

And even the very best in our field—C. Vann Woodward, Perry Miller, and Richard Hofstadter come to mind—all too often survive as intellectual roadmaps to earlier ways of thinking rather than as a creators of a bracing encounter between past and present. Most of the yearly tide of historical works that pour out from our presses are quickly forgotten as changing fashions and differing assumptions within our society create a new conversation with the past, and it is no more fruitful to lament this reality than to brood over our own physical mortality.

As today's new blend of conservative politics and libertarian culture overshadows the political liberalism of my early life, my interest in the historical nexus between racial and economic inequality and the political economy that sustains it increasingly seems an echo of half-forgotten battles. While there will continue to be scholars (and readers) for whom these questions are important, I am inclined to believe that—absent some striking upheaval in our national and regional life—they are not likely to engage readers over the next thirty years.

Still, I keep remembering that the past, and the present, is not a roadmap to the future. Clarence Bacote joined the faculty at Atlanta University in 1930 and until his death in 1981 taught and published on African American history. During the 1930s he helped revitalize the local NAACP; during the 1940s he was one of the founders of the Atlanta Negro Voters League and created a network of "citizenship schools" to prepare black citizens for registering and voting in central Georgia. On one Saturday after another, he gathered together a collection of pamphlets and leaflets and hit the streets of Atlanta, urging embittered and often defeated black folks to register, to vote, and to become involved in civic and community life. This began in 1931, at a time when only a handful of African Americans could vote. He went out on those streets for year after year after year with almost no results. Year after year he taught students who were going out into a fiercely segregated South that seemed immovable.

I once asked him how he did it and he laughed as he always did: "Easy, you just get up out of bed: you put on your britches one leg at a time and you go." He was a good storyteller, and the punch line always followed the joke. "Remember John Quincy Adams, one of those 'good white guys,'" Clarence said with a wink. "Remember? 'Think of your forefathers; think of your posterity.'"

Whatever the future, I remain convinced that we can learn something about ourselves — how we have lived and how we should live — by continuing to wrestle with our past, the myths as well as the harder truths. I hope I have contributed to that conversation in my writing and in my teaching of forty years, but the truth is: the study of the South and its fierce encounter with our nation's history has been reward enough.

Notes

1. Portions of this essay appeared in different form in "Reflections of a Reconstructed White Southerner," in Paul A. Cimbala and Robert F. Himmelberg, eds., *Historians and Race: Autobiography and the Writing of History* (Bloomington and Indianapolis, 1996), 33–50.
2. Shakespeare, *The Tempest*, act 3, scene 2, line 155.
3. "Memory," line 1, in Arthur Quiller-Couch, ed., *The Oxford Book of English Verse, 1250–1900* (Oxford, Eng., 1927), 544 [selection 468].
4. David C. Carter, "Outraged Justice: The Lynching of Postmaster Frazier Baker in Lake City, South Carolina, 1897–98" (B.A. thesis, University of North Carolina, 1992).
5. *Strange Career* (New York, 1955); *Burden of Southern History* (New York, 1960); *The Souls of Black Folk* (Chicago, 1903); *Southern Heritage* (New York, 1958); *Mind of the South* (New York, 1941); *The Other America* (New York, 1962).
6. William Faulkner, *Absalom, Absalom* (New York, 1936), 357–58.
7. David Harlan, *The Degradation of American History* (Chicago, 1997), xv–xxxiii.
8. Dan T. Carter, *Scottsboro* (Baton Rouge, 1969).
9. Dan T. Carter, *When the War Was Over: The Failure of Self-Reconstruction in the South, 1865–1867* (Baton Rouge, 1985).
10. Quoted in Arthur M. Schlesinger Jr., *Robert F. Kennedy and His Times* (Boston, 1978), 2:779–80.

11. Dan T. Carter, *The Politics of Rage: George Wallace, the Origins of the New Conservatism, and the Transformation of American Politics* (New York, 1995).

12. John Egerton, *The Americanization of Dixie* (New York, 1974).

13. *New York Times*, April 4, 1986, p. A30.

14. It is an argument I developed in the Fleming lectures I gave at LSU in 1991 and elaborated upon in *From George Wallace to Newt Gingrich: Race in the Conservative Counterrevolution, 1963–1994* (Baton Rouge, 1996).

15. George Packer, *Blood of the Liberals* (New York, 2000), 350–51, 388–89.

16. Richard Hurd, ed., *The Works of the Right Honourable Joseph Addison* (London, 1856), 3:16.

From Here to There and Back Again

Adventures of a Southern Historian

CHARLES JOYNER

I look back on my boyhood through a haze of memories. My earliest recollections of Myrtle Beach, South Carolina, evoke the smell of salt spray and the touch of beach sand, damp and cool against my bare feet. My world was bounded by the woods, a dirt road, and the Atlantic Ocean. Behind us were the woods; but Thirty-eighth Avenue, unpaved until the 1950s, ran right by our house and two blocks down to the beach. My brothers and I made the beach our playground.

I remember nights by an open window, listening to the sounds of the surf rising in the darkness as my brothers and I tried to fall asleep in those hot southern nights before air conditioning. I was certain that the sound of those waves held the secret of life. Some people believe the sea divides, but I knew somehow that the sea unites. I knew that the waters that washed our shores connected me to people across the ocean whose shores were washed by the same waters. The coast, where the sea meets the land, is a good place to ponder connections: the connections of sea to land, of nature to human beings, of Europe and Africa to America, of tradition to change, of environment and economy to culture.

In those saltwater years of my youth I had vague and mostly mistaken ideas of what lay beyond the horizon, but it already inflamed my imagination. I used to stand at the edge of the sea and think to myself that, if I looked hard enough, I could see England. But England is not directly across the Atlantic from South Carolina — Morocco is. And because I was peering across the Atlantic toward a point exactly perpendicular to the slanting shoreline of South Carolina's upper coast, I was actually looking even further south — toward Nigeria and Ghana.

I inherited a strong sense of place from my mother's family, who were early settlers in South Carolina.[1] Carolinians began as many peoples. More than any English mainland colony, however, South Carolina's roots were Caribbean. Many of her early settlers were English by way of the West Indies, especially by way of Barbados. Barbadians controlled the provincial government and determined the course of South Carolina's politics for almost half a century. One of the Barbadians was Robert Daniel, who arrived in 1690 and quickly established himself as a leading figure in local politics. An authentic military hero of the St. Augustine expedition of 1704, he was a highly controversial acting governor of South Carolina in 1716 and 1717.

The Huguenots, a group of French Protestants, were an ethnic group of special importance in early South Carolina. Suffering what they regarded as acute persecution during the reign of Louis XIV, thousands of Huguenots fled to America at the end of the seventeenth century. One of them was Daniel Horry. A native of the ancient province of Angoumois, Horry arrived in Charleston in April 1692. Soon he married another Huguenot, Elizabeth Garnier, from the Isle de Ré off La Rochelle. The couple applied for English citizenship, but by the time their naturalization was granted several years later, Daniel Horry had died.

Three different groups of Scots were important in early South Carolina — lowlanders, highlanders, and the ambiguously designated Scotch-Irish, who were known in Britain as Ulster Scots (and other less pleasant names). Lowlanders were among the earliest Charleston merchants. In the early eighteenth century tens of thousands of Scotch-Irish came to South Carolina, becoming the great pioneers of the upcountry. Following the infamous highland clearances in the old country, large numbers of kilted highlanders came to the Pee Dee region of South Carolina. Among the Scotch-Irish was young John Beaty, a native of County Cavan, Ireland, who emigrated to Carolina from Belfast around 1723. The name Beaty had been indigenous to the Scottish border since the fourteenth century. John Beaty's decision to emigrate to Carolina apparently did not meet with parental approval. His father left him one pound in his will in 1741, because of his alleged disobedience. Nevertheless, by 1736 John Beaty was a landowner in the newly created Kingston Township.

The Barbadians, the Huguenots, and the Scotch-Irish often despised one another in the crucible of the growing young colony. But as the generations passed, Europeans of various ethnic groups mixed here in ways that rarely occurred in Europe. Barbadians, Huguenots, and Scotch-Irish were able to put aside at least some of their ethnic prejudices. The great-granddaughter of the Huguenots Daniel and Elizabeth Horry married the grandson of Scotch-Irish immigrant John Beaty. Their daughter married the great-grandson of the Barbadian Robert Daniel. And *their* granddaughter married a descendant of Scottish highlanders connected to Clan Cameron. The names of this last couple were Mary Eady Wilson and Nathan Paul. They lived in Horry County, and their granddaughter Kelly was my mother. The fusion of folk cultures in South Carolina is more than an abstraction to me.

The Joyners have been ramblers at least since 1635, when young Thomas Joyner left Bere Regis, Dorset, in England for Isle of Wight County, Virginia. Abraham Joyner, his great-grandson, moved from Virginia to Northampton County, North Carolina, in the early eighteenth century. And Giles Joyner, my great-grandfather, moved from North Carolina to Alabama in the 1850s. His son Will was born in Alabama in 1857 but grew up in an orphanage in Mississippi. Will's son Winston, my father, was born in Sucharnoochie, Mississippi, in 1901.

My people had been farmers for generations, but Winston Joyner wanted to make a more lasting mark on this earth than the furrow of a plow through the soil. He fled the drudgery of farm life in the Mississippi flatwoods to become part of South Carolina's bulldozer revolution: he helped build concrete highways. He covered much of the landscape of South Carolina with them in the 1920s and 1930s, and he built them to last. He took pride in the roads he constructed, and he was very pleased that the last three concrete highways in South Carolina to be covered with asphalt were highways he helped to build. He met my mother, Kelly Paul, while he was building Highway 701 between Conway and Georgetown in coastal South Carolina along the Waccamaw River, and they married in 1930. I, their firstborn, came into the world in 1935 in the midst of the Great Depression. Ultimately they would have four more sons and finally a daughter. Until World War II we lived all over South Carolina, wherever highways were being built.

My formal education began with first grade in upstate Pickens in 1941. Even then I was interested in history. My parents had given me my first book when I could barely read, before I went to school. It was a book of the American presidents, with a picture and a short biography of each president from Washington to Franklin Roosevelt on facing pages. I practically memorized it. I completed the first grade at what was then called Inland School, near Bucksport, where my mother grew up in coastal South Carolina. One teacher taught the first three grades. During about a third of each school day, we first graders had to wait or read on our own while the second and third graders recited. It was a valuable lesson in patience and self-education.

My primary school years coincided with World War II, and I was very conscious that history was taking place in my own lifetime. My family spent the war years in Mt. Pleasant, near Charleston, where my father was involved in war work at the Charleston Navy Yard. I wrote frequent letters to my Uncle Odell, a Seabee in the South Pacific; and I listened to the radio newscasts with my father. I quickly came to recognize the voices of Edward R. Murrow, H. V. Kaltenborn, and other newscasters. I also kept a scrapbook of newspaper clippings about the war, from Pearl Harbor through North Africa, Anzio, Normandy, Iwo Jima, and Hiroshima, from "a day that will live in infamy" to D-Day, VE-Day, and VJ-Day.

My earliest introduction to the relationship between history and folk culture came from a wonderful local historian in Mt. Pleasant named Petrona Royall McIver. "Miss Petey" not only tutored me in the Presbyterian Shorter Catechism but also stirred my youthful imagination with the history of Gullah culture, the culture created by African Americans who had labored on the rice plantations along the Cooper River. She told me of the beautiful hand-coiled rice "fanner baskets" they made there, like the ones their ancestors had made in Africa. It was she who first suggested to me two close relationships that have influenced my approach to history. The first was the bond between history and folk culture. The second was the connection between places, the same connection that I had first sensed gazing across the Atlantic. She made it clear to me that in order to understand this one small place, one had to know a great deal about the history and culture of three continents—Europe and Africa as well as America. I did not at the time connect the kind of microhistory I was learning informally from her with the kind of generalized macrohistory I loved in school. But later it would become very influential on the way I would approach my work as a historian.

After the war we moved to Myrtle Beach, where I was fortunate to study history not with the coach (who taught math) but with Mary Miller Long, who taught history with an emphasis on movements and motivation. She introduced me to history as an intellectual activity by assigning me the task of defending the English side in a debate on the American Revolution. It had never before occurred to me that there might be any justification for the English effort to hold on to their colonies until I began to prepare my arguments. That was the first time it had ever dawned on me that the study of history was something more than just memorizing interesting facts, that it involved issues that were intellectually exciting. From then on I was hooked.

My parents were part of that southern generation that grew up on farms and moved to the towns. So I was a town boy, in a Myrtle Beach of approximately four thousand year-round souls. But I always looked forward eagerly to visiting my cousins on my uncles' tobacco farms over at Bucksport, where my mother came from. I worked some of the children's jobs at harvest time — or "putting in," as we called it. I "drove a crate," guiding a mule pulling a high-sided wagon on sledlike runners between the rows of tobacco, where it was loaded by "croppers" with leaves of tobacco carefully picked, or "cropped," from the very bottoms of the stalks. I was too young to crop, but from observing the adults I concluded that cropping tobacco — bent double in the hot sun picking sticky tobacco leaves from the bottom of the stalk with one hand and stuffing them under the other arm until one could hold no more — must surely be the hardest work ever devised for human beings. My job was to guide the mule back to the barn and to unload the tobacco for the "stringers," who attached the leaves to sticks that would hang in the curing barn. On each side of the stringers stood "handers" — kids like me who "handed" the sticky leaves to the stringers with the stem ends up. Some days I was a hander instead of a driver. I always marveled at the speed with which the stringers could fill a stick with tobacco.

Before oil replaced wood for curing tobacco, someone had to stay up all night to regulate the heat in the tobacco barns. Often there was a party to help keep that someone awake, with chickenbog and other delicacies to eat, with banjo-picking and storytelling. I always thought the grownups made me go to bed too early. And I have never lost my interest in banjo-picking and storytelling.

When I was a boy, I used to love the hunting and fishing stories of Archibald Rutledge, although I was too poor a shot to be a hunter. If I could ever hit a target with my Red Ryder BB gun, my brother Paul could always shoot a circle around the spot. But I grew up in a hunting and fishing society, and my cousin Laird Staley and I devoured Archibald Rutledge's stories of hunting and fishing excursions with his black companions. Laird used to complain that I spent too much time *reading* about hunting and fishing and too little time trying to *do* any. But I shall never forget one fishing expedition with Laird when I was a boy.

One spring in the 1940s we had a great freshet, or flood, in the Waccamaw Swamps. The water was so high that the Bucksport dock was under water, and so was about a mile of the road to it. To get to Bucksport, we had to go down the road in a boat. Laird and I built a raft so we could paddle out in the swamp and hang fishhooks in the trees, hoping to catch some mudfish. Our raft was more or less like Huckleberry Finn's, except that ours was smaller and less stable. And ours tipped over. I could not swim. But it was a good day to learn.

Music was always an important part of my life. As a young boy I listened to country music on the radio and plunked away on the banjo my mother gave me, the banjo she had played as a young girl. We got a piano when I was about seven, and I quickly learned to play by ear. We did not have a record player, but I was especially drawn to blues and boogie-woogie on the radio.

I also loved the music I heard each Sunday at the First Presbyterian Church, about two miles south of our house in Myrtle Beach. It was good that I did, for my attendance was never optional. In my family it would have done no more good to have minded going to church than to have minded heat in the summertime. But I loved the old hymns and the sounds of the harmonies as we sang. I joined the church choir in my early teens, as soon as my voice changed from my childhood alto to a deep bass. I learned to read music (at least one line at a time) while in the choir.

Our church held its first desegregated service about 1950. A Boston Braves farm team held its spring training in Myrtle Beach. One Sunday an African American baseball player appeared with several of his white teammates. They were seated and worshipped among us without incident. There was a good deal of talk afterward about what should or should not be done if they returned. But they did not return, and for the time being instinctive good manners prevailed over prepared bigotry.

I remember many of our pastor's sermons fondly. I was especially impressed with the way he could illustrate theology through good stories. I think my early recognition of the power of storytelling to clarify complex situations has had a lasting effect on how I try to write history, even (or perhaps especially) when my purpose is more analytical than narrative, as it would be years later when I was trying to write what would become *Down by the Riverside*. Perhaps because I was quick to season my manuscript with the various stories I found in my research, I eventually came to recognize the *big* story that all the *little* stories helped to tell.

Storytelling is a very southern mode of discourse; and our pastor, the Reverend Cecil Brearley, was a gifted storyteller. I recall vividly one of his sermons, disguised as a story about a man who did his work so thoroughly that he could "sleep when the wind blows." I have remembered that sermon during several hurricanes in my hometown. I think of Hurricane Hazel, which struck Myrtle Beach in October 1954, as a calamity of mythic proportions. Even today it continues to mark the dividing line in my consciousness between the past and the present, between what we were and what we have become, between the home I loved in my youth and the unforeseeable entity it is becoming.

Work was woven into our lives as deeply as religion. It may seem peculiar that the work ethic was so strong in Myrtle Beach, where so many tourists came to play. The tourist industry offered the opportunity — and the necessity — for summer jobs. Some folks in Myrtle Beach back then liked to say that "they work us to death all summer and starve us to death all winter."

I first worked for newspapers on a paper route at the age of ten, then sold papers to tourists on Ocean Boulevard the summer after I turned twelve. That fall I took a job in the print shop of our local weekly. After that I worked at a self-service laundry until at thirteen I took a better-paying summer job as a grease monkey in the Myrtle Beach municipal garage. One of my tasks was to lubricate the police cars. A policeman complained that I missed grease fittings. I said that I could not remember where all those grease fittings were. My father, who had become superintendent of the Myrtle Beach Street Department, told me that I did not need to remember where the grease fittings were located, I merely needed to remember what they were there for. Wherever two pieces of metal rubbed together, I should look for a grease fitting nearby. It was a breakthrough for me from a world of education as memorizing to a world of education as disciplined thinking. And I was able to extrapolate from the grease fittings to the real meaning of his lesson: If I could learn how things work, I could figure out how to deal with them. I have never forgotten that. It was perhaps the single most important lesson of my life.

At fourteen I obtained my driver's license and became a truck driver for the city during the summers and on Saturdays during the school year. Usually I drove a dump truck back and forth to an area where a marina was being dug beside the inland waterway. Several times a day I backed down a long narrow fill under a dragline that deposited a mixture of sand and shell known as coquina into the bed of my truck. In Myrtle Beach in the 1940s and 1950s we paved streets with this mixture. Although I came within ten miles of the North Carolina line several times a day for the next two years, it would not be until after I had graduated from high school that I would see what lay north of that border.

In the fall of 1951, during my senior year in high school, I was employed by a new real-estate and investment company. That led to another office job in the summer of 1952, one I would hold for the next six years. While the Myrtle Beach Farms Company actually owned some farms, its main business was resort development. It was, in fact, the company that had first developed Myrtle Beach. My main job was to count the money that came in from the rides and concessions at the Myrtle Beach Pavilion, at that time the hub of Myrtle Beach. In 1955 I took on an additional night job as box-office manager of the Myrtle Beach Playhouse, a professional summer stock company offering live theater to tourists and local residents, mostly light comedies with stars whose careers by then were largely behind them.

So part of my parents' legacy to me was a strong and very Calvinistic work ethic, a charge to achieve, to subordinate pleasure to duty. I can well remember my mother telling me, when I was about fourteen years old, that if anyone had told her when I was born that I would not be *at least* governor by now.... She did not finish the sentence. She did not need to. My parents imposed no blueprint for what I was supposed to become when I grew up, but they made it clear that they expected me to amount to *something*.

As I look back over my boyhood, I absorbed without reflection the breathtaking beauty of my state from the mountains to the sea. And with no greater contemplation I soaked up the traditions of those Barbadian Anglicans, French Huguenots, and Scotch-Irish dissenters who had been my ancestors — their contradictory faiths in liberty, equality, and white supremacy, their embrace of human bondage in a new nation consecrated to freedom, and their elevation of the natural right to property over the natural right to liberty. I knew that my ancestors fought with the rebellious thirteen colonies that proclaimed their secession from the British empire and with the rebellious eleven states that proclaimed their secession from the United States of America. But *my* country was the United States, not the Confederacy. I was a boy during World War II, and I was the patriotic product of a time as well as of a place. I was an American, at a time when my country was engaged in a great global war with the Axis powers to determine whether our nation, or any democracy, could endure. My efforts to confront my own contradictions and complexities required that I confront those of my region as well. It was not easy for me to understand how *my* ancestors, who had fought for the Confederacy, could have fought against *my* country.

I received one of my first lessons in what racism cost the South when I learned as a youngster that my Uncle Giles had been murdered in Mississippi in 1935. He was a game warden, barely thirty-five years old when he was killed by a poacher he was attempting to apprehend. The only witnesses were the killer's two black employees. They reported what they had seen to the investigating officers, but my uncle's killer went free because the law would not allow black men to testify against white men in Mississippi courts. So as a boy I was touched with at least a tacit knowledge that we southerners had a deeper and more tragic past than the one purveyed in the history textbooks I encountered in high school. I knew somehow even then that our Southland was a complex and contradictory society, one that had kept much of its folk culture well into the mid-twentieth century — along with a sense of continuity, a sense of the enduring past, and an awareness in our bones that history was not just something unpleasant that happened someplace else.

Eventually I went away to college. Nobody in my family had ever graduated from college before. In fact, neither of my parents had finished high school. To this day, I do not understand why they were so fiercely determined that their children would have college educations. But the abundance of summer jobs for their children in Myrtle Beach helped to make their dream financially possible. I went away to Presbyterian College, in the upstate college town of Clinton, South Carolina, where I majored in history and English. The new freshman class brought the student enrollment to just over five hundred. We were a homogeneous lot on the whole, overwhelmingly male and almost all southern white Protestants. Sprinkled among us were fewer than a dozen women, a few Catholics, and a handful of northerners. When I arrived at Presbyterian College, World War II had been over for less than a decade, and there were still a good many veterans in the student body. They lent an aura of seriousness to our classrooms.

These were years of striving for self-discovery, trying to attain a clearer personal understanding of life's essentials. Most of us experienced personal crises of love, faith, friendship, and death among friends or family while at Presbyterian College. But little in the classrooms challenged our provincialism, or our complacency, or our racism in those placid years of the 1950s.

The real challenge to my provincialism came from an unexpected quarter —

the college choir. Dr. Edouard Patte, our Swiss-born choir director, announced early in the spring of 1954 that on our spring tour through the Deep South we were going to sing at Stillman College, a black Presbyterian institution in Tuscaloosa, Alabama. We would be guests of Stillman, he said; and as they would be gracious hosts, we must be gracious guests. He expected us to be friendly, shake hands, and live up to the South's reputation for good manners. Without preaching (although he was an ordained minister), Dr. Patte did more to instill in his choirboys a Christian understanding of the relationship of all God's children to one another than either our chapel services or our formal education. But southern etiquette at the time did not countenance interracial handshaking. Dr. Patte left it up to us, but he did not make it easy to dodge the dilemma. If we were unable, or unwilling, to be gracious guests, we were not required to come along on the trip. But of course we knew that if we did not make the trip, we would miss our visit to New Orleans.

The choir members reacted in varying ways. I remember one student who dropped out of the choir then and there, although he never acknowledged his reason. Another announced that it did not bother him one bit. He had got on well with "darkies" all his life, he said. That student would later move beyond such condescending paternalism to become one of the most eminent ministers in our denomination and a personal friend of several important civil rights leaders. Despite my heterodox notions about the Civil War, I was no rebel against segregation then. Segregation, after all, still prevailed all over the country. In my quiet and timid bigotry I said nothing; but inwardly I determined that I would not enjoy it, and that I certainly was not going to shake hands with any black students.

Against my better judgment, I relished our visit to Stillman College immensely. We ate with our hosts in the college dining hall and attended their choir rehearsal. Their singing put us to shame. At our own concert that night, the "Amen" we sang following Dr. Patte's benediction was so dreadfully out-of-tune that even Stravinsky would have found it discordant. The "Stillman Amen" became legendary in the choir. Despite our embarrassment, we all enjoyed our visit to Stillman. For me it was life-changing. Despite my earlier resolution, I did shake hands with black students. The color did not rub off, but I know *something* had.

After graduating from Presbyterian College I went to the University of South Carolina to study for a master's degree in history. USC started its Oxford Visiting Professor program the year I arrived, and I was able to study Tudor-Stuart England with a distinguished retired Oxford professor, David Ogg. The following year I studied the French Revolution with an up-and-coming young visiting Oxonian named John Roberts, who would go on to become a famous scholar and "telly don" on the BBC.

In American history I studied with William Best Hesseltine, who was visiting from the University of Wisconsin. To say that Hesseltine was eccentric is to understate. He had little respect for teaching, only for scholarship. If a graduate student asked him to direct his dissertation, he had a stock reply: "I don't direct dissertations. Can you write a book?" Hesseltine believed in "publish or perish" even for high-school teachers. His scholarship has not stood the test of time well, but he was certainly a stimulating teacher. I had earlier encountered teachers given to sweeping (and dubious) generalizations, but I had never before studied with a teacher who would deliberately lie about factual details and then berate students for failing to challenge him.

I first recognized the potential of folklore as a means of researching history in Howard Quint's seminar on American social movements. We in the seminar tried to emphasize public opinion, but we were all impatient with the inadequacies of newspaper editorials, political speeches, and sermons as evidence of public opinion. We regarded such sources as examples of what the public was being told, not evidence of what the public was thinking. Writing a master's thesis on the radical response of early-twentieth-century Rocky Mountain miners to the industrial system, I stumbled upon songs made up by the miners themselves and sent in to labor newspapers. While details were not always accurate, I recognized the value of such sources as clues to the mentality and motivation of the miners. But I did not recognize a larger significance in my subject than the obvious dissonance between the rights of freedom of the press and the rights of defendants to a fair trial.

Soon afterward I heard similar songs on a record by a group called the Weavers. The Weavers also sang songs from other historical movements, as well as many of the very same songs I had heard around the tobacco barns in Horry County. And they called all those songs *folk songs*. Since in the late 1950s I still considered history to be mainly the study of political events and movements, I did not immediately recognize any potential usefulness in the nonpolitical songs. But I realized that these movement songs could be important sources. Thus from the time I was a graduate student in history in the late 1950s, my research interests were already being shaped by a leaning toward studying the lives of the folk, the men and women earlier ignored by mainstream historical scholarship.

I was drafted into the army in 1958, first for basic training at Fort Jackson, South Carolina, then as a personnel clerk in Officers' Records at Fort Belvoir, Virginia, and finally as a military historian at the Army Chemical Center in Maryland. Because I had already earned a master's degree in history, I was assigned to a team writing a history of the Army Chemical Corps in World War II. Cranking out the "official version" of Chemical Corps history struck me as a form of intellectual dishonesty. One of my fellow conscripts on the team advised me simply to write my drafts honestly and save my carbons. The army had level upon level of censors who would be only too happy to revise my words into the "official version." That helped for a while, but eventually I wanted my own words to stand. It was easy for censors to remove adjectives, but harder to remove verbs, since they had to be replaced. So I tried to develop a writing style with strong verbs, a writing style harder for them to change.

Military service was not without its compensations. It was not until I was in the army that I actually knew any black people on racially equal terms and was thus able to form any real interracial friendships. Three of my closest friends in the army were black, and I played piano in an interracial jazz combo that played clubs around Washington and nearby Maryland and Virginia. By then the army no longer made concessions to segregationist sensibilities. I succeeded in keeping America safe during my watch, but I believe that the experience did more for me than I did for my country.

When my active duty was up in 1960, I returned to South Carolina to pursue a doctoral program in history. But I brought a lot of new experiences and new insights with me. And I was now eager to do my part in the new movement that was trying to do something about the social system that had held my native region back for so long.

Back at the University of South Carolina I studied with Avery O. Craven, visiting from the University of Chicago. Craven was then the country's leading scholar of the coming of the Civil War. Inclined toward pacifism as a Quaker, Craven had found the Civil War eminently "repressible." He was already in his late seventies, well past what was then considered "normal" retirement age. But intellectually he was not only still alert, he was still growing, still a hands-on historian, still researching in the archives. And, in the light of what was taking place in the world around us, especially the Civil Rights movement, he was rethinking the implications of his having earlier minimized the role of slavery as a cause of the Civil War. I shared with Craven a sense of being caught between conflicting values. One was a kind of pacifism that recoiled at the sheer bloodletting of the Civil War. The other was a contradictory sense that, horrible as war is, some causes are worth fighting for. I had responded to my military experience with an outburst of antimilitarism. But, as an idealistic young graduate student, fresh from two years of integrated experience in the army, I was also deeply involved in the quest for racial equality, deeply involved in efforts to organize a statewide biracial student movement.

I shared an apartment at 1015 Henderson Street in Columbia with three remarkable young southerners—Selden Smith, Dan T. Carter, and Hayes Mizell. All four of us were graduate students in history, and we shared idealistic visions of a better South as well as grandiose dreams of professional success and dire apprehensions of personal failure. We also shared the experience of coming of age when one kind of South was falling and another kind of South was struggling to rise, when the present was as exciting as any time in history. We were no longer willing to accept the old definitions of southern history as "the glorious deeds of the glorious dead." We knew that precious little of the past was glorious, and we knew that southern history was still happening all around us. Nor were we any longer willing to accept the old definitions that depicted "the South" (meaning whites) versus the "Civil Rights movement" (meaning blacks). We knew that blacks were as "southern" as whites; and we knew that there were white southerners *within* the Civil Rights movement as well as *opposed* to it. We knew, because we were four of those participants. We shared much more than an apartment; we became lifelong friends. Another lasting friend from those years was William W. Freehling, a young graduate student from Berkeley, who spent a year in South Carolina researching his dissertation on the nullification crisis.

Helping to organize a statewide interracial student movement, the South Carolina Student Council on Human Relations, we were powerfully influenced by an extraordinary group of men and women we came to know whose deep love of the South, as Dan would later write, had included a long hard struggle "to keep alive the dream of racial justice during the height of racial reaction in the 1950s and early 1960s."[2] They included Alice Spearman and her associate, Elizabeth Ledeen, of the parent body, the South Carolina Council on Human Relations. They also included James McBride Dabbs of Maysville, South Carolina, president of the Southern Regional Council and author of *The Southern Heritage*. Like an Old Testament prophet, Dabbs called upon his fellow southerners "to face up to their racial as well as their individual sins, and to repent." He said it was our *responsibility*—as southerners—to build a new South of racial reconciliation and to offer the wider world an example of racial harmony.[3]

Our apartment became something of a crossroads of the Civil Rights movement in South Carolina, host to various civil rights workers as they came through the state. In Columbia, as well as in conferences at Penn Center on St. Helena Island, South Carolina, we also encountered somewhat younger activists, such as the remarkable young preacher Andrew Young, the dedicated Connie Curry, the inimitable Will Campbell, the committed Casey Hayden and her pugnacious husband, Tom. We engaged in long and intense discussions with Modjeska Simkins, founder of the South Carolina Conference of the National Association for the Advancement of Colored People (NAACP), and with Ella Baker, the first executive director of the Southern Christian Leadership Conference (SCLC) and the unofficial godmother of the Student Nonviolent Coordinating Committee (SNCC). I was her chauffeur when she was in Columbia, and I learned a great deal while "driving Miss Baker."

Music played an important part in my involvement in the Civil Rights movement. Time and again I witnessed the overwhelming power of traditional African American preaching styles in mass meetings. Time and again I felt the heart-stirring inspiration of the magnificent old spirituals with their exciting new "freedom" lyrics. Perhaps because I had learned to play the guitar in the army and knew so many freedom songs, I was elected the first president of the statewide biracial student movement—the South Carolina Student Council on Human Relations.

As the movement grew, sit-ins and other antisegregation protests intensified across the state—in Columbia, in Greenville, in Orangeburg, in Rock Hill. The segregationists mobilized for all-out resistance. Red-baiting was organized on a statewide scale by such groups as the Citizens Councils, the John Birch Society, and Operation Alert. SLED (the State Law Enforcement Division) was called out to investigate the so-called "subversives." A friend who worked in the governor's office said he saw our pictures on the governor's desk. Hayes Mizell and I lost our teaching assistantships at the university. Ella Baker urged us not to be cowed by the red-baiting and harassment. She said that our problem in the South was neither radical thought nor conservative thought but simply a failure to think at all. If we were ever going to break the pattern of segregation, we must no longer let the opposition control our thoughts.

The segregationists called us traitors to the South, but I believe the black and white participants in the Civil Rights movement were the most truly loyal southerners the region has ever had, most loyal to the best of the South. The racists represented the region at its worst. Whether rich or poor, educated or ignorant, they were all dangerous to the South they claimed to love. But we understood their alienation, understood their frustration and their hatred, understood their need for someone to blame. My parents also did not share my views on civil rights, and this caused some tension in our relationship, but it was mitigated by our love and mutual respect. I was not without some sympathy for those forced to change the racial assumptions of a lifetime, and my parents were not without the capacity to change.

As a young southerner during the Civil Rights movement, I considered it a moral imperative to reexamine the history of my region. James McBride Dabbs, both in person and through such writings as his book *The Southern Heritage*, helped me to understand the South in a broader sense than was generally assumed in those days. Journalists typically depicted "the South" in monolithic, all-white terms: "the South" versus "the Civil Rights movement." That was not completely wrong, of course; but it would have been just as accurate to say "the South" versus "the racists." Southerners did not all come in one color, nor were all southerners racists. Dabbs helped me to understand "the South" as the aggregate of all its people, enabling me to perceive that, even as our politicians had been trying to preserve a social system that had separated the southern people, there was nevertheless a shared southern culture of incredible richness that had been created by the interaction of all the southern people, black and white alike.[4]

While it would have been impossible for me to leave my own white culture behind, even if I had wanted to, I consciously began in those years to try to teach myself what would later come to be known as African American Studies. I read fiction by Ralph Ellison and Richard Wright, folklore by Zora Neale Hurston, and history by W. E. B. Du Bois and John Hope Franklin. I read jazz criticism and listened to such jazz, blues, and gospel artists as Dizzy Gillespie, Muddy Waters, and the Dixie Hummingbirds. So the informal part of my graduate education — to an even greater extent than the formal study — gave me a broader approach to southern history than I might otherwise have had.

I had read C. Vann Woodward's *The Burden of Southern History* in the army. In his essay "The Irony of Southern History," Woodward had grounded the South's claims to a distinctive heritage in its historical experience.[5] But the heritage itself remained unclear because he did not explore the culture within which that history was experienced. His friend David M. Potter, in his famous essay "The Enigma of the South," proposed that the South's essential distinctiveness was embodied in what he called "the culture of the folk," a culture that had withstood all the homogenizing onslaughts of commercial popular culture. He considered the relation between land and people "more direct and more primal" in the South than elsewhere in the nation. "The relation of people to one another," he wrote, "imparted a distinctive texture as well as a distinctive tempo to their lives."[6] While Potter never explored the implications of his insight, I believed that his insight was sound.

I have spent most of my career, since earning my Ph.D. in history from the University of South Carolina in 1968, trying to build on the wisdom of Woodward and Potter in an effort to understand the interplay of history and folk culture in the South. I have found in folk culture insights into the history of men and women previously ignored by mainstream historical scholarship, and I have found in history insights into the folk culture created by such men and women. The history of the South is above all the history of the folk, who were more than merely the central characters in the drama. They were the very embodiment of society itself.

In 1963 I married Jean Dusenbury of Myrtle Beach, who had graduated from Columbia College in 1962. Shortly after our marriage we took part in the March on Washington. As we stood across the reflecting pool from the Lincoln Memorial, we were increasingly pushed back and crushed together as more and more marchers arrived. But the hopes of all of us soared to the sky as we hung on Dr. King's inspiring refrain: "I have a dream!" It must have been the grandest assembly for the redress of grievances that Washington had ever witnessed. After forty years it remains an unforgettable experience. Nothing could substitute for being there. Nor could there have been any alternative to our experiencing, as young teachers in North Carolina and Tennessee, areas of the South we had only read about before—the Appalachians, the Ozarks, North Carolina mill villages, and west Tennessee cotton patches.

I met John Hope Franklin in the spring of 1964 when he came to speak at a convocation in my first year of full-time teaching at Pfeiffer, a small Methodist college in Misenheimer, North Carolina. I had already been influenced by his writing. In fact, I had adopted his new book on Reconstruction for my Civil War and Reconstruction course.[7] I was honored when he visited my class, and even more honored when he asked me to join him for lunch. I can still remember our discussion of his friend Melville Herskovits, whose *Myth of the Negro Past* I had been reading.[8] Even more indelibly engraved on my memory is his advice to me that day to be a historian, not just a history teacher. He was the first historian ever to utter such advice to me. I did not know then whether I would be able to follow his advice; but John Hope Franklin was a most important influence on my career, not only for his scholarship but also for showing how a scholar with insight into the moral dimension of the past could serve the needs of both scholarship and citizenship.

A year or so later I met Willie Lee Rose and her mentor, C. Vann Woodward. Willie had recently published her *Rehearsal for Reconstruction,* a pioneering example of the kind of history I have since come to call exploring "large questions in small places."[9] She and I soon became friends, but I remained in awe of Woodward. He was always cordial when I saw him at annual meetings of the Southern Historical Association, but it would be another decade before he would call me "Chaz"—and still another before I would presume to call him "Vann."

Convinced as I was that southern history was intimately bound up with folk culture, I was eager to learn more about white traditions as well. Soon, with support from the National Endowment for the Humanities, I was recording white tradition-bearers—banjo pickers, ballad singers, and dulcimer makers in the Appalachians and the Ozarks. In 1965 I toured around the South with the Southern Folk Festival, an interracial folk music tour combining traditional folk musicians from the Sea Islands, the Appalachians, and the Ozarks with young activists such as Bernice Reagon, one of the founders of the SNCC Freedom Singers. Later I explored some of the sources of southern culture by taking my portable tape recorder to Great Britain. I recorded in Sussex pubs, Aberdeenshire homes, and Orkney crofts. I recorded Hebridean weavers, Northumberland shepherds, Midlothian miners, Dorset farmers, Ulster housewives, and Newfoundland fishermen as well.

By this time I had accepted a position at St. Andrews Presbyterian College in Laurinburg, North Carolina. I taught there for nearly fifteen years, from 1966 to 1980. "Christianity and Culture," St. Andrews's interdisciplinary core program, and the interdisciplinary faculty who were my colleagues there—such as George Melton in European history, Carl Bennett in American literature, and Leslie Bullock in religion—contributed greatly to my education. The teaching team for the semester called "The American Experience," which I chaired after 1968, wrestled with the influence of Christianity on ideas as we taught such works as Reinhold Niebuhr's *The Irony of American History,* William Faulkner's *Absalom, Absalom,* and C. Vann Woodward's *Strange Career of Jim Crow.*[10]

My first book, *Folk Song in South Carolina,* was a fledgling effort to study the men and women who had been tradition-bearers in my native state through their cultural creations.[11] In 1969, in the Library of Congress, I discovered the Federal Writers Project interviews with living ex-slaves. They included interviews at Murrells Inlet and Pawleys Island, both in Georgetown County, South Carolina, not far from Myrtle Beach. The interviewer, Genevieve Willcox Chandler, was still living; and soon I was driving into her yard full of questions about Hagar Brown and Ben Horry and the other ex-slaves she had known. I thought that if I could put her interviews together with census and other records it might make an interesting article. I could not know then that it would become a book, or that it would consume most of my time for the next fifteen years. But as I pursued my research on slave life in this Gullah-speaking community in the South Carolina lowcountry, I realized I had found an epic story. It was the story of the creation of African American folk culture, one that would call upon everything I ever knew and—as it turned out—a great deal more that I would have to learn.

Although I had already earned a Ph.D. in history, and although I had already read widely in folklore, I soon realized that I needed more systematic study than self-directed reading could provide. If I were really serious about understanding the history of the folk, I felt that I needed to undertake further graduate study in order to draw upon the insights of anthropology and folklife studies. By the mid-1970s I had decided to enroll in the graduate program in folklore and folklife at the University of Pennsylvania for a second doctorate. Supported by a fellowship from the Social Science Research Council and a sabbatical leave from St. Andrews, I studied cultural anthropology, sociolinguistics, African folklore, and ethnomusicology. Each reinforced my conviction that anthropological approaches would be useful in the kind of history I wanted to write, but each also opened new ways for me to think about history as well.

After earning a second Ph.D. at Penn, I undertook postdoctoral study in comparative slave societies at Harvard with the Jamaican historical sociologist Orlando Patterson. He was then writing his major work on the subject, *Slavery and Social Death*.[12] His preference for broad macrocomparative studies broadened my perspective and gave a new and comparative dimension to my efforts. Despite my continuing preference for microstudies, I found that the comparative method enabled me to ask larger questions of my small places.

Since completing my studies at Penn and Harvard, I have been profoundly influenced in my approach to the study of folk culture by contemporary developments in the fields of folklore, linguistics, and anthropology, as well as history. I held a joint appointment in history and anthropology at St. Andrews for several years. During the academic year 1979–80 I was a visiting professor at the University of South Carolina — in the history department during the fall semester and in the anthropology department in the spring. I have drawn on anthropological theory and method in most of my writing ever since. Like my friend Willie Lee Rose, I have tried to combine the ethnographer's preference for spatial concentration with the historian's commitment to examine change over time.

As I continued my research it became increasingly clear that the undertaking would require research in the field as well as in the archives. Genevieve Chandler and her daughter, Genevieve Peterkin, and the Reverends George Besselieu and Abraham Nelson helped me to track down children and grandchildren of the slaves Mrs. Chandler had recorded, enabling me to conduct my own interviews with them. In addition, June Wesley Elliott, Patricia Doyle, and Arthur H. Lachicotte shared with me their deep knowledge of the local history. In those years I made frequent trips to the South Carolina coast from our home in North Carolina.

Jeannie and I had come to love Laurinburg. Our daughter, Hannah, and our son, Wesley, were born there, and some of our close friends are still there. Laurinburg was close enough to Myrtle Beach for us to visit our families often. But Laurinburg was not home. In 1980 I accepted a position in the history department at Coastal Carolina University, near Myrtle Beach. My family and I joined the waves of people who kept coming as relentlessly as the waves of the sea. Our move greatly facilitated my continuing research on a South Carolina slave community. All Saints Parish, between the Atlantic Ocean and the Waccamaw River in Georgetown County, is immediately south of Horry County, the place of my youth.

When I completed the manuscript I sent it to the University of Illinois Press because of my respect for its director, Richard Wentworth, one of the giants of academic publishing. I had known him for several years from various meetings of historians and folklorists. At Illinois I was especially fortunate to have my manuscript accepted by August Meier for his series Blacks in the New World. Augie's editorial skills are legendary, and the book that emerged from his close reading and astute suggestions was infinitely better than it would have been otherwise. I cannot imagine any other editor as demanding, as thorough, or as generous with his time and wisdom. As my manuscript had grown longer and larger, my analysis had drawn more and more on such jargon-heavy disciplines as linguistics, anthropology, and folklore. Augie encouraged the interdisciplinary analysis but insisted the manuscript needed to be translated into English. Setting out to write another draft I realized that there is no such thing as an "audience" for a book. Reading a book is a solitary activity. I decided to write this final draft for one reader — my daughter Hannah. She was sixteen then, and I wondered if I could explain everything I had learned from my interdisciplinary research and analysis to her. I knew she was intelligent enough to understand the ideas, but I also knew she was not so experienced as to know the jargon. I *know* the effort to write especially for her played a part in improving my prose.

When the book was published as *Down by the Riverside: A South Carolina Slave Community* in the summer of 1984, it enjoyed a warm critical reception and brisk sales both locally and nationally.[13] By the time I faced my colleagues at the annual meeting of the Southern Historical Association in November, it was already in its third printing. The favorable reception of the book led to invitations for visiting professorships. I taught in the history department at the University of California, Berkeley, during the fall of 1986; and I was Ford Foundation Professor of Southern Studies at the University of Mississippi during the spring of 1987. Longstanding friendships with Lawrence W. Levine and Leon F. Litwack at Berkeley and with William Ferris, Winthrop D. Jordan, and Charles Reagan Wilson at Ole Miss were deepened, and new friendships were developed. In the meantime I accepted a tenured senior professorship in southern history at the University of Alabama in Tuscaloosa, to begin in the fall of 1987. The highlight of that fall for me was the session at the annual meeting of the Southern Historical Association, "Pursuing Large Questions in Small Places," on *Down by the Riverside* and *In My Father's House Are Many Mansions*, by my friend Vernon Burton. The panel, chaired by C. Vann Woodward and consisting of William S. McFeely, Nell I. Painter, Clarence E. Walker, and Bertram Wyatt-Brown, drew a large audience.

At this point it was wonderful good fortune that Coastal Carolina University invited me in 1998 to return as the first Burroughs Distinguished Professor of Southern History and Culture. I gratefully accepted the chair, endowed by Henry Buck Burroughs in honor of his parents, Franklin A. and Iola B. Burroughs. The mission of the Burroughs Chair was research and dissemination of studies in southern history and culture in the form of publications, presentations to professional meetings and community groups, and sponsorship of lecture series and symposia. The Burroughs Chair not only afforded me time for research and writing through light teaching duties and freedom from committee assignments but also contributed funds for travel and research. Among my publications after coming back were *Remember Me*, a short book on slave life in coastal Georgia in 1989, and *Shared Traditions*, explorations of relations between southern history and folk culture in 1999, as well as essays on William Styron and William Faulkner. I also contributed introductions to new editions of *Drums and Shadows*, Guy and Candie Carawan's *Ain't You Got a Right to the Tree of Life?*, Elizabeth Allston Pringle's *A Woman Rice Planter*, and Julia Peterkin's *Green Thursday*.[14]

In addition to my own work, through the Waccamaw Center for Historical and Cultural Studies I was also able to support reduced teaching loads for colleagues working on southern topics in various disciplines and to provide guidance and support to local historians in researching, writing, and publishing their work. And I was able to sponsor the Horry County Oral History Project, consisting of more than seventy interviews with the men and women, black and white, rich and poor, who constituted our county's living libraries, all recorded on broadcast-quality videotape. Four half-hour anthologies from the collection have been broadcast on public television. And the Waccamaw Center sponsors the monthly meetings of the Rivertown Bluegrass Society.

The Burroughs Chair has also afforded me the opportunity to reach out to a larger public audience. It has allowed me to bring to Coastal Carolina University a number of distinguished visiting speakers, including such old friends as Bertram Wyatt-Brown, David Hackett Fischer, Drew Gilpin Faust, Daniel C. Littlefield, Jack Bass, Vernon Burton, Anthony J. Badger, Rhys Isaac, and Bill C. Malone. It also made possible the participation of Carol K. Bleser as a distinguished visiting professor during the first semester of Coastal's Southern Studies Concentration. In addition, I have been able to organize a number of conferences and symposia, including "Pursuing Large Questions in Small Places," bringing together scholars from Australia, Canada, Europe, and the United States in 1989; "Southern Writers of Fact and Fiction," bringing together novelists, poets, and historians in 1996; "William Faulkner and Southern History," bringing together historians and literary critics in 1997. Coastal Carolina University also hosted meetings of the Southern Intellectual History Circle in 1995 and of BRANCH (British American Nineteenth-Century Historians) in 1999 and co-sponsored, with the University of South Carolina, the James McBride Dabbs Centennial Conference in 1996 and, with the Citadel and Avery Institute, "The Civil Rights Movement in South Carolina" in 2003.

It was also possible to reach a larger public audience through television production, such as *Legacy of Conflict*, a miniseries on South Carolina's role in the Civil War that I produced for the South Carolina Educational Television Network, and *I'd Like to See What's Down There*, a documentary on historical archaeology I co-produced with George McDaniel, for the National Trust for Historical Preservation. It was shown nationally on the History Channel. That kind of outreach would have been inconceivable without the lighter teaching duties afforded by the Burroughs Chair.

Since my return I have had the opportunity to participate professionally at a level that would never have been possible otherwise. I have been able to accept visiting appointments at the Du Bois Center at Harvard in 1990 and at the University of Sydney, Australia, in 1993. And the Burroughs Chair has allowed me to lecture and publish, to "tell about the South," on every inhabited continent.

Late in his life, when he had outlived such close friends as David Potter, Richard Hofstadter, and Robert Penn Warren, C. Vann Woodward and I became friends and traveling companions. And I had the honor to chair the plenary session at the Southern Historical Association honoring his ninetieth birthday. My favorite memories of him concern two of his visits to Myrtle Beach. One was a 1995 conversation he had with William Styron and me on the continuing ironies of pursuing southern history. The other was a walk on the beach he, Peter Parish, and I took during a 1999 meeting of BRANCH, in which Woodward spoke of the conservatizing of southern history, not only by court decisions chipping away at *Brown v. Board of Education* but also by certain historians who had completed, as he put it, a well-traveled road from radical youth to reactionary superannuation.

Thinking back, it is easy to see that my participation in the Civil Rights movement and my commitment to southern history both sprang from the same impulse. The realization that southern history embodied both the past and the present forced me to rethink most of what I thought I knew. This process of reevaluation was more than an attempt to use the past to justify the present, for the past has as much to teach by admonition as by example. I found it exciting to apply the insights of the history I was living to the history I was studying, while at the same time I was trying to apply the lessons of the past to the present, to strike past and present against one another like flint.

When I took my stand against the racist divisions of segregation nearly half a century ago, I never thought that I was doing anything especially dangerous; but in the comfort of hindsight, I realize it was more dangerous physically than it seemed at the time. I really did believe, though, that what I was doing put my future career as a historian at risk, but I knew that it was important for white southerners to link arms with black southerners and stand up for justice in our native region. So I did it anyway. In retrospect, I now see that not only did that involvement not endanger my career, it made me a better historian. If anyone had told me then that I would later become a visiting professor at Berkeley, an associate of the Du Bois Center at Harvard, a Ford Foundation Professor at Ole Miss, and that I would have been chosen at least partly because of my experience in the Civil Rights movement, I would never have believed them.

My old friends from graduate school, with whom I had shared such idealistic visions, such grandiose dreams, and such dire apprehensions, were as marked by the experience as I was. Selden Smith became a professor of history at Columbia College and a recipient of the Order of the Palmetto, the highest honor bestowed by the State of South Carolina, for his efforts to improve interfaith and interracial relations. Hayes Mizell has been a lifelong human rights activist. In 1979 President Jimmy Carter appointed him Chairman of the National Advisory Council on the Education of Disadvantaged Children. In 1987 he became director of the Edna McConnell Clark Foundation's Program for Student Achievement. When Hayes told us in 1963 that he had "cracked the code," that instead of *writing* history he was going to be *written about* by historians, we smiled. Now the Hayes Mizell Papers comprise one of the larger collections of the South Caroliniana Library at the University of South Carolina. The library recently received a $100,000 grant to expedite its processing.[15] Dan T. Carter would go on to an illustrious career as one of the leading historians of the South. His books — *Scottsboro, When the War Was Over*, and *The Politics of Rage*, a biography of George Wallace — have won numerous awards. And he is the only historian to have won an Emmy, which was awarded for his script of *Settin' the Woods on Fire*, a documentary based on his Wallace biography.[16] After serving as Mellon Professor of History at Emory University and president of the Southern Historical Association, he would return to the University of South Carolina in the fall of 2000 as Educational Foundation Professor of History. And Bill Freehling published such prize-winning books as *Prelude to Civil War, The Road to Disunion: Secessionists at Bay*, and *The South vs. the South: How Anti-Confederate Southerners Shaped the Course of the Civil War*.[17] After teaching at the University of Michigan and Johns Hopkins University, he accepted the Singletary Chair in the Humanities at the University of Kentucky.

In 1993, while I was a visiting professor at the University of Sydney, I was asked (in an interview since published in the *Australasian Journal of American Studies*), "What are the difficulties of being a southerner and writing southern history?" I responded that I thought of it less as a difficulty than as an opportunity.[18] Of course all history is difficult. The great French historian Marc Bloch said that history is impossible. And there are particular hazards in writing the history of "Ourselves," whether we define "Ourselves" in national, regional, ethnic, racial, or gender terms. If we confuse history with hagiography, if we write history to glorify "Our" ancestors, we are likely to write some pretty bad history. But there are equal hazards for those who specialize in writing the history of the "Other," the history of those who are postulated to be "different." I think any history studied only by insiders — or any history studied only by outsiders — is only half studied. As we say here in the South Carolina lowcountry, we need both "binyas" (who have been here) and "comeyas" (who have arrived more recently).

In any event, for good or ill, I am a southerner who writes of the South, of his own native region, often of his own native state. I am of the South, and I love the South — not only the sands and salt marshes of our coasts, the red clay of our Piedmont, and the hills and hollers of our mountains, but also the rich diversity of our people, *us, all* of us. That love cannot help but show, in some way, in my writing. I love the South, but I reject the notion that the test of legitimacy is filiopietism. As a historian I am also part of the larger world, and I cannot help but hold the South and the larger world up against each other in mutual comprehension and in mutual criticism.

Comparisons with other parts of the world inevitably illuminate the southern past, but increasingly comparisons with the southern past also illuminate the present of many parts of the modern world. For example, in 1989 I took part in an anthropological congress in what was then Yugoslavia.[19] It was obvious to anyone then that the country was coming apart. I asked some of my newfound Croat friends if their agitation might not destroy the union. "Well, we certainly hope so!" they exclaimed. I ventured that perhaps we should discuss this, since I am from South Carolina and we have had some experience with such matters. I come from a region of secessionists, I told them, and I have studied secession's causes and consequences for most of my adult life. I told them I did not see much to recommend it. I warned them that they might be in for a bit of trouble. But my warning went unheeded.

Time has changed my hometown of Myrtle Beach, South Carolina, almost beyond recognition. Streets have been renamed, closed, and even moved. Old landmarks have been moved to new locations or torn down. The house I lived in during high school has been moved inland across the Waccamaw River to Bucksport, occupying now the site where my mother grew up. And Oak Street, which once intersected Thirty-eighth Avenue beside our house, now runs straight across the lot where our house used to stand. My children have grown up. My daughter, Hannah, has become a historian herself, graduating from Harvard with honors in history and earning a Ph.D. in history at the University of Pennsylvania. My son, Wesley, earned bachelor's and master's degrees in anthropology and is currently pursuing a Ph.D. in history at the University of South Carolina.

To my surprise and delight I was invited — at the instigation of Edward L. Ayers — to deliver the Page-Barbour and James W. Richard Lecture Series at the University of Virginia in November of 2001. I knew that nearly half a century earlier C. Vann Woodward had first presented his *Strange Career of Jim Crow* as the Richard lectures there, in the shadow of Monticello. In my three lectures I examined the mutual influence of European and African influences on all the forms of southern music, from traditional folk music to formal classical compositions, jazz from New Orleans to avant garde, country music, blues, bluegrass, and rock. I am continuing my study of southern music, drawing on memories of evenings listening to banjo-pickers at the tobacco barns, of my early listening to the Grand Ole Opry and the boogie-woogie pianists on the radio, of late-night jazz jam sessions in the army, of freedom songs in mass meetings and marches during the Civil Rights movement, of folk-song concerts and bluegrass festivals—drawn, in short, from a lifelong love affair with southern music.

I have lived, and still live, much of my life at the intersection of the urbane and bookish academic world that I now inhabit and the oral culture of the folk among whom I was reared. Pondering that folk culture is more to me than merely a venerable pastime; it is a passageway into the past. Echoes of the old ballads and spirituals still reverberate in my ears and in my memory, growing fainter, sometimes barely audible, like a magical incantation, fusing the predestined and the contingent into something deeper than my conscious levels of thought and feeling. I am perpetually standing at the crossroads, at the same intersection between home and travel, between the conflicting tugs of my rootedness and my urge to ramble, which have preoccupied me ever since those long-ago days when I stood on the Carolina shore gazing out across the sea, pondering the connections between myself and the world beyond the horizon.

Notes

1. Eudora Welty makes much of the "sense of place" in southern consciousness. See especially "Place in Fiction," in her *The Eye of the Story: Selected Essays and Reviews* (New York, 1978), 6.

2. Dan T. Carter, "Reflections of a Reconstructed White Southerner," in *Historians and Race: Autobiography and the Writing of History*, ed. Paul A. Cimbala and Robert F. Himmelberg (Bloomington, 1996), 42.

3. Edgar T. Thompson, foreword to *Haunted by God: The Cultural and Religious Experience of the South*, by James McBride Dabbs (Richmond, 1972), 7.

4. James McBride Dabbs, *The Southern Heritage* (New York, 1958); *The Road Home* (Philadelphia, 1960); *Who Speaks for the South* (New York, 1964); and his posthumous *Haunted by God*.

5. C. Vann Woodward, *The Burden of Southern History* (Baton Rouge, 1960), 167–91.

6. David M. Potter, "The Enigma of the South," *Yale Review* 51 (Autumn 1961), 142–51 (quotations on pages 150–51).

7. John Hope Franklin, *Reconstruction: After the Civil War* (Chicago, 1961).

8. Melville J. Herskovits, *The Myth of the Negro Past* (Boston, 1941).

9. Willie Lee Rose, *Rehearsal for Reconstruction: The Port Royal Experiment* (Indianapolis, 1964). I believe I coined the phrase "Large Questions in Small Places." I first used it in the title of a session I proposed to the program committee of the Southern Historical Association in the fall of 1986. The session, "Pursuing Large Questions in Small

Places," was accepted and appears in the SHA 1987 program book. I organized a conference under the title "Large Questions in Small Places" at Coastal Carolina University in 1989, bringing together biographers and scholars of community history, endeavors then considered at opposite ends of the historical profession.

10. Reinhold Niebuhr, *The Irony of American History* (New York, 1952); William Faulkner, *Absalom, Absalom* (New York, 1936); and C. Vann Woodward, *The Strange Career of Jim Crow* (New York, 1955).

11. Charles Joyner, *Folk Song in South Carolina* (Columbia, 1971).

12. Orlando Patterson, *Slavery and Social Death: A Comparative Study* (Cambridge, 1982).

13. Charles Joyner, *Down by the Riverside: A South Carolina Slave Community* (Urbana, 1984).

14. Charles Joyner, *Remember Me: Slave Life in Coastal Georgia* (Atlanta, 1989); *Shared Traditions: Southern History and Folk Culture* (Urbana, 1999); "Styron's Choice: A Meditation on History, Literature, and Moral Imperatives," in *Southern Writers and Their Worlds*, ed. Christopher Morris and Steven G. Reinhardt (Baton Rouge, 1998), 78–119; and "Sutpen's Honor: William Faulkner and the Historians," in *Faulkner: Achievement and Endurance*, ed. Tao Jie (Beijing, 1998), 105–16; and introductions to *A Woman Rice Planter*, by Elizabeth Allston Pringle (Columbia, 1992); *Drums and Shadows: Survival Studies among the Georgia Coastal Negroes* (Athens, 1987); *Ain't You Got a Right to the Tree of Life?*, by Guy and Candie Carawan (Athens, 1989); and *Green Thursday*, by Julia Peterkin (Athens, 1997).

15. See Hayes Mizell, *Shooting for the Sun: The Message of Middle School Reform* (New York, 2000).

16. Dan T. Carter, *Scottsboro: A Tragedy of the American South*, rev. ed. (Baton Rouge, 1979); *When the War Was Over: The Failure of Self-Reconstruction in the South, 1865–1867* (Baton Rouge, 1985); and *The Politics of Rage: George Wallace, the Origins of the New Conservatism, and the Transformation of American Politics* (New York: 1995).

17. William W. Freehling, *Prelude to Civil War: The Nullification Controversy in South Carolina* (New York, 1966); *The Road to Disunion: Secessionists at Bay, 1776–1854* (New York, 1990); and *The South vs. the South: How Anti-Confederate Southerners Shaped the Course of the Civil War* (New York, 2001).

18. Shane White, "'Down by the Riverside': An Interview with Charles Joyner," *Australasian Journal of American Studies* 13 (July 1994), 45–55 (quotation on page 49).

19. Charles Joyner, "A Tale of Two Disciplines: Folklore and History," Twelfth International Congress of Anthropological and Ethnological Sciences, Zagreb, Yugoslavia, July 24–31, 1988, published as "Prica o dvije discipline: Folkloristika i historija," in *Folklor i povijesni proces*, ed. Dunja Rihtman-Augustin and Maja Povrzanović (Zagreb, Yugoslavia, 1989), 9–22.

Accidental Historian

PETE DANIEL

Nothing in my family history suggested that I would become a historian. When I was growing up, I did not even know that there was such a thing as a historian, much less "an historian." There were history teachers, of course, but they read out of boring textbooks that smart people far away assembled. Authors were not deemed important, nor film directors. Actors, both in fact and fiction, were more important than the creators. Books, films, magazines, and religion were all formulated in distant and mysterious places. I eagerly consumed this packaged culture with no thought of its origin. I lived on a smooth surface, and it seldom occurred to me to question this tranquility. Religion and segregation in particular were sacrosanct. Living on the surface had great attraction, but as I grew older contradictions erupted, and this glassy veneer shattered. The experiences of my youth shaped a unique view of race and class, different from my parents and from other adults and even from my close friends.

Some twelve hundred people lived in my hometown of Spring Hope, North Carolina. A railroad track, a spur line from Rocky Mount, divided the town, and a steam engine made a daily round trip through town. Spring Hope had barber shops, food markets, a hardware store, dry cleaners, a cotton gin, filling stations, dry-goods stores, a bank, lawyers and doctors, pool halls, a movie theater, car salesmen, and two sawmills. On Saturdays rural people crowded the streets. A group of white men congregated in front of Sykes Feed Store discussing the weather and fouling the sidewalk with tobacco juice. Women warily picked their way through the brown minefield. Waves of laughter rolled from Williams Pool Hall in the black section of town. Spring Hope was a good place to grow up, but between the time I left to attend college in 1957 and when I completed my Ph.D. in 1970 the vitality had drained away. Small farmers were disappearing, and the town's modest businesses were no match for Rocky Mount's shopping malls. This drastic transformation shocked and puzzled me and raised questions that would later shape my historical interests.

Both sides of my family came from rural Granville County, North Carolina.

The Hunts moved south to Nash County in the 1890s as part of the spread of the flue-cured tobacco culture. My mother, Stella Hunt Daniel, completed nursing training in Baltimore in the midst of the Great Depression. Without pocket money and alone in the big city, she made friends, worked hard, and only occasionally went out socially. She loved to tell stories of those days.

The Daniel side of my family settled in Rocky Mount. As a child, I spent many Sunday afternoons either in Rocky Mount with the Daniels or in Seven Paths with the Hunts. The Daniel children grew up hard. When my grandfather, James Leonard Daniel, died, most of the children went to work in a textile mill. My father, Peter Edward Daniel, never went to school a day in his life. After working in a factory, he became a carpenter and as a young man traveled across the South. He learned to read and write, he told me, by going out with literate women who mentored him. He was an attentive student. After establishing himself as a carpenter, my father settled in Spring Hope in the 1920s, bought an old tobacco warehouse, and went into the sawmill and building-supply business. His first wife, Ethel Derby Daniel, bore him five children and died in childbirth bearing Frederick Eugene Daniel. Fred and I were separated by five years, and my younger sister, Linda, by four years. Stella Hunt Daniel, much younger than my father, married into a household that did not make things easy for her or her children. Growing up I always felt outside the older family circle.

I was an introverted kid and loved to build model airplanes. I can still feel the excitement of going to Joyner's Toyland in Rocky Mount and selecting a new model. In my memory, I can smell the Testor's airplane glue and dope, see the fragile balsa sheets, wield the exacta knife, and feel the long strips notch into place along the fuselage. And I can recall the disappointment after gluing the tissue paper to the skeleton and painting it with airplane dope only to watch it sag into a sad copy of the picture on the box. Model airplane construction taught me patience and focus — and disappointment. Even with the most patient and careful work, the knife slipped, parts did not fit, decals tore, and the final product was imperfect. In retrospect, the intense hours spent on model airplane construction were good training for writing history. Both are solitary and often frustrating pursuits. By the time I was in high school, the models were plastic and clipped together easily with a touch of glue. The plastic models looked exactly like the box picture of an F-80, F-86, or MIG 15. Yet these easy-to-assemble models were unsatisfying in their plastic perfection. The shiny plastic models underlined the injunction that you couldn't appreciate something unless you worked for it, a proverb often aimed at welfare recipients and the idle rich.

By the time plastic triumphed, I had moved on to other interests. It is possible that I would have become a hopeless introvert addicted to books, model airplanes, and stamps had not my brother Fred dragged me away from the glue-fumed indoors and tossed balls at me, wrestled, and forced me to defend myself. At first I detested this physical world, but the shy part of me gave way to an increasingly competitive nature. As I grew older, I barned tobacco, drove trucks, worked at the sawmill, played sports, drag-raced, and avoided inside work. Far into college I wondered if I could ever be content with an inside job.

As a child, I spent many a Saturday afternoon in the Spring Hope Public Library, which was a wing of the WPA-constructed community building about a hundred yards from my house. It sat on the fat end of a triangle of land that ran past our house. Miss Sally May Wood was our librarian and my neighbor, and the library was directly across from her house. I lost myself in magazines and books, and I provided Miss Sally with some company. I loved the smell of books. One of my fondest memories is sitting in a chair at home with a book in one hand and a bologna sandwich in the other.

As I grew older, I graduated to the drug-store reading room. Southside Pharmacy, owned by my friend Gus Neville's father, stocked a wide variety of magazines and comic books. After school we would drop by the drug store, get a coke, take a magazine or comic book off the stand, settle into a booth, and chat and read for an hour before going home. I read *Life, Look, Colliers, The Police Gazette*, comic books, and the other magazines. Eclectic reading became a habit. Mr. Neville put in a rack of paperbacks with suggestive covers, but the local clergy pressured him to remove it.

The Joyce Theater, located about two hundred yards from my house, featured B-westerns and detective films on Wednesdays and Saturdays, along with serials, comics, and newsreels. The stentorian newsreel voice narrated war, peace, the atomic bomb, communists, sporting events, and personalities. Before television, the newsreels were our nightly news viewed a week late. There were many "war pictures" that featured American heroism and enemy perfidy. The Joyce Theater expanded the town limits and transported me to places filled with turmoil, excitement, and mystery. I was regular in my attendance. Perhaps some of the Hollywood storytelling technique sank in, but by the time

I started writing history such scenarios became cautionary. The big newsreel voices suggested objectivity, and the war and cowboy pictures invincibility. My experience in Spring Hope as well as historical research suggested an imperfect world and unhappy endings.

It is impossible to recapture exactly how schooling planted a historical seed. I attended a segregated public school and had excellent teachers. They coped with students from a cross-section of classes. One of my first-grade friends, we heard, lived in an abandoned tobacco barn. Some of my rougher friends taught me to curse fluently, and by the second grade I was extremely foulmouthed. I had no idea what most of the oaths meant and stupidly mispronounced words. Neither my parents nor my teachers knew of this vile vocabulary.

While writing this essay, I called my fourth-grade teacher, Vera Lewis Edwards. She remembered me as a quiet and conscientious student who would complete an assignment, place it on the edge of the desk as she required, and then read a book till the other students finished. Miss Lewis arrived in Spring Hope in 1948 fresh out of college, and we were her first class. She was young and beautiful, and we were all in love with her. She was lively and demanding, almost like a movie star set down in our classroom. Later she married Joe Wayne Edwards, and they became our neighbors when they moved two houses away.

What little history I heard in secondary school is lost in a haze. I remember studying the mythological history of North Carolina, memorizing the one hundred county seats, and learning that Civil War governor Zebulon Vance and educational governor Charles Brantley Aycock were the state's major heroes. Ruth Douglas introduced me to U.S. history in high school. Although I cannot recall specifics, she ignited my interest in the subject.

In ninth grade, Mrs. Patterson taught English, and I sat on the front row beside a kid whose dad was the warden of the nearby prison farm. We competed with each other good-naturedly, and Mrs. Patterson made English class exciting. When she assigned an essay on some event in our lives, I wrote on my comic first date. Steve Edwards was two years older than I and had his driver's license. My date, Danielle Lewis, lived fifteen miles away on the other side of Middlesex, in what was called the Gallberry. Her sister, Janie Edwards, was a neighbor, and Danielle and her parents visited almost every weekend. In the essay I explained the arrangement with Steve, the anticipation, arriving at Danielle's house, her dog terrorizing me as I got out of the car, and my awkwardness. Mrs. Patterson told me later that the essay won a competition, but I never learned, or have forgotten, the details. Her encouragement varied markedly from that of my other English teachers, who paid no attention to my writing. Indeed, with the exception of Mrs. Patterson, I do not recall anyone during these formative years encouraging my writing.

When I was about thirteen, I got a newspaper route delivering the *Durham Sun*. Many of the subscribers were African Americans who probably preferred a Durham newspaper, given that Durham was the headquarters of North Carolina Mutual Life Insurance Company and the home of a large black middle class, things that I certainly did not know. Each afternoon I rode my bike to Dewey Liles's service station/bus station to pick up the papers. This was during the Korean War, and I recall reading the headlines and looking at the arrows that indicated U.S. advances or retreats. Along the route, I delivered papers to the white pool hall, the barbershop, the Grill (the drive-in that I frequented when I got a driver's license), and to Mills Barbecue, a black-owned restaurant. I rolled my bicycle into Spring Hope Recreation Center, the white pool hall, and personally handed the paper to Mack Marlowe behind the bar. There were some tough folks there who shot pool or sat sullenly in the dim recesses of the bar.

My paper route took me to many African American houses both to deliver and to collect, so I observed black culture at close range. This encouraged my outsider feeling, for when all of the racist talk exploded after the *Brown v. Board of Education* decision in 1954, it made little sense to me. I knew a lot of black people, and racist talk conflicted with what I observed. Yet there was not a soul in town with whom I could talk about issues along the color line. Nor can I remember exactly what was going through my mind in those days, but I had some fairly strange ideas. The complex segregation laws and doomsday talk of integration totally confused me.

When I was about thirteen years old, my father sent me to paint Neil and Tinsey Evans's house. Neil, the logwoods foreman, was bald, solid, and resourceful. Later, I often drove him to Louisburg to get the chainsaws filed. As I painted the house exterior, I heard the radio playing as Tinsey did her ironing. The music was unfamiliar to me; it was rhythm and blues. In my ignorance I thought that black peoples' radios were also segregated and tuned in different music. Given the other segregationist rules, it made a certain amount of sense. When working on the "Rock 'n' Soul" exhibit in Memphis, I learned how important it was that the airwaves could not be segregated.

After *Brown*, school integration became a burning issue. Adults whispered their thoughts not quite out of the earshot of children. I do not recall a single white person coming out for integration. The Supreme Court, the president, many northern leaders, and the NAACP were transformed into wicked communist agents bent on destroying southern traditions. Much later, through the NAACP Papers, I discovered not only that Spring Hope had an NAACP chapter but also that I knew several members. One worked for my father. From other sources I learned the racist activities of a local lawyer, a man who when I was a kid promised me a dime to take my turn in the barbershop queue and left without paying me.

The contradictions introduced by *Brown* were upsetting, not just because I knew so many black people who in my eyes were goodly people, but also because of religion. Bible lessons did not square with the hate and meanness that I witnessed among Christian white people. In Sunday school we sang about how Jesus loved the little children of the world, red and yellow, black and white, and there was a precious picture of Jesus instructing a colorful group of children. If Jesus had showed up with that group of kids in a Nash County school, it would have provoked violence.

Although Spring Hope, like the rest of the South, was segregated, blacks and whites moved among each other in many of their daily rounds. My father's workforce was half African American. From an early age I knew all the workers; and as I got older, I worked with them. When I reached fourteen years old, my father gave me an afternoon job cleaning up the converted tobacco warehouse of the blocks, sawdust, and shavings created by the millwork and planing crews. While shavings from the larger planer were blown across the street to the sawmill boiler room, shavings and sawdust from the smaller machines piled up and usually filled a sixteen-foot truck bed. Fortunately, the truck had to be moved from pile to pile, so I quickly learned to drive.

The back of the warehouse faced black homes and Williams Café and Pool Hall, a small-town juke joint. The work force knocked off Saturday noon, and by that time the pool hall was rocking. Trying to catch a breeze on hot summer days, I would stand shirtless at a window and look out on the black life of Spring Hope.

Some summers I worked on the green end of the sawmill, toting off outsides, ripping tobacco sticks, hauling lumber to the planer, or delivering building supplies. In addition to trucks, I learned to drive tractors. Will Allen Perry, a black worker, became my mentor, and with his patient instruction I learned to back a four-wheel buggy. He also taught me to unload freshly sawn boards from the buggy. It seemed effortless when Will Allen unloaded 2x4s. In one graceful motion, he grasped the end of the board, lifted it to the stanchion, levered it with a whip of his hand, and when he released it, it fell neatly onto the pile. Clumsily, I lifted one end of the board, prized the other, and eased it onto the pile. After many tries and much coaching I felt the magic. The motion had to flow, so that the lift, twist, and levering created a whip in the green 2x4. Both Will Allen Perry's skill with the tractor and his magic with boards taught me more than good work habits. He brought to any job at the sawmill, including sawing, the same grace and command. Work bent to Will Allen's touch in a transcendent, even aesthetic fashion.

Just as Will Allen Perry inspired graceful perfection, Monroe Hopkins instructed me in the application of brute strength. Monroe was a large man who was never without a dip or chaw. Before I got my driver's license I often rode with him to deliver building supplies. He was incredibly strong and taught me how to get advantage of Sheetrock, bags of cement and plaster, shingles, and sills. Although he had little of Will Allen's flair, Monroe taught me how to move bulky objects without straining myself. These two men, one black and one white, shaped my work ethic. Their different skills when combined created an approach to labor that I continue to draw upon for inspiration. My father's example added another dimension. "Don't do a job just as good as anyone else," he advised. "Do it better."

Religion played a crucial role in my formative years. I followed my father to First Baptist Church while my mother and younger sister, Linda, went to Gibson Memorial Methodist Church. In Spring Hope the Baptist pastor, Dr. James H. Blackmore, was the most educated person in town. He was called to the pulpit of the First Baptist Church when I was almost a teenager. He had been a chaplain during World War II and completed a Ph.D. at Edinburgh. Indeed, his eastern North Carolina drawl had been corrupted with Scottish enunciations. Dr. Blackmore greatly influenced the group of boys that I grew up with. There were a half dozen of us who hung out together, an unusual pack of well-mannered, intelligent, and ambitious kids. Dr. Blackmore did not have the same impact on girls our age, although many of them were at least as intelligent as the boys. In the 1950s, girls were not expected to pursue careers. Given their intelligence in the classroom and their success on the basketball court, girls could obviously hold their own. I was impressed with Dr. Blackmore's learning and for a time his piousness. For a few years, I fell so far under his influence that I contemplated becoming a preacher. Having a scholar (he wrote several books) as a mentor influenced my reading, for Dr. Blackmore favored some titles and frowned on others. He also pushed our group to aspire to the God and Country Award of the Boy Scouts. Most of us were already Eagle Scouts. When I look back on my boyhood friends, I realize that our parents, our pastor, and our teachers had high expectations.

Dr. Blackmore sponsored a campaign, "Read the Bible through in 1952." Being fourteen years of age, I eagerly took on the King James Bible. I cannot recall what my young mind was making of the laws, wars, poetry, genealogy, beatitudes, and prophecies, nor do I remember how long it took me to complete it. Several adults finished before I did, but none of my friends had the stomach for the good book. The King James Bible influenced my writing style. While writing *Breaking the Land*, for example, I was editing a section and jolted to a halt.[1] Why did this sentence sound familiar? I read it again, aloud. The cadence, I realized, was from a New Testament passage that was seared into my mind. I have no idea how many other literary debts I owe to the Bible or, for that matter, to William Faulkner, Flannery O'Connor, or Thomas Pynchon.

The local square dance furnished another set of contradictions involving religion, music appreciation, and class. The community building, with its library wing, contained a large open room suitable for meals or dances. The triangle of land that we used for sandlot baseball and football served as a parking lot, and people also parked along the street and sometimes in our yard. The Saturday night Junior Chamber of Commerce–sponsored square dance drew people from all over eastern North Carolina. The Jaycees were making a killing off "setups," soft drinks used to chase the liquor. The loud music, calls, and shouts shook our house, and my folks detested the square dance. It was, we children were told, the music of untamed heathens driven into a frenzy. Much later I learned that Lester Flatt and Earl Scruggs were at the time appearing on WPTF radio in Raleigh and playing gigs around the area. Surely they played this square dance. The dance closed down at midnight to a screeching of tires and rebel yells. Then we could sleep.

Of a Sunday dawn two of my notorious neighbors could be seen on the field at daybreak moving among the discarded bottles and pouring the leavings into a Mason jar. On Monday afternoon we cleaned the field of the bottles and rubbers and resumed our games. Our parents never knew about the rubbers. We understood exactly what was going on at the square dance, although we did not know what to make of it. The preachers finally closed it down and brought respectability to our neighborhood. Several black cafés gave the square dance a run for its money insofar as wildness was concerned. I grew up knowing that there was a forbidden world that was kept from me, and studying that world became one of my historical missions.

Respectable music was often boring. When Danielle Lewis, my first girlfriend, would visit her sister, Janie, we would often watch the Pall Mall "Hit Parade," with four artists covering the latest hit tunes. Rock 'n' roll strangled that program, for it exceeded the skills of the artists to replicate Little Richard and Jerry Lee Lewis. My group of friends did not care for anemic Pat Boone covers either. Even at that age and in that place, we realized that most covers were lame versions of the real thing. This evolved into a cautionary tale that warned how any genuine article of popular culture or, for that matter, history, could be tamed to fit into an acceptable mold. *Readers Digest* condensed books epitomized another example of cultural dilution. Again and again I find historians and curators more comfortable with mythology than with fact, with pleasant and predictable exhibits than fact-based presentations, and with an obsession for Hollywood endings.

When I was almost a teenager, I picked up my father's name as my nickname. Jimmy Pearce, who nicknamed everyone in my class, started calling me Pete. I was named for my grandfathers, James Daniel and Calvin Hunt, and at first did not appreciate being called Pete because of the sexual teasing that came with it. The name stuck. For people looking for obscure facts, my first article was published under James C. Daniel. It was the only thing that he ever published.

We did well in football for a small high school that usually dressed out fewer than twenty players. When a player got hurt, the coach would send in a freshman or sophomore, and the player from the other side of the line would tell him whom to block. Our basketball team my sophomore year went undefeated in league play, won the county tournament, but lost in the district finals to an excellent Youngsville team. We started three sophomores and two seniors. Our gym burned down between my junior and senior years. It was a small brick gym with three rows of seats on each side intersected by potbellied stoves. There was no hot water in the dank dressing room. We wore our suits to home and away games. None of the gyms we played in had shower facilities. The rafters were so low that we shot line-drive jump shots, and the floor was so short that the half court line actually started before midcourt. The separate-but-equal gym at the African American high school was even smaller and more dismal.

Although I did not learn about history from playing sports, I did learn about teamwork. This is not useless information for a museum curator called upon to work on exhibit teams. I favor a small, tightly organized, highly motivated team, each player, as it were, knowing all of the positions. My small-town upbringing has forever biased me against hierarchical, specialized, and labyrinthine bureaucracies.

Playing ball was part of being in high school, as was dating, driving fast, cruising the grill, and listening to music. We all thought we were totally cool, and certainly we passed through high school at a wonderful time, 1953 to 1957. McCarthyism and the Cold War registered in our minds but not so much as girls, fast cars, and rock 'n' roll.

Looking back at my life before college, there was little to predict that I would become a historian. Because most of my classmates wanted to study science or technology, I toyed with that idea, although science was not my best subject. Still, I headed off to college hoping that medicine, law, or teaching would be in my future. Not long after I arrived, the segregation crisis exploded at Little Rock, and a short time later the Soviet Union launched *Sputnik*. One night I went out to a field beside the dorm and watched *Sputnik* spin through the sky.

It did not take long for historians to make an impression on me at Wake Forest University (which was then a college). Dr. Thomas Mullen taught me freshman world history. Like my fourth-grade teacher, Vera Lewis Edwards, Mullen was young and exciting. Unlike in high-school history courses, the past came alive in Mullen's lectures. It took a year of mediocre grades to cure me of my science fantasy. Other students would have to challenge the Soviets in space. Then I studied American history with Percival Percy, Buck Yearns, and Henry Stroupe.

I was a junior before I took David Smiley's Civil War and Reconstruction course. I had heard of Dr. Smiley, the blasphemous, eccentric, and demanding professor who students either worshipped or despised, sometimes simultaneously. Smiley challenged my naïve view of the past as in class he slaughtered sacred cows, sneered, joked, dropped best-seller titles and characters from fiction, and played intellectual games. Reared in Mississippi, Smiley had studied with William B. Hesseltine at the University of Wisconsin. Smiley's lectures were innovative, thought-provoking, and challenging, just the thing to shock and challenge someone from my sheltered background. I would not miss a class. For the first time, I realized that history was the study of ideas and points of view that often challenged the conventional story. He ridiculed southern icons, releasing ideas and questions that lay unarticulated in my mind. History, it turned out, was far from boring. I had naïvely thought that all history books were equally accurate, but Smiley entertained the heretical notion that some history books were more equal than others. He taught us always to be skeptical of sources. As he reminded us when using newspapers, "You know they are lying; you just have to figure out why they chose those particular words to lie with." Even though I was completely intimidated intellectually by this man, he made me think. He insisted that an education was obtained between the library and the coffee pot, between learning ideas and defending or refuting them. To this day I value the informal conversation over coffee or beer, where ideas flow unimpeded by academic pretension or jargon.

Visiting scholars came to campus, and at some point Arthur Schlesinger Jr. addressed an audience mostly of history students and faculty. Although I do not recall the topic of his lecture, I do recall his demeanor. Small, bald, scowling, arrogant, and bowtied, he cut quite a figure at Baptist Wake Forest. His father, we learned, was an important historian, and Junior Schlesinger had studied in the best schools and had written important books. He was an intimidating figure. By a singular coincidence, in the late 1960s I sat on a civil rights panel with Schlesinger and several area students at Arena Stage in Washington. He had by that time served in the White House, so our questions focused on the Democrats' civil rights record. I prefaced my question with a review of the race riots, the lack of school integration, and continuing friction along the color line. Then I asked Schlesinger how his alleged claims of "progress" could be reconciled with these facts. He replied that with the civil rights legislation—public accommodations and voting rights—changes for the better were inevitable. Having studied Reconstruction, I was not convinced.

During registration for spring semester my senior year, one of the history professors asked if I would apply to Wake's new M.A. program in history. Until that moment, graduate school had never entered my mind. With mediocre grades from my science adventure and no confidence in my intellectual ability, graduate school seemed an impossible dream. Surprised, even flattered, I applied. Wake's best students, of course, were off to schools with established graduate programs. My score on the Graduate Record Examination that summer disappointed me, but it embarrassed Dr. Henry Stroup, head of the history department who became the head of the graduate school. I sensed that he believed he had made a grave mistake admitting me before that score arrived. My revenge on the Educational Testing Service came at the University of Maryland, where I passed the German reading exam by guessing my way through it. I had never studied German. I also had a 4.0 GPA at Maryland. So much for ETS's reliability and predictability. It still upsets me when I consider how many people's lives have been changed, altered, or ruined because of test results and how many peoples' self-esteem has been crushed. My entry into graduate school, then, was providential and inauspicious.

Although I had written term papers, Smiley assigned a seminar paper the first semester in graduate school. Using the Wisconsin formula (I encountered it again in Horace S. Merrill's seminar at the University of Maryland), Smiley taught us how to write a historical essay. I wrote on Albion W. Tourgée, the North Carolina carpetbagger, judge, and novelist. Although I hoped to make Tourgée the subject of my M.A. thesis, I discovered halfway through research on the seminar paper that Otto Olson had recently completed a dissertation on him. For my paper, I focused on Tourgée's legal career in North Carolina. I used newspapers and, because Tourgée was a judge, court cases, and also read his Reconstruction novel, *A Fool's Errand by One of the Fools*. I feared that my paper was narrow and horrid, and given my experience in English classes at Wake, that I would somehow screw up the essay.

I still recall the night at Smiley's house when he returned the papers, and, amid the ample penciled suggestions, he had written an A. His careful reading constituted a writing lesson as arrows rearranged sentences into active voice, and his comments offered fresh insights on content and style. That seminar paper quickened the English that I had studied, and for the first time writing took on a purpose. It would be difficult to overstate the impact of that seminar and that A. It was the first time since the ninth grade that a teacher had made positive remarks about my writing.

Even as I was learning about the South, Balkrishna Gokhale arrived at Wake Forest to teach the history of India and Southeast Asia. Because he was Indian, Gokhale taught his courses from an Asian viewpoint. When Subaltern Studies emerged years later, it seemed similar to what Gokhale had taught us decades earlier. For a Baptist like myself, Gokhale's discussion of Hinduism, Islam, and other religions proved exciting, if not heretical. Having been brought up on U.S. and European history, the study of Southeast Asia opened another historical window. Before a seminar one afternoon, we speculated whether Gokhale ate beef, given the status of sacred cows in India. When a student asked him, he smiled, "Yes, only the Indian cow is sacred."

Just after graduating from college in 1961, I married Bonnie Sullivan. We were both naïve Baptists and, of course, thought we were quite mature. When we were engaged, graduate school had not yet appeared on the horizon, so we began our marriage as a threadbare graduate couple. Two months after the marriage Bonnie was pregnant. We moved to the Wake Forest trailer park and spent two eventful years there. Elizabeth Anne Daniel (Lisa) was born on May 18, 1962. Being an excellent English student, Bonnie helped me by reading and commenting on my seminar papers. We still brag about having lived in a trailer park. I've stopped laughter after several condescending trailer-park jokes or stories by adding, "Yeah, I've lived in a trailer park."

After I completed my M.A. in the summer of 1962, I took a job at R. J. Reynolds Tobacco Company and trained to be a foreman. My options at that time were RJR or a high-school classroom. Married and with a young daughter, I wanted to earn more money than high-school teaching paid. The job taught me a lot more than how to make cigarettes. A foreman at RJR ran a production floor where up to a hundred workers either made or packed cigarettes. Foremen apprenticed by operating machines, picking up cigarettes, and finally learning the calculus of keeping a balance among the millions of cigarettes moving between rooms that made cigarettes and packed them. At the beginning of a shift, foremen and department heads tallied the trucks of cigarettes on hand and decided on how many making and packing machines to run in order to maintain an equilibrium between those two operations.

Working with people each night as a line foreman proved both challenging and frustrating. Many of the workers were conscientious, but there were those who goofed off. Each factory had its own rhythm. I worked at one factory that made filter cigarettes, and the intricate filter drums broke down regularly. Mechanics would fool around and get them going only to have them crash. We were not getting our production quota, and things were tense. One night the worker who poured glue into reservoirs atop the spinning filter drums came back from dinner drunk. On his next round, he missed a reservoir and splashed glue into the intricate clips and springs of the filter drum. It was such a spectacle that everyone stopped by to marvel at the mess. This event broke the tension for a while. The worker kept his job but got a letter of reprimand. I had more sympathy for this man than I did for the foremen and mechanics who goofed off, for their laxity was calculated.

Reynolds was facing integration at this time, and management was terrified. We were briefed on how to handle demonstrations or disruptions. In one meeting my suggestion that it might be beneficial to talk with the black workers about the situation met incredulous silence. Until this time there were not only separate black restrooms but also segregated making and packing rooms with white overseers. RJR management understood that integration, even in the restrooms, would go smoothly if they blamed it on the federal government. The word was circulated that RJR would lose its government contracts if it did not integrate. There was grousing, but integration came smoothly at RJR.

I worked the night shift, and we ate dinner about 9:00 P.M. Often the conversations among us foremen turned to matters of segregation. I was a hardcore integrationist while most of my colleagues believed in segregation. This led to spirited discussions. Charlie Grubbs, an extremely intelligent department head, liked to establish scenarios on a desert island. "Suppose we were shipwrecked on a desert island with several black men," he would begin, "and there was only one gun." One man allowed that he could tolerate integration anywhere but in swimming pools. We talked about segregation often, and these good-humored conversations among white foremen encouraged me to stand up for my convictions. Unlike other segregationists I have known, these men did not dwell on intermarriage fantasies. Because I argued with passion and good humor, they respected me. In these dinner-booth discussions, my arguments took on an edge that has served me well, with some people. Others in academic, business, and museum work shy from even good-humored disagreement. My museum career, I am sure, has been stunted by managers who see me as a troublemaker because I passionately argue my convictions.

Our dinner-booth conversations were not isolated from the reality of civil rights. Chris, who ran the Greek restaurant where we dined, refused to serve a black man one night. I could sense Chris's tension as he weighed his white clientele against seating a black customer. After the black man left, I observed that Chris had been in the United States less than ten years and had just refused service to a man whose ancestors had been here before the Civil War. That comment lit a spirited discussion. Chris needed a federal contract so he could blame the federal government for making him serve black people.

More than anyone else at RJR, Mr. McIver (I cannot recall his first name) fascinated me. He was a short man with a bull neck and a small potbelly, and, instead of turning his head, he turned his entire body to follow conversations. He talked with a nasal snarl that underlined his sarcasm. The first time I encountered him, Mr. Mac, as he was called, was making vile remarks about Martin Luther King Jr. I immediately detested him. Earlier in his career, I learned, he had been foreman of one of the segregated black production floors. Naturally, I ended up with Mr. Mac as my department supervisor. To my surprise we got along well, and gradually I learned that he was far more complex than I had first thought. Other foremen told me that black workers held him in high regard. Many nights as the floor roared into production and we waited for the cigarette count, I would end up talking with Mr. Mac for a quarter hour or more. I cannot recall if we ever talked about integration, and I do not understand how he balanced his steady stream of racist comments with his reputation for dealing fairly with black workers. He was extremely intelligent and, like myself, distrusted the factory supervisors. In many ways, Mr. Mac personified the contradictions that permeated white ideology. His speech implied that he was a diehard racist, but his words did not match his deeds. When I was writing *Lost Revolutions* and attempting to explain southern racial thinking, I thought often of Mr. Mac and his contradictions as well as the uninhibited dinner conversations about integration.[2] When I left RJR at the end of the summer of 1963, the college students on my floor gave me a copy of James Baldwin's *The Fire Next Time*, an indication both of how open I was with my thoughts about civil rights and the tenor of student life at that time.[3]

Bonnie, Lisa, and I moved to Wilmington, and I taught at the University of North Carolina at Wilmington for three years. Teaching the U.S. history survey was excellent preparation for graduate school. UNCW was just emerging from its junior-college past, and it needed bodies to teach. A group of us arrived that fall with fresh M.A. degrees and full of energy. By that time, the Civil Rights movement was roaring at full throttle, and every night on the news, black people demonstrated against southern sheriffs and water hoses. This behavior of white southerners infuriated me.

Hearing that the Ku Klux Klan was holding a rally, I naïvely called the FBI to ask if it would be safe to attend. Bonnie and I and another couple showed up at what was a thinly disguised George Wallace rally lighted by a large fiery cross. The Grand Dragon's speech was filled with malapropisms. When he bellowed, "The federal government is enroaching on our rights," we sneaked glances at each other but knew that a smile or laugh would be a mistake. Some time later I was sitting in the waiting room at the VW repair shop and struck up a conversation with a Pembroke Indian woman from Robeson County. In the late 1950s the KKK had held a rally there and gotten chased out and humiliated by Indians. Since there had been rumors that the KKK would return, I asked what folks there thought. They wanted the KKK to return, she explained. "We want to kill them."

Later I went with a colleague to the founding meeting of the Citizens Council. Wilmington was ten years behind most of the South in organizing its "respectable" segregationists. The speaker assured us that we all knew why we were there. The audience seemed to understand the veiled references to big government, corrupt justices, the coming takeover by blacks, and how the Civil War fit into the equation. We were encouraged to take a stand and defend the white race before it was too late. These experiences allowed me a glimpse of segregationists in action. When I was writing *Lost Revolutions*, I wished that I had paid more attention. My experiences at UNCW made it clear that if history were to be my career, I would need a Ph.D. This created mixed feelings, for some of the "doctors" at UNCW were hardly role models.

After three years teaching at UNCW, in the fall of 1966 I became a Ph.D. student at the University of Maryland. The history department hosted a coffee-and-cake social to introduce incoming graduate students to the faculty, staff, and senior graduate students. I met Louis R. Harlan there. I neither knew he had moved to Maryland nor had I read his work. Yet within minutes of meeting, we fell into a spirited discussion trashing Charles B. Aycock, one of North Carolina's two great heroes. I came to realize that he was not only knowledgeable but, in his quiet and effacing manner, profound.

At that time the history department had over a hundred teaching assistants, and that night I met, among others, Ray Smock, Jim Lane, David Goldfield, and Dennis Burton. Ray and I played tennis the next morning, beginning a close friendship with Ray and his wife, Phyllis, that has lasted for over thirty-five years. Both Ray, who had studied with August Meier at Roosevelt University in Chicago, and I ended up in Harlan's seminar on African American history. Having previously studied the South primarily from the white point of view, the seminar grounded me in the best scholarship in the field and allowed me to see the South from yet another vantage point.

Although it would be tempting to settle accounts with some of the professors at Maryland, for the most part my course work progressed smoothly. When I arrived, some of the senior graduate students warned me to avoid Paul Conkin's difficult and demanding intellectual history course. They lived in mortal fear that Conkin would end up on their prelim committee and ask a complex question on Puritans or pragmatists. I audited Conkin's course that first semester and took it for credit in the spring. Although I would like to boast that I understood intellectual history, Paul Conkin overwhelmed me with the breadth of his knowledge. Two of the most gratifying moments of my life came when Conkin publicly mentioned my work. The first came at the Chancellor's Symposium at the University of Mississippi in the early 1980s, when I gave a paper on economic aspects of the New Deal's Agricultural Adjustment Administration. Although Conkin was not commenting on my paper, I sent him a copy for his information. When he gave his talk, he not only mentioned my analysis of the AAA but also observed how it paralleled the experience of his rural Tennessee family. He also mentioned my work in his presidential address to the Southern Historical Association.[4] At the SHA in Baltimore in 2002, while Conkin and I were talking about my recent work on pesticides, he paused and shook his head at one of my remarks. Ever the mentor, he invited me to sit down while he explained to me where I had erred in my analysis.

Paul Conkin left for Wisconsin before my second year at College Park, but in the fall semester of 1967, Louis Harlan began the Booker T. Washington Papers. He was not sure that he could justify a white assistant, but in the end, with John Blassingame coming on as assistant editor, I was hired to work on the BTW project instead of doing classroom work. Although I had used editions of collected papers, I had no idea about style, selection, annotations, or methodology. We decided that the first step would be to read through several major editions to discern a style that would suit the Washington project. Then we plunged into the editorial sea.

As the project geared up, I met Louis and Sadie Harlan twice a week at the Library of Congress and began photocopying selections from the massive collection of Washington papers. Louis, who was writing what became a Pulitzer Prize–winning biography of Washington, had been through the entire collection and indicated to us the significant documents. Sadie, who managed the daily operations, had become a Washington expert in her own right. Given that there were some one million items in Washington's papers, we were selecting only a small percentage for publication. Working in the Manuscript Room for two days a week taught me about editing and research, but Louis's friends added another dimension to the experience. He seemed to know every scholar there. August Meier and Elliott Rudwick, who were working in the NAACP Papers, became steady lunch companions. The lunch conversations were as spirited there as the dinner talks had been at RJR.

Louis later sent me to the National Archives to find Washington letters in the various record groups. Washington, of course, was a powerful southern Republican politician, so he had written many letters of recommendation and had other contacts with the federal government. I met the National Archives staff and, more important, learned my way around the archives. Louis eventually sent me to Howard University, Tuskegee Institute, and the Schomburg Collection of the New York Public Library. When we started annotations, I learned to find the "chestnuts," those hard-to-crack identifications of obscure people who appeared in the papers. A stack pass gave me access to shelves of books that I could quickly move through looking for my list of chestnuts. (Under James Billington, the Library of Congress later closed its stacks to all researchers, needlessly complicating annotation research and other scholarly projects that have legitimate claims for stack access.) Writing annotations taught me conciseness, a valuable lesson employed later when I wrote exhibit labels. Working on the Booker T. Washington Papers with Louis Harlan and having him as my Ph.D. adviser offered advantages far beyond the experience of most graduate students.

After prelims, I continued to search for a dissertation topic and was reading through *Crisis* and *Opportunity* magazines as well as secondary sources that might produce leads. It was while reading *Crisis* on the fifth floor of the Library of Congress Adams Building (then the Jefferson Building) that I came across an article on peonage. I had seen the term but had only a hazy understanding of it. It occurred to me that if peonage was important there might be material in the NAACP Papers, two floors below in the Manuscript Room. Indeed, there were several boxes containing clippings and correspondence. Many of the letters came from the Justice Department. Then I went to the National Archives and asked Don Mosholder, who worked in Justice Department records, if there were materials on peonage. Mosholder was a quiet and resourceful archivist, and he mused a moment before confiding that there were substantial peonage records. He explained that he had to screen out the federal-agent reports before I could see the material. The first box he brought out gave me chills. No one had seen this material since it was filed, and it was rich beyond anything I had ever seen.

Peonage had a rich legal history, so I realized that I would need to read cases. The first citation I checked was to *Bailey v. Alabama*, 219 U.S. 219. I entered the Law Library at the Library of Congress and warily approached the gentleman at the reference desk. I asked where I could find this case. He looked over my head from his elevated station and said, "If you will turn around and go to the shelves just behind you labeled *U.S. Reports*, and go down to volume 219 and turn to page 219, you will find your case." Blushing at my ignorance, I meekly turned around and found the case. Later I discovered that by using the same case number, I could access briefs and records. There were five briefs filed on behalf of Alonzo Bailey, several of them engineered by Booker T. Washington. This trip to the law library began a long association with legal records, sources that historians too often ignore. My essay on the *Bailey* case won the Louis Pelzer Memorial Award in 1970.[5]

Maryland was not all academic work. Several of us played penny poker or, lacking pennies, played heroic games of Monopoly. Ray Smock, Jim Lane, Dennis Burton, Don Miller, and David Goldfield usually sat in. During the first year, Ray and I would often go to the Varsity Grill, a seamy bar on Route 1, and drink beer and play the pinballs. Later, the Rendezvous became the history department hangout. *The Maryland Historian* was born at the Rendezvous and grew out of a conversation among Ray, Dennis Burton, and myself. Ray and Dennis followed up and founded this unique graduate-student history journal. By the late 1960s, go-go hit College Park, and the Varsity Grill had a back room with shimmering young women in cages above staggering and blasphemous undergraduates. I loved going back there. Buried in bedlam and sleaze, I found it the most relaxing place in College Park.

When the Varsity caught fire one day, my daughter Lisa returned home from school asking Bonnie if her dad was in the fire. Lisa and I would sometimes go over to Cole Fieldhouse to see basketball games. In my second year at College Park, Lisa was to start kindergarten. Bonnie and I attended a PTA meeting at the College Park school, at which administrators and parents aired the problem of overcrowding. Either the kindergartners would go on split shifts or kids would have to be bused to Lakeland School. Since most of the kids Bonnie and I went to school with back in rural North Carolina had been bused, we were having a difficult time grasping the gravity of this problem. After about half an hour of obscure talk, an administrator explained, in case everyone did not know, that

Lakeland was an entirely African American school, right down to the teachers. We looked at each other and were immediately on our feet. Bonnie and I explained that in the South, whatever its other faults, people did not hide segregationist feelings behind code words. (This was before the "Southern Strategy.") Our southern accents promoting integration and damning hypocrisy must have confused, if not alarmed, many of our fellow parents. Naturally, the school administrators sent the kids who lived in graduate-student housing to Lakeland. Lisa made good friends at Lakeland and doted on her kindergarten teacher, Mrs. White. On July 8, 1968, Laura Elaine Daniel was born, and she joined a family engaged in integration and antiwar work. She later followed me to Wake Forest University and came to revere it as I had. Our family still shares causes.

While at College Park, I marched in every antiwar demonstration held in Washington. Ray Smock lent me an old camera and gave me some instructions. Photography became a passion, and my mother bought me a camera for my birthday in 1969. In the spring of 1970 on a warm and beautiful day, I took photographs on the Mall as we marched against the Cambodian invasion. Jim Lane and I broke away from the main crowd in front of the White House and walked up to the Washington Monument. From there we saw people splashing in the pools and lying on the grass. My favorite photograph was of a buck-naked man carrying an American flag, chanting, "If you're not in the pool, you're part of the problem." My friend Grace Palladino used the photograph in her book *Teenagers*, but editors tastefully cropped it at his navel.

During one march, the *Washington Post* the next day carried an overhead photograph of the crowd at the Washington Monument taken, the caption read, at noon. I looked down at the sparse crowd, at the monument's long shadow across the image, and knew it was not taken at noon. I had been there at noon to meet friends and could barely squeeze through the crowd. Weeks later a correction appeared, noting that the photograph had actually been taken at five in the afternoon. Memories of David Smiley: I knew the *Post* was lying, and I knew why it chose that particular caption for its lie.

In the spring of 1970 I defended my dissertation, completed most of my work on volumes 1 and 2 of the Booker T. Washington Papers, was separating from my wife and daughters, and would shortly be leaving for the summer to teach race relations to troops in Berlin. I spent the next year on a National Endowment for the Humanities postdoctoral fellowship at Johns Hopkins

When I completed my Ph.D. dissertation on peonage, I sent it off to August

Meier, who at the time was editing a series in African American History for Atheneum. The manuscript came back with mostly favorable remarks but, the editor suggested, the book should end at World War II, not in the 1960s. Meier suggested that I revise and resubmit, which I did six months later. Having found more evidence of peonage in the 1950s and 1960s, I had strengthened the last chapter. It was rejected. I then sent it to Dick Wentworth at the University of Illinois Press, and it was accepted.[6] This experience suggested the power of editors and publishers in shaping history. When recent Ph.D.s ask me about revisions or readers' reports they find unfair or uninformed, I encourage them to consider the good advice but to stick by their ideas and research.

I left Baltimore in the fall of 1971 and went into exile in Knoxville, Tennessee. I often drove the five hundred miles to Columbia, Maryland, to visit my daughters, and I became a regular houseguest of the Smocks. The seven years at the University of Tennessee were a disturbing blend of alienation, desperation, and self-destruction. I gave impressive parties at my apartment that sat atop a ridge with a spectacular view of the city and of the Cumberland Mountains beyond. In 1976 I held the first Broken Heart Ball, my notion of the proper Valentine party, and the tradition has continued every year since. I became close friends with my neighbors, the Wiklunds, and we nightly watched the Watergate saga unfold. At the university, I offered courses in African American history and felt tension and hostility from some African American students. By the mid-1970s, many students added downers to the drug mix, and, as American history survey students in the 125-seat classroom stumbled into and tumbled out of their chairs, I discovered an interior voice asking why I was carefully writing lectures that attempted to bring interesting material to the classroom when most of the words flew unintercepted and splattered into the back wall. On the other hand, when I returned to the University of Tennessee in the fall of 1975 after a year as a visiting professor at the University of Massachusetts at Boston, I discovered a new crop of first-rate graduate students; many became my friends. Nan Woodruff and James Burran completed their Ph.D.s under my direction, and working with them was my most satisfying teaching experience. Yet I felt a palpable discontent and a gnawing sense that my fate lay elsewhere, as if settling down in Knoxville would be a death sentence.

I can still recall my exhilaration in the spring of 1978 when I learned that I had won a National Endowment for the Humanities fellowship for independent study. That summer I packed my belongings and moved to Washington, never to return to the University of Tennessee. It was not so much teaching as the teaching environment that drove me away — the departmental politics, the bonsaied intellectual community, the lust for tenure, the worship of rank and status. I won tenure my second year, but it meant little to me. I have frequently been asked why I resigned from a tenured position. It was a puzzling question. Why would I have remained in a position that offered more punishment than reward? It was, as the saying goes, a no-brainer.

I moved into an apartment near Union Station and began research at the National Archives and the Library of Congress. I was back home. Over the year I completed most of the research for *Breaking the Land*. As my year of leave was expiring, U.S. Senator Robert Morgan from North Carolina hired me. Being a legislative aide and a speechwriter was good work, but it ended in the election of 1980 when Morgan lost to John East in the Reagan landslide. Having resigned from UT as full professor a year earlier, I was unemployed. Expecting that Morgan's staff and other unemployed Democrats would be weeping, I was surprised to discover them calmly updating their résumés. I could only imagine the hand-wringing at a university had a similar overthrow happened.

For several months, I worked in the Department of Education and will always have compassion for public servants facing deadly nine-to-five jobs. In a final stroke of good luck, I ended up at the Smithsonian's National Museum of American History in the summer of 1981 working on the one hundredth anniversary exhibit on Franklin D. Roosevelt. After a year at the Woodrow Wilson International Center for Scholars writing *Breaking the Land*, I returned to the museum and became a curator.

Curatorial work appealed to me. Accidentally, I had stumbled into a challenging and multifaceted job, one that involves answering public inquires, attending countless meetings, and fretting about the intellectual decline of the Smithsonian Institution. It also requires me to collect and restore objects, to work on exhibits, to advise fellows and interns, and to research and write. The ideal project combines collecting, research, exhibition, and historical writing. In the "Rock 'n' Soul: Social Crossroads" exhibit about Memphis music, for example, I used video interviews that we did with people connected to the Memphis music scene of the 1950s and 1960s both in the exhibit and in a chapter of *Lost Revolutions: The South in the 1950s*. Interviewing rock 'n' roll and soul music stars of my teen years was a special moment in my life, as was later doing interviews with the stock-car community. Both communities were composed primarily of working-class people blessed with talent. They reminded me of my favorite museum colleagues, who, like my childhood mentors, possessed vast repositories of common sense, wisdom, and useful knowledge. Temperamentally, I am a curator, not a professor. That I have been allowed to work for two decades in the National Museum of American History has been extremely good fortune.

When I was a junior in high school, our class took a trip to Washington. We saw a D-Jaguar, rode the roller coaster at Glen Echo Park, and toured the Smithsonian Institution. At that time, I was incapable of even fantasizing working in a museum. Now, for more than twenty years, I have ridden my bike to work down East Capitol Street, cut through the Capitol grounds, and pedaled down the Mall to the museum. Reflecting on my background, I know the odds of my moving through this landscape each day. I was the beneficiary of tremendous luck and good fortune. It was while I was working at the National Museum of American History that my mother and I were talking about how different I turned out from other family members. "Sometimes I think you were switched at the hospital," she said. Then she paused and smiled. "But you were the only baby there."

Notes

1. Pete Daniel, *Breaking the Land: The Transformation of Cotton, Tobacco, and Rice Cultures since 1880* (Urbana and Chicago, 1985).
2. Pete Daniel, *Lost Revolutions: The South in the 1950s* (Chapel Hill, 2000).
3. James Baldwin, *The Fire Next Time* (New York, 1963).
4. "Hot, Humid, and Sad," *Journal of Southern History* 64 (February 1998), 3–22.
5. "Up from Slavery and Down to Peonage: The Alonzo Bailey Case," *Journal of American History* 57 (December 1970), 654–70.
6. Pete Daniel, *The Shadow of Slavery: Peonage in the South, 1901–1969* (Urbana and Chicago, 1972).

"Hey, Man, Where Did *You* Come From?"

Reflections on My First Three Decades

PETER H. WOOD

          I recall vividly an evening talk in Princeton University's Firestone Library in the fall of 1971. I was living in Princeton, New Jersey, working to finish my Harvard dissertation concerning slavery in colonial South Carolina. The speaker, Professor Stanley Elkins, had published a controversial book on slavery a dozen years earlier. It suggested that enslaved blacks, like concentration camp victims in recent times, found it difficult to resist in the face of total and arbitrary control. Professor Elkins had received harsh criticism — not all of it justified — for his suggestive exploration, and this evening was no exception. A small audience, including most of Princeton's few black undergraduates, had turned out to challenge the historian, who continued to argue that overt resistance was rare among North American slaves.

    As a visiting graduate student, I had slipped into the back of the room to listen. The students were asserting that not all slaves were Sambos or Uncle Toms, and that there must have been other rebels before Nat Turner. They brought considerable vehemence and self-confidence to their case but very little evidence. Frustrations were growing, when I finally got up the nerve to raise my hand; it was the first time I had discussed my research in public. "I have been doing work on early South Carolina," I said, "and I have come across an incident in 1739 called the Stono Revolt. Very few people besides Herbert Aptheker have even heard of it, but I have found enough material to write a whole chapter about this event."

    The room fell silent. I explained briefly how a group of rebellious slaves had broken into a store near Charleston to take arms, killing the white owners and leaving their severed heads on the doorstep. The rebels marched south in the direction of Spanish St. Augustine, waving a banner and rallying scores of additional slaves to their cause before they were finally pursued and massacred.

The heads of the leaders were displayed on posts along the road leading back to Charleston. My brief account provided the students with just the kind of grim and detailed information they had been looking for. A young man with an Afro seated several rows in front of me turned around in his chair and gave me a friendly and quizzical look. "Hey, man," he asked in surprise, "where did *you* come from?"

Where indeed? It was not a question I could answer easily at the time. My wife, Ann Douglas, already had her Harvard Ph.D. in hand after writing a medieval dissertation about *Piers Plowman*, and she had just become the first woman in the Princeton English department. I was still finishing my own thesis, and I was under contract to start teaching early American history at Princeton the following year. But it was a hard time for each of us, and I never took up the Princeton post. The previous June, on the same day that Ann received her doctorate, my mother died after a seven-year battle with cancer. The following February, Ann and I separated, ending a seven-year marriage that had started too early for both of us. Several weeks later, my father suffered a third and fatal heart attack.

In my twenty-eight years, I had had remarkably little experience with disappointment and heartbreak, so I needed a drastic change if I was to regain my footing. When the Rockefeller Foundation in New York City offered me a post as a humanities officer, Princeton generously released me from my contract so that I could take the job. Within months I finished my dissertation, signed a contract with Alfred A. Knopf for its publication, and threw myself into work at the foundation. By the time I left there in 1974, the book had appeared as *Black Majority: Negroes in Colonial South Carolina from 1670 through the Stono Rebellion*. A year later I accepted a Duke University teaching position that has lasted over three decades. I bought a house in nearby Hillsborough, a small town where pieces of the eighteenth-century past still remain remarkably visible, and I began a new life in North Carolina.

I have now lived in the South as long as I lived beyond its edges. Much of my own research over the last three decades (and the work of many of my terrific students) has focused on the interaction of Europeans, Africans, and Native Americans in the southeastern region. Not surprisingly, I have also taken an interest over the years in nonsoutherners who have spent time in the region, such as the French explorer René-Robert Cavelier de La Salle in the seventeenth century, the Quaker naturalist William Bartram in the eighteenth century, and the New England painter Winslow Homer in the nineteenth century.

It is always easier to try to make sense out of the experiences of others than to fathom the nature and trajectory of one's own life. But perhaps I am somewhat better equipped now than I was thirty years ago to answer the query, "Hey, man, where did *you* come from?" When I consider how a colonial historian, trained in New England and Old England, became fascinated with race relations in the early South, I first think back to my St. Louis childhood; I remember formative experiences that cluster around a magnificent river, a magical ballpark, and an unusual home. Then I recall years of training and preparation, much of it unplanned and unintended, that finally landed me in North Carolina teaching, and learning, southern history. Looking back, the first three decades of my life prepared me surprisingly well for what would follow.

A college friend who grew up in Bayonne, New Jersey, told me that until he was eight he assumed that the world was made out of asphalt. Not so for me, born in suburban St. Louis, Missouri, on May 1, 1943. Our home was a handsome, modern creation that had been designed by a student of the great architect Frank Lloyd Wright, so it was filled with strange angles and redwood paneling. In the 1990s the house was leveled to expand a park in the increasingly affluent and crowded suburb of Ladue, but sixty years ago my early childhood unfolded on the edge of fields and neighborhood woodlots. And a river ran through it.

It was not just any river that ran through my boyhood; it was the Father of Waters, the mighty, south-flowing Mississippi. From the angled roof of our house, beyond a distant farm field, we could see the trees that lined Deer Creek. In the summer, we fished in this small, rambling stream and looked for animal tracks along the muddy banks. The raccoons, like the neighborhood kids, spent hours hunting for tiny lobster-like "crawdads" among the slippery rocks. All the rainwater that rolled off our roof and down our driveway eventually seeped into Deer Creek and flowed steadily eastward for ten miles into the Big Muddy.

Perhaps children growing up today near whatever is left of Deer Creek feel little connection to the Mississippi. The lines of force may pull along six-lane highways instead, toward the massive Lambert–St. Louis International Airport. Charles Lindbergh flew mail planes there when it was tiny Lambert Field, and he christened his tiny aircraft *The Spirit of St. Louis* before setting off for New York and Paris to make aviation history in 1927. I had been to an air show at Lambert Field, watching the sleek, noisy fighter planes built by McDonnell Aircraft — the kind of Phantom jet that Ted Williams would fly in Korea. I had waved good-bye from the airport balcony when my father, an infectious-disease specialist and professor of medicine at Washington University, took off for Seoul in 1950. (The Army had asked him to visit a MASH unit and investigate the mysterious hemorrhagic fever that was devastating U.S. soldiers in their trenches near Korea's 38th parallel.) But it was the riverfront, not the airport, that captured my imagination. After all, I had never gone up in a plane, but I had been on the river.

One of my earliest memories involves a day trip up the Mississippi on one of the few remaining steamboats, the *Gordon C. Greene*, to visit Mark Twain's boyhood home in Hannibal, Missouri. I spent much of the journey peering over the stern rail, mesmerized by the gigantic paddle wheel that churned up foam and spray as it drove the boat north against the powerful current. We saw the muddy Missouri River tributary pouring in from the west. We strolled the streets of Hannibal to see Tom Sawyer's picket fence and to hear about the adventures of youngsters not much older than myself. Several years later I made my way through a series of orange-covered biographies about the childhood exploits of famous Americans. I still recall my embarrassment, halfway through the book on Mark Twain, when I complained to my mother that "so far it is all about some boy named Samuel Clemens."

Twain's river took on a deeper historical dimension when I was six years old. In the fall of 1949 my mother took me to the City Art Museum of St. Louis to explore an exhibition called "Mississippi Panorama." The museum's director, a family friend named Perry Rathbone, had helped to create the exhibit, which concerned the river's heyday during the century after Jefferson's Louisiana Purchase. I looked in wonder at the bright-green landscapes of George Catlin, the drifting riverboaters and trappers of George Caleb Bingham, and the busy steamboat scenes of Currier and Ives. But the most memorable item was the exhibit's centerpiece, an enormous muslin sheet, 90 inches high and nearly 350 feet in length, that had been painted in 1850 by Montroville W. Dickeson and John J. Egan to convey the saga of the river to popular audiences. The lengthy panel scrolled slowly across a narrow stage to reveal a series of melodramatic scenes, including the nighttime burial of the explorer Hernando de Soto, the Natchez Indian uprising of 1729, wolves attacking settlers, a devastating tornado, and the excavation of an ancient Indian mound.

The exhibit also contained a 28-inch model of the *Golden Eagle*, a sternwheel river packet built in 1904 that had run aground for a final time near

Grand Tower, Illinois, in 1947. Some of the big boat's jigsaw wooden trim, known as "gingerbread," was on display as well, courtesy of Miss Ruth Ferris of the Community School. That just happened to be the small private elementary school that the Wood children attended, and Miss Ferris was the legendary teacher whose class was synonymous with the Mississippi River. Each year her fourth- or fifth-grade students visited the cobblestoned riverfront, built model steamboats, and studied English, arithmetic, music, social studies, and everything else through the medium of the river. Shortly after the *Golden Eagle* ran aground, Miss Ferris arranged to salvage the entire pilothouse and have it brought to the school on a huge flatbed truck. There, it was installed on the playground, complete with whistle and bell, and christened by the students with jars of river water from the Mississippi and its great tributaries, the Missouri and Ohio.

Students five years ahead of me, including my older brother Bill and his friend John Hartford, enacted a skit at the dedication, complete with a rendition of "Ol' Man River." During high school, the two of them would form a bluegrass band. John went on to become a Grammy-winning musician in Nashville, but he never lost his love for riverboats, developed at the Community School. Before his death in 2001, John wrote a song dedicated to Miss Ferris, which still appears on the Web site maintained by his fans:

> But her very favorite, as you all know,
> Was the *Golden Eagle*, Captain Buck's old boat
> This old stern-wheeler sank and went to heaven,
> When I was in the fourth grade in 1947. Uh-huh . . .
> Well, she did some politicking that was tricky and hard,
> And she got the pilothouse for the schoolhouse yard.
> And so instead of studyin' I became a dreamer.
> Dreamin' about boats on the Mississippi River. Uh-huh . . .

You couldn't study the river without discussing cotton, and you couldn't explore cotton without touching on slavery. But elementary-grade students at an all-white private school in the early 1950s received little more than a glimpse of the topic. I remember that one of our class trips to the riverfront included a visit to the imposing Old St. Louis Courthouse. (It was not yet dwarfed by Eero Saarinen's soaring Gateway Arch, completed in 1965.) In the dim interior, under the huge iron dome, a guide mentioned briefly that a century ago this had been the site of two historic trials concerning a slave named Dred Scott. The haunting name itself prompted further questions, but the answers were vague and incomplete. I sensed that while the adults in the rotunda wanted us to understand the importance of "The Dred Scott Case," they seemed quite uncertain whether we should be rooting for or against Mr. Scott. Their confusion only piqued my interest.[1]

General William Tecumseh Sherman once described the Mississippi as "the spinal column" of the American nation. For me, the great river was a vital centering force; it oriented my small world like a huge compass needle, pointing north and south beneath the giant Eades Bridge as we headed east each summer to visit relatives in New England. On memorable childhood visits to Chicago and Louisville and Kansas City, I took my crude mental bearings from the river, knowing that I would return to its west bank. I could not, of course, actually haunt the river itself in the way that young Sam Clemens had done. Still, I had access to one thing that Huck's generation of Missourians had not had. By the time I was seven, baseball had become my consuming passion, and Sportsman's Park, home of the Cardinals and the Browns, had become the fixed center of my expanding universe. I would not have traded the dark-green outfield fence, with its ads for Sealy mattresses and Falstaff beer, for all the whitewashed fences in Hannibal.

Naïvely, I assumed that St. Louis was called the Mound City because Harry Brecheen and Ned Garver worked their magic from the mound at Sportsman's Park. I wore my battered Cardinal cap day and night, and I visited the ballpark every chance I got. Otherwise, I listened to Cardinal games on the radio, with the devotion that some people reserve for soap operas. Broadcaster Harry Caray narrated each daily installment in detail, sponsored by the local Griesedieck Brothers Brewery. His distinctive voice reached avid Cardinal fans in ten states, many of them living west or south of Missouri, where no major league franchise had yet been established. I recall sitting by our Motorola console listening to a long Sunday double-header in 1954, when my hero, Stan Musial, became the first batter ever to hit five home runs on a single day. I still have the baseball he signed for me, though the green ink has completely faded, and even now I can recall the hometowns of most of his teammates, many of them from the South: Enos Slaughter from Roxboro, North Carolina; Howie Pollett from New Orleans, Louisiana; Wilmer Mizell from Vinegar Bend, Alabama.

Like so many other kids, I learned elementary geography and mathematics through baseball. I also learned about ethnicity. (A fascination with Eastern

Europe that took me to Poland after my junior year in college no doubt began with following the Cardinals' Polish American stars, such as Musial, Ray Jablonski, and Rip Repulski.) But most importantly, I learned about race. I remember the first time I saw the ever-powerful Brooklyn Dodgers; I was sitting with my father on the third-base side of the field. When a visiting player reached first base, all the fans facing us in the distant right-field pavilion began to cheer. I turned to my father in disbelief that anyone from St. Louis could be pulling for the Dodgers, and he explained to me that the player, named Jackie Robinson, was a Negro, as were all the spectators in right field. Simple economic segregation had put them in the cheapest seats, and Robinson was their man.

As the right-field fans chanted "Go, Jackie, go," Robinson danced off first. On the first pitch, he dashed for second, and when catcher Joe Garagiola threw the ball into center field, Robinson continued running, losing his cap and sliding safely into third base amid a cloud of dust. The right-field bleachers erupted in wild applause, and I realized for the first time that there must be something even bigger than hometown loyalties dividing Americans. What was it, and how had it come to be? During art class at the Community School the next day, I took a wide strip of brown paper and painted a dramatic mural of Jackie Robinson sliding toward me into third base. He had *Dodgers* written in blue script across the front of his uniform, his cap was flying, and the fans in the bleachers were cheering him on. To say that he had made an impression on me is an understatement.

Before long, I had resolved the Robinson Paradox to my satisfaction: clearly all black Americans, at least in St. Louis, rooted for the Dodgers. Imagine my surprise the following year (October 3, 1951) when I returned home from school to listen to the National League playoff game between the Dodgers and the Giants. I settled in the kitchen with Wilma, the African American woman who came twice a week to prepare dinner, knowing that she must be pulling for Brooklyn. But when Bobby Thomson won the game for the Giants with a ninth-inning homer, Wilma was elated. When I asked how that could be, she explained that she had loved the Giants ever since they added two Negro stars, Hank Thompson and Monte Irvin. From then on, I paid special attention to black players when they came to Sportsman's Park — Roy Campanella, Don Newcombe, Larry Doby — and I was excited when owner Bill Veeck brought Leroy "Satchel" Paige to the Browns' bullpen late in the great pitcher's career.

Baseball was more than a spectator sport, of course, because I grew up in a household filled with sports. Both my parents enjoyed outdoor activity, and my father (William Barry Wood Jr., 1910–71) had been a renowned athlete. His father, a Boston cotton broker who traveled annually in the South, had played college baseball; his mother played amateur golf competitively. As a varsity athlete at Harvard, he earned an unprecedented ten letters over three years, competing in football, baseball, hockey, and track. In the fall of 1931, as an All-American quarterback, Barry Wood appeared on the cover of *Time*, and he earned a national ranking in tennis. The fact that he was also a scientist who earned straight A's made him a prominent scholar-athlete in his generation. (When I arrived at Harvard in 1960, a classmate from Massachusetts told me that he had been named Barry after my father.) After graduation, he passed up an offer to play hockey for the Boston Bruins in order to attend medical school. The proceeds from his book, *What Price Football: A Player's Defense of the Game* (Boston, 1932), helped pay for his medical education. Dad enjoyed physical exercise, but he encouraged his children to play sports only if it was fun.

For me, nothing was more fun than baseball—perhaps (as my mother later pointed out to me) because it provided a good way to capture my father's attention. For several years I played the outfield for a Little League team, sponsored by the local American Legion Post. The day my heavy flannel uniform arrived, I had my mother take my picture, leaning on a bat as though posing for a baseball card. The club was economically, if not racially, integrated, and most of my teammates were tougher and more worldly than I was. But I had a wonderful coach in my father, and there was a big field beside our house. We built a crude backstop by stretching spans of chicken wire between two locust trees; I fashioned a home plate out of wood and painted it white. On spring evenings, I would wait for him at the end of the driveway with two gloves and a ball, eager to play catch or shag fly balls when he returned from his work at the Washington University Medical School.

My dad's laboratory research involved the relation of white blood cells to fever. The interest went back at least as far as his training days at the Johns Hopkins Medical School in the 1930s. During a postdoctoral year, he studied pneumonia cases among black steel workers who were confined to a segregated ward in Baltimore. Later, he devised a way to observe the bloodstream of a rabbit by placing a glass chamber against one of its wide, thin ears. Then he could peer into it through his microscope to observe how the flow of white cells increased when the animal developed a fever. He would count the red and white cells passing through a narrow capillary and calculate their changing rates. Working in an era before video, he connected a movie camera to his microscope and recorded the process on film. Occasionally, when he was preparing a lecture, he would bring home the film, and the whole family would watch it in the darkened living room.

When I recall my fascination with these unusual home movies, I suspect they contributed somehow to my later interest in documentary film. They certainly prepared the way for my attention to the relation between sickle-cell trait and resistance to malaria, a link that I examined in *Black Majority*, my book about slavery in early South Carolina.[2] Perhaps they even laid the foundation for the concern with historical demography that underlies most of my work. During the 1980s, for example, I drew up the first full estimates of the population of the eighteenth-century South, divided by race and region, calculating changes over time in the number of red, white, and black inhabitants.[3] Strange as it sounds, I suspect that the historian son was subconsciously following the footsteps of his scientist father, whose laboratory films had suggested the importance of counting carefully by color and observing change across time.

Like my father, my mother had grown up in Boston. She too was athletic and scientific (with a Ph.D. in bacteriology from Hopkins), and she too was an outstanding teacher who loved books of all sorts. She raised a big family; I was the third of five children, with two brothers and two sisters. There was no early-vintage television set in the house to distract us; instead, she would read aloud to some of us every day, and to all of us together on Sunday evenings, from carefully chosen books. On long four-day drives to New England to visit relatives in the summertime, she would read whole books to us, mile after mile, to keep us entertained, and at least once on each trip she would recite Longfellow's poem "Paul Revere's Ride" from beginning to end. One of my earliest memories is of holding her hand as we ascended the winding stairs to the belfry of the Old North Church in Boston (still open to the public in those days), where lanterns for signaling Paul Revere had hung "on the eighteenth of April in '75." An enthusiasm for colonial history, therefore, goes back to my earliest years.

As soon as she could discern our individual interests, my mother would nurture them with books and articles, nudging us to be aware of broader issues in the world around us. I recall the day in May 1954, shortly after my eleventh birthday, when I grabbed up the sports page to read about Olympic shot-putter Parry O'Brien, who had just broken his own world record and become the first person ever to "put the shot" more than sixty feet. "You might want to look at this story too," my mother observed, pointing me back to the front page of the newspaper. "It is going to make a big difference in this country." There, above a picture of Chief Justice Earl Warren, was a headline proclaiming the Supreme Court's school desegregation decision in the case of *Brown v. Board of Education*. That night, I paid closer attention than usual to the evening news as read by newsman Edward R. Murrow, who, along with sportscaster Harry Caray and comedian Edgar Bergen, was the other esteemed and distinctive voice that spoke from inside our Motorola.

Another major news item made a more immediate impression. During the summer of 1954 I spent several weeks playing ball and fishing with a boy about my age who had come north from the town of Greenwood, in Tallahatchie County, Mississippi, to visit his relatives in St. Louis. He was white like me, but his accent was different from mine; and the world he came from was strikingly different too. The following year, in late August, the newspapers announced the gruesome murder of Emmett Till. The fourteen-year-old black youth from Chicago had gone south to Mississippi for the summer, and he had been lynched and thrown in a river for allegedly whistling at a white woman in a grocery store. The violence occurred in Tallahatchie County just north of Greenwood. Till's mutilated body was returned to Chicago, and his grieving and outraged mother demanded that the casket remain open for all to see. The newspapers carried pictures of anguished mourners. In Mississippi, an all-white jury acquitted the killers after deliberating for less than an hour. The death of someone almost my age, in a county that I had heard about, got my full attention.

My mother had been immersed in several books by southern writer Lillian Smith—*Strange Fruit* and *Killers of the Dream*—and she began giving me more things to read about the South and history. Stephen Vincent Benét's monumental poem about the Civil War, "John Brown's Body," made a big impression on me. For the first time I heard stories about my mother's paternal grandfather, George Hutchins, born in Massachusetts in 1844, who became a drummer boy in the Union Army and spent much of the conflict assisting surgeons as they performed operations on the battlefield. After the war he married a woman he met in Atlanta, and they returned to New England, where their son, my grandfather, was born in 1877. Henry T. Hutchins would train at Johns Hopkins to become a surgeon, serve in France in World War I, and then operate for many years at the Boston Women's Hospital before moving to St. Louis to live with us in the early 1950s, after his wife died. Separated by two-thirds of a century, he and I became fast friends. Until his death in 1960, the year that I went off to college, I had a third supportive older mentor in the house besides my mother and father.

Most teenagers undergo sudden and disorienting changes with regard to their parents, their peers, and their own personality. Whatever shifts occurred for me were overshadowed by a wrenching geographic, academic, and social change. I didn't rebel; I moved to Baltimore instead. In the summer of 1955, a year after the St. Louis Browns moved to Baltimore and became the Orioles, my father accepted a position at the Johns Hopkins Medical School, where he had been trained, and we moved back to Baltimore, where my older brother and sister had been born. In highly mobile midcentury America, the move was nothing special, but for a twelve-year-old from the Midwest, it seemed like a journey to another planet, and not an especially hospitable one. Having just finished the seventh grade, I felt uprooted from the friendly co-ed school named for American naturalist John Burroughs. Gilman, the spot where I landed, was another segregated, private school full of white suburban youngsters from professional families, but it could not have seemed more different. It was a demanding, all-boys institution, where the students wore coats and ties and addressed their teachers as "Sir."[4]

The transition was painful in the extreme. I missed my St. Louis friends, and I feared that I could never adjust to the high academic demands and stultifying atmosphere at Gilman, with its dark hallways, strict rules, and boisterous students. But after months of agony, I adapted to my new habitat — first reluctantly, then enthusiastically. We lived in Owings Mills, in the attractive Greenspring Valley, and I made new neighborhood friends. My parents and my grandfather offered patient support, and even my ever-competitive siblings seemed sympathetic. Also, I used sports as an entryway, joining my classmates to play football and basketball. In the spring, most of them turned to lacrosse, a game I had never heard of. I drew the line there, electing to stand in center field for years as part of a struggling baseball team, watching with increasing envy and fascination as my friends played top-notch lacrosse on the adjacent field. (Only as a college sophomore would I finally switch to lacrosse, pushed by my low batting average and pulled by the chance to excel at a sport that my athlete-father had never played.)

To drive away the clouds, I learned to cheer for the Orioles in the newly built

Memorial Stadium — after all, they had come from St. Louis and started slowly, just like me — and I became a fan of the Baltimore Colts, the city's rapidly rising professional football team. Predictably, I knew their roster by heart, and I was present when a young Lithuanian American named Johnny Unitas replaced George Shaw as the starting quarterback to begin an unparalleled career. But the biggest burst of sunshine came in the classroom. Even as a slow reader, I found that I could keep up. The classes were small, the teachers were outstanding, and the subject matter was challenging. Most exciting of all was an ancient-history class taught by Ludlow Baldwin, a frustrated archaeologist who grew misty-eyed explaining the magical significance of ziggurats in Mesopotamia.

Though we had moved due east, in cultural terms we had moved a few degrees south and several decades back in time. Gilman's school colors were blue and gray, as if to remind us all that the Civil War was still being fought. President-elect Lincoln had slipped through Baltimore at night on the way to his inauguration, fearing a hostile reception, and a century later the town's elite still seemed unduly dedicated to the Lost Cause. As in St. Louis, I was living in a "border" society built around large measures of outward bluster and inner ambivalence. But now I had some purchase on my situation; a youthful migrant-newcomer vantage point helped me know this was not the only America. Later, I would feel fortunate to have grown up in two different places. It gave me a certain double vision or added perspective — an early sense of cultural relativism — that made it easier to become a historian.

My formal historical training began during my first week at Harvard College, in the fall of 1960, and lasted for more than a decade. In what could have been a perfunctory initial session, my academic adviser took the time to go over my schedule and steer me toward a class in American social history with Oscar Handlin. I had never heard of Professor Handlin, nor of social history, but I soon became enthralled with the man and the subject. Handlin was small, balding, and rotund. (Students had fondly dubbed him "The Big O" in comparison with basketball great Oscar Robertson.) He spoke slowly, with a nasal New York twang to his voice, and he formed his words into perfect sentences and paragraphs, as though he were dictating a book. The rumor that he had once been a catcher in sandlot baseball remained unconfirmed, but it was certain that a decade earlier he had won the Pulitzer Prize in history for *The Uprooted*, his compassionate overview of American immigration from Europe. As he read from *The Great Gatsby* and discussed Al Capone and Billy Graham, I sat in the front row and took notes furiously. My roommates, amazed at my zeal, claimed that I had become a convert to the historian's faith.

The next semester, a seminar in art history proved equally exciting, but I elected to major in history. Sophomore year I was drawn toward early American history by my excellent tutor, Philip Greven. He was among the cohort of young historians who were conducting pioneering demographic studies of early Massachusetts towns, using primitive computers to sort their data, so our reading and discussions had a New England slant. Later, a course on colonial American history with Professor Bernard Bailyn confirmed my interests, though I did notice that his engrossing lectures on British America rarely ventured further south than Virginia. The department's class in southern history (referred to derisively as "Mint Juleps") remained on the books, but the post in that subject had not been occupied for more than a decade, and few seemed to notice. I did catch a memorable glimpse of the early South when my junior tutor, John Thomas, assigned an old book by Verner Crane called *The Southern Frontier*.[5]

After my junior year, I went to Poland during the summer of 1963 with the Experiment in International Living. My small group stayed with families in Kraków, where the Jagiellonian University (associated with Copernicus) was preparing to celebrate its six hundredth anniversary. Living in the ancient city suddenly made life in colonial America seem surprisingly recent and accessible to me. I traveled back through western Europe with a Catholic friend, staying in several ancient monasteries that were like nothing I had ever experienced, and I returned to Baltimore in August, only days before the famous March on Washington. It drew more than 250,000 people, but I was not one of them. The South, both past and present, remained only at the edge of my vision. I wrote my senior honors paper on the Puritans' relations with the Indians.

Just as northeastern history suited my New England college, where I graduated in 1964, British history was the mainstay of the English university where I landed next. The Rhodes Scholarship that took me to Oxford that fall aboard the *France* did little to open my eyes to early southern history. In the next two years I earned a second B.A. at Merton College, majoring in a program called "Modern History." That turned out to be an overview of English history from Caesar to Churchill. I knew that learning about the evolution of the British empire would be excellent background for studying colonial history, but I worried that it would be hard to master enough Anglo-Saxon history, since I would be starting from scratch. Fortunately, my "don" was familiar with Yankee shortcomings and made the decision that we could lop off one millennium and concentrate on the second one. "In your case, Wood, we shall begin in 1066," he said to me as he handed me a list of books on the Norman Conquest. When I asked naïvely which was the "right" one, he patiently explained the subtleties of historiography that had eluded me as an undergraduate. It was the first of many wonderful Oxford lessons.

When I returned to Harvard Yard to pursue a graduate degree in 1966, I found a country that had been transformed. The Civil Rights movement had expanded and changed; so had the war in Vietnam. There were thirty-eight urban riots that year, leaving eight people dead, and in 1967 the racial violence escalated dramatically, with more than 160 insurrections, 8 involving intervention by the National Guard. In July, forty-three people were killed during a week of rioting by African Americans in the Detroit ghetto. I was in Cambridge studying Spanish in Harvard's summer school at the time. I recall vividly watching the CBS Evening News on a small Sony television set and seeing the Motor City in flames. Correspondent Roger Mudd was hovering above the smoke in a helicopter, peering down on the devastation from the air, much as the American correspondents were covering the war in Southeast Asia. I realized at that moment that the "authorities" who were supposed to be explaining the events to us had little sense of who these people were, what had brought them to Detroit, and what they were thinking and feeling.

Starting that evening, I wondered whether the story of these urban residents and other black Americans, traced back far enough, would intersect with my interests as an early American historian. Could I get close to the lives of uprooted African ancestors in the way that Handlin had revealed the lives of immigrants from Europe? I went to the stacks in Harvard's Widener Library and visited the shelves concerning England's North American colonies. They were arranged geographically, so I began in Maine and worked my way southward, looking for books or articles that concerned the initial history of African American newcomers, slave or free, in each colony. The monographs were few and far between, but they increased as I approached Virginia; then they dropped to almost nothing. When I reached the South Carolina shelf, I had located the void that every young historian hopes to find, an intriguing and significant subject that has somehow been overlooked. I was excited, and my enthusiasm for the task only increased when I opened several books on early South Carolina. They all made clear, in their righteous prefaces, that only individuals who had been born and raised in the Palmetto State could properly write its sacred history.

The challenge, of course, would be finding sufficient primary material to explore the topic of Africans in the earliest years of colonial South Carolina. Professor Bailyn, as my adviser, was skeptical but very supportive, and I threw myself into the task. Before long it was clear to me that one of the thirteen English mainland colonies was more than half black at the time of the American Revolution, yet no one had studied, or even noticed, the lives of these people. The odyssey that began in the Widener stacks would take me to archives in Columbia and Charleston, South Carolina, and those trips would confirm the availability of materials and the viability of the subject. A Deep South dissertation topic would have the advantage of throwing me into a realm that was far from New England and entirely unfamiliar to my admired parents and teachers. I would need to be independent and resourceful, and I relished the opportunity.

From that point on, two amazing worlds would open up to me in the years ahead. One involved the early southern past, a domain of Indians, Africans, and Europeans that existed long before there was a New South, or even an Old South. For all but a few historians, this varied and changing place had long been covered up or blotted out, mythologized, marginalized, or forgotten. In the past four decades it has drawn a resurgence of interest, and I have been fortunate to share in this renaissance. The other would be the world of the southern present and future; in the early 1970s it seemed promising, contradictory, and frequently inspiring, the more I got to know and understand it. It was also filled with an endless supply of shrewd, talkative, resourceful, and committed people, a considerable number of whom I have been lucky enough to meet and know.

I could see these two worlds come together when I described the Stono Rebellion to black Princeton students in 1971. And both realms have continued to rub together and reinforce one another in my life ever since. Traveling through the South for the Rockefeller Foundation, taking a job at Duke, and settling in Hillsborough, North Carolina, all helped to braid the different strands of my life more tightly together. These opportunities also opened up a whole new chapter of learning that continues to the present day. For much of my first thirty years I did not live in the South, and I could barely glimpse the importance and depth of its past. Three decades later, all that has changed.

Notes

1. A half-century later, students can visit elaborate Web sites, download a play based on the trial transcript, and read the infamous verdict handed down by the U.S. Supreme Court in 1857.

2. Peter H. Wood, *Black Majority: Negroes in Colonial South Carolina from 1670 through the Stono Rebellion* (New York, 1974), chap. 3.

3. Peter H. Wood, "The Changing Population of the Colonial South: An Overview by Race and Region, 1685-1790," in Peter H. Wood, Gregory Waselkov, and M. Thomas Hatley, eds., *Powhatan's Mantle: Indians in the Colonial Southeast* (Lincoln, 1989), 35-103.

4. I have reminisced about Gilman in the 1950s in Patrick Smithwick, ed., *Gilman Voices, 1897-1997* (Baltimore, 1997), 177-84.

5. I later wrote about this experience of discovery in my preface to a Norton paperback edition of Crane's 1928 book: Verner W. Crane, *The Southern Frontier, 1670-1732* (New York, 1981), vii-xvi.

Southern History from the Outside

ANTHONY J. BADGER

Jim Holt, a fine New Zealand historian of U.S. Progressivism, claimed there was always one book that so captured your interest in a subject that you would always be able to remember where and when you first read it. What made Jim an American historian was reading Richard Hofstadter's *The Age of Reform* (1955). Twenty years later he could still remember the exact location in his university library where he had found the book and first read it. In my case the book was William E. Leuchtenburg's *Franklin D. Roosevelt and the New Deal* (1963). It was 1966 after my first-year exams at Cambridge; the book had just come out in paperback, and I was going to be taking my first-ever course in American history the following year. I devoured the book in the pub behind Sidney Sussex College while England won the world cup at soccer and Tom Graveney, my schoolboy hero, made a triumphant return at the age of thirty-eight to the national cricket team. Leuchtenburg's dramatic narrative, the sheer scale of the Great Depression, the personality of Roosevelt and other colorful politicians, the bewildering range of bold government programs — all seemed so different from what, at that time, I took to be the gray conservatism of the National Government in Britain in the 1930s. My response to Leuchtenburg's historical reconstruction, I later discovered, was the same as that of young British intellectuals like Isaiah Berlin and Denis Brogan to the New Deal at the time. Herbert Nicholas, the first Rhodes Professor of American History at Oxford, recalled the hopes invested by the younger generation of academics in the 1930s, who contrasted the "positive affirmations of the New Deal" with "the appeasing record of the Chamberlain government":

> Yet partly because the Democrats had succeeded in presenting themselves as a party of hope (there was *no* British party of hope in the 1930s), partly because of FDR's personal dynamism (there was *no* dynamic British party leader in the 1930s except Sir Oswald Mosley), one could and did nourish

the conviction that one now realizes to be partly illusion that the America of Franklin Roosevelt would, somehow or other, either avert the war or, when it came, rescue the democracies of Europe from their common foe.[1]

Leuchtenburg's book made me want to be an American historian. I did not suspect that a quarter of a century later I would be organizing a conference in Cambridge — a stone's throw from the pub where I had first read it — to mark the thirtieth anniversary of the book's publication. Bill responded at that conference to British and American historians who reflected on writing about the New Deal "In the Shadow of Leuchtenburg." Even less did I suspect that I would later crisscross the South working in the archival collections of southern congressmen in the vain hope of beating Leuchtenburg to one of those collections.[2]

Leuchtenburg's book also reintroduced me to Huey Long. I had read about the Kingfish when I was twelve in a book on my father's shelves, *America Came My Way*, by a young English baronet who toured the United States in 1935. Sir Anthony Jenkinson had crossed the United States, from the America's Cup races off Rhode Island to Hollywood. Armed with influential introductions, he met and wrote about celebrities from Walter Winchell to Shirley Temple. Long afterward I discovered that the book had been dismissively reviewed by the doyen of British commentators on the United States, Alastair Cooke. Cooke, his biographer noted, "swiftly spotting an interloper on his territory, accuse[d] [Jenkinson] of making sweeping statements based on a highly superficial experience of the country."[3]

Jenkinson's chapter on Huey Long stuck in my mind, not only because of its title, "Huey Long Takes His Shirt Off," but because of the footnote that pointed out that he had subsequently been assassinated. To a twelve-year-old in 1959, assassinations of politicians in democracies seemed exotic rather than all too frequent, as they would in the years to come. When I discovered in Leuchtenburg's narrative of the New Deal that Huey Long was an important political figure, my curiosity was piqued. I read Allan P. Sindler and Harnett Thomas Kane and gave a paper on Long to the college undergraduate history society, largely relying on anecdotes about Huey that, to the England of Harold Wilson and Ted Heath, made politics in Louisiana seem from another planet. T. Harry Williams was actually in Oxford that year as Harmsworth Professor, and I acquired a copy of his inaugural lecture, which previewed his massive biography of Huey. In the modest way of 1960s liberals, I championed Long's record for poor whites and accepted that his corruption and power grabs were necessitated by the ruthlessness and conservatism of his enemies. Subsequently, I was suspicious of Williams's wide-eyed acceptance of the most specious defenses of Long's behavior. Almost twenty years after that first undergraduate paper, I finally had the chance to publish an essay that was a modest contribution to the revisionist interpretation of Long more vigorously and convincingly undertaken by Alan Brinkley, William Ivy Hair, and Glen Jeansonne. Thirty-five years later I had the chance to be a visiting professor at Tulane University during the trial of Governor Edwin Edwards and to chronicle the havoc wrought with governance in Louisiana by conservative segregationists and Republicans, on the one hand, and corrupt Long-style welfare liberals on the other. In my Mellon Lecture there in 2000 I summarized my new understanding about the state: "The future for the have-nots in Louisiana and for the state's economy looks bleak. The legacy of corrupt welfare liberalism and racial moderation has produced a system of public governance that has proved incapable of delivering a modernized economy. The legacy of good government and racial and economic conservatism has equally failed to produce a vision that can see beyond the next tax cut or the next toxic waste dump. Politics as TV wrestling is a great spectator sport and it has been for me a subject of endless fascination over the past forty years, but I have to confess, as I head to the airport, that the quality of governance it provides is more easily coped with at a distance of three thousand miles."[4]

Leuchtenburg's reawakening of this dormant interest in Huey Long did not make me a southern historian. It did make me want to look at the New Deal in the South. The British, used to national, ideologically distinct, and coherent political parties, found the association of New Deal liberals and southern conservatives in the same party strange. How that relationship functioned in the 1930s, when that tension became so apparent, was what I wanted to understand. Armed with one survey course in American history and this sketchy ambition, I set out to do a Ph.D. in American history at the University of Hull, which had given me a three-year studentship.

In Cambridge, American history had been championed by Frank Thistlethwaite, but he was in the economics faculty and had left to be the first vice-chancellor of the University of East Anglia; by Denis Brogan, an idiosyncratic professor of political science who retired in 1967; and by Pitt professors, distinguished but transient, on annual appointments from the United States. The history faculty had sent William R. Brock, a noted historian of Lord Liverpool, to the United States to retool as an American historian, but he left in my final year to go to Glasgow. J. R. Pole, initially appointed on outside funding, was only rather grudgingly taken on the university's payroll when that funding ended. For all the very considerable scholarly distinction of these Americanists, it was difficult to avoid the feeling that, for Cambridge, American history was not a proper subject. "American history is not a fit subject for a gentleman," intoned one college director of studies in turning down the request of an undergraduate, Harry Porter, to take the optional course on American history.

In Hull, by contrast, American history was taken seriously. Hull had an American Studies department, established in the 1960s on the model of the pioneering interdisciplinary programs at the Universities of Manchester and Keele. The excellence of the Hull Library's American holdings was due in part to funding from the USIA, in part to the energy and bibliographic interests of members of the department, and in part to the benign support and encouragement of the university's librarian, the poet Philip Larkin, who shared historian John White's passion for jazz.

There was no critical mass of graduate students: I was the only one. There was no coursework, no training in historiography, and no training in research methods. My supervisor was a specialist in immigration history. Of vast swaths of American history I was wholly ignorant. Yet it was a wonderful time. I read widely in New Deal historiography and in contemporary American politics. The members of the staff seemed to treat me as a colleague rather than as a student. Philip A. M. Taylor was a model supervisor. Like William Brock, Taylor marched to his own intellectual drumbeat. Both had an inner self-confidence as historians that their interpretation of the sources, whatever the subject, would be of value. Their independent conclusions at critical points intersected with simultaneous developments in American historiography. Brock's careful reading of congressional debates during Reconstruction — in which he took the rhetoric of Radical Republicans seriously — led to the landmark *An American Crisis: Congress and Reconstruction, 1865–1867* (1963), which appeared just as the revisionist historiography of Reconstruction came to fruition. His later work on state government agencies in the late nineteenth and early twentieth centuries coincided with the explosion of work on "state development" in the United States. Taylor's whole approach to immigration, summed up in *The Dis-*

tant Magnet: European Migration to the U.S.A. (1971), paralleled the work of Rudolf Vecoli and others that stressed the persistent importance of European experiences and values in the immigrant experience. Taylor had few qualms about supervising a Ph.D. on the New Deal. He read whatever I wrote quickly and carefully. He consistently prodded me to greater clarity and to be certain about what questions I was trying to answer. He was immensely encouraging, gave me the chance to lecture to undergraduates on the New Deal, and displayed a reassuring if, in retrospect, foolhardy confidence that I would obtain an academic job at the end of the three years. He also arranged for me to fund a year's archival research by asking an old friend to give me a teaching assistantship at North Carolina State University at Raleigh. In September 1969 I set off for the first time to America and to the South.

In 1997 I was invited back to North Carolina State to give the Harrelson Lecture. I flew in direct from London to Raleigh-Durham Airport, an airport now almost identical to any other major international airport. I sat next to a Swedish telecommunications specialist from Ericcson who was visiting his company's office in the Research Triangle. I was entertained in excellent restaurants and held up in endless traffic jams—all the trappings of a modern city. It had been very different in 1969. Then I had flown in from New York, walked from the bottom of the aircraft steps to a small, single-story building, and gone outside to pick up my baggage from a carousel open to the elements. The first night I spent in the Carolina Hotel, now demolished, which, unknown to me, had been the campaign headquarters for the liberal faction in the state's politics, the headquarters of Kerr Scott and Frank Graham. (Candidates of the Shelby dynasty used the Sir Walter). Searching that night for a meal, I could only find an indifferent Chinese restaurant. Asking that Sunday evening for a drink, I was given my first, and last, root beer. Looking at the wallpaper paste on my plate next morning at breakfast, I tasted my first, and last, grits.

But if the Triangle in 1969 was not a gourmet or beer drinker's delight, it was an archival treasure trove at the State Archives in Raleigh and over at the Southern Historical Collection at Chapel Hill. In a year I knew more about the New Deal tobacco program, I suspect, than anybody has ever wanted to know with the exception of Pete Daniel. Teaching the history of Western civilization to textile majors equipped me for anything I was ever likely to face in a classroom in the future.

I left North Carolina as a New Deal historian who happened to be studying the South. My interest in the tobacco program was in the policy options available to New Dealers, in the implementation of those policies at the local level, and in what that said about the radical opportunities or the constraints that confronted Roosevelt and his advisers. I just happened to be studying that question in North Carolina rather than Montana. My consciousness of race was intermittent and marginal. In my dissertation, African Americans were acted upon; they had no agency, if they appeared at all. My concern was with sharecropping as an object of policy, not with the life of the sharecroppers themselves. I did manage to capture, from a 1946 dissertation and its interviews, the sense of a greater breathing space that alternative sources of credit and votes in crop-control elections gave African Americans, but the experience of sharecroppers, black or white, did not loom large as it would later for Pete Daniel and Jack Kirby. I was working at a tokenly integrated university. Only one African American started on the basketball and football teams. The Atlantic Coast Conference was only on the edge of the desegregation that Charles Martin has so expertly described. Concern and awareness about race relations in general, not about race relations in my own community, was my dominant emotion. As a schoolboy in Bristol in 1963, I had waxed suitably indignant about apartheid in South Africa. Only thirty years after the event did I discover that there had been a bus boycott in my own city by West Indians that same year. In Raleigh in 1969–70, I could not avoid being aware of Jesse Helms, of Nixon's southern strategy, of the strike of cafeteria workers at the University of North Carolina, or of substantial school desegregation for the first time in early 1970 when the greatest white flight from the public schools occurred in the areas inhabited by Duke faculty. But I met few black students, and I did not understand the daily humiliations of segregation in the way that white southern students radicalized by the Civil Rights movement did. While I was in Raleigh, eleven-year-old Tim Tyson was told that his friend's father had killed a "nigger." My recollection is that I was entirely unaware of the rioting that followed in Oxford. Oxford, North Carolina, was known to me only as the home of New Deal congressman and 1938 senatorial candidate, Frank Hancock.[5]

I returned from my year in North Carolina (I would go back there every summer in the 1970s), started writing up my dissertation, and applied for a university lectureship — advertised in British history with a preference for someone who could also teach American history — at Newcastle University in the north of England. I turned up in the administrative offices of the university at the appropriate time, was interviewed for thirty minutes, told to come back in two hours' time, and then sat in a small room with the other candidates while the committee made up its mind. It transpired that the department really wanted an Americanist but all the other applicants were British historians. So an administrator came out and announced that the committee wished to offer the job to me — and I set off to the train station with one of the defeated candidates. At the age of twenty-four, with an unfinished dissertation and still ignorant of vast chunks of American history, I was a tenured university academic and determined to make my reputation as a historian of the New Deal — and that is what I published on for the next twenty years.

But teaching undergraduates made me a southern historian.

In Newcastle I taught a survey course on American history from 1965 and a final-year special subject on the New Deal. That specialist course was the basis of my later general overview of the New Deal. But in the early 1970s any American historian was conscious that the most exciting work was being done in the field of slavery. As one after another major studies by John Blassingame, George Rawick, Robert W. Fogel and Stanley L. Engerman, Eugene D. Genovese, Peter H. Wood, Edmund S. Morgan, Herbert Gutman, Lawrence N. Levine, and others appeared, there was a powerful imperative to engage with this literature. To me, it seemed the best way to make sure that I read these books was to promise to teach a seminar course on them myself; subsequently I introduced a course on "The South and Race: From Slavery to Civil Rights." In the first couple of years the students and I taught each other. There was no copy, for example, of Gutman's book on the black family in Newcastle, and the students had to rely on my laboriously typed-up notes. In time, the course became a large lecture course and the staple of my teaching at Newcastle in the 1980s.

There were a number of consequences from this indirect way into southern history. First, unlike so many southern historians, I did not come to southern history through C. Vann Woodward's *The Origins of the New South* (1951). I had read it as an undergraduate, but I did not grasp why the book was so important. Not having been exposed to traditional southern historiography, I failed to understand how it challenged the conventional pieties and why it was such an eye-opening book to that generation of southern historians immediately preceding me. The book that shaped my teaching of the course on the South was *The Strange Career of Jim Crow* (1955) and the debate about the forgotten alternatives to segregation, which was ideally suited to small-group class discussion. By contrast, Michael O'Brien, like me an undergraduate in Cambridge, had gone to Vanderbilt University to take a master's degree, and he addressed from the start of his career questions of southern identity and southerners' sense of self. Unknown to each other, we followed each other round southern archives on very different quests. For O'Brien, Vann Woodward loomed large, and in 1974 he published an article in the *American Historical Review* quizzically exploring Woodward's liberalism.[6]

Second, my introduction to the historiography of slavery (and later women) changed the way I wrote about the history of the New Deal. It was my first serious engagement with the new social history, with the history of "the inarticulate many rather than the articulate few." I began to appreciate the limitations of my political and administrative approach to the history of the New Deal, no matter that I was stressing the local and state impact of the New Deal and the implementation of its programs. I therefore tried to incorporate the new work on rank-and-file labor militancy, on the unemployed, on Native Americans, and on blacks into my New Deal account. I have to confess that my study of women came later. In 1974 Carl Degler came to Newcastle and gave a version of his Harmsworth inaugural lecture at Oxford, "Is There a History of Women?" In Newcastle the answer in 1974 was definitely no. Only slowly did I fully understand the implications of this omission. History in Britain was a notably "stag" affair in the 1970s. We lacked that cohort of older American women historians who reentered graduate school and the profession in the 1970s in the aftermath of the women's movement in the United States. We also lagged in equal opportunity employment policy. Again, teaching women's history was my entry point into belatedly incorporating women into my New Deal narrative.

Third, my engagement with the modern South was slow. The historiography of slavery, Reconstruction, and the New South was so rich that a course based on seminar discussions of major historiographical issues inevitably focused on the earlier period. The historiography of the Civil Rights movement, for example, was largely stillborn at that point. When the course became a lecture course, I had to address the Civil Rights movement more substantively; and it became clear that that was what the students wanted to hear about. I therefore replaced the final-year New Deal special subject with a course on "Martin Luther King Jr. and the Civil Rights Movement." The subject matter made it the most popular special subject in Newcastle before I was appointed — to my surprise — to the chair at Cambridge in 1991. The appointment process at Cambridge was even more austere than it had been at Newcastle. In 1991, two years to the day after the closing date for applications, I received out of the blue a letter from the vice-chancellor indicating that the electors wished to offer me the chair. In the intervening twenty-four months there had been no communication from Cambridge, no interview, and no meeting with the electors.

Once there, however, my priority in Cambridge was to try and make American history more central to the faculty's provisions for students so that some of the best Cambridge undergraduates might choose to stay on for research in American rather than early modern British history, for example. Teaching a popular course on civil rights that now had a rich and rapidly developing historiography seemed one way of achieving that goal. The faculty board was skeptical but tolerant. Teaching King and the Civil Rights movement was, said one member, "dreadfully modern." Another wondered if any student would choose the course, given that the students could choose to study, for example, charters in medieval Florence. As a result I was assigned the smallest room in the building. When seventy-five students crowded into a room with sixteen chairs, my hopes were justified, and over the next four years the course broke records for the number taking a Cambridge special-subject paper.

It was one thing to teach the Civil Rights movement, another to change tack and carry out research in the modern South. Having written a local case study of the New Deal, my thoughts first turned to a local case study of the Civil Rights movement in Mississippi, modeled on William Chafe's study of Greensboro. James T. Patterson swiftly disabused me of that notion: John Dittmer was already at work on just such a study. I also doubted that any British scholar could spend enough time in the United States to carry out the necessary archival and oral history work. Subsequently, Adam Fairclough and Stephen G. N. Tuck, with their studies of Louisiana and Georgia, respectively, triumphantly proved me wrong. My next thought also sprang from my New Deal specialization. When Norman Thomas chided Roosevelt for being so fearful of upsetting southern conservatives in tackling the plight of sharecroppers in the Arkansas Delta, Roosevelt explained that they had to be patient: there was, he said, a new generation of southerners on the horizon. I wanted to know how that new generation of southern liberals handled the race issue when civil rights came to center stage after 1945. I set out to look at the liberal governors in the postwar South who appealed on economic issues to a biracial coalition of lower-income whites and the small but slowly increasing black electorate. Were politicians like Jim Folsom, Sid McMath, Kerr Scott, and Earl Long simply overwhelmed in the aftermath of *Brown* by the overwhelming forces of popular mass racism? I tried to understand this relationship between constituency pressure and political stances on race by looking also at the Southern Manifesto of 1956. What happened to those southerners who refused to sign the Manifesto, particularly the three North Carolina congressmen whose early careers I had been familiar with during the New Deal and who faced primary elections immediately after they refused to sign?[7]

But could I be an effective historian of the South? Could I understand the South, if, unlike Quentin Compson, I had not been born there? Like other British Americanists of my generation, I had consciously tried to make my work indistinguishable from that of U.S.-based historians. Unlike many of our predecessors who saw their role as interpreting the U.S. to a British audience or pursuing distinctive Anglo-American themes, we had tried to produce works as well researched as those of our American counterparts, on domestic American topics at the heart of American-centered debates, published by American university presses, and reviewed in the leading American journals. But, when I started to write about the South, could I overcome the handicap of not having been born there?[8]

A number of critics, whose work I greatly respected, believed not. In 1993 I spoke at the Southern Historical Association as a member of an all-British panel on civil rights. The commentator warned the audience not to be seduced by our "charming British accents," because the study of southern race relations hid many traps for unsuspecting outsiders. (I apparently had fallen into these traps more heedlessly than the other panelists, Brian Ward and Adam Fairclough.) Four years later at an excellent conference on the fortieth anniversary of the Little Rock crisis, another commentator on another all-British panel thought that our outsider status prevented John Kirk and me from displaying enough empathy with the dilemmas faced by white southerners trapped by a paralyzing racial culture. (The belief that one could not adequately write American history without being born there had also been held by the electors of the Paul Mellon Chair at Cambridge in 1991. As the vice-chancellor wrote to me, they had been seeking an American-based historian for the chair "as a matter of principle, not *simply* [emphasis mine] because of doubts about the quality of the British Americanists."[9] A distinguished Ivy League historian made a subtly different point to me when a great friend of mine and noted southern historian refused to move to his university. The best southern historians, the Ivy Leaguer argued, were those who were born in the South but moved north and achieved a certain detachment. He cited David Potter, David Donald, and C. Vann Woodward.)

Such criticisms of our outsiderness, gently and charmingly made, gave me pause. Far from being unsympathetic to the plight of white southerners, I had imagined myself a sort of honorary good ol' boy described recently by James C. Cobb as "a disarmingly downhome, diehard Braves fan who prefers Budweiser to Guinness." I believed that I was as likely to spring to the defense of white southerners criticized by supercilious Yankees as any native. I could understand how C. Vann Woodward reacted at the Selma-Montgomery march. He and other historians on the march rather self-consciously gathered round to give three cheers for Martin Luther King. As he told Willie Morris, he looked over to see the raw hatred of the white Alabamans watching from behind the ranks of the National Guard. And part of him sympathized with their view. In 1984 Alger Hiss took me to see some of his white liberal friends on Long Island. He told them that I had wonderful things to report from the South. (I had been telling Alger about what John Shelton Reed described as the transformation of day-to-day race relations in the South.) I was listened to with the careful attention and astonishment that a missionary returning from a foreign country would receive. One couple worried about the physical safety of their son, who was going to Montgomery to clerk for an African American federal judge. Should he discard his New York car tags? Would we provide a safe house for him in Atlanta when he made his journey south? I suppressed the desire to reply that he was less likely to be attacked by rednecks in Alabama than by his fellow New Yorkers on the streets of Manhattan.[10]

My work argued that both conservatives and moderates in the South believed that public opinion was arrayed against them. Conservatives believed that ordinary white southerners were entirely too indifferent to the threat posed to white supremacy. Moderates believed, on the contrary, that ordinary whites were entirely too stirred up over the race issue, and that defiance of that popular sentiment would be fatal politically. The difference was that the conservatives were prepared to mount a righteous crusade to stir up white opposition to desegregation, to persuade ordinary whites that the Supreme Court could be defied, but the moderates and liberals for the most part were silent, fearing that too much agitation would harm the prospects of gradual racial change. In a contest between conservative dynamism and liberal fatalism, there could be only one victor. As critics rightly noted, there was an undoubted implication in my argument not only that liberal failings mattered and enabled the triumph of Massive Resistance, but that they did not need to be so supine. I had to acknowledge that it was all too easy for historians to second-guess politicians and to ascribe a freedom of maneuver that may have been illusory. It was undoubtedly true that to second-guess courageous politicians like Frank Smith, Carl Elliott, or Hale Boggs from a distance of three thousand miles was even easier.

Nevertheless, I retained some hope that an outsider's perspective might not be crippling. Part of that optimism lay in the achievements of a remarkable trio of graduate students who came to Cambridge as my first Ph.D. students there in 1992. Tim Minchin, Stephen Tuck, and Clive Webb left me in no doubt as to the value of British scholars working on southern history. The British Ph.D. undoubtedly has its faults. The absence of course work and an empirical emphasis may contribute to the tin ear that many British Americanists, as Richard King notes, have for theory. Our work can seem traditional and even old-fashioned. But there are compelling virtues in the British system as well. On a prosaic level, the concentration on the dissertation enables students to complete their dissertations quickly and to enable a scholar like Tim Minchin to have written four substantial research monographs within ten years of starting as a graduate student at the age of twenty-two. That speed does not come at the expense of archival research. Most of them have spent well over a year in southern archives during their Ph.D. studies — archival research that was unhindered by teaching responsibilities. The oral-history interviews that Tuck conducted, the voluminous National Labor Relations Board hearings that Minchin explored, and the geographical range of the collections that Webb consulted all testify to the thoroughness of their research. Even more important, the freedom granted to highly intelligent students to pursue their own topic is valuable. Would an American Ph.D. student have been given the license to study an entire state for a case study of the Civil Rights movement as Tuck was; would such a student have been allowed to follow Webb's determined path to cover black-Jewish relations in the South all the way from slavery to the present? Distance perhaps also allowed them to challenge the conventional pieties and to undermine rather celebratory accounts of resistance and protest in the South. Tuck was as interested in Georgia communities where there was no civil rights protest as in those that were hotbeds of activism. Webb made it impossible to sustain easy generalizations about mutual black and Jewish interests in civil rights in the South. Minchin found the failure of textile unionism in the South not in a distinctive culture of southern workers but in the structure of the industry and the circumstances of wartime and postwar prosperity.[11]

The obvious obstacles facing an outsider observer and some possibly compensating benefits from a measure of detachment were brought home to me at the 2003 conference organized by Vernon Burton and Winfred B. "Bo" Moore Jr. at The Citadel, the first major conference to examine the Civil Rights movement in South Carolina. I could not help but feel an interloper as I listened to the moving testimony from African American participants in the movement, particularly survivors of the Orangeburg massacre, about the violence and intimidation they faced. I could also not match the eloquent appraisal of white South Carolinians who, as students in the early 1960s in Columbia, had courageously been part of the small interracial movement in the state: Selden Smith, Charles Joyner, Dan T. Carter, and Hayes Mizell. Could I bring anything to this family reunion?[12]

To be asked to talk about the reaction of South Carolina governors to racial change and to do so on the same platform as former governors Fritz Hollings and John C. West was certainly likely to expose any comfortable academic second-guessing of southern moderates. I noted that it took "no little courage and no little political skill to reorient the state toward economic development and peaceful racial change." I did, however, raise questions about what I described as the "self-exculpatory model" of massive resistance in South Carolina—that the responsibility for massive resistance lay with everybody *except* the white political leaders of the state. I also queried the more panglossian versions of the "self-congratulatory model" of the state's peaceful adaptation to racial change in the 1960s. How much congratulation was due to a white leadership for eventually and belatedly complying with the law? How much credit was due the white leadership for averting the threat of violence, a threat that that leadership had unleashed in the first place? Critics have argued that I, as a nonsoutherner, have failed to understand politicians like Hollings and West on their own terms. What I argued in Charleston was that we do need to understand, not patronize or demonize, the white southern leaders of the 1950s and 1960s. But to understand them is not to absolve them of responsibility.[13]

Jack E. Davis recently exclaimed in effect that "the British are coming" as he noted the large number of British scholars publishing on the Civil Rights movement.[14] In fact, southern history as a whole, not just the post-1945 South, disproportionately engages the interest of American historians in Britain. From Betty Wood on colonial Georgia to Mike Tadman on the slave trade to Adam Fairclough on modern black protest, many of the leading British Americanists work on the South. They do so at a time when interest in southern history appears to be on the decline in the United States. Fewer posts in southern history and literature seem to be filled in American universities outside the South than they were a generation ago. In southern universities like Emory and Georgia, leading southern historians acutely feel the scorn of their Ivy League–trained colleagues in American and European history who regard southern history as mere "local" history.

Why does the South exert such a pull over British academics? It may be the universality of the southern experience of war, poverty, defeat, and guilt that C. Vann Woodward identified. Michael O'Brien noted that Columbia, South Carolina, burned to the ground by Sherman, was instantly recognizable to someone who grew up in a Plymouth flattened by the Luftwaffe. Stephen Tuck claimed an affinity between the British West Midlands and the South as marginal regions. A former imperial power coming to terms with its own history of racial oppression might be seen to have a special interest in a region coping with slavery, its own form of apartheid, and the dramatic collapse of white supremacy. The trials and tribulations of a fledgling nation-state have powerful contemporary European resonance. The Civil War has had a never-ending fascination for British observers interested in the constitutional workings of federalism and the scale of the military conflict. The southern roots of so much American popular culture attracted scholars like Brian Ward.

Contingency also plays a part, however. The presence of expatriate scholars who happened to work on the South, Bill Dusinberre and Richard King, has been enormously important. Teaching demands turned Peter Parish into a southern historian as they had me. His head of department in Glasgow, Esmond Wright, who was tired of teaching a special subject, told Peter to introduce one instead. When Peter suggested his own specialty, the Age of Jackson, Wright told him to teach instead the American Civil War, which would be more popular with the students. The results, some years down the road, were Peter's magisterial studies of the Civil War and of slavery and its historians. The paucity of graduate awards in Britain in the 1970s and 1980s led historians like Mark Newman, Richard Follett, and Keith Mason to pursue their Ph.D.s at southern universities. The accidents of appointments and funding opportunities allied to student demand have shaped the importance of southern history in British universities as much as the universality of the southern historical experience. Indeed, for many scholars and students, what has always been attractive about the South has been the appeal of its difference, rather than its similarity: its exotic politics, its brutal race relations, its compelling nonviolent social protest.

Jack Davis compared the "invasion" of British historians to the arrival of the Beatles in America.[15] He rightly doubts that we will have the same impact, though he is generous about our work. The outsiders' perspective has perhaps some value for the pursuit of southern history at this particular time. The interest in the South in Britain and Europe should bolster the confidence of southern historians that theirs is not a parochial subject. But the outsider can also challenge the sense of proprietorial ownership of their own history by southerners, especially white southerners. The outsider status neither guarantees authenticity not precludes it. The outsider may state the obvious, rediscover the wheel, or miss the nuances, but the outsider may also interrupt the familiar. To prefer Budweiser to Guinness does not prove the British historian has a special empathy for the South as a pseudo-Confederate common man. To pull no punches on the platform at The Citadel about white southerners in the 1950s does not make the outsider coldhearted to the dilemmas of white southerners in their own place and time. As an outsider, I may have no personal stake in southern history, but I hope I can bring to it great interest and sympathetic — which is not to say uncritical — eyes and ears.

Notes

1. Herbert Nicholas, "The Education of an Americanist," *Journal of American Studies* 14 (April 1980), 15–16.

2. I did manage to get to the papers of Albert Gore Sr., at Murfreesboro, Tenn., first. It seems likely that I may also have been first to use the papers of Jack Brooks in Beaumont, Tex., since the boxes were still in the cellophane wrappers that they had been in when they arrived from Washington. But otherwise, Bill has beaten me every time.

3. Sir Anthony Jenkinson, *America Came My Way* (London, 1936), 143; Nick Clarke, *Alastair Cooke: The Biography* (London, 1999), 115.

4. Anthony J. Badger, "Huey Long and the New Deal," in Stephen W. Baskerville and Ralph Willett, eds., *Nothing Else to Fear: New Perspectives on America in the Thirties* (Manchester, 1985), 65–103. Tony Badger, "'When I Took the Oath of Office, I Took

No Vow of Poverty': Race, Corruption, and Democracy, 1928–2000" (Mellon Lecture Series, 2000), copy in the author's possession.

5. Anthony J. Badger, *Prosperity Road: The New Deal, Tobacco, and North Carolina* (Chapel Hill, 1980); Michael Sewell, "British Responses to Martin Luther King, Jr., and the Civil Rights Movement, 1954–68," in Brian Ward and Tony Badger, eds., *The Making of Martin Luther King and the Civil Rights Movement* (London, 1996), 206; Charles Martin, "The Rise and Fall of Jim Crow in College Sports: The Case of the Atlantic Coast Conference," *North Carolina Historical Review* 76 (July 1999), 253–84; and Timothy B. Tyson, *Blood Done Sign My Name* (New York, 2003).

6. Michael O'Brien, "C. Vann Woodward and the Burden of Southern Liberalism," *American Historical Review* 78 (June 1973), 589–604. Michael has explored his own intellectual history with characteristically stylish irony and self-deprecation in the introduction to the paperback edition of *The Idea of the American South, 1920–1941* (Baltimore and London, 1990), ix–xv, and "The Apprehension of the South in Modern Culture," *Southern Cultures* 4, no. 4 (1998), 3–18.

7. Tony Badger, "Southerners Who Refused to Sign the Southern Manifesto," *Historical Journal* 42 (June 1999), 517–34 ; "Whatever Happened to Roosevelt's New Generation of Southerners?" in Robert A. Garson and Stuart S. Kidd, eds., *The Roosevelt Years: New Perspectives on American History, 1933–1945* (Edinburgh, 1999), 122–38; "'Closet Moderates': Why White Liberals Failed, 1940–1970," in Ted Ownby, ed., *The Role of Ideas in the Civil Rights South* (Jackson, Miss., 2002), 83–112. Harold Cooley, future chair of the House Agriculture Committee, had been elected as a pro-New Dealer in 1934. Charles Deane, elected in 1946, had first run in 1938. Thurmond Chatham was a prominent Liberty League member and supporter of Wendell Wilkie in the 1930s.

8. Tony Badger, "Confessions of a British Americanist," *Journal of American History* 79 (September 1992), 515–23.

9. Sir David Williams to Tony Badger, May 29, 1991 (copy in the author's possession).

10. James Cobb, "European Scholars Can't Get Enough of the South," *University of Georgia Alumni Magazine* 82 (June 2003), 4; Willie Morris, *North Toward Home* (Boston, 1967), 399. Alger Hiss, who drafted the first AAA contract for flue-cured tobacco in 1933, understood the South perfectly well. He liked to be read to, as he had read aloud to Oliver Wendell Holmes. I read to him that summer of 1984 chapters of Patricia Sullivan's Emory Ph.D. dissertation that became her pathbreaking book, *Days of Hope: Race and Democracy in the New Deal Era* (Chapel Hill, 1996). Old southern New Dealers who loomed so large in that book, like Clark Foreman and Virginia Durr, had been old friends of his.

11. Timothy J. Minchin, *What Do We Need a Union For? The* TWUA *in the South, 1945–1955* (Chapel Hill, 1997); Clive Webb, *Fight Against Fear: Southern Jews and Black*

Civil Rights (Athens, Ga., and London, 2001); Stephen G. N. Tuck, *Beyond Atlanta: The Struggle for Racial Equality in Georgia, 1940–1980* (Athens, Ga., and London, 2001).

12. Henry H. Lesesne, *A History of the University of South Carolina, 1940–2000* (Columbia, S.C., 2001).

13. Tony Badger, "From Defiance to Moderation: South Carolina Governors and Racial Change" (Paper given at "The Citadel Conference on the Civil Rights Movement in South Carolina," March 7, 2003, copy in the author's possession); *The (Charleston) State,* March 8, 2003.

14. Jack E. Davis, review of *Beyond Atlanta: The Struggle for Racial Equality in Georgia, 1940–1980,* by Stephen G. N. Tuck, *American Historical Review* 107 (December 2002), 1595–96.

15. Davis, review of *Beyond Atlanta,* 1595.

Living History

DREW GILPIN FAUST

We create ourselves out of the stories we tell about our lives, stories that impose purpose and meaning on experiences that often seem random and discontinuous. As we scrutinize our own past in the effort to explain ourselves to ourselves, we discover—or invent—consistent motivations, characteristic patterns, fundamental values, a sense of self. Fashioned out of memories, our stories become our identities.

Historians tell stories too. But we who consider ourselves professional practitioners of the craft have been trained to mistrust the tales people tell, even as we fill pages with our renderings of others' lives. We cast a critical eye on what our long-dead informants tell us about their experiences; we check their assertions about themselves against other sorts of evidence. Are statements in diaries and letters borne out by legal and public records? Are they supported by the writings of contemporaries with different perspectives and agendas? We challenge the narratives of our historical colleagues as we endeavor to find the truth, and we build careers by revising interpretations, by piecing together data in new ways that yield a new plot, a fresh account, a richer understanding about a segment of the past.

To be a historian is thus to be in some sense a living contradiction. We are at once the agents and the objects of history. We are on the one hand individuals—like all others—struggling to fashion a coherent and stable narrative of our own lives that will provide the foundation of a self. Yet we are, by education and inclination, compelled to be skeptical of such stories. We must paradoxically place ourselves both outside and inside of history.

Arnold Toynbee wrote about this complex relationship with the past when he remembered witnessing Queen Victoria's Diamond Jubilee procession as a small boy. History, he felt then, was "something ... that happens to other people." Triumphant imperial Britain seemed in 1897 above history. But, he continued tellingly, if he had been a small boy in the American South instead of in London, he would have known that "history had happened to my people in my part of the world." He would have been inside it.[1]

I knew from the time I was a small child in Virginia that I lived in history. When I was born, a half century after the Diamond Jubilee, the South was still breathing the air of war and defeat. The Lee-Jackson highway took me to school; ubiquitous Confederate-gray historical markers memorialized battles like Cedar Creek, Belle Grove, or Bethel or skirmishes along the Opequon and the Shenandoah; seven small marble slabs noted the presence of unnamed Confederate dead just behind my grandfather's grave in the Old Chapel cemetery; and my grandmother sought to inspire and instruct us with choruses of "I'm a good old rebel / That's just what I am / For this fair land of freedom / I do not give a damn," impressing us in no small part by the entirely uncharacteristic use of profanity to underscore her passion. But my sense of history was more immediate as well. By midcentury, the Civil War's unresolved legacies of race had assumed new urgency as the 1954 *Brown v. Board of Education* Supreme Court decision challenged the customs of racial segregation that had been legally enshrined by *Plessy v. Ferguson* in 1896. Now integration was to become the law of the land; schools, and then all of southern society, were to be transformed with "all deliberate speed."

I have always known that I became a southern historian because I grew up in that particular time and place. My sense of self, my story about how I became who I am, has always been situated in events now nearly a half century old and the subject of academic study for many of my fellow historians. I developed a narrative about my childhood, about my identity as rebellious daughter, that I offered to all those who asked — and to some who didn't — a narrative that explained my redemption as a white southerner and my resurrection as civil rights advocate and activist. In the preface to *Mothers of Invention*, published in 1996, I committed to print the story I had repeated so often.

> My professional historical interest in the South grew out of those early years . . . for I lived in Harry Byrd's home county during the era of *Brown v. Topeka* and "massive resistance" to school desegregation. . . . It was not until I heard news about the Brown decision on the radio that I even noticed that my elementary school was all white and recognized that this was not an accident. But I quickly penned a letter to President Eisenhower to say how illogical I thought this seemed in the face of the precepts of equality I had already

imbibed by second grade. I confronted the paradox of being both a southerner and an American at an early age.[2]

Seeing this explanation in print was jarring, for it juxtaposed my own narrative with the stories that filled the rest of that book — stories I had subjected to the historian's critical eye, had researched and footnoted. Not a few of those footnotes cited letters written by women of all ages to their president — to Jefferson Davis, in this study of Confederate women. But if these letters, not to mention those written to Lincoln, to FDR, and to every other American president had been saved and archived, why not my letter to Eisenhower? It had never occurred to me. But I could no longer simply stand outside the past and make my judgments about it. I had to look at my own memories. I had to make myself the object as well as the agent of history. I had to find the footnote to document my own life.

It seemed a long shot. Perhaps the letter had been lost or misfiled. Perhaps it had never existed. Perhaps I had just thought about writing it or perhaps I had entirely invented a legendary past in order to root my rebellious teenage years of the 1960s in a dramatic childhood epiphany and a personal myth of origin. Perhaps I had indeed written to Eisenhower, but not with the enlightened integrationist and egalitarian document of my memory. Perhaps I had sent something more consistent with the conventional segregationist views of the white society in which I lived. Perhaps the letter would be horrifying.

The papers of the Eisenhower Administration are not stored, like those of the nineteenth-century presidents with which I was familiar, in the National Archives in Washington. Instead, they have been collected in the Eisenhower Library in Abilene, Kansas. And there, among 23 million pages of manuscripts, was my letter. "I have located a letter," wrote archivist Herbert Pankratz in an e-mail titled "Letter by a School Child," "in the White House Central Files. In the letter Miss Gilpin expresses her feelings about how Black Americans are treated and urges the president to make schools more open to minorities." But the letter was written in 1957, not 1954. Mr. Pankratz offered to mail me a copy.[3]

As I waited for the envelope from Abilene, I continued to wonder and worry about what I had written. Why 1957? Clearly I wasn't responding to *Brown*. Yet one thing I did know. In 1957 I would never have written about "Black Americans." That must have been a description of my letter composed much later by an archivist who was creating a calendar of materials in the Central Files.

"Black" was a usage introduced in the mid- to late 1960s; I had probably, I thought ruefully, written about "colored people."

"Dear Mr. Eisenhower," the letter began. "I am nine years old and I am white, but I have many feelings about segregation." I greeted the letter with some relief, with surprise — and at the same time with the eye of the historian who has subjected thousands of such documents to critical scrutiny. I have taught classes that have spent hours discussing a single text like this one — providing context, analyzing word choice, sentence structure, shape of argument, looking for what it has to reveal about another place and time. I have been deeply moved by discovering in a collection of family papers a bloodstained communication from a soldier announcing his own impending death. I have been excited to recognize that the slave names in a white owner's account book represent not just his record of profit and loss but tell a subversive story of black family ties maintained in face of slavery's oppressions. I have always felt that documents somehow magically connected me to the past; reading manuscripts has always been my favorite part of being a historian — even though I have always been slightly ashamed to enjoy such antiquarianism and sentimentality — both highly suspect in the eyes of professional historians. Now here was a copy of a letter I had written, a letter about which I had only vague and inaccurate memories, a letter that not only represented some earlier version of whoever I am but was available to any historical researcher as part of the Dwight D. Eisenhower Library of the National Archives of the United States. This was no longer just my letter, it had officially become archival; it was now what historians respectfully call a Primary Source.[4]

The letter is written on lined five-hole notebook paper, which I must have taken out of my school binder. This seems consistent with my memory that I never told my parents I was writing to the president. They discovered what I had been up to only when a formulaic acknowledgment arrived from the White House. They were stunned — both that I should have written to the president and that I should have expressed the thoughts that I did. I printed in block letters, perhaps worried that my handwriting would otherwise be illegible. I wrote the letter, fittingly — though I doubt I knew this — on Lincoln's birthday in 1957. I was, as the first line of the letter proclaimed, nine years old. I also wanted the president to know — in my first sentence — that even if I was very young, even if I was not among those feeling the force of discrimination, I felt strongly about segregation.[5]

I grew up in a privileged family in the rural Shenandoah Valley. Much of the western part of the state of Virginia had a very small black population, but my county, Clarke, had been home to younger sons of Tidewater gentry families during the eighteenth and early-nineteenth century, and these Burwells, Byrds, Randolphs, and Carters had brought their slaves with them to the valley. The descendants of the white owners and the black laborers remained, joined by newer families like mine, which had come to the valley at the turn of the twentieth century. In 1950 Clarke County's population of 7,074 was 17 percent black; in adjacent Warren and Frederick Counties, the proportions were 8 and 2 percent; in Loudoun and Fauquier, slightly to the east, the percentages were 19 and 26. This was not the Deep South, and I remember no signs designating water fountains or waiting rooms as "Colored" or "White." But it was a community of rigid racial segregation nevertheless, with lines drawn by custom and common understanding. There were separate black and white schools; such restaurants and other public facilities as existed in the largely rural county were restricted to whites. In our own house, the black cook and handyman had a separate bathroom. When I once used it, my mother reprimanded me for invading their privacy.[6]

In February 1957 I was in the fifth grade of an all-white school in Millwood, a village of a few hundred, the nearest settlement to our farm, and the site as well of the all-white Episcopal Church to which my family belonged. The county seat, Berryville, eight miles away, had 1,401 inhabitants; Washington, D.C., was sixty miles to the east. I am not sure where we got our news. We had no television, but I remember the almost constant chatter of the radio — especially in the car as I was driven to school or church or piano lessons. The *Washington Post* was the nearest major newspaper. Somehow I managed to feel engaged with what was happening in the world. I worried in 1956 about refugees from the Hungarian Revolution and wrote about them in school; I would worry in 1957 that the launch of *Sputnik* meant the Russians might try to take over America. Cold War anxieties had made their way to rural Virginia. And I worried about what was happening in the South.

In the winter of 1956–57, the news was filled with stories about the growing conflict over civil rights. The preceding fall the *Post* had reported regularly on the progress of the Montgomery Bus Boycott and the rising prominence of Martin Luther King Jr. In Washington itself, battle was being joined over what ultimately became the 1957 Civil Rights Act, the first significant piece of civil rights legislation since Reconstruction. But in February, Congress was still in the midst of hearings and confronted threats of a Senate filibuster from the South. Alabama state judge George Wallace testified on February 6 that the bill would make federal judges "dictators" and undermine precious rights of the states; the attorney general of Georgia claimed that in creating a Civil Rights Division charged with protecting civil and voting rights, the bill would transform the U.S. Department of Justice into a "Soviet-type gestapo." Yet while the *Post* editorialized in favor of guarantees of rights for black Americans, even its own advertising pages testified to rather different assumptions. Help-wanted notices specified "Colored Men" or "Men. Over 18 (White)." And housing ads announced "Sale D.C. Houses. Colored — Upper NW. True Splendor" or "Colored — Bargain. Modern 2 Family Brick. Only $395 Down."[7]

When Eisenhower traveled to Georgia in early February 1957 for a weekend visit to the plantation of his secretary of the treasury, the local Presbyterian minister greeted him with a Sunday-morning sermon describing "racial tensions that hang over our southland like a heavy thunderbolt." These tensions were nowhere heavier in early 1957 than in Virginia.[8]

Virginia was not an obvious leader for southern opposition to the Supreme Court's rulings on desegregation. In many ways the state had become increasingly oriented toward the North; its population was less than one-quarter black, and political scientist V. O. Key had in 1949 proclaimed the state's race relations as "perhaps the most harmonious in the South." Integration of higher education was already quietly underway with the admission of a few black students to the University of Virginia and Virginia Polytechnic Institute. State officials, including Governor Thomas B. Stanley, initially responded to the announcement of the *Brown* decision with calls for compliance. Stanley promised to work toward "a plan . . . in keeping with the edict of the court."[9]

But the most powerful man in Virginia politics, U.S. Senator, former governor, and Clarke County resident Harry Byrd, took a different perspective. The Court decision, he proclaimed, posed "the greatest internal crisis since the War Between the States." The actions of the Court threatened so to extend federal power as to establish "totalitarian government." Byrd's militant and unyielding opposition and the political effectiveness within the Commonwealth of the fabled — indeed notorious — Byrd Machine would derail efforts by moderates to design a workable plan of compliance and place Virginia at the head of the South's battle against *Brown*.[10]

Harry Byrd had entered politics just after the turn of the century and had controlled a powerful statewide Democratic machine for four decades. After serving as governor, Byrd joined the U.S. Senate in 1933 where he became a national figure, a leading opponent of FDR and the New Deal, and the embodiment of the increasing alienation of southern Democrats from the growing liberalism of the national party.

Byrd had long claimed the role of champion of the Constitution against the expansion of federal power, and in the tradition of his states' rights forebears who had defended the prerogatives of the South in the decades before the Civil War, Byrd embraced two doctrines to serve as the foundation for what would prove a last-ditch battle against integration after *Brown*. "Interposition" and "massive resistance" became the watchwords of the Byrd movement and of the growing struggle against desegregation across the South. Invoking John C. Calhoun's early-nineteenth-century language of nullification, the first doctrine argued that the contractual provisions of the U.S. Constitution provided for the interposition of state sovereignty between the dictates of federal courts and the actions of local school boards; the second doctrine, of "massive resistance," became a rallying cry for states to use this power to block the implementation of *Brown*.

In early February 1956 the Virginia legislature adopted an interposition resolution and urged "our sister States" to join in "prompt and deliberate efforts to check this and further encroachment by the Supreme Court, through judicial legislation, upon the reserved powers of the States." In the course of the next year seven more states followed, passing their own interposition measures. Under pressure from Byrd and his allies, Virginia governor Stanley abandoned his earlier moderation and convened a special session of the General Assembly in August 1956 to consider a program of massive resistance. With Byrd forces in control, the legislature adopted twenty-three segregationist laws, including five measures explicitly designed to intimidate the NAACP. At the core of the program of massive resistance was a law that removed control over any school integrated by court order from its local authorities to the Commonwealth of Virginia. The governor would then close the school, thus enshrining state power over either federal or local prerogatives. This policy assumed that no public education at all was preferable to desegregated schools. In September 1958 the threat of massive resistance became reality when the governor shut down Warren County High School in Front Royal, just eighteen miles southwest of Millwood, rather than permit twenty-two black pupils to enroll under federal court order. As the state pursued its intransigent course, high schools in

Charlottesville and Norfolk were closed as well, denying public education to more than thirteen thousand of its black and white citizens. But in January 1959 both the Virginia Supreme Court of Appeals and the federal district court in Norfolk declared the state's school-closing measures unconstitutional. Within days, Virginia's governor broke his long and deep ties with the Byrd Machine and appeared before the General Assembly to call for an end to massive resistance.[11]

When I had written to President Eisenhower nearly two years earlier, I did not know how the battle over Virginia's schools would turn out. Nor, of course, did I anticipate the struggles that would follow across the South as Eisenhower sent troops to uphold federal authority in Little Rock the next fall, or as the movement extended well beyond school issues and spread to Greensboro, Albany, Orangeburg, Birmingham, Selma, and Mississippi. So what was it that prompted me on a February day in 1957 to appeal to the president? What I remember is that I heard something on the radio as I was being driven home from school by Raphael Johnson — a black man who worked for my family doing everything from mowing the lawn, shining shoes, and washing floors and windows to transporting my brothers and me around the county, entertaining us all the while with quizzes on state and world capitals or the order of the presidents. I was in the car with Raphael when I heard something that made me realize that black children did not go to my school because they were not allowed to, because I was white and they were not.

I may well have heard a story about that day's decision by Norfolk federal judge Walter Hoffman to set August 15 as the deadline for integration in the Tidewater city of Newport News. Or I may have heard reports of Virginia's appeal the preceding day to delay federal desegregation mandates for Arlington and Charlottesville. But why did I respond to these reports rather than news the preceding fall of Montgomery bombings? Or of the massive resistance legislation passed in Richmond in August and September?

In my memory, in the story I had often told of that trip home from school, I asked Raphael if what I had just understood was true, whether I would be excluded from my school if I painted my face black. I came home and wrote these very words in my letter, not now as a question but already transformed into a declaration of outrage to the president. "If I painted my face black I wouldn't be let in any public schools etc. My feelings haven't changed, just the color of my skin."

What I remember is that Raphael did not answer my question. My probings about the unarticulated rules of racial interaction made him acutely uncomfortable; he was evasive. But his evasion was for me answer enough. How was it possible that I never asked that question or saw those realities until I was nine years old? How could I have not noticed before? Why did I notice then? And given my long obliviousness, why did these discoveries make me so upset? How did I know how to read Raphael's response and not to press him? Why did I have, as I wrote Eisenhower, "many feelings about segregation?"

It was not because race was a subject much discussed in my household. I lived in a world where social arrangements were taken for granted and assumed to be timeless. A child's obligation was to learn these usages, not to question them. The complexities of racial deportment were of a piece with learning manners and etiquette more generally. There were formalized ways of organizing almost every aspect of human relationships and interactions—how you placed your fork and knife on the plate when you had finished eating, what you did with a fingerbowl; who walked through a door first, whose name was spoken first in an introduction, how others were addressed—black adults with just a first name, whites as Mr. or Mrs.—whose hand you shook and whose you didn't, who ate in the dining room and who in the kitchen. But to a young white child sorting through this array of behavioral rules and expectations, the dictates of racial etiquette hardly stood out from all the others.

Partly this was because the iron fist of prejudice in my 1950s Virginia was sheathed in the velvet glove of paternalism. I do not think I ever heard the word *nigger* as a child; I never witnessed any physical cruelty of whites toward blacks. The white adults around me treated "colored people" with what they considered to be good manners. Yet there was at the same time an undeniable assumption of superiority—of greater intelligence, of entitlement, of earned social position—that took its most pernicious and overt expression in occasions of humor or gentle mockery, disguised, or perhaps rationalized, as patronizing affection. When I became a historian and began to read about black and white interaction in the Old South of a century earlier, much seemed startlingly familiar.

No one talked openly about race in my family. It would have been considered rude—not unlike discussing sex, another prohibited topic. That the Supreme Court or Martin Luther King Jr. would raise such issues was above all a breach of decorum. Such rare references as I heard from my elders about the emerging civil rights revolution consisted of clucking dismissals of impropriety and ill-mannered presumption. The elephant sat unmentioned in the living room. Even in the political arena, the discussion of race in Virginia was coded. Harry Byrd's program of massive resistance never directly invoked race or attacked blacks; instead he spoke of constitutional abstractions, of states' rights and federal encroachments.

Yet somehow I knew that, as with sex, talking about race was not just rude but dangerous. When I asked Raphael about my school, I crossed both those lines — of propriety and of safety. To acknowledge race was the first step toward change. Raphael knew far better than I the dangers involved in any questioning of his place. But even at nine I knew enough to recognize my questions as a transgression.

Like a majority of white Virginians, my parents had voted for Eisenhower in 1952 and 1956. The solidly Democratic South was beginning to break apart, recognizing the Republican Party as the more natural home for its conservatism. Harry Byrd had in a sense given his permission for such realignment, refusing to support Adlai Stevenson's Democratic presidential candidacy. When Eisenhower won the election, Byrd hailed the new administration as a "ray of hope" that federal power and spending might be curbed.[12]

I understood little of this in 1957, but I had been taken the preceding fall, as part of the 1956 campaign season, to an Eisenhower rally in nearby Middleburg. The candidate himself appeared, and although I remember nothing of what he said, the man's benevolent mien and generous smile made me glad to wear my "I Like Ike" button. I had seen the president; the White House had a human face; I could certainly write to him. I would address my letter to "Mr." not "President" Eisenhower.

What surprised me most about the letter when I was reunited with it after more than forty-five years was that the argument it offered against segregation was fundamentally a religious one. I had not remembered that at all. "Long ago on Christmas Day Jesus Christ was born. As you remember he was born to save the world. . . . Colored people aren't given a chance. . . . So what if their skin is black? They still have feelings but most of all are God's People!" For years, I had told myself and others a quite different story about the sources and logic of my racial views. I thought that the combination of the merciless rationality and the political innocence of the child had led me to see the inconsistencies between the American creed of democracy and equality and the cruel realities of race in the mid-twentieth-century South. Perhaps I had been encouraged to make these assumptions about my motivations by the literature of southern history and by books like Gunnar Myrdal's 1944 classic, *An American Dilemma: The*

Negro Problem and Modern Democracy, which emphasized the emerging awareness after World War II of the contradictions inherent in American racial attitudes. I thought that the paradoxes of freedom and unfreedom that had plagued Virginians since the slaveowner Thomas Jefferson penned the Declaration of Independence had prompted me to understand — even as a nine-year-old — the hypocrisy of the white South. But my letter did not invoke American values; it assailed a different sort of hypocrisy. It was suffused with Christianity.

Perhaps I took this perspective because of the widely reported news of a declaration in early February 1957 from sixty of Richmond's Protestant clergy, who decried the sacrifice of the state's public school system "on the altar . . . of prejudice" and called for a "Judeo-Christian framework . . . of moral resolution" for the crisis. I certainly seemed to share their "Judeo-Christian" approach. But I have never thought of my childhood or my family as particularly religious. Ours was the detached faith of Episcopalianism, not the enthusiastic piety of the evangelical South. Talk about God was confined to Sunday-morning church, Sunday school, and a daily rendition of the Lord's Prayer — recited so fast at bedtime as to be almost one long word, "whoartinheavenhallowedbethyname." Any other invocation of religion was almost as indecorous as discussing sex or race. We did not even say grace at meals. Yet here I was writing to the president demanding justice for "God's People."[13]

Neither race nor the Civil Rights movement was ever mentioned in our all-white local church. By the middle years of the 1960s my outrage at this stunning silence would lead me to abandon organized religion permanently. But in 1957 I was too young to notice how much less progressive our local minister seemed to be on the segregation question than many of Richmond's clergymen. When I learned much later about the colonial Virginia "right of advowson," which gave landowners effective control over the appointment and retention of clergy, I came to look upon the behavior of our rector, his failure to question the assumptions of the small circle of Clarke County residents who served as his vestry and set his salary, as part of a very long and ignoble tradition. His timidity and conformity, his failure to speak out against — perhaps even to see — twentieth-century racial injustice, were of a piece with the church's willful blindness, even complicity, in the establishment of slavery in the seventeenth century and in its defense up to the moment of its abolition.

Yet I imbibed some sort of egalitarian message from the church nevertheless. Was it from weekly Bible stories in Sunday school? The only one of these classes I specifically recall was memorable for rather different reasons. One day, my father came to teach my class, substituting for the regular instructor — I think the minister's wife — who was sick. That Sunday's tale was Samson and Delilah. When we got to the end, my father asked if we children could identify the moral of the story. When no one supplied it, he offered his interpretation. "Never trust a woman." It seems Sunday school was no more likely to liberate my mind in questions of gender than of race.

Yet Christianity bore a message of freedom and justice and human worth that even the legacies of slavery and the inhumanity of segregation and racism could not silence. Jesus Christ, I informed Eisenhower, was born to save "not only white people but black yellow red and brown." In their segregated churches, white southern Christians sang:

> In Christ there is no East or West
> In Him no South or North;
> But one great fellowship of love
> Throughout the whole wide earth.
> Join hands, then, brothers of the faith
> What e'er your race may be;
> Who serves my Father as a son
> Is surely kin to me.[14]

In the leatherbound Common Prayer and Hymnal that I was given as a child, this is Hymn 263. The words are attributed to "John Oxenham, 1908"; the notes appear above the stanzas on two treble staves marked simply "Negro Melody." Christianity in the mid-twentieth-century South, as in many other times and places, contained powerful ambiguities.

Slaves a century earlier had found in Christianity a message of self-affirmation and a promise of ultimate liberation that provided a critical foundation for community, identity, and survival. In the mid-twentieth century, Christianity would serve as the weapon of the weak, an ideology for mass civil rights activism, a lever of change that would make the transformation of southern race relations possible. Martin Luther King Jr.'s effectiveness depended on the existence of thousands of Americans like me who could be confronted with the contradictions between their fundamental religious and moral commitments and their participation in the South's systems of racial oppression.

In his famous "Letter from Birmingham Jail," written in 1963, King articulated his challenge to the Christian South to live up to its professed ideals. "The contemporary church is often a weak, ineffectual voice with an uncertain sound. It is so often the arch-supporter of the status quo.... But the judgment of God is upon the church as never before. If the church of today does not recapture the sacrificial spirit of the early church, it will lose its authentic ring, forfeit the loyalty of millions.... I hope the Church ... will meet the challenge of this decisive hour."[15]

King explained the strategy that had shaped his efforts in Montgomery, in Albany, and in Birmingham. His movement depended on its appeal to "the light of human conscience" and its commitment to ending the silence of consent to the status quo. "Nonviolent direct action seeks to create such a crisis ... that a community ... is forced to confront the issue. It seeks so to dramatize the issue that it can no longer be ignored."[16]

As I grew older, King would successfully appeal to my conscience. I am not sure what, if anything, I knew of his efforts in Montgomery when I wrote to Eisenhower in 1957. But his message spoke to exactly the sentiments that prompted my letter. And it was these same sentiments that encouraged me by my later years in high school to get involved with Quaker activists and to spend the summer of 1964 on a civil rights initiative in Orangeburg, Atlanta, and Birmingham. Eight years after I wrote President Eisenhower, I responded to Martin Luther King Jr.'s dramatization of the injustices at Selma in exactly the way he hoped and intended. Like thousands of other Americans, I found the television images of Bloody Sunday on Selma's Edmund Pettus Bridge intolerable. I could not stand by as peaceful citizens were clubbed and gassed as they marched for the right to vote. A college freshman, I cut my spring midterms and went to Selma. As with my letter to Eisenhower, I never told my parents. Even as I differed from them on issues of race and civil rights, I seem to have been less successful in challenging their rules about silences. For all the changes that came to Virginia and the world in the 1960s and afterward, we still never talked openly about race, religion, or sex.

The nine-year-old writer closes her letter with emotion, as if the effort to advance the logic of her position has for a full page only just managed to contain the intense "feelings about segregation" she described in the first paragraph. "Please Mr. Eisenhower please try and have schools and other things accept colored people." This letter takes its place within the tradition of entreaties and petitions from women to their rulers. Indeed it was within the nineteenth-century abolition movement that American women's right to petition was first forcefully expressed, as, between 1831 and the Civil War, women sent three million signatures to Congress pleading for the end of slavery. In 1863 Susan B. Anthony defined the petition as woman's most important political right. "Women," she observed, "can neither take the ballot or the bullet. . . . Therefore, to us, the right of petition is one sacred right which we ought not to neglect." Like all American women until the passage of the Nineteenth Amendment in 1920, just thirty-seven years earlier, this nine-year-old letter writer cannot vote. She is, of course, too young. But it means that, like generations of women who preceded her, she has no political power to exert, no threat to offer, no reward to promise any elected official. She can only plead. This injustice matters to me, she writes, even though I am only nine, even though I am white and it is not being done to me.[17]

Why did it matter so much? Was the injustice in some sense being done to me? There was, of course, a long tradition of white southern opposition to slavery that insisted slavery harmed whites more than blacks. Jefferson himself made this argument. But there is no evidence that I was thinking about segregation in this way. Yet I find something curious and perhaps revealing about the letter's signature. "Sincerly." I was a good speller. This is my one slip. But my name is out of alignment. It looks as if I wrote Drew Gilpin, which was indeed what I was called. And then I decided I should include my real first name, which I never used except to identify myself as female. So "Catherine" is added in front — sticking out from the "Sincerly" and looking quite out of place. I wanted to be known not just as nine and white but as a girl. I am sure that had I not added the "Catherine" the response from the White House would have come to Mr. Gilpin; the description of the letter in the Eisenhower Library catalog would note that "Mr. Gilpin expresses his feelings. . . ." I had begun to learn the realities of having a male name even by the age of nine; I knew I had to take action to claim my femaleness and my own identity. I wanted to speak to Eisenhower as the person I was, and clearly I saw part of that as being a girl.

Did being a girl have a more general importance to the letter and to my "feelings about segregation"? I have often wondered this as I have thought about the years that followed. I was the only daughter in a family of four children; I was the rebel who did not just march for civil rights and against the Vietnam War but who fought endlessly with my mother, refusing to accept her insistence that "this is a man's world, sweetie, and the sooner you learn that the better off you'll be." Did my sense of the privileges allotted my brothers — who did not have to wear scratchy organdy dresses or lace underwear, sit decorously, curtsy, or accept innumerable other constraints on freedom—make me attuned to other sorts of injustice? I grew up in a man's world and a white world. Did I somehow see a connection between the two? The women's movement would certainly help me to make these connections many years later. But I did not have the language or analytic framework to articulate such insights until after I graduated from college. It is extraordinary what one doesn't see. Or perhaps on some level I did see, and the sense of my own place in my family and in the Virginia social order did make me sensitive to the place of others.

The public schools in Clarke County were not integrated until 1966. The vagueness of the Supreme Court's demand for "all deliberate speed" became an ironic betrayal of so many of the Civil Rights movement's hopes. By 1966, I was a junior in college in Pennsylvania. I rarely returned to Virginia—from school or, indeed, ever again. I found its silences both too difficult to maintain and too difficult to challenge. I would wrestle with the dilemmas of race that had suffused my childhood from a distance of both time and space. Living my life north of the Mason-Dixon line, I abandoned activism for history, telling myself that I was searching in the nineteenth-century South's experiences of slavery and war for the understanding that might somehow contribute to change.

At the core of the questions I wanted to ask about the past was the desire to comprehend how human beings become so imbedded in the taken-for-grantedness of their world that they cannot see it clearly, how people come not just to accept but to defend slavery or segregation—or any of a host of other insupportable injustices. If we understand how others have failed to see or failed to speak, perhaps, I thought, we can come to recognize our own blindnesses, our own processes of rationalization and self-justification. Perhaps history can help us to see the contingency of our lives, our beliefs, and our social worlds. Perhaps history can help us understand that it could have been, we could have been, we could still be otherwise. In history we might find a sense of possibility.

But as I think of my nine-year-old self, I am acutely aware as well of the opportunities given—or denied—by specific historical moments. I wrote my letter because the radio, the newspapers, the Richmond clergy, the Supreme Court, and the NAACP had begun to break the silence. Had I been born a decade earlier, I would never have asked those questions, written that letter, or been privileged to lead what has become my life. My actions—my letter, my protests, my marches — mattered very little to the cause of racial justice in the twentieth-century South; but they freed me — to speak, to see, and to escape from a world of dehumanizing silence.

Notes

I would like to thank Charles Rosenberg, Donald Gilpin, Steven Lawson, Jeremy Knowles, and Homi Bhabha for invaluable advice on matters of both style and substance.

1. Toynbee, quoted in C. Vann Woodward, *The Origins of the New South, 1877–1913* (Baton Rouge, 1951), xiii.

2. Drew Gilpin Faust, *Mothers of Invention: Women of the Slaveholding South in the American Civil War* (Chapel Hill, 1996), xi.

3. Herbert Pankratz to Drew Gilpin Faust, "Letter by a School Child," e-mail, November 20, 2002.

4. Catherine Drew Gilpin to Mr. Eisenhower, February 12, 1956 [1957, letter is misdated], White House Central Files, Dwight D. Eisenhower Library of the National Archives, Abilene, Kansas.

5. The letter was answered with a formulaic response from Maxwell Rabb, Secretary to the Cabinet, written to "Dear Catherine" and dated February 26, 1957.

6. Maral S. Kalbian and Leila O. W. Boyer, *Final Report: African-American Historic Context, Clarke County, Va.*, CLG Project # 66014 [National Park Service] (Washington, D.C., 2002), 29.

7. *Washington Post*, February 7, 1957, B1; February 8, 1957, A2; February 11, 1957, A14; February 11, 1957, B10, 12.

8. *Washington Post*, February 11, 1957, A2.

9. V. O. Key, *Southern Politics in State and Nation* (New York, 1949), 32n; Stanley quoted in Numan V. Bartley, *The Rise of Massive Resistance: Race and Politics in the South during the 1950s* (Baton Rouge, 1969), 80.

10. Ronald L. Heinemann, *Harry Byrd of Virginia* (Charlottesville, 1996), 341 (first quotation); Bartley, *Rise of Massive Resistance*, 109 (second quotation). On Byrd, see Matthew D. Lassiter and Andrew B. Lewis, *The Moderates' Dilemma: Massive Resistance to School Desegregation in Virginia* (Charlottesville, 1998); J. Harvie Wilkinson III, *Harry Byrd and the Changing Face of Virginia Politics, 1945–1966* (Charlottesville, 1968); James W. Ely Jr., *The Crisis of Conservative Virginia: The Byrd Organization and the Politics of Massive Resistance* (Knoxville, 1976); and Benjamin Muse, *Virginia's Massive Resistance* (Bloomington, 1961).

11. Muse, *Virginia's Massive Resistance*, 22; entire resolution appears in *Race Relations Law Reporter* 1 (April 1956), 445–47.
12. Byrd quoted in Heinemann, *Harry Byrd*, 355.
13. *Washington Post*, February 3, 1957, E3.
14. *The Hymnal of the Protestant Episcopal Church in the United States of America* (Greenwich, Conn., 1940).
15. Martin Luther King Jr., *Letter from Birmingham City Jail* (San Francisco, 1994), 2, 9, 30.
16. King, *Letter*, 17 (first quotation), 6 (second quotation).
17. Anthony quoted in Susan Zaeske, *Signatures of Citizenship: Petitioning, Antislavery, and Women's Political Identity* (Chapel Hill, 2003), 10.

Up South in the Middle West

Toward a Cultural and Intellectual Autobiography

DARLENE CLARK HINE

The Quest for a Richer Perspective

In 1970 Albert Murray argued that "student requests for courses in black heritage, including African history, should be met because such courses also provide instructors additional opportunities to develop a richer perspective on the world-at-large for all students. A black or honey-brown student with his head buried in a book by Frantz Fanon, Che Guevara, Malcolm X, or Eldridge Cleaver may be searching for intellectual equipment for modern living."[1] Just such a quest for suitable "intellectual equipment" in order to develop "a richer perspective on the world" led me into the historical profession. My search continues for even more complex understanding, but now there is a difference. Perhaps more so than in my earlier years, I have a deeper appreciation for the knowledge and insight about the world that emanates from outside of the academy. There are myriad sites of knowledge production. The challenge is to balance the formal education with the life instructions that are firmly embedded in culture and experience, in the teachings of family, and in the lectures of favorite undergraduate professors.

I am about as middle-western as they come. I was born in Missouri, raised and educated in Illinois and Ohio, and have taught history at Purdue University (in Indiana) and at Michigan State University for the past three decades. Yet I have always thought of myself as being, first and foremost, a southerner who was part of the southern diaspora. This paradoxical identity is only one of many complications that underpin my ongoing search, as Albert Murray put it, for "intellectual equipment" and "a richer perspective on the world-at-large." My work in southern history was shaped in part by a childhood spent in rural Villa Ridge, Illinois, by the professors I encountered at Roosevelt University in

Chicago, by my graduate-student days at Kent State University, and by my academic teaching positions. Throughout this odyssey I acquired the "intellectual equipment" from meaningful engagements with significant family members, teachers, friends, and mentors.

This brief autobiographical essay does two things. In it I excavate the southern cultural origins and then examine the midwestern intellectual forces that forged my orientation toward specific research topics in southern history, politics, black women's studies, the professions (especially nursing, medicine, law), and civil rights. My graduate adviser at Kent State University once observed that "it is the way in which a person's own individual experiences intersect with trends in the larger social and intellectual milieu that shapes the social consciousness and the directions of his/her scholarly research."[2] I expand upon this point to add that one does not have to be from, or to reside in, a specific place in order to represent that region. My southernness resides inside. It is reflected in my values and in the intellectual work that I do. This southern identity has facilitated my interrogations and negotiations of the overlapping diasporas in which I participate and represent.

My life falls easily into two periods: the 1950s and 1960s, and from the 1970s to the present. In the first period the influence of my family, especially that of my maternal grandmother, Fannie Venerable Thompson (1904–2002), looms large. This period witnessed my coming of age in, and subsequent migration from, a rural communal environment in Villa Ridge, Illinois. Chicago, the tumultuous 1960s, the Civil Rights and black power movements, and the black consciousness and Black Studies movement informed my politics and cemented a commitment to black liberation through the study, writing, and teaching of history. As an undergraduate student enrolled at Roosevelt University, I was mightily influenced by the teachings and formal writings of three men, English professor Lorenzo Dow Turner, sociologist St. Clair Drake, and historian Hollis Lynch.[3]

In spite of the strong influence my black professors had on my general intellectual development, I made the specific decision to become a historian after taking a U.S. survey course taught by a white historian, Paul Johnson. The remarkably talented and captivating Johnson was an awe-inspiring undergraduate professor. I never spoke to Professor Johnson while enrolled in his class, but to this day I recall his vivid and exciting lectures about Theodore Roosevelt and the black troops that fought in what was then called the Spanish-American War. Paul Johnson possessed both a dramatic gift, joy, and confidence and an obvious command of his subject matter that, when conjoined with a flair for making history come alive, left his students enthralled. His lecture/performances made freshmen and sophomores, regardless of race, gender, or age, eager for the next installment.

The second phase of my intellectual odyssey commenced with my 1968 departure from Chicago in order to pursue graduate study at Kent State University in Kent, Ohio, under the direction of historian August Meier, who had also taught for a brief period at Roosevelt University. The normal course of graduate study was irrevocably transformed by the killing of four students at Kent State on May 4, 1970, by soldiers of the National Guard. I was traumatized to silence by this event and afterward became much more aware of the ways that class and social status determine how people, white and black, male and female, young and old, gay and straight, rich and poor, are treated by those in power. I doubt that troopers would have entered the campuses of Harvard, Yale, Princeton, Chicago, or Berkeley and left bodies strewn across the lawns.

In each successive decade, the 1970s, 1980s, and 1990s, I sought diverse experiences and opportunities to augment my "intellectual equipment." Before joining the history department of Purdue University, I taught for two years (1972–74) at South Carolina State College in Orangeburg. Throughout the 1970s my concentration on southern black political history obliterated virtually all other concerns. I was critically influenced by my Purdue University colleague Harold D. Woodman (who had also taught for a brief period at Roosevelt University). I forged friendships with a group of young like-minded intellectuals who composed the first full-fledged generation of black academicians on predominantly white university campuses, historians such as James D. Anderson, Joe William Trotter, Jimmie L. Franklin, Armstead Robinson, John W. Blassingame, Nathan Huggins, Robert L. Harris, Mary Francis Berry, and Nell Irvin Painter, among others. Another, equally dynamic cohort of such young black academicians as Alton Hornby Jr. at Morehouse, Bettye J. Gardner at Coppin State, Rosalyn Terborg Penn at Morgan State, Charles Vincent at Southern University, and Merline Pitre at Texas Southern University, to name only a few, joined history departments at historically black universities. Throughout the late 1970s and 1980s we renewed friendships and kept abreast of the latest developments in our field while attending annual conventions of the Association for the Study of African American Life & History and the Southern Historical Association.

Several experiences in the 1980s loosened my obsession with southern black politics and help explain my venture into the field of black women's history. My intellectual shift paralleled the development of a more sophisticated gender perspective among women historians. Historians Gerda Lerner, Anne Firor Scott, and Susan Reverby played a major role in the evolution of my consciousness. I took notice of their example and their scholarship. Meanwhile, several young black women historians, including Rosalyn Terborg Penn, Sharon Harley, and Evelyn Brooks Higginbotham, were launching their pioneering work in the fledgling field of black women's history. In 1980 I joined them in the founding of the Association of Black Women Historians. Concurrently, at the invitation of Betty Brandon of the University of South Alabama, I became active in and eventually the president of the Southern Association for Women Historians. Still, the most resonant catalyst that sparked my transformation into a black women's historian came from individuals outside the academy. Black women community leaders, notably Shirley Herd and Virtea Downey, two local primary-school teachers in Indianapolis and officials of Indiana's chapter of the National Council of Negro Women, literally called me to this subject. This externally generated awakening led to the creation of the Black Women in the Middle West archival project, funded by the National Endowment for the Humanities.[4]

My work on black women's history peaked in the 1990s, abetted by collaborative engagement with two white scholars. Ralph Carlson, who founded his own publishing company in 1990, called me and invited me to edit a historical encyclopedia. I was intrigued by the novelty of the idea and soon joined forces with Carlson. Along with historians Rosalyn Terborg Penn and Elsa Barkley Brown, we co-edited *Black Women in America: An Historical Encyclopedia* (1993). With Chicago writer Kathleen Thompson I co-authored *A Shining Thread of Hope: The History of Black Women in America* (1998). As gender enriched race and was complicated by class analysis in my scholarship, I turned my institution-building energies to the development of the Comparative Black History field of doctoral study at Michigan State University. Jack P. Greene of Johns Hopkins University, whom I had met while a fellow at the National Humanities Center, and David Barry Gaspar, a Caribbean historian at Duke University—with whom I co-edited *More Than Chattel: Black Women and Slavery in the Americas* (1996)—inspired this final transformation. The Comparative Black History program signaled yet another step in my intellectual evolution and has implications for the future of African American history and of southern history.[5]

The dawn of the millennium brings new challenges, most critical of which is the ongoing need to globalize the study and teaching of southern history and culture. Terms such as *transnationalism, comparative history*, the *Black Diaspora*, and the *Atlantic World* represent or capture the desire of many black history professors to transcend nation-state boundaries and geographical limitations in this field. The imperative is to find new ways to educate diverse citizens and to facilitate the acquisition of more meaningful perspectives about the people who make up the world we all inhabit. Events and circumstances in the past half millennium, including the Atlantic slave trade, slavery, and emancipation, and decolonization and global migration, have situated peoples of African descent at the epicenter of the modern world. Never has the need for southern history, broadly construed, been more urgent and the future more promising.

Down South in Illinois

As John Killens observes, "We are a Southern people . . . because that is where our people are closest to Africa. But our literature does not show this."[6] Addison Gayle quotes Killens in order to underscore his own call for urban black nationalists to embrace more fully their southern antecedents. Gayle, who joined with Amiri Baraka to forge an ideological foundation for the Black Arts and Consciousness Movement of the 1960s, laced his remembrance or invocation of the South with romantic overtones. It is a South that exists largely in the black imagination but is nevertheless poignant. Gayle exhorted fellow nationalists to depict "the South where Black women still maintain their proud carriage, where our young people continue to look with defiance upon the white world; a South where the ghosts of Harriet Tubman and David Walker, Sojourner Truth and Martin King remain omnipresent, constant reminders of the greatness of a race of men and women, who, forced to desert their god and their land, struggled and survived the American diaspora."[7] With Gayle's invocation in mind, I invite you to accompany me back to the early 1950s to my life on a farm in Villa Ridge, a small hamlet near Cairo, in a region of southern Illinois known then and now as Little Egypt.

After World War II, my maternal grandparents, Robert and Fannie Venerable Thompson; my parents, Levester (1921–83) and Lottie Mae Thompson Clark (1927–90); and aunts and uncles and cousins collectively moved from Missouri to newly purchased land in southern Illinois. The whole family left its past of Mississippi, Arkansas, and Missouri sharecropping to become landowning black people. This was merely the next-to-the-last-stop in a decades-long migration process that Fannie Venerable Thompson of Charleston, Mississippi, initiated when one night, at the age of fifteen, she surreptitiously left her home and without parental knowledge or approval was married to World War I veteran Robert Thompson, whose only visible possession was a white mule.[8]

The privileged only daughter of the more affluent Venerables, Grandmother could scarcely have imagined the fate that awaited. (According to Aunt Clotine Thompson Mason, the Venerables [also misspelled "Venable"] owned three hundred acres of land and a house in town.) Young Fannie's choice of husband provoked a crisis within her family. Robert and Betty Lee Venerable decreed what must have been a gut-wrenching and distasteful verdict made palatable, perhaps, by anger and most likely a sense of deep humiliation as a result of Fannie's rebellious rejection. They disinherited her. According to Grandmother, her parents had dreamed of her marrying a minister or a teacher. They certainly never anticipated that she would elope with a man, albeit tall, dark-skinned, long-haired, and undeniably handsome, a man who had a white mule but no land or anything else.

Grandmother had made her bed hard, and now she had to lie in it. Too proud to beg for forgiveness and too much in love to admit regret, she eventually bore fifteen children, eleven of whom reached majority, and all of whom, to differing degrees, shared in the farmwork—driven by the need to survive but, more importantly, by Fannie and Robert's grim determination to own their own land. They yearned for the kind of upward mobility that only land ownership could confer. The amount of productive and reproductive labor Fannie delivered makes this modern woman's head swim. Across the hard decades of the Great Depression and World War II, indeed for the remainder of her life, Grandmother sustained an unshakable determination to regain the status she had lost by marrying white-mule-owning Robert Thompson. Once the couple acquired the Villa Ridge farm, the acquisition of an education became the touchstone of Fannie's gospel, and she taught her children and grandchildren to strive to excel. She grew to revere professionals, advising me, when I was but a child, that if I could not become a professional, the next best thing was to marry one. Many of her children became teachers and physicians, and the process of the professionalization of the family continued into the third and fourth generations.

It took me a while to piece together the details of Grandmother's story of lost and found respectability and even longer to understand black family silences about social class and caste issues such as skin color. The awareness of secrets and feelings undisclosed dawned quite abruptly. I vividly recall that there happened a storm of activity, a flurry of cleaning and cooking, by a usually calm grandmother who was suddenly anything but reserved. In this instance of Grandmother's frenetic preparations, Grandfather was uncharacteristically subdued. She was everywhere at once singing her favorite song, "This Little Light of Mine." I asked Grandmother what was the matter, why she was cleaning an already and always clean but rambling farmhouse with a porch that wrapped around two sides of it. She said her mother, Betty Lee Venerable, was coming to visit. Well, the reverent tone she used made it seem as if the Queen of Sheba were on her way. To be sure, mother and daughter had reconciled earlier, but this was apparently the first time Betty Lee Venerable was visiting Fannie in Villa Ridge, on her own land.

Things seemed to have been turned upside down. For instance, Grandfather's shotgun, and those of his sons, were nowhere to be seen. More ominously, he had ceased talking about the mysterious Mr. Charlie and the dangerous peckerwoods who were always threatening, at least by his accounts, to take his land. "Mr. Charlie" was what he called rich and powerful white men. "Peckerwood" was a word he used when talking about all those white people who were neither rich nor powerful. Grandfather's determination to retain his land at all costs grew out of the fact that without the land and the income derived from selling the cotton, the family was doomed. Most assuredly there would not have been sufficient resources to pay for anyone's college education.

However, in this particular instance, what was even more disquieting was Grandfather's failure to mention the latest exploits of President "Ike," the only white man he grudgingly appeared to admire. Grandfather's curious silence underscored the importance of the impending visit. And when Betty Lee Venerable arrived, to my child's eye, she was a light-brown-skinned, slightly built woman with a distinctly regal bearing. It was the only time I ever saw Betty Lee Venerable, but fifty years later the memory is still as fresh in my mind as a snapshot. Only later did I learn that Betty never accepted Robert and that the darkness of his skin color was one of the unstated reasons why they were never warm toward each other.[9]

Another snapshot in my mind has at its center a little red-brick, one-story school building named after a nineteenth-century Alton, Illinois, abolitionist newspaper editor, Elijah P. Lovejoy. My parents migrated on to Chicago, where my father, Levester Clark, found a truck-driving job with the Chicago Fire Brick Company. I remained on the farm in Villa Ridge. I was assured that as soon as they had earned and saved enough money to purchase more property, everyone would return to Pulaski County. As things turned out, I was the one who later moved to Chicago, but not before putting in three years at Lovejoy. I remember riding the yellow school bus from my grandparents' farm, past a huge school with a playground full of white girls and boys en route to Lovejoy, with its two rooms and two teachers who were also sisters. One of the sisters was the wife of the only black physician in the area. Grandmother held them in high esteem.

My teacher, either Mrs. Hayes or Mrs. Buckley (I'm not sure which) was responsible for the first five grades. Each row in the room represented a grade. When I completed first grade, I moved across the aisle. I liked my teacher and classmates, so I didn't want to exchange them, but I did not understand why our school building was not as pretty as the one passed every morning and afternoon. Grandmother never provided a satisfactory answer when I asked why my school was so small and hidden away in the woods. The silence that greeted my question suggested that something was not quite right, but I couldn't figure it out. Eventually, I stopped asking about differences in the allocation of resources and facilities and concentrated on the little Dick, Jane, Sally, and see-Spot-run books used to teach us how to read. I never asked anyone why all the children in my book looked just like those on the school playground that my yellow bus passed.

Learning to read was its own reward. I do recall, however, that I pursued the quest for literacy with a special urgency, in part because I thought it was a way to help Grandmother and not just a tactic to win her approval. Every night Grandmother read pages in the Bible; sometimes she read them to me. I could never figure out how a person could read a book for as long as she did and never complete it. I reasoned that if I learned how to read, I could help Grandmother finish the Bible, and then she would be able to read other books.

In addition to learning how to read, I managed to figure out two important things while living with my grandparents and attending Lovejoy. The first lesson was a simple one. If I misbehaved in school I would be punished; and somehow Grandmother would know about it almost before I arrived home, and then I would receive another punishment. Grandmother's form of punishment was especially effective because it involved refusing to give me a piece of her favorite, most cherished treat, a banana. (Bananas were native to Indonesia. The fruit traveled across the Indian Ocean to East Africa and arrived in the New World during the era of the slave trade.) It seemed unfair to be punished twice for the same misdeed, therefore good behavior made more sense. My second discovery was equally as self-serving. I found that if I was still and worked fast to complete assignments, then I could listen, unnoticed, to what Mrs. Hayes taught all the other grades. There was an advantage to having five grades in one room. It made it easy to learn more than expected.

At age eight or nine, I rejoined my family in Chicago, but I brought along an internalized luggage of core values that encapsulated the essence of my southernness. Ten of those values established codes of public presentation and prescribed beliefs and appropriate behavior in private practice. These then are the values instilled by my grandparents in southern Illinois: (1) Respect elders. Revere the old people because even though they may not know it right, they always know more. (2) Remain close to family and community and love those who love you first. (3) Pay close attention to personal appearance because people are watching even though you may be unaware of their scrutiny. (4) Respectable people never put their business in the street. (5) Learn when to fight and when to fold. But if you must fight, make the first blow count because you may not get to deliver another lick. (6) Acquire as much education and learning as possible, but be skeptical about everything. Above all, do not become an educated fool. (7) Make very few promises, but keep your word. Be fair and honest and treat everyone the same. (8) Strive for excellence to bring honor and pride to your family, and to reflect well on teachers, ministers, and the community. (9) Speak up for yourself and for those incapable or unable to do so for themselves. (10) Read the Bible, be good, share with others, practice silence, and embrace solitude.

Family and College Up South in Chicago

I would like to report that my transition from rural Villa Ridge to urban Chicago was an easy one, but that would not be entirely accurate. It was wonderful to be with my sisters and brother and parents in the extended family compound on the West Side of Chicago. Each summer, until I was seventeen, I returned to Villa Ridge to stay with my grandparents, thus attenuating the impact of the move. In addition to transporting the above enumerated core values, I also packed a number of, according to my family, "country" vestiges. Every time I opened my mouth, some aunt or younger sister rushed to "correct" my speech, grammar, accent, or pronunciation. I was always, or so it seemed, calling things by the wrong name. When I referred to Warren Boulevard as a road, someone would insist that it was a street. When I asked permission to go "to town," someone would say that I meant "the store." These frequent lexical interventions along with the disapproval of my taste for homemade clothes made me acutely self-conscious about language and dress. Fortunately, some of the male relatives provided a measure of escape from all of the "correcting."

One of my truly good fortunes was the fact that Uncle Dennis Perry lived with Aunt Fannie on the top floor of the two-story compound on Warren Boulevard. Uncle Dennis was a professor of microbiology at Northwestern University Medical School in Chicago. He was a brilliant scientist who, most importantly, never seemed to tire of answering my endless questions. Throughout my years at Crane High School, Uncle Dennis played an active role in my intellectual development. He assisted me in the creation of a science project that attempted to find a way to detect and eliminate carbon monoxide. Uncle Dennis was always available to help solve algebra, geometry, and trigonometry problems. I learned from him the importance of meticulous research and the necessity to pay close attention to the details.

Uncle Dennis and my hardworking father, Levester Clark, were my most ardent cheerleaders. My father challenged me to think critically. He applauded any clever turn of phrase I managed to concoct. He shared with me his passionate interest in Chicago politics. Neither my father nor my uncle appeared to harbor any interest in how I sounded or in what I wore. They both were very proud when I graduated at the head of my high-school class. A few months after graduation, however, my father quietly co-signed my application for a charge card at a downtown Chicago boutique called The Fashion Plate. The saleswomen were more than a little eager to complete the divestment of my "countrified" dress and to launch me on the path to designer clothing. So, my father had been aware of the "correcting" process. Later, Uncle Dennis would register his own disappointment with me when I changed my major from biology to history.

As a high-school valedictorian I received a scholarship and admission to

Roosevelt University. Shortly after arriving at the downtown campus, I found a work-study job in the library. This position, more than anything else, fueled my acquisition of an informal education to complement my formal one. I had intended to major in biology when first I enrolled at Roosevelt, but, much to Uncle Dennis's consternation, that original intent soon yielded to American history.

At the conclusion of my first year at Roosevelt I gave birth, in August 1965, to my daughter Robbie Davine. It was not her birth that provoked such family angst as it was my decision not to marry her father. My distraught parents, especially my mother, interpreted such willful behavior as a sign of their maternal and paternal failure. Only the timely intercession of Grandmother placated the family. She assured everyone that Robbie's birth was a blessing. Privately she instructed my mother to assume responsibility for the undeniably adorable grandchild. She advised me not to have any more children, deeming it incompatible with professional pursuits. Robbie's birth signaled the end of adolescence and marked the emergence of a "no-nonsense attitude" about my education and future career that became a cornerstone of my adult personality.

The high tide of the Chicago Civil Rights movement overwhelmed me. I could not shake an insatiable curiosity and desire to learn what had caused so much white fear and black rage. As a biology student I knew that "race" had no physiological meaning. But as a cultural assumption it certainly carried weight in the larger world. I wanted to understand why and thus went searching for suitable "intellectual equipment." My American history survey course taught by Professor Paul Johnson quickened my desire to know more and inspired me to commence a private quest for different perspectives on the country's past.

It was while working in the library that I came across a book published in 1934 by Carter G. Woodson (a former West Virginia coal miner who received his Ph.D. in 1912 in history from Harvard University and is widely considered the "Father of African American History") concerning black professionals with a specific focus on physicians, lawyers, and some attention devoted to nurses.[10] This book resonated with my inner core values and my grandmother's fixation on the importance of professional occupations as a source of status and mobility. Woodson's most polemical work, *Miseducation of the Negro*, also captured my attention. I sought more information about this scholar, but no one had yet written a biography.[11] My professors at Roosevelt mentioned Woodson but did not assign any of his books. My discovery and reading of his books was very much a matter of personal drive.

On the formal level, it was Lorenzo Dow Turner who significantly influenced my intellectual development by emphasizing the importance of the African past. He insisted that Africa still held sway over a great deal of black culture, much more than anyone was prepared to admit. I took more courses with Turner and had more conversations with him than with either historian Hollis Lynch or sociologist St. Clair Drake. To be sure, I was fascinated by Lynch, whose British Caribbean accent, dapper dress, and insistence on the importance of an international context for the study and teaching of black history gave my classmates and me pause. I learned a great deal about pan-Africanism from Lynch. The vastly popular Drake had the most commanding presence of any scholar at Roosevelt. Like dozens of other undergraduates who did not actually take his courses but hung on to every word he uttered in public spaces such as the corridors and cafeteria, I was enthralled by the erudite and chain-smoking Drake. He was an outspoken radical sociologist who believed that investigations of the lives of the working class in African American communities should command greater attention. He advocated listening to those who had been silenced because of their social location, disfranchisement, employment status, and a host of other markers that rendered them the outsiders.

Turner's influence on my search for meaning and solutions to race problems in America was indelible. Turner (1895–1972) was the first African American, professionally trained linguist. He entered Howard University in 1910 and earned an M.A. in English at Harvard University in 1917 before returning to Howard to serve as professor and chairman of the English department. In 1926 he completed his Ph.D. at the University of Chicago and journeyed to Nashville to assume the headship of the English department at Fisk University. The summer of 1929 proved to be the turning point in his quest for "intellectual equipment." He taught summer school at South Carolina State College in Orangeburg and encountered the Gullah dialect. Turner embarked upon a course of international travel and study that resulted, twenty years later, in the publication of his most enduring work.[12]

In *Africanisms in the Gullah Dialect*, Turner analyzed the African antecedents and non-Western components of Gullah, a language developed and spoken by enslaved Africans in the sea islands along the coasts of South Carolina and Georgia.[13] In order to understand this language, Turner studied with Hans Kurath, director of the Linguistic Atlas of the United States and Canada project, and attended the Linguistic Society of America Summer Institute at New York University. In the late 1930s he studied African languages at the School of Oriental and African Studies at the University of London and learned Arabic at Yale University. In 1940 he traveled to Brazil "to study the persistence of African cultural features, especially folklore and music, in a culture quite unlike that of the Gullah in North America." He returned to Fisk University and in 1944 became a lecturer in linguistics and director of the Inter-Departmental Curriculum in African Studies. Two years later, in 1946, Roosevelt University hired Turner, making him "the first Negro scholar to be retained on a permanent basis with a full professor status in a white institution of higher learning."[14]

Turner is now frequently credited with facilitating the development of African American culture as a legitimate field of study. Indeed, Turner's study of the language and culture of the Sea Islands and of Brazil complemented the religious and cultural ethnographic work of his friend, Northwestern University's Melville J. Herskovits. These scholars cultivated what may today be called an "Afrocentric" approach to the study of the past of Americans of African descent before Molefi Asante gave the concept its contemporary currency. The opening sentence of *Africanisms* declared, "Persons interested in undertaking the study and interpretation of the speech of uneducated Negroes in the coastal region of South Carolina and Georgia would do well to acquire some acquaintance with several languages spoken in those sections of the West Coast of Africa from which the Negroes were brought to the United States as slaves."[15] Turner went on to list 3,595 African personal names, 251 general conversational words, and 92 expressions found in the stories, songs, and prayers of the Sea Island blacks, thus proving the African antecedents in Gullah.[16]

I enrolled in my first Lorenzo Turner course in 1966 and then in additional ones that he taught until I graduated in 1968. In the first course, Turner played the aluminum disc recordings of Gullah speakers that he had recorded in the 1930s and 1940s. The passage of time never dimmed his passion for the study of the linguistic past of African Americans. But it was the course that he taught about African American antebellum writings that made an indelible impression on me and augmented my "intellectual equipment." Only later did I learn how much of the information conveyed in the course appeared in his first book,

Anti-Slavery Sentiment in American Literature Prior to 1865, which Carter G. Woodson published in 1929 under the imprint of the Association for the Study of Negro Life and History.

In *Anti-Slavery Sentiment*, Turner identifies five pivotal dates in American history: 1808, the abolition of the African slave trade; 1831, the founding of William Lloyd Garrison's *Liberator*; 1850, the passage of the Fugitive Slave Act, which he argues "was responsible for the conversion of thousands of persons to the cause of abolition"; 1861, the beginning of the Civil War; and 1865, the end of the Civil War and the ratification of the Thirteenth Amendment to the United States Constitution, abolishing slavery.[17] According to Turner, opposition to slavery as reflected in a vast array of primary sources and expressive cultural productions evolved from moral and religious arguments to the espousal of the doctrine of natural and inalienable rights of man. It was during that later evolutionary phase that opposition to slavery embraced sentimental and humanitarian arguments. Turner paid attention to the consistent appeals abolitionists made that emphasized arguments based on social, economic, and political necessity.

But there was one particular abolitionist whose writings I found especially riveting. Turner introduced me to David Walker's *Appeal* (1829), a volume that commanded my attention much as had *The Confessions of Nat Turner*. Walker was a free black from North Carolina who moved to Boston in 1827 and published his *Walker's Appeal in Four Articles; Together with a Preamble, to the Coloured Citizens of the World, but in Particular, and Very Expressly, to Those of the United States of America* (Boston, 1829). Walker defiantly called for slaves to rise up and overthrow the yoke of slavery. But he also called to white Christians, "O Americans!! Americans!! I call God—I call angels—I call men, to witness, that your destruction *is at hand*, and will be speedily consummated unless you repent."[18] In the fourth section, entitled "Our Wretchedness in consequence of the colonizing plan," I found the topic on which I would write my M.A. thesis under the direction of August Meier at Kent State University, "The Propaganda of the American Colonization Society from 1816 to 1840" (1970).

I did not fully appreciate how much Turner had influenced me until I began to write this essay. Like most undergraduates, I took for granted his knowledge and teaching and quickly forgot about him as I embraced the rigors of graduate school. And because I did not trust completely my recollections, I sent for my Roosevelt University transcript and, sure enough, I had signed up for nine credit hours of course work with Lorenzo Dow Turner.

Becoming a Southern Historian

In 1968 I left Chicago to enter graduate school. I believed that there were many stories to be told and that it was my responsibility to find the most effective way to give voice and visibility to the ordinary, everyday people, mostly those black men whose past deeds had made my present and future possible. In other words, while I did not subscribe to the "great man" approach, I still understood history to be about men's experiences and exploits. I did not possess a feminist consciousness. Meanwhile, events back in Chicago made me skeptical about the efficacy of social-change activism. I was especially devastated by news of the murder of Fred Hampton and Mark Clark, two leaders of the Black Panther Party in Chicago. The killings at Kent State on May 4, 1970, were all the more sobering because I stood on the grounds, along with William C. Hine and other graduate students, and watched the horror unfold.

My adviser, August Meier, possessed an encyclopedic knowledge of the black past. Former Northwestern University graduate student John Bracey once claimed that Meier had forgotten more history than most of us would know in our lives, and in this case the cliché was undoubtedly true. I wondered after taking seminars with him whether there was anything worthwhile left to do. Meier was a demanding professor and somewhat intimidating. He expected perfection and was disappointed when it was found to be in short supply. Eventually, Meier and I had the dreaded discussion about a dissertation topic. I indicated a desire to write a biography of a post-Reconstruction era activist, T. Thomas Fortune, militant editor of *The New York Age*. Meier vetoed the idea because Emma Lou Thornborough was working on the definitive Fortune biography. Next, I offered that I wanted to write on the Populist movement and agrarian radicalism. My grandfather's radicalism remains a vibrant memory to this date. But Meier had no interest in this subject. He countered with the recommendation that I write a history of the National Association for the Advancement of Colored People's legal campaign to overthrow the Texas "white primary" and efforts to prove the unconstitutionality of claims by Democratic Party leaders that it was a private organization open only to white members. In the one-party South, to be denied the right to vote in primary elections was to be disfranchised. I accepted Meier's recommendation and set to work.

I approached research and writing about the NAACP with misgivings, however. After all, my generation considered the organization to be hopelessly irrelevant to the black liberation movement. We often castigated leaders such as Roy Wilkins. Still, having no viable alternative, I went to work on the topic and gradually made it my own. In fairness to Meier, I conceded that I had been ignorant of the truly radical and significant accomplishments of the NAACP. It was a riveting topic that allowed me to bring together all of my disparate interests in politics, movements for social change, and black professionals. I found that the story of the white primary campaign could best be told through the lens of the local black Texas leadership (and a couple of local white lawyers). These were the unsung, strong-willed, determined, and courageous men and women who served as plaintiffs in numerous suits, who raised the money to pay court costs, and who mobilized the people behind the NAACP national legal committee.

It was while working on the dissertation, "The NAACP and the Destruction of the Democratic White Primary, 1924–1944" (1975), that my interest in the history of the black professional class, especially physicians, nurses, and lawyers, took the shape of a research project and has haunted me for the past twenty-five years. My dissertation became the basis of my first book in southern black history.[19] The 1944 U.S. Supreme Court decision in *Smith v. Allwright* gave black southerners the right to participate in Democratic Party primary elections and represented a major victory in the battle for political empowerment. By examining the lives and work of noted black lawyers Charles Hamilton Houston, William H. Hastie, and Thurgood Marshall, I developed a greater appreciation of the antecedents to the classic Civil Rights movement of the 1950s and 1960s. These professional men forged relationships with local Texas activist professionals, businessmen and club women, and community NAACP and religious leaders to mobilize diverse constituencies as a necessary precondition to attacking all manifestations of white supremacy and Jim Crow segregation in public institutions and in American electoral politics. My interest in questions of black political power and the processes through which African Americans transformed their subordinate status in the South found full expression in *Black Victory*.

My second monograph, *Black Women in White: Racial Conflict and Cooperation in the Nursing Profession, 1890–1950* (1989) focused on the history of black women in the nursing profession in the nation, with particular attention devoted to the South, and for good reason. Most of the scores of black hospitals and nursing training schools were located in the South. The history of black women nurses was as much a work in southern history as it was in American history. I am now revising my study on blacks in the medical and legal professions and the origins of the Civil Rights movement.

Call it coincidence or serendipity. In 1972 I accompanied my historian husband, William C. Hine, to Orangeburg, where I taught African American history and served as coordinator of Black Studies at South Carolina State College. Because Professor Lorenzo Dow Turner had supplied me with sufficient "intellectual equipment" with which to make sense of the world I encountered, I was not at all perplexed when I heard Gullah speech.

In this essay, I have returned in space and time to the 1950s and 1960s, to reclaim my formative southern culture experiences and to recall the intellectual influences that gave me the equipment to become a historian who writes and teaches in order to introduce into the ongoing professional conversation fresh perspectives on the world and the place of African Americans in it. The musings of Albert Murray provided cautious inspiration for this retrospective essay. "In any case," he wrote in 1971, "such is the fundamental interrelationship of recollection and make-believe with all journeys and locations that anywhere people do certain things in a certain way can be home." He added, "So whoever says you can't go home again, when you are for so many intents and purposes back whenever or wherever somebody or something makes you feel that way."[20]

Our personal family experiences have value, and through the sharing of these stories we expose our memories of home and open windows of understanding about our worlds. It is as important to cross generational boundaries that separate historians as it is to bridge the gap between those who live and work outside the walls of the academy and we who are within. Myriad forces shaped the historian I have become, and it is illuminating and disconcerting to excavate the events and recall the people, many of whom are too easily forgotten, who accompanied me on my journey across the southern diaspora. While I may have been born in the border South of the lower Middle West, I know deep in my heart and soul that I am and will always be southern.

Notes

1. Albert Murray, *The Omni-Americans: New Perspectives on Black Experience and American Culture* (New York, 1970), 212–13.

2. August Meier, *Negro Thought in America, 1880–1915: Racial Ideologies in the Age of Booker T. Washington* (2nd ed., Ann Arbor, 1988), iv.

3. See Lorenzo Dow Turner, *Anti-Slavery Sentiment in American Literature Prior to 1865* (Port Washington, N.Y., 1966). The author's first book was originally published in 1929 by the Associated Negro Press, founded by Carter G. Woodson who also founded the Association for the Study of Negro Life and History and launched the *Journal of Negro History* (renamed in 2002 *The Journal of African American History*). Turner's best-known work concerns linguistic "retentions" among African Americans; see Lorenzo Dow Turner, *Africanisms in the Gullah Dialect* (Chicago, 1949).

On St. Clair Drake, see "Studies of the African Disapora: The Work and Reflections of St. Clair Drake," in Benjamin P. Bowser and Louis Kushnick, eds., *Against the Odds: Scholars Who Challenged Racism in the Twentieth Century* (Amherst, Mass., 2002), 86–110.

One of Hollis R. Lynch's most influential books remains *Edward Wilmot Blyden: Pan-Negro Patriot, 1832–1912* (New York, 1967).

4. Darlene Clark Hine, *When the Truth Is Told: Black Women's Culture and Community in Indiana, 1875–1950* (Indianapolis, 1981). Also see Darlene Clark Hine and Patrick Biddleman, eds., *Black Women in the Middle West Project* (Indianapolis, 1984).

5. Darlene Clark Hine and Jacqueline McLeod, eds., *Crossing Boundaries: Comparative History of Black People in Diaspora* (Bloomington, 1999). This anthology includes papers that were presented in 1995 at the first Comparative Black History symposium at Michigan State University in East Lansing. Key contributors to both the program and to the volume were historians Jack P. Greene and David Barry Gaspar.

6. John Killens quoted in Addison Gayle Jr., "Reclaiming the Southern Experience: The Black Aesthetic Ten Years Later," *Black World* 23 (September 1974), 20.

7. Gayle, "Reclaiming the Southern Experience," 20–29 (quotation on page 22).

8. In his autobiography, South Carolinian Benjamin Mays offers a glimmer of insight into the advantage young black men at the turn of the century may have derived from owning a white mule. "My brother John was the sporty one in our family. He worked and saved until he could buy a white rubber-tired buggy and a beautiful white mule which he named Kate. John and Kate created quite a sensation in the community and at Mount Zion. When the boys came to church alone, they were expected to take their girl friends home — a duty which they did not find at all burdensome" (Benjamin E. Mays, *Born to Rebel: An Autobiography* [New York, 1971], 13–14). I thank William C. Hine for bringing this passage to my attention.

9. Oral interview with Clotine Thompson Mason, February 8, 2003, Chicago, Illinois; and with Maplean Thompson King and Fannie B. Thompson Perry, February 8, 2003, Chicago, Illinois.

10. Carter G. Woodson, *The Negro Professional Man and the Community: With Special Emphasis on the Physician and the Lawyer* (Washington, D.C., 1934).

11. Now there is a biography: Jacqueline Anne Goggin's *Carter G. Woodson: A Life in Black History* (Baton Rouge, 1993); also see Pero Galo Dagbovie, "Black Women, Carter G. Woodson, and the Association for the Study of Negro Life and History, 1915–1950," *The Journal of African American History* 88 (Winter 2003), 23–41, for the most recent historical scholarship on Woodson.

12. For a brief description of the unique features of Turner's work, see William S. Pollitzer, *The Gullah People and Their African Heritage* (Athens, 1999), 23, 109. Also see Margaret Wade-Lewis, "Lorenzo Dow Turner: Beyond Gullah Studies," *Dialectical Anthropology* 26 (2001), 235–66.

13. Lorenzo Dow Turner, with a new introduction by Katherine Wyly Mille and Michael B. Montgomery, *Africanisms in the Gullah Dialect* (1949; reprint, Columbia, 2002), xi.

14. Turner, *Africanisms*, xiv–xxv.

15. Turner, *Africanisms*, 1; Melville J. Herskovits, *The Myth of the Negro Past* (New York, 1941); Lorenzo Dow Turner, *An Anthology of Krio Folklore and Literature with Notes and Interlinear Translation in English* (Chicago, 1963). Also see Margaret Wade-Lewis, "The Impact of the Turner/Herskovits Connection on Anthropology and Linguistics," *Dialectical Anthropology* 17 (1992), 391–412; Wade-Lewis, "Lorenzo Dow Turner: Pioneer African-American Linguist," *Black Scholar* 21 (Fall 1991), 10–24.

16. Pollitzer, *Gullah People*, 109.

17. Lorenzo Dow Turner, *Anti-Slavery Sentiment in American Literature Prior to 1865* (Port Washington, N.Y., 1966). Originally published by the Association for the Study of Negro [African American] Life and History in 1929 and based upon his 1926 Ph.D. dissertation at the University of Chicago.

18. Walker's *Appeal* quoted in Turner, *Anti-Slavery Sentiment*, 36. Italics in original.

19. Darlene Clark Hine, *Black Victory: The Rise and Fall of the White Primary in Texas* (Millwood, N.Y., 1979). In 2003 the University of Missouri Press published a new edition of *Black Victory* with new essays by Darlene Clark Hine, Steven F. Lawson, and Merline Pitre. The new edition coincided with my being the president of the Southern Historical Association (2002–3) and allowed me the opportunity to comment on the 2000 presidential election that witnessed the disfranchisement of some members of the black community in key Florida cities.

20. Albert Murray, *South to a Very Old Place* (New York, 1971), 3–4.

Stranger in a Strange Land

Crossing Boundaries

VERNON BURTON

Call me Vernon. As I am interested in identity, let me start with my name. I was to be named after my father's youngest brother, Lloyd George Burton, killed in World War II. Since I was born on my father's birthday, however, my mother and my paternal grandmother insisted I be named after my father. My father was Orville Verner Burton, but he did not want me called "Junior," so he changed the spelling of my name to Vernon. My father was Orville, and I was always called Vernon. Only in two brief stints with the U.S. Army was I Orville, and sometimes when my mother wanted to get my attention. My first publications were under the name of Vernon Burton. A few publications use O. Vernon Burton, but that is not my choice. Some years ago, when the University of Illinois put "O. Vernon Burton" on my office door, one of my daughters asked, "Daddy, why did they put a zero in front of your name?" People may assume that an initial is the way southern historians should begin their names because of C. Vann Woodward. The "Orville" came about for my first two edited books on southern community, when Greenwood Press asked very specifically for my first name, and published work has used Orville Vernon Burton ever since. My mother liked seeing the "Orville," and I was willing to do anything to please my mother.[1]

My life has been one of crossing boundaries, boundaries of race, geography, class, and status. I crossed boundaries from southern rural–small town to northern urban. I crossed the boundaries from farm and working class to professional. In my work as a historian of the South, I did not limit myself to one time period. I also crossed interdisciplinary boundaries, drawing on social sciences, literature, and quantitative techniques. With my work in both history and computers, I crossed strict academic boundaries into public history, trying to democratize access to information and computers. I crossed boundaries from the classroom to the courtroom, where I worked with some of the greatest civil rights lawyers to fight segregation and to increase minority representation in government. I have been invited to cross two oceans to give talks on the South in Europe and Asia. I have crossed so many boundaries that sometimes I no longer know where I belong.

But I do know where I am from. I grew up in Ninety Six, South Carolina, an old colonial town, the "garden spot of history." Like many people, rather than learning history, I absorbed it from the memorials that surrounded me. We had two local historical markers. One celebrated native son and U.S. congressman Preston Brooks and his brutal caning of Massachusetts abolitionist senator Charles Sumner in the Senate chamber. The other was Star Fort from the Revolutionary War. About three miles outside of town, Star Fort was an open field where children played and teenagers got into mischief; it was not until later that it was developed into a tourist attraction under the National Park System. Most of what our community thought of as "History" concerned the Revolution. Although both sides of my family fought for the Confederacy in the Civil War, it was never a topic of conversation, except for the rare mention that my mother's grandfather had apparently been affected for the worse and returned home with a drinking problem. For the most part, the current interest in the Civil War and the Confederate flag is not something I grew up with. Nevertheless, although the African American community did not participate, the centennial of the Civil War was a fairly big event in Ninety Six. At that time, no monument in Ninety Six commemorated our most illustrious citizen, Dr. Benjamin E. Mays. President of Morehouse College and spiritual mentor of Martin Luther King Jr., Mays was well known in the African American community and almost unknown among whites. Ninety Six now has a monument to Benjamin E. Mays.

The community of Ninety Six was my world, and the First Baptist Church was the hub around which other activities revolved. With joy we attended every church activity, Sunday mornings and evenings, choir practice, youth activities such as SunBeams or Royal Ambassadors, and Wednesday-night prayer meetings. (I caused a stir by being the first young person to join in the actual saying of prayers, and it was not until years later that women did.) My favorite hymn was "Jesus Loves the Children of the World, Red and Yellow, Black and White, They Are Precious in His Sight," a song that reinforced my mother's belief about all God's children. Yet churches were segregated. Churches also reflected status and perhaps class, but Ninety Six had no real "aristocracy," so there was no Episcopal Church in the town. Social lines were not clear-cut, but few if any mill workers attended our church, although quite a few farmers did. My mother often drove out into the country to bring others to church, and on one occasion there was some grumbling that the guests did not wear proper clothes. My mother seldom spoke out at church meetings, but when she did, people listened. This was one of those times, and the complaining ceased. Another time my mother chose to speak out was in my defense. It was in 1965 at a student-run service; I was the student preacher and used as my text the parable of the Good Samaritan but turned it into the story of African Americans and whites in Ninety Six. One deacon accused me of being a communist and stormed toward the door. When my mother calmly said that if I were a communist, so was Jesus Christ, he sat back down.

I learned at an early age that conflict can characterize community, that chains of exploitation as well as ties of charity and cooperation bound people in a community. I saw that there was much that was not right with race, gender, and class. I realized firsthand the immorality of inequities in my hometown, and I learned to separate the people for whom I had affection from some of the things they did. As a religious child, I was perplexed about the animosity some whites felt toward African Americans. I wondered why the white people in my church did not want African Americans to attend our church, and that "why" question, which led me into thinking about the history of race relations, still animates my research.

One of the greatest blessings in my life was my mother, Vera Beatrice Human Burton. She was incredibly strong and independent. She was proud; she liked to help others but had a hard time accepting help. Her strong belief in education kept me in school, including graduate work in history. My mother was the greatest influence on my life. She instilled in me a love of God, of education, of hard work.

My mother and father were childhood sweethearts from rural Georgia. My mother was one of ten children, four girls and six boys, in very rural Madison County, and my father was one of seven brothers from nearby Dewey Rose. While my grandfather Burton was sharecropping in Madison County, he led the singing at Mill Shoals Baptist Church, where my mother played the piano. All the boys in my dad's family played musical instruments, and they all headed for the military service as soon as they could. The VFW post in Elberton, Georgia, is a reminder of this family military tradition; it is named for my father's two youngest brothers, who were killed in World War II. My mother's family was very different from my father's family: more country, more religious, less likely to spend time reading (except for the Bible), and much more reluctant warriors than my father's family. In one case, the MPs had to come and get one of my mother's brothers to serve in World War II. My father, on the other hand, ran away as a youngster to join the Marines. He lost his leg while on duty in San Diego before World War II. Because a very bad job of amputation left an exposed nerve, Dad was in constant, excruciating pain. For the rest of his life, he was in and out of veterans hospitals; he drank to ease the hurt, and my mother had to give him shots of morphine.

Earlier, after my father had left home for the Marines, his family moved to the town of Elberton, Georgia, and my paternal grandfather, James Burton, became a barber. My maternal grandfather, Jones Lewis (Seab) Human, was a blacksmith who saved his money to buy a farm. On his acreage he also built a shingle- and sawmill. Both of my grandfathers died before World War II, so I never knew either one. I did get to spend a lot of time with both of my grandmothers, and I was struck by the differences in the very isolated rural life of Granny Bess, my mother's mother (Dexter Ann Christian Human), and the town social and intellectual life of Carmama, my father's mother (Carrah E. Faulkner Burton). I would later explore these differences between town and country in my historical research. It also seemed strange and unnatural to me that both of my grandmothers buried the majority of their children. Most of my father's brothers were killed, and I did not have much contact with my cousins on my father's side of the family; nor did I learn much about them till later in my life. But I was especially close to my cousins on my mother's side of the family. Their ages ranged so that some of my first cousins were my age while others had children who were my age.

My mother must have been the adventurous sister in her family; at any rate, she was the one who left home. With the death of my grandfather and the onset of the Great Depression, the family was hard put to keep the farm going, and my mother accepted a job so she could send money home. A former neighbor who had moved to Abbeville, South Carolina, hired her in his store, and soon my mother was the manager. In 1940 my father and mother were married in Abbeville. My father, determined to work, posted bond to become an insurance salesperson. Unfortunately, he had to go into the Veterans Hospital, and, to keep from losing the bond, my mother took the job. That is how the family got to Ninety Six; my mother went there to start an insurance route, or debit as it was called. My parents were part of a white migration from Georgia to South Carolina, looking for jobs as farming was playing out. South Carolina had textile plants, and relatives came to live with us while they found work in the cotton mill or with the power company. Two cousins stayed in South Carolina, but most returned home to Georgia. Actually, each of my mother's sisters had a son who either built a home next door to his mother or built his mother a home next door to him. None moved more than five miles from the homeplace, except my mother, two hours away by car. And then me—a world away.

I knew Ninety Six was rural, but my cousins from Georgia thought they came to the city when they visited us. When we could get Granny Bess to visit, she refused to drink water from the faucet, and I had to go to the spring in the woods. (In an interesting departure from segregated race relations, African Americans and whites shared this spring and often got water at the same time.) My grandmother did not have indoor plumbing in her home, so during our frequent visits to her place, we used an outhouse. Cotton was still grown in Ninety Six, but it was at my grandmother's that I would try to pick cotton, and I remember playing in the bolls lying on the front porch of her small house. These visits to rural Georgia taught me that there were many different Souths and many different statuses and economic variations among people in the neighborhood or even in the same families, even within a short distance of each other.

Many of us who study rural society can see urbanizing changes in our own family histories. When I was a boy, nearly everyone who did not farm worked in the cotton mill. Nowadays, pine trees have replaced cotton and corn, and there is no cotton mill; the largest employer in Ninety Six is Fuji Film. My cousins stayed on the land in Georgia, but my children grew up in a midwestern city. The cousin who farms made his living teaching shop so he could keep the farm going. The other, a race-car driver, became an auto hauler and mechanic and junkyard dealer. These cousins take pride in maintaining their rural values even when they relate less and less to the work of agriculture. My mother always kept a garden that was larger than city folks can imagine. My mother represented those rural values that I continue to treasure: integrity, hard work, independence, and community.

I was born in Georgia in 1947. My father hated the Georgia demagogue Gene Talmadge so much that he took my pregnant mother from their home in

Ninety Six and traveled some eighty miles across the Savannah River so that I could be born near the family homeplace in rural Georgia and thus be in a better position to challenge Talmadge's son Herman for governor. (I never got this opportunity as Gene Talmadge died in 1948, and his son Herman just sort of assumed the chief executive position.)

In Ninety Six, Mom sold insurance for the Nashville, Tennessee–based Life and Casualty Insurance Company. As she drove her insurance route out into the country collecting payments and visiting families, my mother would sometimes pile me in the car with a load of books, and I would read for hours. My memories of visiting rural folks on their farms and in their homes are vivid. We often returned without being paid for the insurance premium, but we had a trunk full of garden produce, sausages, beef, etc. Her insurance route also included the mill village, where my mother would park the car to save gas and walk from home to home. While a youngster I noticed the unfair treatment my mother received as a woman working in a man's world, and it filled me with anger.

On other days, I would stay with my father. I am told by folks that he had me memorize baseball statistics and car makes and models and then would wager with friends on my memory. At any rate, in later years I had a fairly easy time regurgitating lectures or what I had read. My father was something of a political junkie and loved to listen to the radio, especially the news. He wrote and sold crossword puzzles. He read all the time—newspapers, magazines, books; perhaps that is why I was reading before I entered the first grade. My father also loved to tell stories, often about his years in the Marines, of being in China three years in an undeclared war, or just good southern yarns and jokes, and I loved to listen. Sometimes I went with him to the local honky tonks and enjoyed all the men's tall tales.

Because my mother worked, I had what was euphemistically called a nurse, an African American woman who minded me, prepared meals, and helped with the housework. If my mother were still alive, I would never say that we were poor because she would vehemently deny it. But we had very little money. And yet we had an African American woman working for us. Even poor white families in the mill village had African American domestics working for them and caring for their children. It was a sad and unjust situation when working in the homes of unaffluent whites was one of the few economic opportunities for African Americans.

As an only child, I enjoyed very much being with my nurse and her friends wherever we went. When we went to the movies, we sat in the loft area. I later discovered that was the segregated section for African Americans, but at the time I had no idea that I was integrating the movie theater. These memories are those of a child, and, although I have interviewed some of the African American women who worked for my mother, I cannot pretend to understand their true feelings. I do know that I cared deeply for them, and they all still seem to care for me and for my parents. Mrs. Pat Williams spoke eloquently at my mother's funeral in 2001.

Something very important to me growing up was my friendship with Charles Willis Williams; like everyone in his family, I called him "Brother." I was pretty naïve; it took me a long time to know why some whites teased me about my "black brother." Our homes were near each other's, only across the cow pasture, and we ate meals together at each other's homes and had overnights together. Brother was a few years older than I was, and before I started school I went with him from time to time to the segregated, so-called "colored" school, where his mother, Mrs. Catherine Williams, taught. He and I were pretty much inseparable. Brother was better at everything than I was. When we boxed, I always had to be the white guy that Joe Louis or Floyd Patterson beat up. In the miles of woods behind our homes, known as "Little Mountain," we had wonderful and dangerous adventures, one with an escaped convict, another with poisonous snakes. This interracial friendship was not in the least strange to me, and it continues to this day, though Brother and I live and work far apart (he is in upstate New York).

My mother believed from the Bible that we were all descended from Adam and Eve and therefore we were brothers and sisters. I can still remember her telling me that there was no difference between black and white and that God could have easily made me black and Brother white. My mother was very quiet but held firm in her beliefs of equality and fair treatment. Only later was I told that my father would not eat at the table with Brother, my mother, and me when we ate together. Although he had ambiguous personal feelings, he never stopped me from spending time with my friend. And I was never allowed to use the "N" word—I never have in my life. He also insisted that I address adult African Americans as Mr. and Mrs., very uncommon for the time. The African American community appreciated my father because of the time he confronted and dispersed the Ku Klux Klan at Brother's house. My father's reputation for being a racial liberal may or may not have been real. Maybe it was for his day and time, I just do not know. But the reputation hurt him, and me, within the white community. Whites complained that my mother, Brother, and I sat together in the car, problematical because it was in the public sphere.

From my African American friends, I learned other versions of history, other views of my community, and other people's motivations. Even more complex, I grew up with triple segregation; African Americans went to one school, white rural and town kids went to my school, and, through the grammar-school years, kids whose parents worked in the cotton mill, who lived in the "mill village," went to the mill school. I recognized early on the boundaries of class as well as race, and I did not like boundaries.

My father died when I was seven years old, the week before Christmas. My mother and I had little income and many medical bills. We never received any financial assistance, not even social security. Because my father had been in the Marines for thirteen years, we were probably entitled to continue receiving his pension from the Marines, but Ninety Six had no attorney. More important, my mother was too proud to ask. I remember her saying that if she took nothing from the government, they could not take her son for the military.

Life in the patriarchal South was confusing for a boy without a father. I suspect that growing up without a father led to my interest in matriarchy/patriarchy. (Having written a book on patriarchy, I now realize that God is a Female with a sense of humor because She has gifted me with five daughters.) I believe I took up hunting and fishing as some way to define myself in a culture that emphasized "masculinity." But we also ate what I hunted and caught. I began setting rabbit boxes when I was eight. I eventually accumulated the best pack of running beagles in the area. I also played sports. Ninety Six was a great football and baseball town. Of course, the high-school teams were segregated, but I grew up playing with black and white kids, whoever was available to get enough to make a team. I participated in Scouts from the time I could join Cub Scouts until I received my Eagle and God and Country awards. I was also active in 4-H club, raising all sorts of animals to show at the county fair. I started with a hundred chickens and moved on to cows and steers. This hands-on experience clearly influenced my views of rural life. Church organizations, 4-H and Boy Scouts, sports teams, high-school band, all were institutional means of defining and making a community, something that I would learn and would also study for the rest of my life. It was clear to me that, although I was raised with only a mother, I was expected to absorb patriarchal values. Ironically, my mother tried to keep me from doing housework, and yet when I went to work in the cotton mill, I had to sweep for miles, and when I went to Furman University, I worked in the dining hall.

After my father's death, my mother told me that I was now the "Man of the House." I believed it, took that responsibility seriously, and immediately sought to bring in some income. Folks in Ninety Six called me a "working fool." I loved to work. I began working at a dairy and then sold *Grit*, a weekly newspaper, from door to door in African American and white neighborhoods. When I was nine years old, I got a morning paper route delivering the *Greenville News*. I added the *Atlanta Journal and Constitution* on Sundays to my regular paper route. As I rolled newspapers for my paper route each morning in the entrance of the old movie theater that was closed (with the poster advertising *God's Little Acre* staring at me), I read two different papers with totally contrasting political views. This intrigued me, and I think the different interpretations of events by the newspapers helped me develop a healthy skepticism. I would not be held within the boundary of a certain interpretation.

In addition to newspaper delivery, I did any sort of odd job. One summer I planted an acre of peanuts on our land. After harvesting, I boiled those peanuts with my mother's help, and we packed them in individual bags for sale. I used the proceeds to buy a mule, and the following summer, in partnership with an elderly African American man, I used the mule to plow people's gardens. In high school I was paid to write a weekly column about Ninety Six for the *Index Journal*, serving the county of Greenwood. As a young teen I went to work for our church choir director, Barry "Mac" McAdams, a World War II hero, a supermacho southern male, a great hunter and fisherman. I worked on his farm, bush-hogging and plowing. While atop his tractor I spent many long hours in simple contemplation. I also worked in his store in Chappels, a crossroads village even smaller than Ninety Six. I cleaned, mopped, butchered, pumped gas. McAdams also taught me about auto mechanics and carpentry. Lots of truckers and other men congregated in Mac's store, and I thoroughly enjoyed hearing them tell stories. When McAdams died right before I graduated from high school, his widow, Mrs. Louise McAdams, came to my mother and offered to send me to college. My mother appreciated the gesture but refused any help. Another person to offer financial support to me in college, which again my mother appreciated and refused, was Mrs. Nellie Pollykoff, a Jewish merchant in Ninety Six. (I was unaware of any anti-Semitism in that small town.) So, although I witnessed the "petty tyrannies" and injustices of rural/small-town life, I also saw firsthand the generosity and support that comes from a true community.

When I was sixteen, I got a job in the cotton mill, its high fence topped with barbed wire ever since the textile strike of 1934. The cotton mill was supposedly segregated, so they had no need for "white" and "colored" restrooms. Yet, on the weekends, I worked with several African American men who did odd jobs and cleaned up at the mill. We used to laugh when we all used the same restroom when the mill was closed. That same restroom posted a handbill where I first heard about "evil" unions; the poster deplored the horrible effects of unionization. (I have wondered since then if we would have been better served to have called them Confederacies of Labor.) My senior year I was given lots of extra hours at the mill, often more than forty a week. Sometime later Mr. Ransom Yonce, the mill superintendent, told me that he had done this not because he was helping me to make extra money, as I had thought, but because he figured that if I were tired my grades would slip, and his daughter, a friend of mine, would become valedictorian instead of me.

One of my many jobs was as a lifeguard at the local state park. While in college I was asked to come back to be the head lifeguard because it was the summer of integration, and the other white lifeguards had refused to work in an integrated swimming area. I had to train a new group of lifeguards and have them all swear to accept anyone who came to the park to swim and to save anyone needing help and to treat every person with courtesy. I am still proud that we integrated without any problems and offered a welcoming attitude for all citizens of the state.

My "formal" schooling got off to a very rough start, with a record number of whippings for the first day of school. My playmate Danny Price had a crippled arm from polio, and his mother had asked me to look after Danny at school. When, on that first day, another student told the teacher, Mrs. Persley, that Danny had his eyes open for the beginning prayer, I volunteered that Danny should not be punished because the tattletale must have had his eyes open also. Mrs. Persley gave me fair warning not to meddle, but soon thereafter I asked to speak to the class. I asked them to be very careful with how they treated our new schoolbooks because later they would be passed down to the "colored" schools, and we should make sure the books were in good condition. That speech earned me my first spanking. Sometime later that day, about as long as it takes a duck to waddle three miles, my pet duck came into the classroom and straight to me. That earned me a second spanking. I also got my first sense of status in a small southern town when I was placed in a lower group of readers. I made the mistake of asking Mrs. Persley why I was not in the first group since I could already read, and her answer was another spanking.

Mrs. Persley also detested my father. At that time my father was running a pool hall on Pender Row, literally on the other side of the tracks in Ninety Six. I spent some time in my dad's pool hall and one day took blue chalk to school so that Mrs. Persley would have some variety. Mrs. Persley, however, threw it to the floor and stomped on it, yelling that it was evil and dirty just like my father and his pool hall. The spanking that day hurt a lot less than the words about my father. Not surprisingly, I hated school. Fortunately for me, that changed in the second grade with Mrs. Mattie Arant, who took a special interest in me. Mrs. Arant taught me from the second through the fourth grade, and I credit her with changing my attitude about school. I learned the difference a teacher makes.

In high school I was curious about life and people, but the study of history held no special appeal to me. The high-school history teacher was our football coach, and those of us on the team sometimes went to the gym or had team meetings instead of attending class. We did have a very good football team and won the state championship, but I learned very little history. In 1965, when I was president of the student body at Ninety Six High School, we members of the student council caused quite a stir with a resolution that said that any student, no matter what color or race, who wanted to attend our school would be welcome. Accompanying the resolution was a petition signed by a majority of the students. I learned early that some teachers, even those I liked, did not really want student government; they opposed a different way of doing things, particularly on race. I was especially crushed by the reaction of the school superintendent, Mr. J. C. Boozer. Mr. Boozer was called "Fox" because he was quite a fox hunter and sportsman and had been a successful and "cagey" coach. He had been especially good to me, and I had been thrilled when he gave me a pedigreed bird dog pointer. I held Mr. Boozer in such esteem that I was shaken to the core when he called me to the office and told me how disappointed he was in me. I learned young that certain stands could get me in trouble, and that it could be a real mistake to put someone on a pedestal.

Although I was valedictorian and class president, I received no academic honors. I was given the leadership award, the one for which the students themselves chose the recipient. Until my senior year, the awards for each subject had been given to the student who had the highest average in that subject, but for my year they changed the rules so that "attitude" mattered as well. I became very suspicious of the way awards were given and what they meant. I still remember how surprised I was when I received so many awards and honors at Furman University. I really did not think that people from my status received recognition and awards from those who held the power to give them.

One day, as president of the student body, I introduced our local congressman, William Jennings Bryan Dorn, to our high-school assembly. After his speech denouncing Castro, he announced that he was appointing me to the Naval Academy at Annapolis. With this good news, I did not apply to any colleges. I went to Paris Island, took my physical, and had everything ready to go when Congressman Dorn announced that he was delaying my appointment for one year (so the grandson of a wealthy constituent could attend). I was furious and resolved not to go to college at all. It was well past the deadline for applications, and I was enjoying work with Daniel Construction Company. By working overtime and "shutdowns" for eighty-hour weeks, I was making a huge amount of money for that day and time. The welders and pipe fitters I worked with, a rough but good-hearted crowd, planned to go to work on the Alaska pipeline, and I wanted to go with them. Since neither my mother nor father had finished high school, and since few students from Ninety Six went on to college, I decided not to go.

But my mother had a different idea. My mother had always wanted me to go to Furman University, then a Baptist school. She told me that she prayed me into Furman, and I think that she probably did. After my first semester at Furman, when we ran out of money to pay the tuition and costs, Furman offered me a federal scholarship grant. My mother only had to sign a form that said something to the effect that she could not afford to send me. I remember the financial office at Furman explaining to my mother that doctors and lawyers signed this form for their children and that it signified nothing. But my mother refused to sign. Her religious faith assured her God would provide. And God did provide. I received a full scholarship from a private foundation.

Once at Furman, I absolutely loved it. I appreciated that the faculty challenged my ideas and forced me to think and grow, to expand my horizons. I learned at Furman that the academy forms a very special kind of community, one where students and teachers benefit from cooperating with one another and with the larger community. The Furman teachers cared for me, encouraged my curiosity, and were patient with my grammar and lack of sophistication. Because the Furman faculty believed in teaching, they were willing to invest the extra time to help a student who had not come from an academic background. One day in his European history survey class, Dr. Winston Babb, a wonderful professor and human being, mentioned that when he first came to Furman everyone knew what a "lint head" was, but that for the last fifteen years not one student knew the term. For some reason, I spoke up and said rather defensively that I had worked in a cotton mill and that I was proud to have been a lint head. From that day forward, Dr. Babb "adopted" me. I became a history major because of his personal attention to me. I certainly had no great interest in history. I did well on tests, but I did not know that history was more than memorizing and giving back expected answers.

My life took a major change in the summer of 1967 when the Ford Carnegie Harvard-Yale-Columbia Intensive Summers Studies Program (ISSP) selected me (I think it was Dr. Babb who submitted my name). Designed for minority students, this program was to encourage students to go on to law, medical, or graduate school. I was one of the very few nonblacks in the program, but I had less in common with the white students than with African Americans from the South. I remember my first sight of New York: giant skyscrapers, the confusing taxi ride to Columbia, subways, the strange and constant noises, a cacophony of sounds that interfered with my sleep and never ceased. I was a total innocent, and the others worried about me as I rushed about in wonderment looking at everything. The day I learned that my cousin Robert Echols had been killed in Vietnam and there was no way I could get back to Georgia for the funeral, my new friend William Woods from Tugaloo College, also on this program, walked the streets of Manhattan with me nearly all night. Only later did we discover that we had been walking through what folks believed to be a riot.

This was my first visit north and the first time I became aware of my region in a new way. Indeed, until I ventured north, I had never really thought of myself as a southerner, just as an American who happened to live in South Carolina. Nonsoutherners made me very aware of another boundary, that as a southerner I was something Other. In my naïveté I had guessed that northerners knew how to live together in racial harmony. I was excited about going to

New York partly because I expected to learn how African Americans and whites lived together in brotherhood, and I intended to use that knowledge to make the South a place of racial equality. Many New Yorkers, and others I met in the Civil Rights movement, were truly exceptional in their commitment to racial justice. Yet in New York I also met right-wing white supremacists and the worst overt racism I had ever encountered!

ISSP enrolled me in two classes. One was a "Great Books" course that I loved, taught by Union Seminary Professor John B. Snook. The other was a Columbia University graduate lecture course on the Old South. I suppose they assumed that, since I was from the South, I would be prepared for the course, but I had never had any American history classes. The course was taught by Eugene Genovese, at the time celebrated at Rutgers for his opposition to the Vietnam War. Genovese's recently published book, *The Political Economy of the Old South*, electrified the profession.[2] From my perspective, the culture that Professor Genovese described did not ring true for either common whites or the African Americans among whom I had grown up. We had to write a four-page paper on W. J. Cash's *Mind of the South*.[3] I was so angry with Cash's depiction of textile workers that I wrote some thirty pages about how smart cotton-mill folks were. Genovese did not like the paper, but he did get me very interested in southern history. Later that summer, after he learned that I was from the South and an undergraduate, Gene wrote me a kind and thoughtful letter. He even knew that Bill Voiselle, baseball pitcher for the old New York Giants during World War II, was from Ninety Six.

The following summer, again selected for ISSP, I attended Yale University. One of the classes was with Professor William S. McFeely and his graduate student assistant, Joe Ellis. I enjoyed learning from these two scholars. McFeely felt strongly about everything; I had never met anyone as passionate about history. Ellis was very approachable and encouraging. The class studied C. Vann Woodward's *Tom Watson: Agrarian Rebel*.[4] That book changed me! That is when I first began thinking about becoming a historian. Because of Woodward, I began to see how history could further understanding and how new understanding could change the world, especially in terms of race relations. I also got to meet C. Vann Woodward, but at that time I was too shy to tell him what his writing meant to me.

Back at Furman, and now very much interested in southern history, I read another book that had a powerful impact on my life. John Hope Franklin's

Reconstruction awakened me to the importance of who is telling the story.[5] While I was at Furman I also learned that scholarly and teaching interests should not be walled off from the broader world. I joined with others interested in advancing the Civil Rights movement. In February 1968 officers of the South Carolina highway patrol killed three African American students and wounded twenty-seven others who were protesting a segregated bowling alley in Orangeburg. This Orangeburg Massacre and the way state officials explained it away had an influence on me; I again realized how powerful the truth is and how important it is to know who was writing the history. Some of us involved with the Civil Rights movement at Furman formed a group called SSOC, Southern Student Organizing Committee. We needed a faculty member to legitimize us, and Dr. Charles Joyner from St. Andrews College in North Carolina came down to charter us. This was my first meeting with Chaz, who would later become a dear friend. Years later someone from the Smithsonian Institution contacted me about an unusual pin with a black and white hand clasping across a Confederate flag. They had heard that I might be able to identify this "strange protest button." Indeed, it was the SSOC symbol. When the Furman SSOC focused more of its efforts toward protesting the Vietnam War and in loco parentis, I became less involved. Even as an ROTC cadet, I was opposed to the war, but I thought SSOC should remain primarily a civil rights group.

Furman had a required convocation and chapel where a young associate minister, Dr. James Pitts, challenged students of faith to think about social-justice issues. Reverend Pitts brought Dr. Benjamin E. Mays as a guest speaker to the Furman campus. When I discovered that this great theologian, the spiritual godfather of the Civil Rights movement, this apostle of peace whose very life represented a heroic struggle for dignity and for civil rights, was from my hometown of Ninety Six, the tragedy of segregation in the South was made known to me in a very personal way. Dr. Mays and I developed a friendship, and he encouraged me to become a historian. Many years later, when his autobiography was out of print, Dr. Mays asked me to write an introduction, help him edit it, and find a new publisher. He passed away before the editing was accomplished, but I do appreciate that the University of Georgia Press published a new edition of *Born to Rebel*.[6]

Professors at Furman encouraged me to go to graduate school, and because of the Harvard-Yale-Columbia ISSP, I was recruited. Now I was torn by the decision of whether to attend seminary or graduate school in history. It seems my religion professors wanted to save Christianity from me because both history and religion faculty advised me to go into history; these were fine people, and I did not want to disappoint them. Bill McFeely, Joe Ellis, and Vann Woodward advised me to go to Princeton to study southern history with Sheldon Hackney. After Sheldon sent me a personal, informative letter, I decided to accept Princeton's offer of a fellowship.

Unconscious of the role I myself was playing in cultural identity and southern violence, when I took the train from Ninety Six to Princeton, I wore in a holster under my jacket Barry McAdams's World War II pistol his widow had given me. It was only at Princeton that I realized how stupid and illegal it was to be carrying a concealed weapon. I was totally unaware of the geographical and cultural boundaries I was crossing.

Princeton University was an exciting place to be in 1969. The faculty told graduate students that our ideas mattered, that we could disagree and challenge, that we were part of the intellectual community. It was a great faculty, many of whom supported us students in antiwar protests. Lawrence Stone was a large presence at Princeton. Filled with ideas and theoretical approaches, Stone championed social history, family history, and quantitative techniques (this, of course, before his famous call for a return to narrative). Many of the history professors at Princeton influenced me and my work. Arno Mayer's work on modern European counterrevolutions was relevant to the Reconstruction South. Arthur S. Link took time to work with my writing, and we talked about history for hours. We shared a rural Carolina background and more; Arthur was also a man of great spiritual faith, and we discussed theology and the role of the Christian intellectual in society. Sheldon Hackney and James M. McPherson were brilliant. What a heady experience to have these two gifted young historians, both Vann Woodward Ph.D.s, in the same classroom! C. Vann Woodward remained my hero. One of the wonderful experiences of my life was when Sheldon arranged for me to attend Woodward's seminar at Yale. Afterward, I was flattered to go to lunch with Vann. I thought Vann did not know my name because when he introduced me he called me "Mr. Bruden." Finally I got up the courage to say, "Mr. Woodward, my name is Burton." He replied, "That is what I said, Bruden." Then he spelled it out for me, "B-U-R-T-O-N." I replied, "Yes sir, I have just been mispronouncing it all these years." He chuckled.

Due to a departmental fluke, I had two dissertation advisers, which was the best of all possible worlds for me. Then as now, no scholar knew more about the Civil War and Reconstruction than Jim McPherson. He has an incredible breadth of knowledge and ability to synthesize and explain different interpretations. He is a model researcher and taught me the importance of details in getting at the larger question. Sheldon Hackney is inspired by ideas. It was his article on southern violence, which I had read as an undergraduate, that convinced me to go to Princeton to study southern history. It applied quantitative techniques and social theory to understanding culture, and it demonstrated his genius in thinking about problems of southern identity.[7] I am still using Sheldon's ideas thirty years later, and they still are fresh and new.

Because the dissertation determines the direction of the career, it is no easy task to decide upon a topic. Sheldon Hackney offered me the opportunity to do a biography of his father-in-law, Clifford Durr, for my dissertation, and I wish I had understood the subtleties of Sheldon's offer (I could have been one of the founders of Civil Rights–movement historiography). With my rural background, however, I wanted to write about tenant farming and began researching the murky literature on the origins of tenantry. I decided that what was needed was a close study of places, and I proposed to study the development of tenant farming in the South Carolina lowcountry and upcountry by comparing two counties. Some professors, never Sheldon or Jim who were always supportive, warned me against studying South Carolina because as a white southerner my work would be suspect as biased, but I thought I could turn a liability into an asset. Scrutinizing a place I knew well provided insights into the geography and the texture and diversity of the place. (I hope I have demonstrated that one can be close to and also critical of a place.) In a class for Jim McPherson, I had written a long research paper on African American Union Civil War hero and congressman Robert Smalls of Beaufort County, so I decided to do a comparative study of Beaufort County and Edgefield County, South Carolina. Since I had already explored sources in Beaufort, I began first with Edgefield. The origins of tenantry brought me to the stories of emancipation and Reconstruction, and I realized that this was a story that had not really been told. Because Edgefield had such rich manuscript collections, because I had done voter registration there, and because it was close to where my mother lived, I turned the thesis to a study of Reconstruction in Edgefield.[8]

This was the heyday of the "New Social History," and while I was most interested in the political developments of Reconstruction, I wanted to understand the details of how Reconstruction affected the people in a local area. Influenced by social theory and non-U.S. history, I wanted to study the political, economic, social, and cultural lives of all the people. I was excited to read about people in letters and newspapers and then find their detailed records in the census, but I soon realized that a systematic study would require a database of massive information contained in the different censuses of population, agriculture, slavery, mortality, industry, and social statistics. Fellow graduate student Myron Gutmann was a lifesaver; I fixed his car, and he taught me about data manipulation on the computer. Realizing that I needed more formal training in quantitative techniques and demography to interpret the statistics I was deriving from the manuscript census returns, I took graduate classes in those techniques. (Later, as a professor, I did a formal "Study in a Second Discipline" with a concentration on demography and advanced statistics.) I had always been good with numbers; maybe being from a town with a number for its name had something to do with it. At the same time, a demographer friend of mine made the accusation that I was not really a demographer, that I just wanted to know about the common people. Guilty as charged. Nevertheless, numbers were an effective tool. Although I enjoyed statistics and found them to be a useful addition to the narrative explanation, attempting to bridge the boundaries between narrative history and statistics and census analysis cost me years of extra work.

My dissertation, "'Ungrateful Servants'? Edgefield's Black Reconstruction: Part I of the Total History of Edgefield County, South Carolina," uncovered a story quite different from the general literature on the history of the transition from slavery to freedom.[9] Perhaps most important was my argument that historians had been looking in the wrong places to assess Reconstruction. Up until this time, historians usually studied Reconstruction at the level of Washington, D.C., or at state capitals. I believed that the entire debate about the "failure" of Reconstruction had focused too narrowly on the legislative seats of power. I wanted to look at the local level to see how African Americans and whites in rural counties actually changed their lives during this revolutionary period in the South. I found that in Edgefield, African Americans fought for change, their new voting rights resulted in political success, those political successes enabled African Americans to advance economically, and ultimately those economic successes altered social arrangements.

At that time, social theory, quantitative techniques, and local studies were controversial, somewhat outside the academic boundaries set for southern history. This seemed especially true at my new position at the University of Illinois. Moreover, when I presented a paper to the Organization of American Historians in 1976, the commentator refused to believe the evidence that the African Americans in this community were the agents of change. He chided me, "Come, come, now Professor Burton, surely you do not believe that blacks challenged whites in the home of Pitchfork Ben Tillman." When I submitted the essay to the *Journal of Southern History*, it was rejected as "so much Marxist folderol." The reviewer did not like that I was crossing another boundary; I was contradicting Francis Butler Simkins. The reviewer objected that since Simkins grew up in Edgefield, I was in no position to disagree with him. I had to wonder why my growing up in Ninety Six, South Carolina, was not just as valid as Simkins's growing up in Edgefield. Instead this essay, "Race and Reconstruction: Edgefield County, South Carolina," was first published in the *Journal of Social History*.[10]

In 1977 Emmanuel Le Roy Ladurie invited me to participate in an international conference of Annales scholars at the École des Hautes Études en Sciences Sociales in Paris. My paper on the development of tenantry was the only one presented on American history. European scholars, who had to dig information out of parish registers and church baptismal records, were astounded and envious at the wealth of data available in the U.S. manuscript census returns. These international scholars encouraged me to mine that data and use the census as the basic source for tracing change over time in a thorough community study. From this conference, I began to think of a story larger than that of Reconstruction. For one thing, I wanted a new periodization linking the two worlds of slavery and freedom. I like bridges better than chasms, and I hope that my work has done something to undermine the *Gone with the Wind* myth of the Civil War as the Great Divide in American history. Certainly it was extraordinarily traumatic at every level in Edgefield County, but much that mattered to Edgefieldians looks very much the same on either side of the war. Defeat and emancipation did not wreck the white community. In fact, ex-Rebels and freedpeople both played crucial roles of renovation and of conservation in the months and years after Appomattox. To understand that very hopeful irony, I wanted to study the antebellum, wartime, and postbellum community as a piece, something that few others were calling for at the time.

Jim McPherson recommended that I work with Augie Meier, who edited a first-rate series on black history for the University of Illinois Press. Augie, however, like many of my friends and colleagues, wanted me to focus only on African Americans, but I thought that what made the South special was the interaction of African Americans and whites in the same community. William Faulkner suggested in *Light in August* that it was the interaction of black and white, and the white demand for dominance, that defined or, better stated, warped white southern men's understanding of manhood. With all the work in African American history in the last forty years, it goes without saying that African Americans have had a tremendous formative influence on the culture of the South, and it was the interaction of African American and white that I was trying to clarify. Moreover, I have always been interested in the common folk, men and women outside the realm of traditional southern history. Women's history was new, and I wanted this study to include gender issues, among which was the question of whether or not there was a black matriarchy after the Civil War. I have never been satisfied with the usual boundaries of historical study, neither a periodization dividing study of the South between antebellum and postbellum, nor a concentration on one group, whether African American or white, male or female, rich, poor, or yeoman. All the people, black and white—the good, the bad, the heroic, and the craven—all who populate the little postage stamp of history, Edgefield County, South Carolina, have stories to tell. Furthermore, they can be properly understood only when told in the context of each other.

In My Father's House Are Many Mansions: Family and Community in Edgefield, South Carolina tells about white and African American families within a local community context.[11] As Eudora Welty suggests in *Eye of the Story*, "One place comprehended can make us understand other places better. Sense of place gives equilibrium; extended, it is sense of direction."[12] Wanting a history in all its abundance and complexity, I aimed at writing about a particular place, describing the fortunes of men and women, whites and African Americans, enslaved and free people, rich and poor, linked together in families, joined in the give-and-take of a single community existing on a variety of planes: religious, political, cultural, economic, social. I would ground it in quantitative records and the federal census returns (so far used mainly to study northern towns such as Newburyport and Poughkeepsie). On this sturdy structure, I would craft my analysis, using every other kind of qualitative source that came to hand— church records, genealogical and legal records, military records, family Bibles and local pottery, folklore and gossip, manuscripts, maps, and the ink-stained debris of economic transactions. My experience contradicted the notion that non-elite southerners kept few family records. Like most agricultural people, African American and white southerners saved everything. Historical records were just hard to find and are often preserved in unusual ways. I discovered several volumes of tax records being used to support boards as shelves in a country store. With a feeling of reverence for the past and family, African American and white southerners have preserved personal documents that link the past to their own recollections and stories.

A historian brings order out of chaos and, in doing so, constructs an artificial presentation that makes sense out of the past. A study of communities allows us to approximate the complexity and confusion of the human experience. One of the greatest values of local studies as a genre is its holistic view, an insight into real life experience writ large. French scholars such as Fernand Braudel had championed *histoire totale* long before I "modestly" subtitled my dissertation "Part I of the Total History of Edgefield District," but the two views shared little in common except for big appetites and a taste for hard work. Whereas the French tediously built up from geography to culture to politics, I wanted readers to get to know the people themselves in the pleasures, conflicts, and heartbreaks of family and community life from the moment they glimpsed the four faces on the dust jacket. I did not want to use a sample, and I wanted to know everything. Who lived where? Who was in the family? How many children? Who owned slaves and how many did they own? Did the enslaved people live in families? Who could read? Who owned what? What crops were grown? What were the daily routines of household, work, play, church, and school? With that concentration on real men, women, and children, on all groups and their stories—for there was not one master narrative, I became convinced—I tried to do justice to the heart of the people whose family and community lives I lay bare. When some complained that the book lacked "punch," I nodded thankfully. It would have been easier to paint a landscape of villains and victims, but I aimed at something more nuanced and true to the community I had studied.

As I read through the manuscript census returns and recorded the information for each and every household, I thought of the excitement that Frank and Harriett Owsley and his students must have felt as they discovered the lives of the plain people of the South in these same records several decades before I began to work with them. Yet the differences between us—in terms of technology and philosophy—were significant. In technology, I had the advantage of the computer, with which I could manipulate huge amounts of data and rethink and rerun the data as I thought of more questions. As part of his philosophy, Owsley did not view African Americans as part of southern culture and economy. Whereas Owsley was determined to forestall the federal government's enforcement of civil rights, my interest in common folk includes both whites and African Americans and sprang from, and I hope fostered, the Civil Rights movement.

In writing *In My Father's House Are Many Mansions*, I had no models to follow. The revolution wrought by the New Social History was still restricted in scope and influence, and whereas most social history basically presented statistical data in tables and then explained it, that did not satisfy me. I wanted to use quantitative methodology in order to understand nitty-gritty human relationships. I wanted to produce the tables, explain what the numbers meant to the people actually living in the community, and also tell a good story that would interest the reader. Moreover, when the devastating attacks on Robert Fogel's and Stanley Engerman's use of quantitative techniques in *Time on the Cross* (1974) tore that opus to shreds and put "cliometrics" on the run, I could see that the problem was not statistics but a lack of awareness of the social, cultural, and political significance of the documents from which one derived statistics and interpretation. Ten years between census snapshot data collections is a long time in the lives of people, and much of significance can occur between decennial enumerations. Unless the scholar working with the census materials is aware of the changes that occurred throughout the decade, it would be easy to miss alterations in the social structure. For example, the federal census of 1870 was taken just as effective African American resistance to white dominance began and therefore did not reflect all the progress they made. No African American attorneys or businessmen appeared in the Edgefield census, but they were documented in other records between 1870 and 1880. The census of 1880 was taken after the reassertion of white political and social hegemony in 1876, and only vestiges of African American advancement were to be found. Although statistical data drawn from the census can tell what people did for a living, the property they owned, the size of their family, and a number of other things that can assist in the creation of a valuable mosaic of the society, traditional literary sources are necessary to understand the nuances of the census manuscripts. Nevertheless, when used in combination with the literary evidence and other records, the federal manuscript census returns provide abundant information and remain the best source from which to reconstruct a picture of a community.

My use of the census meant recording, tallying, and analyzing the microfilm copies of actual notes recorded by the census taker at the time. I initially coded every household head with information about every family head and every spouse and child present. Information put together amounted to 9,877 cases and 47 variables for the 1880 population census alone; more important, it was integrated and cross-connected at the household as well as the township and county levels. I now have separate individual records for every census year. For 1880, for example, I have separate files for each of the 45,844 individuals, whom I am able to link back to family and household. I used all of the census returns to create the Edgefield Database. This database includes every person and farm recorded in the census returns linked from 1850 to 1880 (with some records prior to 1850 and some later than 1880) for old Edgefield District, South Carolina (a region now comprising five different counties). I continue to use it to investigate "large questions in small places."[13]

When I began the data collection on every person, household, and farm from 1850 through 1880, I had to fill out record sheets by hand and then type out punch-cards. Punch-cards had to be kept in careful order, not a one out of place. Hoping none would jam or be out of order, I then ran boxes and boxes of punch-cards, about seventy thousand cards at a time, into a card reader as input into the computer memory. Once in the computer, the card images would be copied onto a tape. Every time I needed to analyze the data, the tape had to be mounted. I used SPSS and SAS to analyze the data. If I discovered a mistake in the data, which definitely happened, I would have to repeat the process from the beginning. At the computer lab I was relegated to the graveyard shift at midnight to run the cards through the mainframe computer at the University of Illinois because it took so much of the computer's time. It was because of my huge data sets that I was invited to join the National Center for Supercomputing Applications, crossing another disciplinary boundary to work with scientists there. My entire life as a scholar has involved Information Technology: doing it, creating it, teaching it, using it, thinking about it, writing about it. *Computing in the Social Sciences and Humanities*, as well as the accompanying CD-ROM with multimedia applications, shows some of the current possibilities and foreshadows the future of computing in history.[14]

My experience with history computing and the census suggests the benefits of working with the original sources themselves. Because I worked with the entire population rather than a sample and because I was so completely engaged in the coding, I began to discern several significant patterns, unnoticed heretofore. I was able to show not just how many households and families owned slaves, but their kinship connections. An overseer with no slaves, but who was the son of a wealthy planter, is quite different from an overseer with no slaves who was the son of a landless yeoman. I found marriages between free African American men and white women, even on the eve of the Civil War. I also found many instances of white male abuse of African American women, including rape. I discovered rural patterns of African American family stability, of both white and African American rural families overwhelmingly headed by two parents; patterns of differences in town/country/village/hamlet; patterns of female-headed households preferring to reside in town for reasons of jobs and safety; and patterns of unrepresentative scholarly samples because academics did not understand rural culture. These findings were possible only because I used a combined approach of demographic, census, statistical work in conjunction with traditional literary, cultural, narrative sources. Without that statistical data, I would not have discovered the connections and interactions that are essential for an understanding of race relations.

I also think that thoroughness of approach and topic in a local study is needed to breech controversy and anger. When studying specifics of one community, scholars may be better equipped to deal with some of the contentious issues endemic to history, and especially the history of the South. Historians of the southern family, for example, enter both a scholarly and a popular battlefield strewn with prejudices about plantation owners, poor whites, and African Americans, and any discussion of the African American family leads into treacherous terrain, into a literature filled with contradictions as well as political implications. The debates are lively because of implications for current-day family and issues such as single motherhood, welfare, and reparations. In a recent barrage, sociologist Orlando Patterson has denounced revisionist historians as "an intellectual disgrace, the single greatest disservice that the American historical profession has ever done to those who turn to it for guidance about the past and the etiology of present problems."[15] Yet these revisionists, myself included, have tried to look at the life of African Americans without the racist lens of some of the earlier scholars. Whereas sweeping generalizations tend to polarize debate, complex patterns can best be studied on a local level, where processes and changes over time can be closely analyzed. As Pierre Goubert has suggested, local studies are important because "they establish certain proofs, limited in some instances but proofs nonetheless; their statistics compiled with a safety-margin, challenge some of the 'general' ideas, prejudices, and approximations that had held sway in the absence of more precise investigation."[16]

The Edgefield Database goes beyond family and community as studied in *In My Father's House*. My students and I use the database to identify with specificity the socioeconomic status of any individuals mentioned in any Edgefield records. My co-authored book on James B. Griffin moves from Edgefield, through Civil War battles, to a new life and new identity in Texas. This narrative in the southern tradition of a story within a story makes use of the database only to fill in some of the details; the work is not quantitative.[17]

In all of my writings on southern history, I try to capture a sense of mystery and contradiction and what C. Vann Woodward has described as the "Irony of Southern History": the legacy of slavery, the cultural combination of African and European roots, the peculiar quality of caste and clan, the enduring stereotypes, the ability under the most unpromising of circumstances to produce figures both black and white of literary rank, the persistence of gracious living and the aristocratic style, the distorted image of the southern politician, the bitterness, violence, and hope of the Civil Rights movement.

Much of my work has been influenced by the fight for civil rights, and I have written extensively about the Voting Rights Act of 1965.[18] Moreover, my professional career has had a most welcome component, expert witness consultation in discrimination and voting-rights cases where the application of history makes an effective difference (beginning in the early 1980s with *McCain v. Lybrand*).[19] I thought this would be a way to help my region, even as I resided elsewhere. The effect I have had in court, and consequently in the political structure of the lives of people, has made me feel connected and still part of the South, still part of the Civil Rights movement. Some in the profession object vehemently to historians' work as expert witnesses, worrying about objectivity. Yet no historian has to undergo such a thorough and mean-spirited peer review of a book or article as an expert witness has to face in a deposition or cross-examination of his or her evidence. But I must admit that I love it. Also, because of my work in voting rights, I became friends with two of my heroes, C. Vann Woodward and John Hope Franklin, both of whom had been experts for the minority plaintiffs in *Brown v. Board of Education*.

History is eclectic, and I hold strongly that there is no one right approach. We learn from one another. Some of this thinking came from a challenge given to me by a colleague recently. He asked me how, in this day when the profession is interested in globalization, I can justify teaching southern history, how I can emphasize regionalism or local community studies. As I see it, people everywhere on the globe are part of a community. Too often scholars address history at what we think of as the national or transnational level without consciously realizing that these "higher, broader" levels are in fact intellectual constructs rather than concrete realities. Still, it is also true that no history, properly understood, is merely local. History by nature as a discipline is comparative, and in order to define the South, one has to understand how it differs. This union of social and cultural history, as well as traditional political and quantitative research and analysis, offers a more holistic view. I have continued to use this philosophy in all my work since *In My Father's House*.

As a young man growing up in the South, one who worked for civil rights and opposed the Vietnam War, I was witness to the abuses of history, a history that justified exploitation and racism. I then felt and have since realized that history should explain the past, not glorify it. I believe that history is a way of life, a way of making sense of the world and of oneself. Now, after more than thirty years of self-imposed exile from my region, I still see the South as home. I identify with the South, and up North I feel like a stranger in a strange land. When I write about southern history, I feel a kinship with other southerners, black and white. I delight in southern hospitality and storytelling, but I hurt for my homeland's harsh treatment of minorities. Basically, I feel humble about trying to capture the meaning of the South or southern history. As I continue to wrestle with the question of American race relations, I am coming to grips with the limits of both quantification and of narratives. In my life I have done many kinds of physical labor and believe that history is harder than anything else I have done; however, it is also more highly rewarding. At this time in my life, I am still learning and developing my historical views. I am getting fresh ideas every day. I have more boundaries to cross, and I think the best is yet to come.

Notes

1. Orville Vernon Burton, *Class, Conflict, and Consensus: Antebellum Southern Community Studies* and *Toward a New South? Studies in Post–Civil War Southern Communities*, both co-edited with Robert C. McMath Jr. (Westport, Conn., 1982).
2. Eugene Genovese, *The Political Economy of the Old South: Studies in the Economy and Society of the Slave South* (New York, 1965).

3. W. J. Cash, *Mind of the South* (New York, 1941).

4. C. Vann Woodward, *Tom Watson: Agrarian Rebel* (New York, 1938).

5. John Hope Franklin, *Reconstruction* (Chicago, 1962).

6. Benjamin E. Mays, *Born to Rebel: An Autobiography*, foreword by Orville Vernon Burton (Athens, Ga., 1987; rev. ed. 2003).

7. F. Sheldon Hackney, "Southern Violence," *American Historical Review* 74 (February 1969), 906–25.

8. People mistakenly believe that I am from Edgefield. Edgefield is about thirty-five to forty miles from Ninety Six, which today is in Greenwood County. Edgefield District was part of the old Ninety Six District, and the town of Ninety Six was near the juncture of Abbeville and Edgefield Districts.

9. The dissertation is not yet published.

10. Vernon Burton, "Race and Reconstruction: Edgefield County, South Carolina," *Journal of Social History* 12 (Fall 1978), 31–56.

11. Orville Vernon Burton, *In My Father's House Are Many Mansions: Family and Community in Edgefield, South Carolina* (Chapel Hill, 1985).

12. Eudora Welty, *The Eye of the Story: Selected Essays and Reviews* (New York, 1978), 128–29.

13. "Large Questions in Small Places" was the title of a session devoted to this book and also to Charles Joyner's *Down by the Riverside* at the 1987 annual meeting of the Southern Historical Association.

14. I am now the Associate Director for Humanities and Social Sciences at this center. See Burton, *Computing in the Humanities and Social Sciences* (Urbana, 2002), riverweb.cites.uiuc.edu.

15. This was directed at all revisionists, but Patterson specified Herbert Gutman. See Orlando Patterson, *Rituals of Blood: Consequences of Slavery in Two American Centuries* (Washington, D.C., 1998), xiii. See Eric Foner, "The Crisis Is Within" [review of Patterson's *Rituals of Blood*], *New York Times*, February 14, 1999, page 12.

16. Pierre Goubert, "Local History," in Felix Gilbert and Stephen R. Graubard, eds., *Historical Studies Today* (New York, 1971), 304.

17. *A Gentleman and an Officer: A Social and Military History of James B. Griffin's Civil War* (New York, 1996), co-authored with Judith N. McArthur. See also *The Free Flag of Cuba: The Lost Novel of Lucy Holcombe Pickens* (Baton Rouge, 2002), co-edited with Georganne B. Burton. Georganne is involved in my work, if not co-editor, as proofreader. She does not want this article to be a love story and insisted that I not wax poetic about her influence in my life.

18. "Legislative and Congressional Redistricting in South Carolina," in Bernard Gofman, ed., *Race and Redistricting in the 1990s* (New York, 1998), 290–314; Burton et al., "It Ain't Broke, So Don't Fix It: The Legal and Factual Importance of Recent Attacks

on Methods Used in Vote Dilution Litigation," in *University of San Francisco Law Review* 27 (Summer 1993), 737–80; Burton et al., "South Carolina," in Chandler Davidson and Bernard Gofman, eds., *The Quiet Revolution in the South: The Impact of the Voting Rights Act, 1965–1990* (Princeton, 1994), 191–232; "'The Black Squint of the Law': Racism in South Carolina," in David R. Chesnutt and Clyde N. Wilson, eds., *The Meaning of South Carolina History: Essays in Honor of George C. Rogers, Jr.* (Columbia, S.C., 1991), 161–85.

19. Discrimination cases have included more than the South. I have done the history and statistical methodology of racial bloc voting and intent in California, Massachusetts, New York, and Illinois, as well as in Texas (for those who think Texas is not part of the South).

Snow Falling on Magnolias

SUZANNE LEBSOCK

How does a daughter of the snowdrifts come to study the daughters of the South?

Inside that question several others jostle for attention. What sends us away from home? How do we find intellectual homes in other places? And how was it that in the second half of the twentieth century, daughters got to study at all — going to graduate school in numbers, churning through archives, writing books — books, no less, on women?

Snow

I was a December baby, born just at midcentury in Williston, in the upper left-hand corner of North Dakota near the Montana line. My parents were regrouping then, returned to their hometown of Fairview, Montana, after disappointment and disaster had prompted my father to abandon graduate school.

That he had made it past high school was a feat in itself. He was born in 1921 on the high plains of Colorado, the fourth child and second son in a family that grew to eleven children. For generations his people had grown sugar beets, first in Germany, then in Russia, and then in Colorado and Nebraska. Dad was eight when a sugar company agent appeared at their (rented) Colorado farm, promising his father land of his own if he would resettle his family in the Yellowstone Valley on the Montana-Dakota border, an arid and ruggedly beautiful place soon to be transformed by irrigation. They moved in 1929.

Skinny and plagued by croup, the red-haired Kenneth was deemed, by his mother especially, the son least suited to a lifetime of farming. But at first no one had a better plan, and although farming (and the grocer at the Valley Cash, who was generous with credit) provided enough food throughout the Depression, there was little money. Ken finished high school in 1938, and for two years worked as a farmhand for his father (for an allowance, not for wages). His break came when his older sister Annabelle moved four hundred miles west to Bozeman with her ambitious, mercurial husband, a math teacher who intended to get his master's degree at Montana State College. They all but kidnapped Dad, promising to help him enroll and to see him through the first quarter.

This would become a pattern in my father's bumpy ride to a Ph.D. in agronomy: someone he trusted spotted his industry and talent, talked him beyond his prevailing modesty, and suggested a specific next step. Once the United States entered the world war, of course, the steps were dictated by the military. In late 1943 Dad enlisted in the Coast Guard (interesting choice for someone who had learned to swim in an irrigation ditch), on the promise that he could finish his degree. But the Selective Service muscled in, and he found himself instead in an Army transportation unit in Antwerp, Belgium, dispatching supplies by rail to the front.

Before he shipped out, he married his high-school sweetheart, Maxine Wells, who with her parents had encouraged his college aspirations. While Ken was in Europe, Maxine worked in Fairview—at the sugar company, the drugstore, and the post office, where she could intercept Ken's letters on Sundays. She did the postmaster's work and her own, saved her money, and dreaded the sight of the depot agent walking up Main Street with a telegram in hand. She vividly remembers her relief that no telegram came for her. Three of the fifteen men in her high-school graduating class were killed in the war. But Ken came home in 1946, his final military assignment driving truckloads of coal to convents in occupied Germany.

Maxine became Ken's staunchest ally in his quest for an education; as the worst hardships would largely fall on her, her backing was crucial. They returned to Montana State on the GI Bill, had their first child, Randall, in early 1948, and Dad earned his bachelor's degree. Encouraged by his professors to seek graduate training, he again headed west, this time in midwinter to an ill-fated semester at Washington State College. The young family had been promised housing, but none materialized. With legions of veterans crowding the universities, the housing market was horrendous. In desperation Ken and Maxine moved into a trailer on a river bottom. When snowmelt and spring rains came, they were flooded out.

They moved into what they now describe as a "dingy" motel, and then a "smelly" house—the adjectives resonating all too well with Ken's souring feelings about his academic program. Tired of school and thoroughly disillusioned, he packed it in at the end of the term.

Ken worked for his dad again that summer, thinking he might grow where he was planted, settling in and farming for the rest of his life. But Maxine couldn't see it, especially after Ken's grades arrived in the mail: despite his miseries, he had earned straight A's. He also had a pivotal visit that summer from two of his former Montana State professors, who were sizing up agricultural experiment stations and took a detour to see their former student. "You're going to ride that tractor for twelve or fourteen hours a day," one of them warned, "and you're going to be awfully bored and sorry you quit school." And then there was the question of whether Ken would ever be able to farm on his own. His father was a small man and soft-spoken, with a layer of gravel in his voice, but very much the patriarch. Ken proposed that they be partners. His father countered with an offer to make Ken his hired man. The discussion ended there, and with it Ken's future as a farmer.

Two of Ken's brothers had meanwhile started a construction business, digging sewer systems in small towns nearby. When the brothers drove east across North Dakota to Fargo to price machinery, Ken hitched a ride. At North Dakota Agricultural College, he found wheat breeder Glenn Smith, an able and impressively kind man who agreed to take him on. The next winter, Ken was back in school.

In the meantime, Ken and Maxine had become the parents of a baby girl (yours truly) and had been evicted from their rented house in Fairview, crowding in with various relatives until it was time to head for Fargo, a 400-mile trek they made in a snowstorm. This time they did get student housing—a collapsible trailer with no indoor plumbing or running water. Imagine this in a North Dakota winter, with two kids in diapers.

But they were well and truly launched. Ken finished his master's degree in a year and moved (once more in winter) straight on to the Ph.D. program at Iowa State College, where he again found an exceptional adviser and legendary married-student housing. For twenty-three dollars a month, which they could just afford on the GI Bill, my parents got a place in Pammel Court, a makeshift neighborhood of Quonset huts and corrugated metal barracks. Maxine remembers perpetual earaches (my brother's), bronchitis (mine), and runny noses (everybody's, including those of three neighborhood children for whom she provided day care). For her it was an especially taxing day-to-day life. But scores of others in Pammel Court were in the same boat; Ken and Maxine made friendships that survive to this day. And they were getting somewhere. Ken worked like crazy, got help from more advanced students, and earned his Ph.D. in 1953.

Fargo: Not the Movie

We moved back to Fargo then, where we experienced one last creative solution to the postwar housing shortage. The houses in "Silver City" were converted wooden granaries, originally manufactured for use on farms, to hold the harvest so that the growers did not have to sell all at once. These little buildings were small enough to haul on a truck (ten feet wide, twenty feet long), and at North Dakota Agricultural College they became home to generations of married students and young faculty.

I remember a little about Pammel Court and a little more about Silver City (I was three when we moved from one to the other) but am not telling a tale of suffering on my part. In the small, square, black-and-white snapshots from that time, my brother Randy and I look clean, snug, and happy. This story instead is meant to be about historical sensibility. My mother did not get to call most of the shots, but as the more talkative of my parents, she did get to construct our family history. From my earliest memory she formulated these years in terms of motion (she counted some twenty moves in three years) and hardship — which meshed perfectly with the pioneer history we soon learned in school and from books. I loved the *Little House* series (until the last one, when the protagonists got all ladylike and boring) and identified completely with the hardy, westering souls who homesteaded the Great Plains.

We did not identify with the indigenous people they displaced, who, alas, figured in settler narratives largely as forces of nature, like the snowstorms, hailstorms, droughts, twisters, prairie fires, and swarming grasshoppers that formed the litany of pioneer hardships. This figuring of Indians was partly offset by homage to Sacagawea, pictured on the cover of an elementary-school history text, gamely showing Lewis and Clark the way west. But it was one thing to ride the coattails of a celebrity and quite another to incorporate her story to complicate our understanding of who we were.[1]

Our identification with the homesteaders, meanwhile, was reinforced by our having to cope with the same spectacular weather. We experienced blizzards (frequent), tornadoes (rare but terrifying), crash-bang thunderstorms (very frequent in summer), and my personal favorite, "snirt." If there came a blowing snow in the spring, after the farmers had begun plowing, the wind picked up the topsoil and blew it over the town, snow and dirt then falling together. In winter, we walked to school in temperatures below zero, the girls with our skirts stuffed into snow pants, and we walked home, often backward against the north wind. We also walked home for lunch — testimony to our toughness and to the prevailing assumption about where our mothers would be.

By the time I entered school, my family was well settled in our own little house on the prairie, still in Fargo, in a growing row of new cracker-box houses, all the same distance from the gravel street (it was a great thing for bike riders later when the street was paved). Each house had two spindly young elms planted in front. The land was utterly flat — before it was our neighborhood it was a wheat field — and nothing protected us from the bitter winds that blew from the north.

My dad had landed a job as a wheat breeder with the federal government's Agricultural Research Service, and he went on to save pasta. Pasta, if it's any good, is made from durum wheat. In the 1950s and early 1960s the durum crops were nearly wiped out by a fungus called stem rust. Ken developed rust-resistant varieties of durum and subsequently was much honored by the growers and by a younger generation of wheat breeders, who named a new durum variety after him in 1997.

My mother, meanwhile, deeply regretted that she had missed out on college. No one had ever suggested she go (her family seemed to beam all its educational aspirations on my father), nor were there funds to send her; after graduating from high school she clerked at the grocery store to pay off her parents' bill. She admired spunky women, though, an attitude she conveyed most effectively by holding up her own mother as a model for me.

This grandmother, Lois Sommers, was born in 1900 and raised on a sheep farm in northern Minnesota near the small town of Warren, where she achieved local fame for assorted high jinks. To wit: suspended from school one day for some now-forgotten prank, she and her comrade-in-mischief disguised themselves as little old ladies and, in a gesture of mock civic engagement, visited the class from which they'd been ejected. They were found out, of course, but they had a marvelous time.

As a young woman, this same grandmother earned a dollar a pop playing piano for otherwise silent movies. Her first teaching job took her further north to the Boundary Waters, where she canoed (or skated) to school on the Rainy River. After that, she once told me, she "wanted to go where the cowboys were." Hence her venture west to Fairview, Montana, where she had been hired to teach music in the high school. Fairview was careful about decorum; among the many rules laid down for its female teachers was that they were not to ride horses in public. My grandmother borrowed a horse forthwith and galloped him down Main Street.

Before long she found her cowboy. Gerald Wells ("I wouldn't name a *cat* Gerald," he would say) was a farmer and later a labor supervisor for the sugar company. He played the violin, too, and Lois, the pianist, played duets with him. In 1921 they eloped, a move that propelled the young teacher out of the classroom and into the strenuous life of farmwife and mother, giving birth to three daughters and a son. In middle age, however, she returned to teaching. Gerald died young, in 1946, after a long struggle with kidney disease. Lois taught grade school until she was in her sixties, when a broken hip forced her to retire. In her last years she was increasingly debilitated by osteoporosis, and Fairview bored her silly, but she never lost her irreverence or her sense of fun.

And so it was fun to visit, Christmas and summer. On our German grandparents' farm, my brother and I jumped in strawstacks, climbed on tractors and the wooden scaffold that held up the fuel tank, learned to shoot a .22 rifle, and took a sledgehammer to dun-colored rocks to see what they looked like inside. We had the most fun when our cousin and ringleader Andi (then Lebsock, now Barnard) came over from Williston. When the dads let us ride in the truck bed behind the combine, we held funerals for the grasshoppers who got harvested with the wheat. At Christmas, when the cold kept us mostly indoors, we put on performances for the grownups: soap operas, musicals (Andi and Randy on piano, me on ukulele or guitar), and boxing matches. Two pair of real boxing gloves hung on a nail in the basement by the furnace, left over from the uncles' younger days. We pounded on each other and performed original commercials for shaving gear ("I wonder as I wander if every man uses Gillette . . .").

When we stayed with my mother's mother in town, there was less to do (in truth, both places eventually got tedious), but we thought the location was cool. The gravel road that ran past our grandmother's house was the state line; we had only to walk across to arrive in a different state and time zone. Eventually we walked farther on our own, usually to the five and dime on Fairview's one paved street. The cashier naturally pegged us as strangers and asked who we were. "Oh," my brother once replied, "we're from Back East."

I found this mortifying (it wasn't as though we were from Cleveland, for Pete's sake), a reaction I see now as an early glimmer of provincial self-consciousness. Fairview, to be sure, was not Fargo. With a population of about one thousand, Fairview was true small-town America, while Fargo was something else. Fargo had about fifty thousand people and was North Dakota's biggest city. Still, as a fairly small kid, I must have thought on some level that Fargo was no great shakes.

I Was a Teenage Republican

Being from Fargo has acquired a certain quirky cachet since the appearance in 1996 of the feature film of the same name. In the middle 1960s, by which time I was in high school, "cachet" was not a word my friends and I would have associated with our home town. The only times we heard about our state in the national news were on the days when some godforsaken spot in North Dakota—and sometimes it was the godforsaken spot where we lived—was the coldest place in the nation. North Dakota politics apparently counted for less than the weather. In presidential elections, the state always went Republican, and had only three electoral votes anyway. Candidates for president did not campaign there (with the exception, proving the rule, of the desperate Barry Goldwater in 1964). Candidates for vice president, having drawn the short straw, made one appearance each and droned dutifully to us about parity—price supports for farmers.

For us young urbanites, this agricultural hegemony was a problem. One response was to rehearse the list of local institutions that seemed to connect us with the culture of the wider world. We have public television! Community theater! A symphony! And (by 1967) opera! Indeed, the music was rigorous, if a tad morbid: our high-school orchestra and chorus performed requiem masses by Mozart and Schubert.

A less lovely response to our situation was condescension to the benighted farmers to the west of us. We used "farmer" as a synonym for ugly and stupid. If, for example, a person got a tan that stopped at the bicep and made her look strange in a swimsuit, that was a farmer tan. You could call someone a moron or an idiot, or you could just say farmer.

What saved us from being totally obnoxious on this point was that some of us sensed that we were provincial ourselves. On New Year's Eve in, I think, 1966, I was listening with friends to the top forty songs of the year gone by. The radio station must have used national rankings; as they played down the top ten, we found ourselves hearing at least three songs we had never heard before. Not once. I later came to imagine this as the Great Soul Barrier, an invisible shield rising from earth to sky somewhere to the east of us. In my mind's eye I saw Motown producers in Detroit, manfully flinging records like Frisbees across the prairies, only to have them cut down fifty miles west of Minneapolis.

Our isolation, meanwhile, did not exempt us from being touched by some of the great events and trends of our time. The event that had the most immediate impact on me was probably the Soviets' successful launch of *Sputnik* in 1957. Fearful that the United States might lose the space race, American educators initiated a speedup in the schools. In Fargo, this meant standardized testing, "accelerated" classes for those identified as promising, and a modernized (at times baffling) curriculum in science and math.

Tracking and testing have since come in for much criticism, but they saved me from brain death. Before *Sputnik*, I experienced school as an exercise in withstanding boredom. Afterward, school got better, especially when the push for accelerated learning slopped over from math and science into history. I found history intrinsically interesting, especially in high school where I had fabulous teachers and (thanks again to tracking) inventive classmates.

That said, I wouldn't claim that school was the center of anyone's intellectual universe. Education was valued, but it tended toward the utilitarian (it was good if you could use it to save pasta). Learnedness itself was suspect, and making a display of learning was simply not done; in school as elsewhere, the worst failure of character was to get "a swelled head."

You could do intellectual work, though, if you called it something else. We called it religion. The life of the mind was played out mainly in spaces created by churches, in intense debates about theology and ethics. I am remembering one particular Sunday school class in which our teacher, an attorney, told us he had defended a man he believed guilty of the murder with which he had been charged. Our teacher stuck to the lawyer's standard line: It was his duty to give the accused the best defense he could. This drove us bananas. Young Methodists brimming with high moralism, we argued from every angle we could that the lawyer should have gotten the murderer convicted. That was something, that we could join passion and intellect and let them loose in a culture that was otherwise anti-intellectual and did not tolerate expressions of strong emotion.

It may have been the church also that fed my growing feeling (I won't quite call it consciousness) that there was a big world out there, one in which my assumptions were not shared, one that Fargo had not equipped me to understand. Our pastor, David Knecht, was ecumenically minded and a deep thinker. He liked and understood kids, taught us about other religions, and encouraged us to ask questions. Although he rarely revealed his own politics, he would broach political subjects where they connected with faith. He taught us about the theology behind the Civil Rights movement, for example, and greatly admired Martin Luther King Jr.

I admired Dr. King, too, and was stunned and puzzled when he came out against the war in Vietnam. How could so noble a man align himself with the other side? Not that I had any near idea of what that other side might look like. North Dakota offered so little exposure to dissenters (from the Cold War, the Vietnam War, and the Feminine Mystique) that dissent lived in my imagination not as a political position or movement but as something more suited to a horror movie, some sinister miasma sliming its way across the landscape. I don't remember when exactly I became aware that the band of political opinion to which I had had access was extremely narrow. I do remember coming to believe that everything that was happening was happening somewhere else.

The movie *Fargo*, by the way, was not shot there. Except for the early scene in the blackjack parlor, where the hapless Jerry hires two thugs to kidnap his wife, it wasn't even set there.

Carleton

It was a tremendous relief when, in 1967, I arrived at Carleton College. From the perspective of any part of the South, or of either coast, there may not be much to distinguish the snowbanks of Northfield, Minnesota, from the snowbanks of Fargo, but to me the difference was radical.

For one thing, Carleton offered an end to the routine cruelties of high school, where any girl who was not a cheerleader felt like a failure. (I had a moment of supreme satisfaction when Carleton cheerleading simply ceased, because none of the women would do it.) I loved Carleton, too, for its terrific athletic program for women. A natural jock but born too soon for Title IX, I had suffered from sports envy ever since the third grade, when the boys were recruited to play ice hockey. From the seventh grade on, Fargo's young men had access to the full array of competitive sports. For young women, the schools offered no sports at all — no intramurals even, to say nothing of interscholastic competition. This is the core of my feminism.

For all my frustration, it had never occurred to me, nor did it occur to my parents, to protest these inequities or to propose even one modest change. This species of fatalism was cultural, not personal — or perhaps I should say it was so deeply embedded in the culture that it was easily ingrained in the person. In any case, the assumption that one had to cope with things as they were, and a concomitant respect for established authority — these, too, would be turned inside out at Carleton, as they would at a thousand colleges and universities around the world in those years.

It was an exhilarating, often scary time to be alive and a great time to be in school. The civil rights struggle, the quest for student power, the counterculture, the antiwar movement, women's liberation — this cascade of life-changing, world-changing causes inspired or at least challenged all thinking people. Carleton itself was changed. But the faculty saw to it that intellectual rigor continued to matter, and they helped us explore in dozens of iterations the relationships between our politics and our formal learning.

During my entire freshman year I lived in a state of suspended conviction, letting some of my Dakota-think fade while I considered what else was available. I learned a huge amount from students whose experience had been different from mine. Easterners. World travelers. Actual radicals. A group of African American women let me hang out with them as long as I was willing to relieve them of the role of the exotic. One of them later told me that on first sight, she had thought I was the whitest person she had ever seen. For a while I was known as Suzie Snowflake.

I discovered women's history in my senior year, all in a rush. Although I had developed considerable intellectual self-confidence by then, it was hard to know in the fall of 1970 just how to be a student. That spring President Richard Nixon had expanded the war in Southeast Asia, sending troops into Cambodia. Immense protests followed, campus activism reaching its apogee in the fatal shootings of students at Kent State and Jackson State. I was in Chicago that semester, crisscrossing the city with fellow students in an urban studies program, one that featured neighborhood organizations and movements for social change. Under the press of events, the program dissolved three weeks early. Carleton, like scores of other institutions of higher learning, simply shut down.

Returning to school that fall, I felt a restlessness so literal that I doubted my ability to sit through classes. I approached Kirk Jeffrey, a brand-new member of the history faculty, to ask if he would be willing to supervise an independent study. He was extremely busy, inventing new courses while finishing his dissertation, but he agreed, provided I would study something he already knew about. "How about women?" he asked. I hope I did not look as blank as I felt. The single image that bubbled up to me was that of a woman who resembled Mrs. Claus, bent over a washtub.

That changed within a day or two. A student of Carl Degler, Jeffrey was writing his dissertation on nineteenth-century gender ideology. With his coaching I soon replaced Mrs. Claus with now-classic articles by Barbara Welter, Gerda Lerner, and David Potter. I zoomed through books on woman suffrage, and when the secondary works ran out, started in on primary sources. I continued reading with Jeffrey in the winter and spring, and wrote chunky papers on Jane Addams and Charlotte Perkins Gilman.

For months I was Turbo-Student. History had been intrinsically interesting to me for a long time — first in the *Little House* version, and later in the European and U.S. sequence in high school, when I acquired the happy illusion that I could eventually learn everything there was to know. That illusion evaporated about halfway through college, but I was equally happy with history's infinity, with the idea that you could study history and nothing would be closed to you.

Still, women's history was like a rocket launcher. For the first time, I felt I was studying *my* past, a process stoked almost daily by the insights of the women's liberation movement, which broke across the land in that same year. Although the National Organization for Women had been founded earlier, in 1966, and consciousness-raising groups had begun percolating then too, it wasn't until 1970–71 that *Time, Newsweek*, and Northfield, Minnesota caught on. Like countless American women, I experienced the women's movement as an epiphany. It took me about six seconds to become a feminist.

With the self-consciousness that often comes with coming of age, I reconsidered my life to that time, gigantically relieved to identify some of the spectacular stupidities that had earlier seemed like givens. I did not claim then, and would not claim now, that men had as much as women to gain from women's liberation, but I did see that the stupidities cut both ways. My brother, for example, was always tall for his age, and although his temperament was fundamentally artistic, someone was always trying to push him into going out for basketball, which he hated. (Randy's forte was acting, and after a career as a police officer—a vocation in which acting experience is extremely useful—he has recently retired and happily spends his time as a musician, woodcarver, actor, and family man.) I would have given almost anything to play basketball, but until college I had no chance.

I marveled, meanwhile, at the courage of the women—historical figures—about whom I was daily reading. To appreciate their magnitude in my surging consciousness, it may help to recall that for a child growing up in the 1950s and early 1960s, leadership among living women was scarcely to be seen. The women who were publicly known were mostly first ladies (Mamie, Jackie, Lady Bird) and entertainers. Women who somehow managed to exercise exceptional leadership tended to get sandbagged in one way or another. Many were ignored. There were magnificent women leaders in the Civil Rights movement, for example, but unless you were there yourself, you were unlikely to know of them. Others were trivialized (Margaret Chase Smith of Maine, for a long time the sole woman in the U.S. Senate) or punished. Coya Knutson, a very effective two-term congresswoman from a district near us in western Minnesota, lost her seat in 1958 after her husband published a bathetic "Coya Come Home" letter (when she had come home from Congress for visits, he had battered her).[2] No women sat on the U.S. Supreme Court; there were no anchorwomen or female astronauts. In my four years at Carleton, I never had a woman professor (though this, I must confess, was partly a reflection of my own consciousness, or lack thereof; Carleton's faculty included several distinguished women, including Ada Mae Harrison in economics, Harriet Sheridan in English, and Eleanor Zelliot in history).

So the women who spoke to me with authority came mainly from the past. After some months of uncertainty about what to do next—law school? grad school? no school?—I settled on graduate school, so that I could go on and teach about the remarkable women whose stories I found so inspirational. I applied to two prestigious Ivy League graduate programs, neither of which accepted my earnest application. It did not occur to me until years later—I mean many years—that my applications might have stood a better chance had I not written in my essays that the purpose of studying history was to foment feminist revolution. The University of Virginia, meanwhile, did not require an essay of any kind. I did not write one, and they took me right away.

Gidget Goes to Grad School

I arrived in Charlottesville in 1971 with no clue about how graduate school might differ from college and no sense either of what it meant to become a professional historian. This would cost me in some ways. I report with no pleasure but for the possible benefit of historians-in-the-making that at the end of my first year I flunked my master's orals. This debacle had several causes, but the one for which I must claim primary responsibility is that I had not yet learned to talk about history. In my family, a conversation about one's work typically consumed only six words. ("How was your day?" "Oh, fine.") Speaking otherwise, in detail or with enthusiasm, was to risk display of the dreaded swelled head.

Talking history was thus an acquired skill for me. By the end of the next semester I had acquired enough to retake and pass the exam; I soon acquired more — and was socialized into the profession — by historians from all over, feminists of many stripes who banded together nationally and in regional groups to try to do something about the wretched status of women in the history profession.

Here is how it was in 1970, when an American Historical Association (AHA) committee chaired by Willie Lee Rose (a committee established as a result of pressure exerted at the AHA's 1969 annual meeting) published its report. In the nation's ten highest-ranked graduate departments, the proportion of faculty who were female was 2 percent. In five of those departments there were no women at all. As for full professors who were female, those ten departments had among them a grand total of two (that would factor out to .7 percent). In the AHA itself, women were 3.7 percent of committee members. At the annual meeting in 1969, women comprised 3.7 percent of participants on the program. Moreover, the Rose Report (as it soon came to be called) made it clear that the status of women had actually declined since the 1920s and 1930s.

From the 1969 protests emerged the Coordinating Committee on Women in the Historical Profession (CCWHP), a membership organization and pressure group, open to men, whose mission was to support women historians and democracy in the profession in any way its members could devise. When the CCWHP put out a call for a graduate-student coordinator (in 1972, I think), I signed up, with Joan Jacobs Brumberg, a fellow student at Virginia who had invited me to the AHA when the annual meeting was held near her home in New York.

CCWHP meetings were a gas. In early days I loved them above all for the visible differences among the women who rose to speak. In the phrasing my kids might use now, they were collectively so-o-o *not* North Dakota. Mollie Davis, elegantly coifed and dressed, could have passed for the quintessential southern lady until she spoke and revealed at once a dramatic drawl and a startling militance. Donna Boutelle, in the more casual mode of southern California, was understated and wry. (On Richard Nixon's taking up residence in San Clemente, for example, "There go the property values.") Peace historian Sandi Cooper from New York City chaired the CCWHP Steering Committee when I joined up. She seemed at first the essence of northeastern sophistication, with her sarcasm and dark beauty. Before long I came to appreciate also the poignancy and humor melded to her radicalism. She was extremely kind to me, as all these women were, without exception.

What strikes me most forcibly as I recall this time — and here my story connects with my dad's — was the indispensable role of mentorship, and in my case a lucky abundance of mentors. Anne Firor Scott, having learned of my work when I applied for one of the early Woodrow Wilson dissertation fellowships in women's studies, announced herself to me at a meeting of the Southern Historical Association. For a long time I thought of her as my fairy godmother, bibbity-bobbity turning me into a legitimate historian. Anne conducted what amounted to a national underground graduate program in those years, corresponding with students from all over. Many of us worked with faculty who didn't mind our doing women's history (this was my situation at Virginia, where I worked with Willie Lee Rose, Josef Barton, Joseph F. Kett, Charles W. McCurdy, and Paul M. Gaston), but only rarely did they have firsthand knowledge of the field. Anne, who had worked on figures like Jane Addams and Emma Willard as well as on southerners, knew plenty. She was also at the ready with sound advice (usually solicited) about career issues, which we paid for by listening to unsolicited advice about haircuts and wearing warm-enough clothes. "I know, I know," she once told Nancy Hewitt, "it's not my job, but . . . I can see you and your mother can't."[3]

One of the CCWHP's first victories, meantime, was getting the AHA to replace Willie Rose's ad hoc committee with a standing Committee on Women Historians (CWH). Two years later that committee decided to add a graduate-student member, and I applied. I was the first student appointed to any AHA committee, a result not of the brilliance of my personal contributions — though I had worked hard to connect with other students and to gather data on our condition — but rather of the democratizing energy of feminism at that time. Other AHA committees would follow suit, the organization increasingly conscious of its need to reach beyond its traditional constituencies.

The women's movement within history saved me from the profound feelings of uselessness I had as a graduate student (teaching would do this, too, once I got to offer courses on my own). The women's movement also saved me from a particular strain of loneliness. Heading to graduate school as a conscious feminist, I had thought, "New York doesn't need Lebsock, Boston doesn't need Lebsock, but Charlottesville, Virginia, probably does." I was right; Charlottesville did. What I didn't know then was how difficult it would be to sustain a sense of momentum and connection in the absence of a feminist community. I made great friends in Charlottesville, but our bonds were different, those of fellow sufferers, making what headway we could toward the Ph.D. despite the undertow of a dismal job market. Travel proved essential. Key to my survival in graduate school were trips to women's committee meetings in other places, where I would gulp in as much sisterhood as I could, and hope it would be enough to keep me breathing during the next semester.

From the women in the CCWHP and CWH I learned to talk history. My first CWH meeting took place in Chapel Hill. On our way to lunch on a stunningly sunny day, Jane DeHart and Linda Kerber engaged in an animated conversation about the Age of Jackson. "Imagine that," I thought, "people actually talk about this stuff outside of class." Not long after, I attended my first AHA annual meeting as a women's committee member and quickly learned the ritual for meeting another historian. The nametag made the first bits of the conversation efficient: one's name and affiliation were readily established, and there might follow an exchange about whether we knew so-and-so at the places our nametags displayed. Then the inevitable next question: "What are you working on?"

Had I been walking the moon instead of the corridors of San Francisco's Saint Francis Hotel, this question could not have seemed stranger. Here was another Gidget moment. My working but (until then) unarticulated assumption was that a significant conversation ought to reveal, or move toward revealing, a person's essence and commitments. It did not seem to me at the time that what one was working on was a very good channel to that.

But I learned to answer the question, partly because the people who asked it (I'm thinking especially of Joan Moon and Joan Kelly) were interested. With the history of women in its infancy (or perhaps toddlerhood by then), everything seemed a revelation, and in those times everyone knew they could learn from everyone else. At first, I had only one thing to talk about, a humble seminar paper on married women's property rights in the South. Other people asked what I was finding as though it mattered, and I began to believe that it might.

The seminar paper was Willie Lee Rose's idea. As one of the very few senior women in U.S. history anywhere, she was at least half the reason I went to Virginia in the first place, and although she moved on to Johns Hopkins midway through my second year, she helped me immeasurably. For one thing, she knew the value of direct encouragement. Before she left, she offered a benediction and a challenge. "I want you to focus your interests," she said, "and become a Scholar." I didn't know yet what she meant by that, but in her rendering, "Scholar" clearly began with a capital S, and I thought I'd better try to be one. Meantime, she helped launch me on the project that would dominate my research life for the next ten years.

Although I had arrived at Virginia clueless about professional matters, I was very clear on what I wanted to do with the history of women. First I wanted there to *be* a history of women. Second, I wanted to find a way to do the social history of women. For all the inspiration I had found, and continued to find, in the lives of great women ("women worthies," as Natalie Zemon Davis would famously label them), I did not want to study worthies myself. The way I thought of it then was that we could not understand what nineteenth-century women's rights advocates were about unless we understood what they were rebelling against; we needed to know about the lives of ordinary women.

This was hardly a stroke of originality on my part. Social history was then approaching its high-water mark, and although the most creative social historians had an exasperating tendency to confine their studies to men, it nevertheless stood to reason that a social-history approach could be applied to women as well, if only we could figure out how to tap into the sources.

That was the problem. Given all we have learned since, it is difficult to convey just how opaque the record of ordinary women's lives seemed in 1972. Willie Rose suggested I begin with the law, that I investigate a claim made in passing by several historians that in the course of Reconstruction the legal status of southern women was improved. This simple beginning led down some circuitous paths. The laws, it turned out, mainly concerned the property of married women, and in every state the laws were different. It was not just a Reconstruction story either. Between 1839 and the early twentieth century, every southern state moved in the direction of equal property rights for women. Not that most southern legislators and judges could be accused of having been champions of equality. By the time I got all this under control in about 1975, it had shaped itself into a riddle: How did southern women get equal property rights in states where there was next to no support for women's rights?

This whole project was in some ways a frustrating enterprise. It was about men, after all — mostly elite white men — who were less interested in the status of women than in four or five other, often incompatible, aims, including debtor relief, the safe transmission of property to one's grandchildren, the extension of protections available to the rich to those of small property, the free flow of capital, and the streamlining of the law. But I learned enough to spot a possible point of entry into the social history of women. Under the common law, married women could not own property in their own names. But a second system of jurisprudence called equity did permit married women to own property. In equity it was possible to set up a separate estate, property a married woman possessed and in some instances actively controlled, depending on the precise phrasing of the instrument that set it up.

Key words: *instrument; precise phrasing; active control.* It looked as though there ought to be vast stashes of documents that would tell us how many married women got their hands on separate estates, and what sorts of control those women had over their property.

This was the germ of *The Free Women of Petersburg*, published in 1984, by which time I had for several years been teaching at Rutgers University in New Jersey.[4] The respectable reasons why I chose Petersburg appear in the book itself; I had reasons less respectable — or perhaps more intuitive is the better phrase — as well. In the 1970s Petersburg had a very fifties look (1950s, I mean); for the most part the town had avoided the preciousness of Virginia's more famous tourist destinations. Because I thought of my dissertation as nitty-gritty social history, Petersburg seemed just the place. Petersburg was also the site of a Brown and Williamson tobacco factory, manufacturer of Kool cigarettes, which, heaven help me, I smoked in great numbers.

The subtitle of *The Free Women of Petersburg* is *Status and Culture in a Southern Town, 1784–1860*. Status and culture were indeed the book's two central concerns, along with method — demonstrating that the sources commonly available for nineteenth-century locales are replete with evidence on women. But it is arguable that although it was set in a southern place, the Petersburg book was not a work of southern history. Had there been in place a historiography on southern women, I would doubtless have framed the evidence in somewhat different ways. As it was, when I finished the manuscript in 1983, the first wave of books on southern women was just beginning to appear. Before then, Anne Firor Scott's foundational work, *The Southern Lady* (1970) and Jacquelyn Dowd Hall's superb 1979 biography of Jessie Daniel Ames (*Revolt Against Chivalry*) stood virtually alone.[5]

So I tried to hook the Petersburg evidence to concepts of national or even transnational scope. The concept to which I hope to return someday is that of women's culture — cast in the Petersburg book as a distinctive women's value system. About halfway through the process of turning my dissertation into a book, I came to see that property records could be mobilized to speak to values. What did men and women respectively do with what they had? Treat their children alike or play favorites? Protect a daughter from her husband's creditors or let her take her chances? Engage in risky business ventures? Leave a legacy to a church? Free a slave?

The concept of women's culture died a fairly swift death after the mid-1980s, in part because it took inadequate account of differences among women. Indeed, in recent years historians and other scholars have come to think of gender in increasingly complex terms, positing multiple femininities, masculinities, and sexualities. This I applaud (see my critique, a few pages back, of 1950s stupidities). But the evidence from Petersburg tugs at me yet. I grouped free men together (this included a significant minority of free blacks) and compared their behavior to that of free women (a group that included a larger minority of free blacks). On every single thing I could think of to count, free women as a group behaved differently from the men. It seems we are not finished with gender analysis in its simpler forms.

The Teflon South

I am meanwhile meditating on how a Great Plains start might have influenced my approach to the South. North Dakota wasn't even a state until 1889. Although we had our Civil War buffs (my brother had a buddy who memorized most of *Lee's Lieutenants*), refighting the war never presented itself as a mission I should take up, either in its military terms or in the debates over what was at stake in the war and in Reconstruction. In the beginning especially, I felt free to surf southern sources without having to address the field's hoariest questions.

At the same time, I certainly understood what it is to live in a region that is commonly condescended to and stereotyped; the South, of course, is often demonized to boot. Congresswoman Pat Schroeder famously labeled Ronald Reagan the Teflon President, as no bad deed would stick to him. The South seems to possess the same quality in reverse: No progressive deed sticks; it's too important to outsiders to maintain Dixie as the region that takes the moral heat for the rest of us.

Try, for example (as I did in a widely ignored article in the *Journal of Southern History*), to tell people that the first states to grant property rights to married women were southern states—Mississippi, Alabama, Arkansas, Florida, and Texas.[6] All of them moved on this issue before New York passed its famous statute in 1848. But to this day I read scholarly accounts that put New York in first place.

Truth is, married women's property reform succeeded in part because it was not perceived primarily as a women's rights measure. When we understand when and why the law changed, New York looks not only tardy but less progressive. And while the South gets no points for feminism, those five states on the southern frontier do take the prize for innovation.

I learned this lesson early. The *Southern* article appeared in 1977, and it reinforced my preexisting impulse to minimize, or at least complicate, alleged differences among regions. I think it also contributed to a compulsively empirical research style. I really did read every single thing I could find that had been written in or about Petersburg. Spout about the South if you will, but bring footnotes; I look for chapter and verse.

It was not clear to me when I finished the Petersburg book that I would continue working on things southern — women, wherever they might live, were still more central to my interests — but a call from Cindy Aron set me on a Virginia course for a long time to come. At her invitation, I signed on as historian for the Virginia Women's Cultural History Project, created by a visionary gang of professional and political women who intended to mount a major exhibition at the Virginia Museum of Fine Arts. Kym Rice was our curator, I was to write the catalog copy, and we were to go to press in a year flat.

At the end of that frenetic year, I had another book, a story or two to tell my grandchildren (Did I ever tell you about the time somebody tried to fire me for writing about slavery?), a couple of ideas for future research, and a commitment to writing history that was racially inclusive. I had just produced a narrative in which the stories of black and white women were interwoven and in which both were central. This was eye-opening for the white women, numbering in the thousands, who came in contact with the project. And it mattered profoundly to the African American women who came in contact with the project. After it was all over, I made a conscious decision that whatever I took up next, it would be roomy; it would make space for black women, for white women, and for whoever else might illuminate their condition.

First stop: the woman suffrage controversy in Virginia. Our understanding of southern suffragism had been dominated for twenty years by Aileen S. Kraditor's *Ideas of the Woman Suffrage Movement, 1890–1920* (1965), a ferociously smart book that incorporated southern leaders only to expose their ugly contribution to the debates — their contention that white supremacy would be enhanced if women got the vote.[7]

Having just buzzed through the papers of the Equal Suffrage League of Virginia, however, I had the impression that they contained little about race. I decided to investigate, making a conscious move toward political history. Like many others, I felt frustrated that despite our mushrooming knowledge about women, we had made little impact on the way history was taught in, say, the typical college survey course. By the mid-1980s it was clear that the teachers of those survey courses were not lining up to do our work for us; if we wanted them to teach about women, we had to show how women's history intersected with the subjects that drove the surveys: politics, economic change, warfare, diplomacy.

My foray into the Virginia suffrage debates quickly brought me face to face with the legislators, editors, and other pontificators who led the charge against votes for women. At first these antisuffragists said little about black women voting. But as the suffrage movement built strength in Virginia and scored victories elsewhere, the "antis" resorted to race baiting on the grand scale, declaring that woman suffrage would mean the death of white supremacy. The white suffragists, liberals by the standards of the time, thought white supremacy a bogus issue and tried to avoid discussions of race altogether. Black suffragists, meanwhile, maintained silence; they could only damage the cause by speaking up for it. They surfaced after the Nineteenth Amendment was ratified, however, mounting impressive voter registration campaigns in several Virginia cities.[8]

I do not think I understood at the time that this project marked a decisive turn toward southern history. As before, I asked questions of general scope: Did woman suffrage live up to its billing as a democratizing movement? How do we understand the simultaneous workings of gender and race? But the suffrage project was also specifically and essentially southern. It was born of a question about southern activists in particular, and as the story unfolded, the dominant players turned out to be the antis, representatives of a new, white-supremacist political order specific to that time and place. Suffrage leaders, white and black, were constrained at every turn, not only by the antis' superior power but also by their boundless cynicism and mendacity.

The worse the antis appeared, the more this project felt like a rescue operation. In this I was in good company, for rescue has been a driving impulse in women's history from the start — perhaps especially at the start, when we looked in the past for people like ourselves and at first saw only a void, or Mrs. Claus. We wanted to rescue women from oblivion — both the women worthies and the ordinary women whose ceaseless life-sustaining labors had been forgotten or taken for granted. We wanted also to rescue women from the straitjacket of the "traditional" family. Anthropology suggested to us that there was no such thing, and we soon got glimpses of new histories — histories of work, family, sexuality, friendship — that made new forms seem not only possible but inevitable.

This was the starting point for "A Share of Honour," the book I wrote to go with the museum exhibition.[9] So far as popular perception went, women's history in Virginia began and pretty much ended with Pocahontas. But social history had come to Virginia in the 1970s; a small band of scholars had done considerable analysis of families in the colonial Chesapeake, and they shared with us work as yet unpublished.

Among them they had turned up enough about women to make possible some thought-provoking generalizations. In the early seventeenth century, peoples from three parts of the world encountered each other in the Virginia

Tidewater. The situation was at first extremely fluid, and *nobody* — neither Indians nor English nor Africans — had what most Americans think of as traditional families or gender roles. (The traditions that eventually prevailed were established later, largely in the nineteenth century.)

Moreover, seventeenth-century English women could do extremely well for themselves if they were strong enough to survive their disease-ridden environment. In the next century, however, the status of English women declined in measurable ways, suggesting another provocative line of inquiry. Note that the eighteenth century has long been portrayed as Virginia's most glorious: the plantation aristocracy rose to its peak; the Founding Fathers led a Revolution and launched a great experiment in representative government. But for women, enslaved women included, the eighteenth century was arguably the pits.

Much of the rest of the book was put together with baling wire and binder twine, but we learned enough to see that comparable reconfigurations are due for later periods as well. The period from about 1890 to 1920, for example, has long been considered a dismal era in Virginia history. Historians have written little about it. But for women, both black and white, it was a time of unprecedented productivity and visibility in the public sphere. So, when the conventional understanding of a state's history is dead wrong for half the population, how much longer do we want to hold on to it?

I spoke above of rescue. The entire project of which "A Share of Honour" was a part was conducted in that spirit; I think it probable that a rescue impulse has been especially intense in the South. The history of southern women got a late start, and it has therefore seemed important to save women's history from its initial northeastern slant. It has at times seemed important to rescue the South itself from outsiders' assumptions about its uniform wickedness. And finally, because so much in a presumably history-conscious region has been forgotten or distorted, it seems especially important that we tell a more inclusive story. (A riddle heard, I think, in the Virginia Historical Society. Q: "How many Virginians does it take to change a lightbulb?" A: "Three. One to screw in the bulb and two to talk about how much better the old bulb was.")

Few feminists and few African Americans would agree that the old one was better. And yet, even in the South's most disheartening moments, instances of creativity and resistance abound — which brings me to *A Murder in Virginia*.[10] My first hint about the Lunenburg case, a sensational and racially charged ax murder, came from a scrapbook in the Hampton University archives (this while

I was researching "A *Share of Honour*"). According to an unidentified clipping, the African American women's clubs of Richmond had formed their first federation in response to the case. "The members worked earnestly to raise $500.00 to assist in the defence of the Lunenburg prisoners (women charged with murder) and succeed[ed] in turning over to the cause $690.00. The women were acquitted of the charge, and set at liberty." The clipping said nothing more about the case, but the outcome seemed strikingly unusual for 1895. I thought it might make an intriguing project — if only I could find the sources. I checked the map and the Library of Virginia's newspaper holdings. Lunenburg is in the Virginia Southside. It has no cities, and I was disappointed to learn that the Library of Virginia had little in the way of newspapers for the small towns in surrounding counties.

Fast forward. When I moved on to the suffrage project, I read the microfilm of several years' worth of the weekly *Richmond Planet*. Along the way I picked up Ann Field Alexander's fine dissertation on John Mitchell Jr., the *Planet*'s militant black editor.[11] There, indeed, was the Lunenburg case. Cranking the *Planet* back to 1895, I found the story, often richly illustrated, jumping off the front page of almost every issue. Lunenburg, moreover, proved to be page-one news in Richmond's white press as well. The white dailies' efforts to out-sleuth each other, together with John Mitchell Jr.'s intimate reporting of the doings of the accused, generated plentiful evidence.

I quickly learned that the murder victim was a white woman, wife of a prosperous but miserly farmer. Four people, all African Americans, were arrested. Solomon Marable, a lanky sawmill hand, was captured after merchants in a nearby town witnessed him spending twenty-dollar bills like those stolen from the site of the murder. Marable in turn implicated three women. I already knew the case had been a catalyst for organization among the black women of Richmond. "This is women's history," I thought, "and there's a book here."

I postponed work on a blurrier study of the politics of exclusion in the era of disfranchisement; with two small kids, it seemed potentially self-defeating to pursue a project of indefinite dimensions. The Lunenburg case, by contrast, had a beginning, middle, and end. It also offered a new channel into the social history of women. Criminal cases often take obscure sorts of people and throw them into the spotlight, illuminating their day-to-day routines as well as the extraordinary events that bring them to public attention. The accused women of Lunenburg — Mary Abernathy, Mary Barnes, and Pokey Barnes — were illiterate and poor. All three were mothers and had also worked as laundresses, general domestics, and farm laborers. Lucy Pollard, the woman murdered, was literate and much wealthier but represented nevertheless a large, hard-working group about whom we know little. As reporters and the courts dug into what had happened on the day of the crime, the patterns of the women's lives clarified. So did their irreducible individuality.

Novelists are typically better placed to develop character than historians are, and by the time I knew enough to begin writing, I was thinking a lot about novels, especially detective stories, and about relationships between history and fiction. I set aside the conventions of monographs and decided to write instead in a fictionlike form, which is to say, to make the book read as much as possible like a novel, without making anything up.

Just weeks after I began writing, I had the good fortune to discuss the project with the thoughtful group of graduate students gathered in Edward L. Ayers's and Paul M. Gaston's southern history seminar at the University of Virginia. Postmodernism was running high then, and the students asked: Why *not* make things up?

At that moment I did not have a very good answer for them. In time I came to understand it thus: Writing in a fictionlike form is what gives the Lunenburg story its entertainment value. But it's the truth that gives it power.

And so, while many of my intellectually adventurous colleagues were engaged in the linguistic turn — exploring the evanescence of truth, the contingent and unstable qualities of knowledge, and the constructedness of everything (and certainly I learned from this) — I rummaged in Southside courthouses, looking for objects that would let me write believable scenes. I got a little kick out of each discovery. Solomon got new shoes — hooray! The judge wore his spectacles on the top of his head. The paint was peeling on the courthouse, and the roof leaked. It mattered to me that these details be documented. If we want readers to trust us on the big things, it seems to me we should strive for integrity on the little ones.

The big things surprised me. "Time and again," to quote the prologue, "people acted bravely and against type." Facing trial without lawyers, the accused women were compelled to defend themselves; the young Pokey Barnes cross-examined witnesses like a veteran trial attorney. All three women stoutly maintained their innocence. Unified African American communities buoyed them up; during a period of several weeks when the women were especially vulnerable to mob violence, volunteer patrols of armed black men guarded them throughout the night. Numerous white men, meanwhile, from the governor to the local farmers who hid the suspects from a roiling crowd, put themselves at political or bodily risk to prevent lynching. And whites and blacks worked in coalition to see justice done.

This is not the South we thought we knew. If I were inclined to reinforce the melodrama of southern sinfulness, I could of course put a different spin on what the Lunenburg case has to teach us. The farmers who sneaked the suspects out the back door would have had no occasion for their heroics, after all, had not an increasingly impatient crowd stood out front, prepared for a lynching. And it is possible to see at least one ulterior motive beneath the apparent virtue of the white men who put the rule of law above the vengeance of the moment. They were perhaps working out the lopsided bargain they hoped to strike with black men: Give up politics, let us run things, and we'll see to it that your people will be treated fairly.

Still, they did the right thing. In the Lunenburg case, a critical mass of white men rose above prejudice to uphold the rule of law. All the while, the accused women stuck up for themselves with extraordinary intelligence and resolve. Together they have given us a transcendent story, one that can speak to any situation in which principle is arrayed against racism and the passions of the moment. It may also be a suggestive story for southern history in particular, signifying (along with work published recently by others) the need for a new interpretation of the period between the general emancipation and the establishment of Jim Crow.[12] Next time I go rummaging, this interpretive endeavor may be the end in view. Meantime, I have acquired another project, or perhaps a hobby, closer to home.

David Herbert Donald opens his biography of Lincoln with one of the best first sentences I know: "Abraham Lincoln was not interested in his ancestry." Lincoln's was a very midwestern attitude, one I used to share. As I've located my work more centrally in southern history, however, I've become more interested in my own family. My mother once told me that her father's parents had come from southern Illinois, a fact that for many years lay dormant in some recess of my brain. Only recently did it occur to me to ask: Would they not likely have come to that part of Illinois from the upper South?

It took only one day to make the initial connections, linking census schedules straight up the begats in the male line. Gerald Wells, the grandfather who died before I was born, was the son of Carl Wells, son of Leonard Wells, son of Lewis Wells, son of another Lewis Wells. The first Lewis Wells fought in the Revolution. Hot damn, I can join the DAR. I don't know yet about the United Daughters of the Confederacy, but these ancestors clearly traveled west along a southern route. Sometime between 1810 and 1820 Lewis Wells and his namesake son moved to Illinois from Kentucky. And before that, in the 1790s, they moved to Kentucky from the upcountry of South Carolina.

So far I have managed to steal only one more day for this research. I spent it on the Internet, hoping to push the story back at least one more generation. It gets spooky here. According to information posted on a genealogy Web site, the first Lewis Wells was the son of one Thomas Wells. Thomas Wells was born near Richmond, Virginia, in about 1699. He died in Virginia in 1755 — in Lunenburg County.

My friend Jacquelyn Dowd Hall — born in Oklahoma, schooled in Tennessee, and a longtime resident of North Carolina — has spoken of "the anguish of writing about a homeland that has such a dark and bloody history."[13] A child of the northern prairie, I thought I had been spared the personal burden of southern history. Perhaps it's time to pick it up, check its heft, and consider the significance of blood.

Notes

1. I am happy to learn that this has been changed considerably. The chronology given on North Dakota's official Web site now begins ca. 9500 BC, with the arrival of Paleo-Indian peoples and the mining of flint, "North Dakota's first export commodity." www.state.nd.us/hist/chrono.htm.

2. Robert McG. Thomas Jr., "Coya Knutson, 82, Legislator, Husband Sought her Defeat," *New York Times*, October 12, 1996, p. 52.

3. Quoted in Nancy Weiss Malkiel, "Invincible Woman: Anne Firor Scott," in Nancy A. Hewitt and Suzanne Lebsock, eds., *Visible Women: New Essays on American Activism* (Urbana, 1993), 383–92 (quotation on page 390).

4. Suzanne Lebsock, *The Free Women of Petersburg: Status and Culture in a Southern Town, 1784–1860* (New York, 1984).

5. Anne Firor Scott, *The Southern Lady: From Pedestal to Politics, 1830–1930* (Chicago, 1970); Jacquelyn Dowd Hall, *Revolt Against Chivalry: Jessie Daniel Ames and the Women's Campaign Against Lynching* (New York, 1979).

6. Suzanne Lebsock, "Radical Reconstruction and the Property Rights of Southern Women," *Journal of Southern History* 47 (May 1977), 195–216.

7. Aileen S. Kraditor, *Ideas of the Woman Suffrage Movement, 1890–1920* (New York, 1965).

8. Suzanne Lebsock, "Woman Suffrage and White Supremacy: A Virginia Case Study," in Hewitt and Lebsock, *Visible Women*, 62–100.

9. Suzanne Lebsock, *"A Share of Honour": Virginia Women, 1600–1945* (Richmond, 1984).

10. Suzanne Lebsock, *A Murder in Virginia: Southern Justice on Trial* (New York, 2003).

11. Alexander's dissertation has now been published as *Race Man: The Rise and Fall of the "Fighting Editor," John Mitchell, Jr.* (Charlottesville, 2002).

12. See the exemplary essays in Jane Dailey, Glenda Elizabeth Gilmore, and Bryant Simon, eds., *Jumpin' Jim Crow: Southern Politics from Civil War to Civil Rights* (Princeton, 2000).

13. Jacquelyn Dowd Hall, "What Difference Does Region Make?: Teaching, Writing, and Living Women's History," a paper presented at a session of that title at the annual meeting of the Southern Historical Association, Louisville, Kentucky, November 11, 1994.

Borders, Boundaries, and Edges

A Southern Autobiography

EDWARD L. AYERS

I should be a better southerner than I am. I have the credentials of family and birthplace, of formative experiences and education, of residence and childrearing, of commitment in scholarship and teaching. And yet, like many in the academy, I stand at some distance from the white southern majority in everything from politics and religion to taste in music and food. Despite my southern background, I have to work to imagine the perspectives of all kinds of southerners in the past and in the present. All the history I have written grows from that effort.

I was born in the mountains of North Carolina of parents who were textile-mill operatives at the time. My father, Tommy Ayers, and my mother, Billie Lou Buckner, had known their days of working tobacco and hooking rugs. My father, although only twenty-one when I was born, was a veteran of the fighting in Korea. The first year of my life we lived on a farm in Micaville, North Carolina, where the red-clay driveway grew so slippery that my mother feared sliding into the ditch every time it rained.

When I was three, in 1956, we moved about an hour and a half north, over Iron Mountain, to Kingsport, Tennessee. There, both my parents worked at the Kingsport Press, one of several industrial enterprises in the booming little city. The town had been designed from the ground up about forty years before by a number of northern-based corporations eager to take advantage of the nearby resources, including the "Anglo-Saxon" labor force. The city fathers hired a leading city planner from Massachusetts, adopted a city-manager form of government, boosted themselves to the press and investors, and prospered. Kingsport called itself "The Model City" and believed it. In the 1950s this Appalachian outpost was a humming, thriving place, with broad streets, a busy downtown, and high hopes. It looked to be a good place to raise a family, and so my parents came.

My parents always worked very hard. One of my first memories was riding at night in the car between shift changes—probably at eleven at night, the beginning of the graveyard shift—sitting in the backseat while mom came in to work and dad took me back home. My mother worked at a linotype machine, my father at a printing press. I recall taking a tour and proudly watching my dad, handsome, wiry, young, and smiling, working a machine that picked up large sheets of paper and swept them high in the air. The press published complicated projects such as the *World Book Encyclopedia*, and I spent many hours poring over the set we bought on discount, virtually memorizing the sections on "Automobiles" and admiring the layered plastic overlays that revealed complexity otherwise invisible.

When it came time to go to school, I caught the bus to Andrew Johnson Elementary. We didn't talk much about what Andrew Johnson actually did, but we knew he was a president of the United States and that he had grown up not far away from Kingsport, about thirty miles down the highway in Greeneville. I loved school and everything about it. In the second grade I had a beautiful young teacher who led us in singing every morning. One song had acting that went along with it: "Stoop down, bend down, pick a bale of cotton." No cotton grew in East Tennessee, and I had never seen cotton plants, but the song and this teacher made it sound like fun.

This teacher liked me, for we shared a high energy level and a certain dramatic inclination. She chose me to appear with the sixth-graders' glee club, putting on a big show for parents. For this show, she covered my face in burnt cork, gave me a tambourine, and made me a tall hat of white cardboard. My job, and that of Eddie Anderson at the other end of the stage, was to beat our tambourine along with the songs of the South performed by the bigger kids. At one point, under the hot lights and between songs, I took off my hat for a moment and was surprised—but pleased, I discovered—by a wave of good-natured laughter from the audience. The burnt cork stopped in a straight line across the middle of my forehead, where the hat had covered.

That would have been about 1960. So far as I know, no one at Andrew Johnson Elementary, segregated as it was, had any problems with a minstrel show. The Civil Rights movement must have seemed pretty far away from the white people of Kingsport at that point. The little city was about 5 percent black, the population carefully segregated. I saw black kids only rarely, though I do recall the marching band of Frederick Douglass High during the Fourth of July parade downtown.

Though we lived in a Republican district in Appalachia and in a quite modern young city, the culture of white supremacy thoroughly saturated us. People I knew did not hesitate to identify bright colors as "nigger colors" and big sedans as "nigger cars." It was not uncommon to see signs that caricatured black men enjoying watermelon. Downtown, signs identified the colored entrance to the Strand and the State Theaters around to the side, leading to the balcony. When we white boys fought, we charged that two on one was nigger fun; when we had to decide the last one chosen for ball, eenie meenie minee moe ended with a nigger's toe. When we wanted to frighten our younger siblings, we told them a big nigger was coming to get them.

We were Southern Baptists and I liked church. An early photograph shows me smiling in front of a portrait of Jesus, sitting at a table with an open Bible before me, white shirt, black jacket, and black bowtie, hair neatly combed with a gentle wave on top. I was saved when I was eleven and baptized at Litz Manor Baptist Church. I joined the Royal Ambassadors and studied my Sunday school lessons. I loved the Cub Scouts and then the Boy Scouts, also based at church. The idea of a clearly defined hierarchy of effort and accomplishment, marked by merit badges and insignia, appealed to me. I became senior patrol leader and was elected to the Order of the Arrow, an honor society that required a truly challenging "ordeal" of initiation, far off in the mountains. (I would write more of the rigors we faced, but I am pledged on my Scout's honor not to reveal any details.)

Much of this, except the minstrel show, could have happened anywhere in America in the late 1950s and early 1960s. But we had a sense of being different. We all knew that despite our extreme coolness, with our surfer shorts, Maltese cross necklaces, and whatever other fad came and went, we were hillbillies in the eyes of the world. The "Beverly Hillbillies" were the stars of television then, and we recognized that the show made fun of us. Even though the show had to arrange for Jed and his clan to come from Texas so that an accidental oil discovery could set the ridiculous plots in motion, the characters talked a lot about Tennessee and had kin from there. And they talked in caricatures of our accents; we knew people who said "see-ment," just like Granny did when she talked about the "cement pond," the swimming pool. We saw that people made jokes about us — right on television — just like we made jokes about black people. Friends came back from vacations up north or in Florida and reported that people outside the mountains wondered if we wore shoes and had indoor plumbing.

While I was quite young my mother went to college in Johnson City and became a fifth-grade teacher. By all accounts, she was a wonderful teacher for the next thirty years. Kids who ran into us at the store were star-struck; parents thanked her profusely; former students recalled her warmly decades after they left Sullivan Elementary or Rock Springs. She went back to teaching quickly after my brother and sister were born.

My father continued to work at the Kingsport Press until a strike came in the mid-1960s. A union member, Dad walked the picket line from midnight until eight in the morning and stuck with his friends as long as he could. But the fifty-dollar-a-week strike benefits didn't go far with three kids. Rather than scab, he just left the press altogether. Fortunately, he had a good idea of something else he could do.

Dad became a car salesman. He could talk better than anyone I ever knew, with jokes and cussing and logic deployed in just the right measure for his audience. He specialized in used cars, which carried more profit; his business card reminded people that "Everybody Drives a Used Car," since a car became "used" as soon as it left the lot, losing much of its value. Dad worked on commission, which meant that some days he might walk the freezing or blazing lot from eight in the morning till six and not make anything; but other days he might sell three cars and would be a lot of fun at dinnertime. He and Mom moved from the tract house where we'd lived throughout my years at elementary school and into a subdivision named, for some reason, Colonial Heights.

Dad and Mom loved fast cars and always drove as new, and as hot, a car as they could afford. NASCAR racing was the only sport in which my father was interested, and racing formed a great bond between us; we both admired Richard Petty and saw him several times at the little track outside of Asheville, North Carolina, and then at the new steeply banked half-mile track in Bristol. On a vacation trip to Myrtle Beach, we stopped at Darlington and I climbed up into the starter's box and imagined that I waved the checkered flag over the electric-blue car #43. (I liked Fireball Roberts and Rex White quite a bit, too, but they drove a Ford and a Chevy, respectively, and we were Mopar guys, hemi guys. Dad, after all, worked at the Plymouth dealership, and we understood loyalty.)

After growing up absorbed in Scouts, Sunday school, and cars, I was hit hard by rock music in the 1960s. It was not that some slumbering talent suddenly awakened, for I could neither play nor sing; every effort at both revealed to me that my love of performance would not be satisfied by becoming the next Hendrix or Morrison. Instead, improbably enough, rock music opened to me a kind of proto-scholarship. I virtually memorized every issue of *Rolling Stone* when it came out (it seemed a lot more subversive then, printed on newsprint and boasting four-letter words and ads for drug paraphernalia), and I spent hours with my best friend poring over album covers and lyrics. That friend, Mike Harris, precociously sophisticated, taught me not to laugh at things I didn't understand. He told me about Captain Beefheart and Frank Zappa, Miles Davis and John Coltrane, music we didn't hear on the radio.

When, in English class, we were told to write a report about a poet, I immediately chose Dylan Thomas because I'd read that Bob Dylan had named himself after him. I went to the public library and found not only Thomas's difficult poetry but also books that told me about Thomas's exciting life of drink and fallibility, and that explained the poetry. I loved this — the context, the explanation, the adding of layers of meaning. I wrote a better paper than I really needed to.

My father would not countenance long hair — I knew through desperate and prolonged debate on the subject — and so, to my disappointment, I looked quite neat for the late 1960s. To complete the image, I edited the student newspaper, played the role of a stuffy professor type in *Up the Down Staircase*, and was a student-council leader. Underneath, however, I knew myself to be a rebel in some way I had not yet learned to express or embody. I sympathized with, identified with, those who struggled for civil rights on television and those who resisted the war in Vietnam. But those struggles seemed far away from Colonial Heights and Sullivan Central High School. I switched to a friend's church, where a young pastor led honest and interesting discussions about the issues of the time, but the debates only led me farther away from religion.

History did not interest me. It was just a boring textbook and a dull coach, a wasted hour. I lived four miles from the great Warriors' Path of the American Indians, five miles from a TVA dam, ten miles from a place where Daniel Boone had hunted, and within easy driving distance of the Cumberland Gap, the coal fields, the haunts of Parson Brownlow, the center of southern abolitionism, and all the other wonders of my fascinating part of the country. I was oblivious to it all. I cared nothing about, and knew nothing of, the Civil War. We had no statues and no memories of that conflict, divided as we had been among ourselves during the Civil War years.

Though I loved to hike and camp in the mountains, my friends and I laughed at country music and had no idea that we went to high school fifteen miles from the birthplace of that music. We liked it when the Byrds or Dylan did country, but the real stuff we saw on Saturday afternoon television—Porter Wagoner with Dolly Parton in shiny outfits and bouffant hair—struck us as everything we wanted to leave behind. We were children of the Age of Aquarius, citizens of the world, open to sitars and African drums, distrustful and disdainful of the politics, style, and accents of the culture all around us. Some kids we went to school with belonged to that culture in ways we did not. I remember one friend, a quiet tow-headed boy, singing "Wildwood Flower" one day at recess, pronouncing "hair" just like Mother Maybelle Carter did. He was amazed that I'd never heard of the song.

Despite my obtuseness, I had long been unintentionally preparing for what would become my life's calling. The most memorable place of my childhood was the home of my paternal grandparents, Fred and Dell Ayers. They lived in Yancey County, North Carolina, where my parents had grown up, high in the mountains. They had long enjoyed running water and an indoor bathroom, but they heated the house with a coal stove that my grandmother had to keep filled one bucket at a time from the woodshed. They did not have a telephone until I was fifteen. The road out front was dirt and, to my grandmother's persistent annoyance, supplied a never-ending cloud of dust that settled over the porch at the side of the house and worked its way through the screen door.

My grandmother had been born in that house (built during the Civil War, I was told) back in 1897, and then she and my grandfather had moved there in the late 1920s after a brief time in West Virginia. My grandfather ("Paw," I called him for some reason) used to joke about how run-down the place had been when they moved in; the briars had grown so thick, he said, that the rabbits had to wear leather jackets. Fred Ayers was funny and sly, a carpenter and a rounder. He was gone from home for months at a time, working on big building projects up in Washington, D.C. When he returned home, he chafed at the limitations of the farm. He gambled and drank hard and would come home late, loud, and mean. I hid his liquor because I hated him when he was drunk and tormented my grandmother. When he was sober I loved him.

Dell Ayers—"Grandmaw"—was about five feet tall but tough. She could bully cows through gates and snap the heads off chickens. I loved her deeply, and we spent a lot of time together while my grandfather was gone. I would stay at her house for weeks at a time in the summer. She spoiled me, letting me sleep late and then watch cartoons and the Three Stooges on the one channel they received on their black-and-white television. She made my favorite apple pies and biscuits. She would walk with me all over the steep hills of the farm, going to the blackberry patch, showing me the origins of the spring, climbing high to look down on Cane River.

At night, after watching whatever was on ABC (it was strange to see "The Jetsons" in such a setting), we would read the Bible together. It seemed that she especially loved the Book of Revelation, which scared the dickens out of me with its images of the apocalypse and retribution for sins large and small. We'd go to bed early and I would lie there imagining Jesus descending through the moonlit clouds and the dead arising from the family cemetery up on top of the hill. I worried about the Matchbox car I had taken from one of my friends. And I worried whether Paw would get to go to Heaven with us when the Day of Judgment came.

On Sunday Grandmaw and I went to Riverside Baptist Church. She couldn't drive, so we would have to hope a neighbor would stop by. One time Paw took us. He got up, shaved, put on his nice blue double-breasted suit, parked his truck in front of the church, and then leaned conspicuously against the front fender, reading the Asheville paper while others walked by into church.

The church was something very different from what I saw back in Colonial Heights. At home, everything was decorous and organized. At Riverside, people sometimes cried and talked in tongues. In the singing, I joined in with the other males on the echoing lines in the hymns, imagining that I was hitting profound bass notes. And I remember shaking hands with one of Grandmaw's friends and her comment when she noticed no calluses; "You aren't a farm boy, are you?" she asked kindly.

I was not. Whenever I visited Grandmaw and Paw I felt a deep connection to the place. I knew every stretch of the creek, every corner of the barn, smokehouse, and corncrib. I handled every old tool in the woodshed and every object and scrap of paper in the cabinets around the house. I fooled around in the fields, picking a few worms off the tobacco and stacking a few tobacco sticks. I went fox hunting with my grandfather, sitting around the fire listening to the dogs chase across the ridges as they bayed in excitement and anticipation.

But I was not a farmer. I did not really belong in Burnsville. Living with an elderly lady, I imagined that the whole county was like that, behind the times.

I had a wonderful aunt and uncle who lived in town, and they had a boy just one year younger than me. He played Little League and had several channels on his television and visited Asheville. But he did talk a little different from me and didn't live in Kingsport, where we had a McDonald's and several theaters and factories. I pictured us as farther apart than we really were. And I suspect that he played up the difference, too, amusing himself with his cousin who knew so little about country life.

To me, Burnsville stood for my family's past. It was close enough to visit and yet far enough away to embody things abandoned. In this, it was no different from the grandparents' farms of many of my generation of southerners. It showed us how far we had come, how quickly things had changed. But that farm did not feel like "history." It was associated with no events, no public acknowledgment. It was just there, fading before our eyes, a lost America. I didn't know what to do with it, and so I just held it close to my heart but away from any future I imagined for myself.

That future, I thought in some vague way, might involve writing. I got a job in a local bookstore when I was sixteen, working for $1.80 an hour. Straightening up the paperbacks and taking them with me to lunch or even home in the evenings, not bending the covers, I learned of Norman Mailer and Philip Roth, of Saul Bellow and Tom Wolfe, of the *Whole Earth Catalog* and the *I Ching*, of Kurt Vonnegut and William Brautigan. I also found, in the classics section, William Faulkner and Thomas Wolfe. I read at every chance and couldn't wait for college.

The University of Tennessee lay about ninety minutes away in Knoxville. I, along with all my friends, intended to go there. The university had open admissions and was virtually free, so there was really no great suspense or deliberation. I applied nowhere else. UT was big and had whatever I would need, I felt sure. I spoke to a reporter at the local newspaper, and he steered me away from journalism school. He told me that I could learn to write in lots of majors, that I should instead study a subject so that I would have something to say. I decided that American Studies would do the trick, since it was basically a disciplined version of what I was studying anyway in *Rolling Stone* and on record jackets and in the borrowed paperbacks. I wanted to be Tom Wolfe, offering hip commentary on the America around me. And the back of *The Kandy-Kolored Tangerine-Flake Streamline Baby* told me he had a Ph.D. in American Studies.

The University of Tennessee in 1971 was hazy with pot smoke, loud music, and too many kids loose for the first time in big concrete dorms. I loved it. And in my very first quarter I found my calling. I somehow ended up taking Honors Western Civilization with a famous young professor on campus, Richard Marius. Marius blew me away. He had grown up in East Tennessee and had gone to UT before attending Yale Divinity School (later declaring himself an atheist) and then graduate school at Yale in history. He knew everything in every language and in every time, it seemed. He wrote learned biographies of Martin Luther and Thomas More, but he had also just published a novel set in our very own East Tennessee in the nineteenth century. The book was out in paperback and looked just like those of Bellow and Mailer and Roth and Wolfe, with glowing reviews on the back. To make it all even better, Marius wrote a weekly editorial for the student newspaper in which he attacked the war in Vietnam and silly university policies.

I couldn't believe Richard Marius's life. People got paid to read books and talk? And he was funny and lighthearted as well as profound. I craved whatever it was that Richard Marius possessed, whatever spark that fired him. Over the next three years I pursued the alluring if vague goal of being a professor, a professor of American Studies. I took mainly literature and confined my United States history to the twentieth century. I was more interested in sociology, philosophy, art history, and economics than history.

And it never occurred to me to study the South. The South, certainly of the nineteenth century, possessed none of the things that had drawn me to academic life in the first place, the rich cultural stew of books, ideas, and music. The South seemed to me to be defined by poverty and injustice, by its very lack of history. I did find James Agee fascinating, for he had lived on my very street in Knoxville and he had written fiction, journalism, and film criticism before dying young. But as for the earlier stuff of the South, what was there to study? In the meantime, while I was a freshman and barely eighteen, my number came up high for the last draft for Vietnam. History had passed me by again, just as it had with civil rights and the summer of love. I seemed a few years late for everything interesting.

In the summer between my second and third years at UT, I worked for a carnival. I lived in my car for an entire summer and worked on the Sky Wheel, a double Ferris wheel. I carried a box of paperback novels with me and felt pretty sure that I was living as Jack Kerouac would have lived. I had never been north of the Tennessee line, and this carnival took me through Delaware, Maryland, New York, and Pennsylvania. The work was hard, but I enjoyed running the ride with loud 8-tracks of Steppenwolf and the Doobie Brothers blasting from enormous speakers twelve hours a day as I "bucked tubs"—loaded riders.

I worked every day but two for the entire summer, when a new friend of mine, Clyde, a young black guy from Flint, Michigan, and I played hooky from the fair in Buffalo to go see Niagara Falls. The docked pay was worth it. Clyde and I got pulled over for no particular reason, and the policeman, looking at my Tennessee driver's license, commented that I would not be riding around with a black boy back home, now would I? Clyde became my best friend in the carnival, and he introduced me to the music of Al Green, who soon started singing from the big speakers on the Sky Wheel, giving it a lot more class.

On the way home from the carnival I went out of my way to visit New Haven and Yale University. A professor at UT had told me it was the best place for American Studies and, just as important, Tom Wolfe's Ph.D. in American Studies came from Yale. And, of course, Richard Marius had gone there.

Yale appeared to be everything I thought it would be. I was unabashed when a couple of students walking their Irish setter in their blazers informed me, after a few minutes of conversation in which I told them that I hoping to talk with the head of the American Studies program the next day, that I might want to clean up my act a bit beforehand, that I looked like Huckleberry Finn. I'm sure I did. I had a Carlos Santana halo of hair, uncut all summer, and Neil Young sideburns. I had a dark tan and had been living in a car. I was probably pretty rough looking, even if I did blow enough money to stay at the Holiday Inn that evening.

The next morning I sat nervously waiting for the chairman of the American Studies program. The Hall of Graduate Studies looked just like *The Paper Chase*, a recent movie about Harvard Law School starring a young actor to whom I imagined I bore a resemblance. The walls were covered with dark oak, and the windows looked like those in a cathedral (I assumed, never having seen one); copies of *American Quarterly* were stacked next to the chair where I waited. I was pretty sure I didn't belong in such a place.

When Professor Sidney E. Ahlstrom arrived, I was a little surprised. He had recently won the National Book Award for his *Religious History of the American People* (1972), but he didn't look much like what I had expected. No pipe, no elbow patches. Instead, he was about five and a half feet tall, with a crew cut, plaid shorts, sandals with socks, and a plastic daisy on his briefcase. Professor Ahlstrom was kind but said about all he could say to a guy who showed up from Tennessee with wild hair, no prior warning, and no record to present: do very well in your courses and get good letters of recommendation and get a good GRE (whatever that was) and we'll be happy to look at your file.

Back at UT, I met my future wife, Abby Brown. Quiet and calm, lovely and self-possessed, the daughter of a pediatrician and homemaker in Kingsport, training to become a teacher, Abby brought to me things missing in myself, a grace I did not possess. When I graduated from UT the next summer, Abby and I married within weeks of finishing my courses. She was going to get her master's degree in Johnson City, at East Tennessee State, where my mother had gone for her degree. For our honeymoon we drove to New York and camped in Maine. Freshly armed, in the middle of a bruising recession, with a B.A. in American Studies, twenty-one and looking even younger than that, I wasn't counting on much of a job in Johnson City. Sure enough, I worked in the credit department of a local tire store and in a factory putting electric heaters in boxes.

But I lucked out and got a position I applied for at the state employment agency: the director of the Johnson City Youth Center. My job was to recruit "problem youth" to the center (a concrete-block shell of a building) and then steer them to job training (which never appeared). I did the first part very well. All it took was free food collected from a local bakery, free pool, free ping pong, free basketball, and free music. Abby helped me paint the place, and I had a poster printed: "No Hassle, No Bull, Just a Place to Be." We soon had a regular group of kids: black and white, male and female. I spent most of my time hanging out with them, learning more about crime, neglect, dysfunction, and broken self-image than I wanted to know. Two kids who had just gotten married, neither of them yet eighteen and both afraid to go home, came to the Youth Center as the best place they could think of to celebrate. And yet I also learned that such kids could be smart, funny, hopeful, and willing to work hard. Labels didn't seem to fit very well.

In the meantime, I sent in my applications to graduate school in American Studies (not history) and read everything I thought might be useful, from Edgar Allan Poe to Daniel Boorstin to Thomas Pynchon. I systematically worked my way through decades of *American Quarterly*, a profoundly disorienting experience that left me sure that I knew absolutely nothing. Despite my ignorance, Yale took me and even offered a fellowship. I was thrilled, of course, not realizing just how unlikely it was that they admitted me.

Abby finished her degree that spring of 1975, and we loaded up a U-Haul and drove to New Haven. My father helped drive up the interstate, and his first words after we found our way to the married student housing complex near the abandoned Olin plant were these: "I wouldn't live here for a million dollars. I'll drive the truck if you want to head back home." We didn't, and we soon began to settle in.

Overnight, Abby and I became southerners. People continually commented on our accents, and some professed not to be able to understand us. When Abby ordered a lemonade our first day in New Haven, the man behind the counter, puzzled, said "ham and eggs?" When an Israeli couple across the hall had us over for dinner along with a couple from Ohio, the Ohio folks asked the Israelis if they could hear any difference in our accents. In all friendliness, the Israelis acknowledged that they could indeed because "We watch *Hee-Haw* all the time." We smiled weakly. Abby and I came to think of ourselves not only as hillbillies but also as southerners. It was easy to traffic in imagined exoticism at dinners with our friends and, I must admit, I did, telling every colorful story I could conjure. Many of them were largely true.

But I still did not want to study the South. I studied European intellectual history (using the Russian I had tortured myself with at Tennessee), American religious history with Professor Ahlstrom, and American literature. I did not take C. Vann Woodward's class or the class on the colonial era taught by Edmund Morgan. Instead, I studied with two brand-new professors who arrived the same year I did: Richard Fox and Paul Johnson. Fox was brilliant, iconoclastic, and political; Johnson, by contrast, was quiet, funny, and sarcastic. He allowed Elliott Gorn and me, taking an independent study with him in the new field of American social history, to read his manuscript, what would become *A Shopkeeper's Millennium*, about the Second Great Awakening in Rochester, New York.[1] It blew me away. I had not known that one could do history like this, history of people who left few records, people who lived through profound social change without knowing it.

I began to think that that this was what I wanted to do, this new social history. I suddenly learned of a burgeoning field of which I had been unaware, of "the history of the inarticulate" and of "quantitative methods." And I began to think that it would be exciting to apply these techniques to people and places I had known. In the meantime, *Roll, Jordan, Roll; American Slavery, American Freedom*; and *Time on the Cross* appeared to adulation and intense discussion, making southern history the center of action.[2]

Though my interest had been sparked, it took months to unfold, and I still did not take Professor Woodward's class on the antebellum South the fall of my second year, my last year of course work. I noted that the students ahead of me whom I most admired, especially Jackson Lears, were advisees of David Brion Davis. They were doing the sort of cultural history I had come to Yale to do. Professor Davis had been on leave my first year, and I had heard over and over again of his brilliance. He had come to Yale not long before, and his overwhelming *The Problem of Slavery in the Age of Revolution* had just been published.³ My classmates and I, along with everyone else who read the book, were in awe. Though relatively young, self-effacing, and exceedingly kind, David Davis had a full dark beard and seemed as imposing as any intellectual I could imagine. We could find no label to define him. He stood above American history, even above European history. I determined that I had to work with him, whatever my dissertation might be about.

Though Davis wrote of the South, among so many other things, he was not a southernist. And when I took my first class with Davis, I wrote a paper on William James, whom I had admired since my undergraduate days. The more I read of James the more I felt an affinity for him. He hated closed systems, hated certainty, hated arrogance; he loved process, possibility, and humility in the face of others' experience. Though our backgrounds could not have been any more different, with his origins in the New England elite and his training throughout Europe, I imagined myself a related spirit to James.

In the meantime, C. Vann Woodward was retiring, and I signed up for his class on the New South, the last class he would teach. I knew almost nothing of southern history, and most of the other students in the class had already worked together for a semester on the Old South. Woodward was reserved, weary of the battles of academic life, it seemed, and grieving for a son lost to cancer at the age of twenty-one, but the books he assigned crackled with life. And none burned with more energy than his own *Origins of the New South*, written twenty-five years earlier.⁴ I could not believe how great the book was — for my money, better even than our Bible of social history, E. P. Thompson's *The Making of the English Working Class*.⁵ Woodward wrote in a way that took my breath away. There was no need to study fiction to read literature, I decided; this was history *as* literature. Professor Woodward was kind to me but took no special interest in this kid from Tennessee. He had seen generations of southern white boys come through Yale, imagining that they were the first to reckon with regional difference.

Visiting my grandparents during graduate school, full of a new self-awareness of the history all around me, I was stunned when my grandfather referred to an ancient apple tree on the place as "Kizzie's tree." *Roots* had been the rage on television in 1977, but surely he had not watched it. In *Roots*, Kizzie was the daughter of Kunta Kinte, the lead character, a first-generation African American. I asked Paw why he called the tree by that name. He told me that "back in slave time, a nigger woman named Kizzie took apples from this tree and hid them in the straw in the barn for her children."

I couldn't believe it. Slaves had lived here, on this mountain farm, a place I had learned the semester before to imagine as the locus of "herrenvolk democracy"? "Well, of course," Paw laughed at his over-educated oldest grandchild. "Who do you think cleared all this land? Your grandmaw's people were big slaveholders." The pieces did not fit. What was slavery doing here, in the highest Appalachians? I had imagined that my family had lived above the worst of southern history, or at least outside it. I took pride in their rugged self-reliance and what I assumed to be their Unionist sympathies. Now, like some bad Faulkner character, I discovered complicity in the great sin of the South.

During that same trip to Burnsville, some of the so-called "Florida People," who were building small houses in the mountains for the summers, came to visit. Paw liked working for them. One family of Floridians drove up the dirt road in a huge RV, and as soon as they got out I could see they had come on an anthropological mission. The father had told his wife and children about this colorful old mountain man who was building their vacation house for them. The kids, teenagers, made no effort to hide their amusement at everything they saw around them: the unpainted and rusty tin roof, the old pictures on the walls, the accents and vocabulary of my grandparents. The visitors patronized their elderly hosts shamelessly. Sitting in the living room, they ignored me for a while, but the mother eventually turned to me and asked where I lived. "New Haven, Connecticut," I answered, in a modulated version of the same accent as my grandparents'. Surprised, and with the other family members suddenly listening, she asked what I was doing there. "Studying at Yale," I said.

I took cynical pleasure in the moment. I had ruined their illusion, spoiled the expedition. These hillbillies lived in time, after all, and their progeny did not always drool on the front porch over a banjo. I was furious at the visitors' casual and undeserved arrogance, their disdain for a culture I understood even if I did not fully share, and of my own similarities to the visitors. I did not reflect on what it said about me that I cared about what these strangers thought of me or that I was so proud to have "transcended" what I claimed to love. But I did now know what I had come to expect: I would have to write about the South.

Back in New Haven, David Davis kindly agreed to advise my dissertation and asked what I was thinking of writing about. I told him that I wanted to do southern prisons. Prisons were a hot subject in those days of "social control." After noticing a brief discussion of the convict lease system in *Origins of the New South*, I had done a little research and it turned out that there were penitentiaries in almost all the southern states before the Civil War. This discovery cut against everything we were being told by Michel Foucault and others about the origins of penitentiaries in modernity and capitalism. Plus, prisons were related to crime. That subject was hot, too, thanks to the English social historians of the 1970s. Everyone had heard of southern dueling, lynching, moonshining, and the like; I could explain this topic to my parents and they might see why somebody would want to write about that. David Davis had written his first book on homicide and found crime interesting; he thought this subject might fly and told me to explore it.

I composed a proposal based largely on a few fugitive references and letters of encouragement from historians Harold Woodman and Eugene Genovese, whom I wrote out of the blue and who kindly responded. When I picked up my proposal from the departmental secretary, she informed me that it had been approved but that the committee doubted that I would find any of the sources on crime that I was looking for. That was alarming, for Abby had decided to take the summer off from her teaching job at the Gessell Institute Nursery School, a job that was sustaining us, and travel with me to archives across the South in a youthful adventure. We bought a tent and a propane grill from Sears and were preparing to live in Kampgrounds of America (KOA, we soon decided, stood for Kamping on Asphalt) at five dollars a night in Jackson, Montgomery, and Nashville. While in Atlanta we would sponge off Abby's sister and brother-in-law, wonderful people who had been two of our best friends. We hoped the friendship would endure weeks of eating their food and getting in their way.

After many dramas of weather and poverty and heat as well as of archival discovery, I began to learn where to look to find the sort of material I was looking for. I researched for another year, returning to Atlanta for weeks. I taught myself statistics from a textbook and videotapes. I taught myself how to use the imposing mainframe computer. I wrote furiously on the typewriter (one of the last graduate students to do so, in all likelihood) and barely filled enough paper to apply for jobs in the fall of 1979.

I suddenly realized that writing about the South had turned me into a southern historian, as far as the job market was concerned, whether I wanted to be one or not. I could not claim to be a cultural or intellectual historian, by the logic of the profession, because I studied the South. I had defined myself as a southern historian even though I knew so profoundly little about the region, only what I had learned in one course and in writing my dissertation. And as it turned out, there was only one job in southern history that year on the job market, at the University of Virginia. Calculating the odds, I worried that I'd be back to stapling boxes for electric heaters or working up credit reports.

Remarkably, I was lucky enough to get a conference interview with Virginia, amazed that they would consider someone with only two chapters of his dissertation done in that buyer's market. I was amazed, too, when they invited me to fly down to Charlottesville for an on-campus visit. (I did not tell them that this would be my first airplane flight and that I had to buy my first jacket or tie.) As soon as I saw the University of Virginia, I loved the place. It seemed to me to combine Tennessee and Yale, public and private, southern and cosmopolitan. I felt right at home on the hilly Piedmont landscape, the Blue Ridge hovering in the distance. Kingsport and our families lay only four hours away down I-81. I got the job at UVA and raced to finish my dissertation before the teaching began. I mailed the manuscript to New Haven on the first day of classes in September 1980.

That dissertation combined social history with cultural history. I had come across the concept of "honor" in my directed reading with Paul Johnson, and that concept became a major theme of my dissertation. At my first professional conference the next spring, where I gave a paper on crime in the South, I met Bertram Wyatt-Brown, who had the page proofs for his book, *Southern Honor*, upstairs in his hotel room.[6] My professional life passed before my eyes as I learned that this senior scholar was about to publish a book with "my" discovery as its very title. He kindly sent me the galleys of his book, and I discovered that we took quite different approaches to the subject even though we agreed on much. Fortunately, I also talked about things other than honor so that the book from my dissertation was not completely overshadowed by Wyatt-Brown.

That book, *Vengeance and Justice: Crime and Punishment in the Nineteenth-Century American South* (1984), revealed certain habits in my way of thinking. It combined quite disparate elements, insisted on the geographic diversity of the South, tried to get close to the experience of daily life, and combined numbers with so-called "literary" evidence. It offered both an indictment of the white South and an attempt to explain things that had seemed to most observers to require explanations based only on cultural dysfunction and innate patterns of injustice, disturbing phenomena such as high rates of homicide, the convict lease system, and even lynching.

Hired to teach southern history (and my new colleague Paul M. Gaston was happy for me to teach not only the Old South but also the second half of the nineteenth century, a topic in which he had lost interest despite his remarkable book on the era), I had no choice but to grow into a southern historian. Fortunately, I loved teaching, which seemed to combine the inherited traits of my conscientious mother and my fast-talking father. And, fortunately, too, I developed a deep and abiding fascination with all parts of southern history, things that had never interested me before and that I had never studied, much less taught. Teaching the history of the South to descendants of the southern aristocracy and descendants of slaves and descendants of hillbillies as well as to the many northerners and non-Americans at UVA revealed to me the power of southern history. That history speaks, I learned, to all of American history, to world history. I have never grown weary of teaching it.

The idea for my next book grew from my research on lynching that I had done for my first book, *Vengeance and Justice*. Searching through pages of microfilmed newspapers, I kept seeing discordant images. On the very pages where brutal murders were chronicled in terrible detail, articles about football games and Coca-Cola and the latest best-sellers and revival meetings hovered. I determined to embrace all of those aspects of life rather than purging them from the story as not really "southern." My work, I determined, would be characterized by listening with respect to everyone, by including as many kinds of people as I could, by showing that everyone, even poor southerners, lived in history.

I decided to see if I could write a history that included politics, religion, music, economic life, literature, popular culture, and daily life. I longed for a story that included as many kinds of southerners as I could fit into the story. *The Promise of the New South: Life after Reconstruction* (1992) was the result of that longing, the same longing for connection across fields that had sent me into American Studies years before. Tackling the same subject as Woodward's *Origins of the New South*, the book that had changed my life, was in part homage, I am sure, as well as faintly patricidal and regicidal. Woodward had published his book before I was born. Surely the new social history, the new cultural history, the new African American history, and the new women's history would provide me with something to add to *Origins*.

With a small fellowship, I drove twelve thousand miles in a $400 car, a vast 1974 Plymouth Satellite with a butterscotch-colored vinyl roof and a bashed-in side I crudely covered with Bondo and a can of spray paint. I moved from one Motel 6 to another as I covered the southern archives, reading everything I could find about the South during the Gilded Age.

Promise was in a way, I suppose, a sublimated autobiography. It translated my own discovery and embrace of the South into a story I could share with others. I came to believe that the categories historians used to analyze the South did its people a disservice, freezing them in time and subjecting them to stereotype. Just as my parents and grandparents were far more complicated and interesting than people from outside could know, so did I believe that the entire southern past held secrets it had not yielded to our analyses.

In the meantime, I was fortunate to work with wonderful graduate students and colleagues at Virginia who continually pushed me to see things in new ways. With John Willis, I edited *The Edge of the South: Life in Nineteenth-Century Virginia* (1991), a collection of essays by graduate students I had advised who dwelled on the perplexing place of Virginia in the South, a place both central and marginal. With my good friend Peter Onuf, I wrote and edited *All Over the Map: Rethinking American Regions* (1996), a series of essays that tried to throw into doubt easy assumptions about regions. With Bradley C. Mittendorf, I edited the *Oxford Book of the American South* (1997), an anthology of "testimony, memory, and fiction" that brought together rich and diverse voices of the southern past from the eighteenth century to the present, all in conversation with one another across generations and divides of race and gender. And I had the good fortune to teach about the South in the Netherlands and in Italy, where I saw my country through different eyes and where my interest in region only grew deeper.

While I was working on these books, my father died a slow death from emphysema and cancer. Long a heavy smoker, for his last years he breathed from an oxygen tank and died far too early. My grandparents died in those years as well, and I felt my connection to the mountains broken.

Yet the cycle began again: Nate and Hannah were born to Abby and me, and we decided that we would live in the country outside of Charlottesville, at the base of Dudley Mountain, where we have cleared a few acres of abandoned farmland with chainsaws and brush cutters. The old road to Lynchburg runs in front of our house, a road where enslaved people and Confederates, farm wagons and hot rods have traveled. Across that road is a plantation house from 1823; down the road is a trailer park, next to farmhouses built in the time of *Promise of the New South* and red-brick ranchers built when I was a child.

As I did the research for *Promise* I found myself almost alone in my enduring interest in computers. While I knew I would hide the numbers in the notes, I held to the belief that it was still necessary to know proportions, timing, and correlations, the patterns on the ground, if we were to write compelling social and cultural history. I worked to master new techniques, including computerized mapping, in the early 1990s, when almost no one I knew in history was interested in such relics of the 1970s. As a result of that interest, I happened to be involved in the creation of the Institute for Advanced Technology in the Humanities at UVA and become an unwitting pioneer in what we came to call "digital history."

Because I had been underfoot for so long in the computer lab in the engineering school working on *Promise*, in 1991 I was asked to serve on a university-wide computing committee. At only the second meeting of that committee we were told that IBM was interested in working with the university if we could think of something interesting to propose. After some discussion, I pointed out that the history and English faculty at UVA did not have computers on their desks; maybe we should see what humanists could do with powerful networked computers. Other committee members were dubious, but the chair of the committee, William Wulf, now president of the National Academy of Engineering, saw merit in the idea and asked what sort of thing I had in mind.

I had nothing in mind other than the merest sketch of a book on the Civil War, but it did not take long for me to combine the idea of that book with the notion of a large digital archive that would permit nonhistorians to have access to all the materials on which a professional historian would write a book. I had long sent my UVA students into the rich primary sources in our library, and I wanted to share that experience with students elsewhere who did not have access to such materials.

I pursued the idea of digital history across ten years, during which the World Wide Web emerged and then boomed. The idea for a digital history project and my next book grew alongside one another. I wanted to get closer to a smaller cast of historical actors, and I wanted to tell a more sustained narrative than I had in my earlier books. I had experimented in *Promise* with some techniques to create the feel of narrative history in what was basically an analytical history. I built that book around quotes and evocative details, trying to recreate the feel of the place I had spent so much time trying to imagine. But I longed for a more unified narrative in my new project.

I also decided that if I was going to live much of my working life in the nineteenth century, that I had to confront its central event. I had resisted the Civil War for as long as I could, put off by the kitsch, fantasy, and politics that surrounded it. But I grew to think that I had to deal with the war. Living among the battlefields and monuments of Virginia year after year, confronting students who knew far more than I did about the history-defining battles that had occurred right under our feet, coming to understand that the Civil War offered the richest opportunity imaginable for American social history, I turned to the war with trepidation.

As I looked for an angle of vision on the war, I was struck by the incongruity between the astonishing beauty of the Shenandoah Valley, just over the Blue Ridge from our home in Charlottesville, and the ferocity of the battles and burning that took place there. I was also struck by the fact that the Mason-Dixon Line cut across the Valley, dividing the same geographic structure into places with sharply differing histories. Influenced by evocative histories of communities such as Emmanuel Le Roy Ladurie's *Montaillou*, I decided that I would write the twinned stories of two communities, one in the North and one in the South, both in the Valley.[7] Once I knew I was writing about the Valley and about the death and suffering war brought, my years of study in Sunday school immediately led me to my title: "The Valley of the Shadow."

The Valley Project proved to be enormous, as hundreds of thousands of newspaper articles, diaries, letters, census entries, tax records, and military reports accumulated. Effective allies and good friends made it possible to sustain such an enterprise across one year after another. Foremost among them were Anne Rubin and Will Thomas, people of remarkable energy and patience. The project we built proved exciting and satisfying, all the more so for being collaborative. Reaching out to high schools and community colleges, to other countries and continents, offered a kind of immediate connection impossible only a few years before.

As I write this brief intellectual autobiography, the book based on "The Valley of the Shadow" Web site is in proofs. That book, called *In the Presence of*

Mine Enemies: War in the Heart of America, 1859–1863, is the culmination of the personal story I have just related. That book returns to my fascination with places that straddle boundaries and cross borders, places like Kingsport and Burnsville and Charlottesville. It dwells on history that has been simplified too much. It cuts against the grain of the reassuring and self-congratulatory history of the Civil War that has become to seem like common sense, even as it also cuts against explanations of the war that blame the South's involvement on anything other than slavery. It tries to put different parts of history—military, social, political, and cultural—into conversation and tries to include many kinds of people.

This new book, like the others I have written, dwells on surprise, uncertainty, and instability, on borders, boundaries, and edges. It focuses on those things not out of some fashionable philosophy but out of something less articulate, something ineffable but real in the South I have known. My work draws from a desire to build bridges and connections between people who might otherwise misunderstand one another, a longing that drives my teaching and my service as dean as well. If I get a chance to write another book, I imagine that it will tell, in one form or another, the same story. It is perhaps the only story I really know.

Notes

1. Paul Johnson, *A Shopkeeper's Millennium: Society and Revivals in Rochester, New York, 1815–1837* (New York, 1978).

2. Eugene D. Genovese, *Roll, Jordan, Roll: The World the Slaves Made* (New York, 1974); Edmund S. Morgan, *American Slavery, American Freedom: The Ordeal of Colonial Virginia* (New York, 1975); and Robert W. Fogel and Stanley L. Engerman, *Time on the Cross: The Economics of American Negro Slavery* (Boston, 1974).

3. David Brion Davis, *The Problem of Slavery in the Age of Revolution, 1770–1823* (Ithaca, N.Y., 1975).

4. C. Vann Woodward, *Origins of the New South, 1877–1913* (Baton Rouge, 1951).

5. E. P. Thompson, *The Making of the English Working Class* (New York, 1964).

6. Soon published as *Southern Honor: Ethics and Behavior in the Old South* (New York, 1982).

7. Emmanuel Le Roy Ladurie, *Montaillou: The Promised Land of Error*, trans. Barbara Bray (New York, 1979).

Contributors

EDWARD L. AYERS (Ph.D., Yale University, 1980) is Hugh P. Kelly Professor of History and Dean, College and Graduate School of Arts and Sciences, at the University of Virginia.

ANTHONY J. BADGER (Ph.D., Hull University, 1974) is Paul Mellon Professor of American History at Cambridge University.

JOHN B. BOLES (Ph.D., University of Virginia, 1969) is William Pettus Hobby Professor of History at Rice University and Managing Editor of the *Journal of Southern History*.

VERNON BURTON (Ph.D., Princeton University, 1976) is Professor of History and Sociology at the University of Illinois and Professor and Senior Research Scientist at the National Center for Supercomputing Applications.

DAN T. CARTER (Ph.D., University of North Carolina, 1967) is Education Foundation Professor of History at the University of South Carolina.

PETE DANIEL (Ph.D., University of Maryland, 1970) is Curator, Division of the History of Technology, at the National Museum of American History.

DREW GILPIN FAUST (Ph.D., University of Pennsylvania, 1975) is Professor of History at Harvard University and Dean of the Radcliffe Institute for Advanced Study.

JOHN HOPE FRANKLIN (Ph.D., Harvard University, 1941) is James B. Duke Professor Emeritus at Duke University.

JACK P. GREENE (Ph.D., Duke University, 1956) is Professor of History and Andrew W. Mellon Professor in the Humanities at Johns Hopkins University.

DARLENE CLARK HINE (Ph.D., Kent State University, 1975) is Board of Trustees Professor of African American Studies and Professor of History at Northwestern University.

CHARLES JOYNER (Ph.D. [history], University of South Carolina, 1968; Ph.D. [folklore], University of Pennsylvania, 1977) is Burroughs Distinguished Professor of Southern History and Culture at Coastal Carolina University.

SUZANNE LEBSOCK (Ph.D., University of Virginia, 1977) is Board of Governors Professor of History at Rutgers University.

BILL C. MALONE (Ph.D., University of Texas, 1965) is Professor of History Emeritus at Tulane University.

Contributors

ANNE FIROR SCOTT (Ph.D., Radcliffe College, 1958) is William K. Boyd Professor Emeritus at Duke University.

PETER H. WOOD (Ph.D., Harvard University, 1972) is Professor of History at Duke University.

BERTRAM WYATT-BROWN (Ph.D., Johns Hopkins University, 1963) is Richard J. Milbauer Professor of United States History Emeritus at the University of Florida.

www.ingramcontent.com/pod-product-compliance
Lightning Source LLC
Chambersburg PA
CBHW011754220426
43672CB00018B/2955